THE BIAS AGAINST AGRICULTURE

Since 1985 the International Center for Economic Growth, a nonprofit organization, has contributed to economic growth and human development in developing and post-socialist countries by strengthening the capacity of indigenous research institutes to provide leadership in policy debates. The Center sponsors a wide range of programs—including research, publications, conferences, seminars, and special projects advising governments—through a network of more than 250 correspondent institutes worldwide. The Center's research and publications program is organized around five series: Sector Studies; Country Studies; Studies in Human Development and Social Welfare; Occasional Papers; and Working Papers.

The Center is affiliated with the Institute for Contemporary Studies and is headquartered in Panama with the administrative office in San Francisco, California.

For further information, please contact the International Center for Economic Growth, 243 Kearny Street, San Francisco, California, 94108, USA. Phone (415) 981-5353; Fax (415) 986-4878.

ICEG Board of Overseers

THE BIAS AGAINST AGRICULTURE

TRADE AND MACROECONOMIC POLICIES IN DEVELOPING COUNTRIES

Edited by
Romeo M. Bautista and Alberto Valdés

A Copublication of the
International Center for Economic Growth
and the
International Food Policy Research Institute

PRESS
San Francisco, California

© 1993 Institute for Contemporary Studies

Publication signifies that the International Center for Economic Growth believes a work to be a competent treatment worthy of public consideration. The findings, interpretations, and conclusions of a work are entirely those of the authors and should not be attributed to ICEG, its affiliated organizations, its Board of Overseers, or organizations that support ICEG.

The International Food Policy Research Institute was established in 1975 to identify and analyze alternative national and international strategies and policies for meeting food needs in the world, with particular emphasis on low-income countries and on the poorer groups in those countries. The Institute's research program reflects worldwide interaction with policy makers, administrators, and others concerned with increasing sustainable food production and with improving the equity of its distribution. Research results are published and distributed to officials and others concerned with national and international food and agricultural policy. The Institute is located at 1200 17th Street, NW, Washington, D.C. 20036-3006. Telephone: (202) 862-5600; fax: (202) 467-4439.

Inquiries, book orders, and catalog requests should be addressed to ICS Press, 243 Kearny Street, San Francisco, California 94108, USA. Telephone: (415) 981-5353; fax (415) 986-4878. For book orders and catalog requests, call toll free in the continental United States: (800) 326-0263.

Cover designer: Irene Imfeld
Copyeditor: Vicky Macintyre
Indexer: Shirley Kessel

10 9 8 7 6 5 4 3 2 1

Library of Congress Cataloging-in-Publication Data

The bias against agriculture : trade and macroeconomic policies in
  developing countries / edited by Romeo M. Bautista and Alberto
  Valdés.
     p.   cm.
  Includes bibliographical references and index.
  ISBN 1-55815-245-8
  1. Produce trade—Government policy—Developing countries—Case
studies.   2. Agriculture and state—Developing countries—Case
studies.   3. Developing countries—Commercial policy—Case studies.
I. Bautista, Romeo M., 1941–   . II. Valdés, Alberto, date.
HD9018.D44B5   1993
338.1'8'091724—dc20   92-36105

CONTENTS

LIST OF TABLES

LIST OF FIGURES

PREFACE

From the 1940s to the 1980s, developing countries saw industrialization as the key to rapid growth. Consequently, when economists studied the trade and macroeconomic policies of developing countries, they focused on how those policies advanced or hindered manufacturing. Some pioneers warned that agriculture plays a critical role in development, and since the 1970s there has been increasing recognition of this fact. Only recently, however, has recognition increased for the general equilibrium context of policy and its effects on agriculture and other sectors of the economy.

In June 1987 the International Food Policy Research Institute (IFPRI) gathered experts in the area of agriculture and economic growth, from both government and academia, to examine how trade and macroeconomic policies have affected agricultural performance. Their findings, compiled in this volume, center on a number of country studies done by researchers at IFPRI's Trade Program and their collaborators. They show that the indirect effects of trade and macroeconomic policies have often diverged from and invariably overwhelmed the direct effects of such policies. The result is that agriculture has faced unintended but severe obstacles. For example, while the government invested in agricultural research and rural infrastructure, its exchange rate policies designed to promote industry worked against agriculture and in fact succeeded in reducing agricultural output.

The Bias against Agriculture, edited by eminent development economists Romeo Bautista and Alberto Valdés, contains important lessons for developing country policy makers who seek to reform their economies. In low-income developing countries, agricultural growth is important for overall economic growth and the alleviation of poverty and food insecurity. Trade and macroeconomic policies, in turn, are important for agricultural growth. Efforts to assure agricultural growth and poverty alleviation, therefore, must not ignore the effects of trade and macro-economic policies. By avoiding the policies that harm agriculture, even indirectly, policy makers have a better chance of achieving their development goals.

Nicolás Ardito-Barletta
General Director
International Center
for Economic Growth
Panama City, Panama

Per Pinstrup-Andersen
Director General
International Food
Policy Research Institute
Washington, D.C.

March 1993

ACKNOWLEDGMENTS

This volume is based primarily on research conducted at the International Food Policy Research Institute (IFPRI) beginning in the early 1980s on the influence of trade and macroeconomic policies on the agricultural performance of developing economies. In June 1987 IFPRI sponsored a workshop on the subject, held in Annapolis, Maryland, that gathered senior policy makers and analysts from developing countries along with the researchers who participated in the country case studies. Most of the papers presented at that workshop, subsequently revised, are included as country chapters in this volume. We also invited the contribution of other chapters, with an eye to lending additional perspectives on the subject.

We would like to thank Miguel Urrutia and the Inter-American Development Bank for providing the basic funding for the Annapolis workshop and the preparation of this volume. The Ford Foundation, the International Development Research Centre (Canada), the U.S. Agency for International Development (USAID), and the Swiss Development Corporation financed some of the country studies and the participation in the workshop of several policy makers and analysts from Africa and Asia.

We are grateful for the comments and suggestions made by the workshop discussants and by the reviewers of the volume as a whole and of the individual chapters: Aiyegboyin Alabi, Kym Anderson, Boediono, Vittorio Corbo, Sebastian Edwards, Ibrahim Elbadawi, Juan Andres Fontaine, Nurul Islam, Juan Jaramillo, John Mellor, Jaime de Melo, Benno Ndulu, Beatriz Nefal, João de Carmo Oliveira, Carlos Rodriguez, Pascal Salin, Eduardo Sarmiento, Grant Scobie, Maurice Schiff, Ammar Siamwalla, and Richard Webb.

We also want to acknowledge the invaluable assistance of David Bruns in organizing the Annapolis workshop and of Marcelle Thomas, Norma Bonifazi, Susan Frost, and Heidi Fritschel in producing this manuscript.

R. M. B.
A. V.

THE BIAS AGAINST AGRICULTURE

I

Introduction

The Relevance of Trade and Macroeconomic Policies for Agriculture

The unrealized economic potential of agriculture in many
low-income countries is large. The technological possibilities have
become increasingly more favorable, but the economic
opportunities that are required for farmers in these countries to
realize this potential are far from favorable.

—Theodore W. Schultz, *Distortions of Agricultural Incentives*

Until recently, the development literature gave scant attention to the
effect of trade and macroeconomic policies on the economic opportunities available to agricultural producers. One reason for this is the nar-
row, sectoral orientation of past agricultural policy analysis; another is
the widespread misconception that agriculture plays a limited role in
economic development.

The main objective of development policy in most developing countries has been rapid industrialization. In actively promoting domestic
industry, however, many of these countries distorted price incentives
against agriculture, substantially diminishing the positive effects of public investment policies meant to support agricultural research and extension, the development of rural infrastructure, and the marketing of
agricultural exports. As a result, their agricultural output has been lower

than it would have been under a more neutral incentive structure, the real purchasing power of the rural population has declined, and many of these countries have experienced a significant demand-side constraint on economic growth.

Development Policies and Agricultural Incentives

Over the years, the share of agriculture in the total output of developing economies has declined. Although this shift is a natural result of economic development, policies emphasizing rapid industrialization—usually by means of import substitution, at least initially—have hastened the process. Developing countries have promoted import-competing industries through high tariffs and quantitative import restrictions. They have also made foreign exchange for the related imports of capital goods and materials available at highly favorable terms.

The import-substitution policies of developing countries have differed in their duration, comprehensiveness, and intensity. In a few places, most notably the Republic of Korea and Taiwan, development strategies became outward-oriented at an early phase of industrialization and encouraged exports of labor-intensive manufactured products. In the 1970s the emphasis shifted to skill-, capital-, and technology-intensive exports, and governments began reducing industrial protection, adopted more realistic exchange rates, and developed export infrastructure. By and large, however, foreign trade regimes remained heavily protective of import-competing industries. In the first phase of import substitution, countries focused on protecting light industry. Later they concentrated on upstream industries requiring skilled labor, substantial capital investment, and more advanced technology. This was the case in most Latin American countries during the 1950s and 1960s and in many Asian countries during the 1960s and 1970s.

In the 1970s developing countries began recognizing the value of exporting manufactured goods and granted subsidies to certain industrial exports. These subsidies did not fully offset the general bias against exports, however, and some incentives were made available only if export producers used imported inputs.

Producers of agricultural exports were in an even worse position. They received no subsidies whatsoever, and most farm products were subject to an export tax (applied either explicitly or implicitly through the pricing policy of state marketing boards).[1] The urban bias in developing country policies also tended to keep food prices down (Lipton 1982), with the result that the general level of wages remained low and industrial enterprises were able to recruit labor from agriculture at a reduced cost. In addition, agricultural producers had to pay high prices for industrial inputs such as fertilizer, pesticides, and farm equipment because of the protection accorded to their domestic production. The subsidies for farm inputs provided little compensation to agricultural producers for the artificially low prices of their output.

Apart from their direct effect on agricultural production incentives, industrial import restrictions reduce the demand for imports and thereby lower the price of foreign exchange. This causes the prices of tradable goods in domestic currency to fall in relation to those of non-tradables and indirectly discourages the production of tradable goods. Industrial export subsidies have the same qualitative effect on the exchange rate (since they tend to increase export supply); agricultural export taxes have the opposite effect. The agricultural sector is particularly vulnerable to distortions in the real exchange rate because the agricultural output of developing countries tends to be highly tradable, whether it is produced by an upper-income developing country such as Chile (discussed in Chapter 9 of this volume) or by a low-income country such as Zaire (Chapter 5). Not surprisingly, trade liberalization and real exchange rate management appear to have a more positive effect on agricultural production than on nonagricultural production (as is shown in Chapter 8 on Argentina).

The real exchange rate can also be affected by an imbalance in a country's external accounts. The unsustainable component of a current account deficit—due to, say, heavy foreign borrowing—serves to defend an overvalued exchange rate, exemplified by the Philippine experience after the oil price shocks of 1973–1974 and 1979–1980 (Chapter 6).

Another factor that may cause the exchange rate to appreciate is the Dutch disease—so named because of the Netherlands' experience with the discovery of natural gas. This disease arises when a boom in one tradable good reduces the profitability of producing other tradable goods by directly bidding resources away from them. The Dutch disease usually refers to the way in which spending and the resource movement connected with the development of a natural resource affect the national economy (Corden and Neary 1982). Chapter 4 discusses how the oil boom in the 1970s affected the Nigerian economy, while Chapter 3 examines Colombia's experience with the 1975–1979 coffee boom.

It is necessary here to distinguish among nominal, effective, and real exchange rates. The nominal exchange rate refers to the relative price of two currencies—for example, the number of units of domestic currency per unit of foreign currency. The effective exchange rate is the nominal (or official) rate adjusted for trade-related taxes and subsidies, that is, the number of units of domestic currency actually paid by importers or received by exporters per unit of foreign currency. By adjusting the nominal exchange rate or trade taxes and subsidies, a government can modify the effective exchange rate for any class of tradable goods in relation to other categories of tradable goods and thereby affect relative profitabilities (see, for example, Chapters 6 and 7 on the Philippines and Pakistan, respectively).

The real exchange rate is the relative price of two goods, represented by the ratio of the domestic price of tradable goods to the price of nontradable goods. This ratio is frequently used to measure the relative profitability of producing tradables compared with nontradables. Often a government changes the nominal exchange rate to modify the real rate (Valdés and Siamwalla 1988). The two rates do not correspond one-to-one, however. If foreign prices and trade restrictions remain the same, the effect of a change in the nominal exchange rate on the real exchange rate will depend on how the price of nontradable goods changes in reaction to the macroeconomic policies being adopted. Thus, a country's monetary and fiscal policies, foreign borrowing, and management of the nominal exchange rate can significantly affect the real exchange rate and hence the profitability of producing tradable goods.

Direct Effects of Trade Policy on Relative Prices

As the preceding discussion indicates, any analysis of the influence of trade policy on relative prices must distinguish between importables and exportables, and between agricultural and industrial exportables. At the aggregate level, a trade regime's price bias in favor of or against the production of exportables compared with importables can be represented by the ratio of the effective exchange rate for exports to that for imports. If this ratio is less than one, a country is promoting the production of importables over that of exportables, which tends to reduce foreign trade. If the ratio is greater than one, prices are discriminating in favor of export production and against import substitution, and therefore the possibilities for trade increase. A value of one indicates that neither exporting nor import substitution is being encouraged and that the relative incentives for home and export sales are "neutral" (Bhagwati 1987). This measure of overall trade bias is used in Chapter 6 to document the gradual weakening of the price discrimination in Philippine trade policy against export producers during the period 1950–1980.

In representing the direct effects of the trade regime on production incentives among tradable goods, estimates of the nominal protection rate are widely used in the empirical literature. This rate indicates the degree to which the domestic price of a product exceeds its free-trade value (that is, its value in the absence of trade restrictions) or border price, evaluated at the official exchange rate. The effective protection rate would provide a more accurate measure, since it takes into account the protection or penalty from the pricing of intermediate inputs, but it is considerably more difficult to estimate, given the limited data available in most developing countries. In any case, the structure of protection would not change significantly if the cost of intermediate inputs were included in the analysis, because such inputs have a small share in the value of agricultural output and because "most input subsidies [are] inframarginal" (Krueger, Schiff, and Valdés 1988, 258).

The import-substitution policies of developing countries have given rise to an incentive structure that discriminates against the producers of exports and of primary products. Among the developing countries of Asia, Bangladesh and the Philippines have had much higher nominal protection rates for import-competing production than for export production; and since the early 1970s their industrial exports have enjoyed greater direct protection than agricultural exports (Chapter 10).

The direct price effects of developing country trade policy have also differed within agriculture. According to the findings of a recent World Bank study (Krueger, Schiff, and Valdés 1988), the most important agricultural exports have been "disprotected" (taxed) more heavily than the principal food products—presumably because of the desire for food self-sufficiency and the administrative and political ease of taxing commercial export crops rather than subsistence food crops. Many developing countries—especially those with higher incomes such as Chile, Korea, and Malaysia—have protected food production through trade restrictions.

Two variables that political economists frequently use to explain differences in agricultural protection among developing countries are per capita income and agriculture's share in gross domestic product (GDP) (Anderson 1986).[2] The need to tax agriculture is perceived to be greater in a low-income developing country in which other economic sectors contribute only minor amounts to total production. In the political market for protection, the smaller, better-educated, urban-based industrialist class is able to lobby the government more effectively than are numerous, widely scattered farmers. As a country grows richer and domestic industry expands, agricultural taxation becomes less necessary, and it becomes easier to organize a political lobby to advance farm interests. Furthermore, urban workers are less likely to oppose higher agricultural prices as their income increases.

This long-run relationship is only partly borne out in the World Bank study, which compares nominal protection rates for two groupings of principal import-competing food crops and exported products in sixteen developing countries during the periods 1975–1979 and 1980–1984. Only nine of sixteen products in the two groupings showed higher average protection rates in 1980–1984 than in 1975–1979. On the whole, it seems that sector-specific price policies during the first half of the 1980s did not improve "economic opportunities," as Professor Schultz refers to them in the epigraph at the beginning of this chapter.

Developing countries have followed various patterns of agricultural protection. Korea, for example, discriminated against agriculture in the early 1970s but then moved toward protection through the mid-1980s. This shift has been attributed to the "social and political difficulties involved in [the] intersectoral resource adjustments" accompanying the rapid shift in Korea's comparative advantage from agriculture to industry (Honma and Hayami 1987, 59).

Malaysia, in contrast, heavily taxed its producers of export crops (rubber and palm oil), who were primarily non-Malays (Jenkins and Lai 1989), but protected its politically powerful, Malay-dominated rice farmers.

Sri Lanka's agricultural pricing policies were initially similar to those of Malaysia. Until the mid-1970s, it taxed the highly successful producers of tree crops (tea and rubber) to finance its large social expenditures. The political cost was relatively small, because the tea and rubber plantations employed a small number of workers, mostly Tamils. At the same time, it protected rice production, which was dominated by the politically influential Sinhalese. When the tea crop surplus began to decline and resource flows from other parts of the economy failed to offset the drop, politicians had to "resort to deficit spending and other quick fixes" (Bhalla 1988, 90). Eventually an economic crisis ensued and in 1977 Sri Lanka adopted a liberalization strategy.

Indirect Price Effects Attributable to Exchange Rate Distortion

As mentioned earlier, trade and macroeconomic policies can also have an indirect effect on agricultural incentives as a result of the misalignments they cause in the real exchange rate. Although frequently unintended, indirect effects can have a greater influence on production incentives than sector-specific government interventions, but they are poorly understood.

Some of the country studies in this volume employ general equilibrium analysis based on a small open-economy model[3] to demonstrate that tariffs on imports lead to a proportionate increase in the domestic price of importables in relation to home goods and indirectly to a decline in the real exchange rate and in the domestic relative price of exportables. Similarly, a tax on exports not only directly reduces the domestic price of exportables, but also indirectly raises the real exchange rate and the domestic price of importables (Lerner 1936), while export subsidies have the opposite effect. The magnitude of these indirect effects depends on the degree of substitutability between tradable and home goods in production and consumption. This factor is called the incidence parameter. In Argentina, Chile, Colombia, Nigeria, Peru, the Philippines, and Zaire, the heavy protection of industrial products has placed a significant indirect tax on agricultural import-competing goods and export production (Valdés 1986).

Tariffs and quantitative restrictions on industrial imports, as well as subsidies for industrial exports, also lead to an overvaluation of the real exchange rate, whereas taxes on agricultural exports have an offsetting effect, except in cases of inelastic foreign demand. The Philippine experience illustrates the dominant influence of trade restrictions on the real exchange rate (Chapter 6).

Unsustainable deficits in the external accounts have been another major source of exchange rate overvaluation in developing countries. Macroeconomic policies that affect the balance of payments therefore also affect the real exchange rate. When Nigeria's oil export revenues increased in the 1970s, government expenditures rose sharply, monetary policy became expansionary, and inflation followed close behind. Since the nominal exchange rate was held fixed or even made to appreciate gradually (Chapter 4), the real exchange rate of the Nigerian naira appreciated considerably.

During the 1970s many oil-importing countries in the developing parts of the world relied heavily on foreign capital to accommodate their large current account deficits during the 1970s. For some, this massive external financing led to serious debt-service problems. In the Philippines, the substantial increase in foreign borrowing and accompanying expansionary macroeconomic policies accounted for about one-third of the estimated overvaluation of the real exchange rate during the 1975–1980 period (Chapter 6).

Colombia, too, experienced a significant appreciation in its real exchange rate, in this case as a result of the Dutch disease that was rampant from 1975 to 1983. The disease was associated with the coffee boom of 1975–1979, which brought marked increases in the government deficit and the money supply and a sharp decline in the domestic price of noncoffee tradables compared with the price of nontradables. The government had a high marginal propensity to spend on nontraded goods, with the result that its expenditures grew rapidly, especially from 1978 to 1983, and helped create an excess demand for nontradables that drove their relative price upward.

Overvaluation of the exchange rate, resulting from both sector-specific trade restrictions and unsustainable deficits in the external account, created a negative indirect effect on the price of major tradable agricultural products in developing countries (Krueger, Schiff, and Valdés 1988). Estimates of these price effects ranged from Malaysia's atypically low average values of 4.3 percent and 9.5 percent for 1975–1979 and 1980–1984, respectively, to the extreme values of 66.0 percent and 89.0 percent for the corresponding periods in Ghana. Many developing countries, particularly those at the lower-income level, maintained high levels of total disprotection (direct plus indirect effects) for both export crops and import-competing food products. Surprisingly, in several cases the indirect price effects were much greater than the direct nominal protection rates. In many instances, moreover, the positive direct protection of food crops was exceeded by the negative indirect price effect attributable to the exchange rate overvaluation.

In the Philippines, the prevailing import and foreign exchange controls had a greater direct effect on the prices of domestic agricultural products than on the prices of nonagricultural products during the 1950–1961 period (Chapter 6). At the same time, the indirect effect of the real exchange rate overvaluation contributed significantly to the decline in the price of agricultural products compared with that of home goods. As trade policy became less restrictive in the 1960s and 1970s, its distortionary effect on agricultural incentives decreased commensurately. Nonetheless, the policy-induced bias against agricultural production remained high from 1975 to 1980, reducing domestic agricultural prices by 20 percent in relation to nonagricultural products and by 12 percent in relation to home goods. This bias was due to the massive trade deficits that helped defend the exchange rate overvaluation, which served to reinforce the effect of falling international commodity prices at the time. As a result, relative agricultural prices in the Philippines fell sharply from the mid-1970s to the early 1980s.

In Peru, the direct and indirect effects of increased industrial protection and agricultural price controls during the period 1969–1973 (compared with 1964–1968) reduced the producer price indexes for agricultural export and import-competing food crops by 38 and 28 percent, respectively (Chapter 2). The trade liberalization measures adopted in 1970–1982, however, lowered the uniform equivalent tariff from 133 to 91 percent and benefited agricultural producers by increasing the domestic prices of their export products (by 34 percent) and import-competing food crops (by 22 percent).

As we have pointed out, the indirect price effects of trade and macroeconomic policies on agricultural production incentives in developing countries, operating through the induced overvaluation of the real exchange rate, are generally unintended. This price bias against agriculture cannot be eliminated simply by adjusting the nominal exchange rate. It can be corrected only at its source, that is, by lowering the import barriers that unduly protect domestic industry and restoring the balance of payments equilibrium.

External Terms of Trade and the Real Exchange Rate

Foreign price movements also affect the relationship among the domestic prices of exportables, importables, and home goods, and hence the real exchange rate. Estimates of the policy-induced effects on the real exchange rate in the studies cited earlier assume unchanging external terms of trade, which, under the small-country assumption, are exogenously determined. An exogenous change in a country's terms of trade affects the real exchange rate in various ways.

Although many economists would agree that a deterioration in the terms of trade leads to a depreciation of the real exchange rate, the relationship between the two is somewhat complicated. When export prices fall in relation to home goods (while import prices remain constant) the supply of home goods increases. At the same time, the demand for home goods declines because of both income and substitution effects. Therefore, the real exchange rate must depreciate to eliminate the excess supply and restore equilibrium in the home goods market. If the deterioration in the terms of trade arises from an increase in import prices, the induced income and substitution effects on demand push in opposite directions; if the substitution effect is the stronger of the two, the real exchange rate will depreciate (Dornbusch 1980). The greater the substitutability between home goods and importables in consumption and the greater the influence of export prices on the terms of trade, the more likely it is that a real depreciation will result from a deterioration in the terms of trade (Bautista 1987b).

Export prices have had a significant effect on the external terms of trade in Argentina and Chile, where a positive relationship between the real exchange rate and the terms of trade would be expected (Valdés 1986). A 10 percent improvement in Pakistan's terms of trade resulted in an increase of 2.4 percent in the real exchange rate for exports (Chapter 7). In the Philippines, the real exchange rate would have been higher by 22 percent between 1975 and 1984 had the terms of trade remained at the level of the 1970s (Bautista 1987b, 52).

Although policy cannot directly influence the terms of trade, changes in the terms of trade can significantly affect the real exchange rate and should be taken into account in assessing the overall incentives for agricultural production.

Effects on Output, Income Distribution, and Intersectoral Resource Flows

The relative price effects of trade and macroeconomic policies have various repercussions on agricultural output and incomes. When agricultural products are underpriced, domestic output suffers—not only because the static efficiency of resource use declines, but also, and more important, there are adverse effects on agricultural labor supply, capital accumulation, and technological change over the long term.

In the short run, the price responsiveness of agricultural output diminishes with increasing product aggregation, since the possibility for resource reallocation declines as products become more differentiated. Clearly, shifting resources in the short run from agricultural to nonagricultural production is more difficult than shifting them from food to export crops, and still more difficult than shifting them from rice to corn. The magnitude of the output loss attributable to lower static efficiency depends not only on the short-run supply elasticity, of course, but also on how depressed agricultural prices are in relation to border prices—which may differ widely from country to country.

A recent World Bank study of trade liberalization in nineteen countries notes that in the period before liberalization their foreign trade regimes typically discriminated against agriculture (Michaely, Choksi, and Papageorgiou 1989). Remarkably, "once this policy was reversed, liberalization produced, from the outset, accelerated growth of the agricultural sector, and increased that sector's share in the country's GNP" (p. 4). This finding suggests that agricultural production responds quickly to changing circumstances.

In addition to this impact on output in the short run, the long-run price elasticity of agricultural supply has dynamic effects associated with the induced changes in factor supplies and in technology over time. It is well known, for example, that the rate of rural-urban migration is a function of the intersectoral income differential, which in turn is determined in part by agricultural prices. Price incentives also appear to stimulate private investment, and higher returns to farming will attract more capital, both physical and human, into agriculture. Relative prices may even influence public investment to some extent. Furthermore, farmers will adopt new technologies and purchase the physical inputs that embody them only if they expect their income to improve. That is, price incentives also influence the diffusion of agricultural technology and the level of productivity. Although rice research in India has been going on for decades, varieties that are responsive to fertilizer were long neglected because of the prevailing high prices of fertilizer and low prices of paddy (Schultz 1978).

Most studies of agriculture's aggregate response to relative price changes have failed to take into account these dynamic effects, let alone the output and income effects beyond the agricultural sector. In order to capture fully the economywide effects of policy-induced price biases against agriculture, one needs to work within a macroeconomic framework that integrates the domestic price structure, production patterns, and income distribution.

That is what the authors of Chapters 8 and 9 have tried to do in developing their dynamic general equilibrium models for Argentina and Chile. They assume that sectoral investment allocation and intersectoral labor migration depend, respectively, on the differential rates of return and labor wage rates across sectors; and that these rates are themselves influenced by sectoral product prices. They also assume that labor productivity in each production sector is endogenously determined by "state variables," such as the level of sectoral investment per worker (representing not only capital deepening, but also new technology embodied in physical inputs) and relative prices. This is a major improvement over the commonly used assumption of exogenous increases in sectoral productivity levels over time.

The simulation model used to investigate the price responsiveness of agricultural supply in Chile takes into account the historical growth of the labor force and capital accumulation. The simulation results indicate an aggregate supply elasticity (after nineteen years) of 1.4, which is quite high. They also show an increase of 11.2 percent in agricultural value added in response to a parametric 10 percent depreciation in the real exchange rate. In Argentina's case, economic performance, especially in agriculture, would have been considerably better under a more liberal trade regime, starting in 1950, together with fiscal and monetary discipline. In 1984, agricultural output would have been 174 percent higher; production in nonagriculture excluding government, 9 percent higher; and GDP, 46 percent higher.

These results for Chile and Argentina strongly suggest that studies that use single-equation specifications of dynamic supply behavior based on adaptive price expectations or partial output adjustment are likely to underestimate the long-run aggregate supply response of agriculture in developing countries.

The usual practice is to estimate the impact of trade and macroeconomic policies on income distribution by their differential income effects on small and large farms by the type of crops grown, and by consumption expenditure patterns. Again, a partial equilibrium framework fails to take into account what happens to sectoral incomes in the face of such adjustments as the response of urban wages to the cost of staple food and shifts in consumer demand toward substitute products. Since most households both consume and produce, what really matters are the *net* effects on them as consumers and producers.

Adelman and Robinson (1978) have developed a dynamic general equilibrium model for Korea to simulate the effects of various policy measures, most of them rural-oriented, for improving income distribution. They found that the economy adjusts to policy interventions largely through price changes and that changes in the agricultural terms of trade have the most significant impact on the size distribution of income. A multisectoral general equilibrium model has been used to show that trade liberalization in the Philippines would lead to a greater expansion of agricultural production than of nonagricultural production and a greater rise in rural than in urban income (Bautista 1986b). These results are consistent with the common assumption that agricultural output in developing countries is more "tradable"—and therefore more sensitive to changes in the real exchange rate—than is nonagricultural output.

For Peru, trade liberalization during the 1979–1982 period would have gradually improved income distribution for the urban populations; within the rural populations those in the relatively better off coastal and jungle areas would have gained in comparison with the highland population (Chapter 2). From a nutritional viewpoint, all population groups would have benefited.

Because the agricultural sector in Colombia produces mainly exportable goods, a more liberal trade regime there would raise agricultural prices and real wages and thereby improve agricultural income and reduce rural poverty (Chapter 3). Conversely, policies that artificially lower the price of domestic food products or subsidize food imports would increase the real income of the urban population and worsen the country's income distribution.

The price bias against agriculture in trade and macroeconomic policies in effect transfers resources out of agriculture. Governments compensate for this resource outflow to some degree through public spending in agriculture. The net transfer in the Philippines between 1970 and 1982 amounted to an annual average of about 25 percent of agricultural value added, whereas in Malaysia (where the real exchange rate has not been significantly overvalued) it came to only 5 percent (Chapter 10).

The concept of intersectoral resource flows put forth in this volume differs from that held by investigators who do not consider the divergence between domestic and foreign prices to be an implicit form of agricultural taxation or subsidy (see, for example, Ishikawa 1967). What they have called an "invisible" source of agricultural transfers over time is actually the deviation of the agricultural terms of trade from the level in some base year. Clearly, in evaluating the distortionary effect of agricultural pricing policy, the temporal movements of the domestic terms of trade are not as relevant as the structure of domestic prices compared with foreign prices (or marginal revenues, if import supply and export demand elasticities are not infinite). Past prices are not particularly useful in such evaluations since they do not represent an alternative set of currently available prices to which the scope for policy action can be related.

Another important factor to consider is how developing countries use the transferred agricultural "surplus" (Myint 1988). Many that have adopted highly protective import-substitution policies and other sources of domestic price distortions have experienced low levels of efficiency in the use of resources in industrial production. Unless such distortions are corrected, agricultural resource transfers are not likely to yield a significant social payoff. There are opportunities to accelerate agricultural productivity and income growth if the capital requirements for improving rural infrastructure and the diffusion of new technologies are met. These opportunities are being neglected, however, as countries continue to discriminate against agriculture in their trade and macroeconomic policies and allow associated resources to flow into nonagricultural production.

The Country Studies and Regional Surveys

The country studies begin in Chapter 2 with a discussion of trade policy in Peru and its incidence on the structure of incentives. Franklin and Valdés develop a quantitative framework to examine the policy effects on farm output and the real income of urban and rural households. They show that the large and persistent decline in Peru's exchange rate after the mid-1960s made it less profitable to produce tradables than nontradables. The authors attribute this decline largely to the sharp increase in trade restrictions, as measured by the uniform tariff equivalent (estimated for each year from 1949 to 1982), which gradually closed the Peruvian economy to international trade.

Using a disaggregative incidence parameter model drawn from Dornbusch (1974) and Sjaastad (1980), Franklin and Valdés find that raising the uniform tariff on manufactured goods by 10 percent (provided that tariffs on agricultural goods do not change) imposes an implicit tax of 5.6 percent (with respect to home goods) on the production of importables such as rice, and an implicit tax of 6.7 percent on exportable agricultural goods such as cotton and sugar. When agricultural prices are compared with the prices of nonagricultural importables, the implicit tax effect on both types of agricultural goods is 10 percent. These results indicate that Peru permits a high degree of substitution between home goods and nonagricultural importables and that exports bear a large part (more than half) of the burden of the tariff on imports.

The three components of the analytical apparatus are the incidence of trade policy on relative prices, agricultural supply, and household expenditures. The authors use a simulation model to assess the short- to medium-term adjustments of a change in the overall level of protection. Their empirical findings indicate that (1) restrictive industrial trade policies rather than the direct price policies for agriculture had the greatest impact on food consumption and income distribution in Peru; (2) as a result of the change in relative prices, there was a noticeable shift in the diet (especially among those living in the highlands) away from traditional foods to importable foodstuffs, together with lower incentives for the production of these goods, a shift that slowed the growth of the production of agricultural tradables and made Peru more dependent on imported food; and (3) as consumers of food, upper-income urban dwellers benefited more in relative and absolute terms than people in the rest of the country, especially those in rural coastal areas.

In Chapter 3 García García explains how Colombia's coffee boom and expansionary fiscal policies contributed to the declining performance of agriculture from the mid-1970s to the early 1980s. (Coffee represents about 44 percent of Colombia's total official exports.) The substantial rise in the world price of coffee between 1975 and 1979 and the subsequent expansionary fiscal and monetary policies led to a sharp increase in the relative price of home goods. The appreciating real exchange rate in turn caused the production of tradables to become relatively less profitable and instead promoted the consumption of tradables, which expanded imports and reduced the export surplus. Thus the coffee boom and expansionary macroeconomic policies biased production incentives against the entire tradable goods component of agriculture.

The large and unpredictable fluctuations in export prices in Colombia have made it difficult to maintain a real exchange rate consistent with long-term growth and export diversification. The paradox for this country—which is associated with the Dutch disease phenomenon—is that even a promising temporary development, such as a sharp rise in the world prices of certain exportables, can have an adverse effect on the rest of the tradable goods sector, including agriculture, for a number of years.

García García also finds that the decline in relative agricultural prices in Colombia, attributable to the coffee boom and continuous budget deficit, significantly lowered agricultural investment and reduced real wages in agriculture.

As Oyejide documents in Chapter 4, the Nigerian government pursued an import-substitution strategy in the 1960s and the early 1970s to promote rapid industrial growth. A subsequent oil boom and accompanying trade, exchange rate, and other macroeconomic policies reinforced this trend toward industrialization. In response—as in Colombia during the coffee boom—the real exchange rate appreciated significantly, and competitiveness, output, and employment in the nonbooming tradable goods sectors, most notably agriculture, declined.

Nigeria is an interesting case because the increased revenue from oil enabled the government to introduce policy reforms intended to favor agriculture. For example, it eliminated export taxes on farm products, reorganized the marketing boards, subsidized fertilizer, and guaranteed minimum prices for farm output. The level of protection at the official exchange rate increased for both food and export crops. In 1982, crop production received substantial protection, ranging from 18 percent for rubber to 14 percent for maize. Only cotton was explicitly taxed. Despite these moves, growth in real agricultural output stagnated or declined.

The reason is found in the way other sectors reacted to these incentives. Between 1970 and 1984, real producer prices declined sharply and then remained constant. In the process, agricultural exports declined by more than 20 percent, to a level less than 3 percent of total export revenues, and agriculture's share in non-oil GDP fell from 60 percent in 1960–1965 to 30 percent in 1978–1981. To a significant extent, labor and capital moved to services and infrastructure. Government spending increased faster than GDP (its share rising from 6 percent of GDP in 1960 to 30 percent in 1980) and caused a massive buildup of internal and external debt.

One of the most dramatic manifestations of the combined effect of the Dutch disease phenomenon and industrial protection was the tremendous flow of labor out of agriculture. Because Nigerian agriculture has been very labor-intensive, peak-period labor shortages and low labor productivity have probably been the binding constraint on production and the main reason for the country's poor agricultural performance. At the same time, as other sectors developed, they provided improved off-farm employment opportunities that pushed up rural wages: their index went from 100 in 1970 to 232 in 1982.

The adverse effect of the oil boom on non-oil tradables was more severe for agriculture than for manufacturing, because of the special labor constraints of agriculture and because manufacturing received more import protection than did agriculture. Thus, both the Dutch disease associated with the oil boom and general trade and exchange rate policies taxed agriculture in Nigeria.

Chapter 5 is on Zaire, which thus far has been the subject of few economic policy studies and has a poor data base. Agriculture employs 80 percent of the labor force and generates 40 percent of GDP; it accounted for only about 16 percent of total exports between 1971 and 1981. Copper is the dominant export.

Using a simple incidence parameter model, Tshibaka examines some of the implications of trade and exchange rate policies for agriculture in Zaire in the context of the substantial structural and institutional changes that followed independence in 1960. He concludes that these policies imposed heavy implicit taxation on all agricultural exportables and some import-competing food crops. He suggests that the production of exportables such as palm oil, cotton, and groundnuts could compete with the major staples such as rice and maize, an important opportunity for Zaire given the thinness of its world markets for white maize and rice.

In Chapter 6, Bautista provides a quantitative analysis of the effects of trade and exchange rate policies on relative incentives in the Philippine economy, particularly in agriculture. Bautista shows that the trade and exchange rate policies in effect from 1950 to 1980 for the most part favored producers of import-competing goods over exports. He computes average effective exchange rates by product category to highlight the differences in the effects on different classes of exports and imports, and his estimates reveal a persistent bias against the production of traditional agricultural exports such as sugar, coconut, pineapple, and tobacco.

Bautista also uses the aggregative incidence parameter model to simulate a free-trade scenario. The results here, too, indicate a heavy bias against the production of exportables relative to home goods and import-competing activities. Traditional exports bear a heavier burden than nontraditional exports.

The study analyzes two sources of real exchange rate misalignment in the Philippines, namely, trade restrictions and sustained trade deficits. In general, trade policy has been a dominant factor in the price bias against agriculture. At the same time, the impact of the trade deficits on the real exchange rate explains why, even after a significant liberalization of trade restrictions in the Philippines in the 1970s, the production of agricultural exportables continued to be taxed, albeit implicitly.

In Chapter 7 on Pakistan, Dorosh develops a quantitative framework to measure the combined effect of trade and exchange rate policies and agricultural price policies on production incentives for agriculture from 1961 to 1987. He presents measures of the implicit trade taxes and effective exchange rates for imports and exports in Pakistan and discusses the movements in the real exchange rate.

This is the only chapter to use regression analysis to examine the determinants of the real exchange rate. It gives particular attention to the endogeneity of some of the explanatory variables (including trade policies, foreign terms of trade, workers' remittances, foreign grants, and long-term borrowing). Some of these variables are not exogenous but are determined simultaneously with the real exchange rate. The results of the regression analysis are used to construct a time series of the equilibrium real exchange rate, which is compared with estimates based on the elasticities and purchasing power parity approaches.

The study finds that the overvaluation of the rupee in the 1960s outweighed the protection provided by the sectoral price policies for wheat, ordinary rice, and cotton and increased the taxation of basmati rice. In the 1970s and early 1980s, the economywide policies reinforced the direct taxation through sectoral price policies for wheat, basmati rice, and ordinary rice, although the influence of the real exchange rate was smaller than in the 1960s. Sugarcane is a different story: it was given substantial direct protection until 1982, and in spite of the misalignment in the prevailing real exchange rate, sugar production received positive total protection throughout the period, except in the years between 1972 and 1977.

The next two chapters—on Argentina and Chile—examine the determinants of agricultural growth from an economywide perspective, with emphasis on the dynamics of economic adjustment. In Chapter 8 on Argentina, Cavallo, Mundlak, and Domenech conclude that agriculture was a strong force behind the country's rapid economic growth from 1913 to approximately 1930. Thereafter, Argentina's economic vitality declined significantly. Although the world prices of its agricultural exports declined continuously in real terms, the authors attribute the slower growth mainly to domestic economic policies.

The hypothesis of the study is that macroeconomic and trade policies were the principal determinants of economic performance. The authors constructed an econometric model to examine the dynamic effects of a hypothetical policy reform in 1930. To simulate the effects of trade liberalization, they estimated behavioral equations for consumption, private investment and its sectoral allocation, factor share, employment, output, and trade flows. This empirical analysis predicts a significantly higher growth rate for agriculture than in the base run, mainly as a result of the induced rapid capital accumulation in agriculture and faster growth in nonagricultural output. To the extent that new technologies are embodied in capital goods, new investments in agriculture have a positive effect on the level of agricultural productivity beyond that attributable to capital deepening. The simulation results also bring out the significant trade-off between the protection of urban real wages and the performance of the economy.

In Chapter 9 on Chile, Coeymans and Mundlak develop a growth model in which the production sectors (agriculture, mining, services, and manufacturing) are linked explicitly through an input-output matrix. The model is formulated in a way that allows the authors to analyze the effects of current events on sectoral growth and therefore resembles the one they used to study Argentina. In Chapter 9, however, the authors present a more disaggregated structure of the links between agriculture and the other sectors. Technological change, sectoral investment, and sectoral labor demand and supply are endogenously determined from an econometrically estimated model for the period 1962–1982.

Although this was a turbulent period for the Chilean economy— owing to changes in the terms of trade, political instability, and changes in economic policies—the model is able to capture the changes in the employment of labor and capital, intersectoral migration, and returns on labor and capital, among other endogenous variables.

The authors present three policy simulations involving changes in the prices of agricultural and industrial products and in the real exchange rate. Using the historical levels of overall investment and labor supply, they find that the hypothetical changes in relative prices affect resource allocation significantly: labor and capital shift to the sectors with higher returns. In this simulation, the capital-labor ratio in agriculture declines continuously and the long-run aggregate supply elasticity for agriculture is 1.4. This elasticity estimate is considerably higher than those obtained for other countries in single-equation regression analysis that does not take into account the effects of agricultural product price changes on factor markets (see Herdt 1970; Reca 1980; and Bond 1983).[4] It is also considerably higher than the estimates put forth by structuralists in the 1950s and 1960s for the aggregate agricultural supply responsiveness to incentives in Latin America.

The regional surveys in Chapters 10 (Asia), 11 (Africa), and 12 (Latin America) review the findings in other studies on the extent to which trade and macroeconomic policies have influenced agricultural incentives in developing countries. A common theme is that agriculture in developing countries, particularly agricultural exports, has borne a heavy implicit tax burden as a result of industrial protection, real exchange rate appreciation, and related macroeconomic policies.

Most countries in the three regions have relatively open economies, with foreign trade contributing 25 percent or more of GDP. Their trade is often dominated by agricultural exports, whose performance has significant implications for their foreign exchange earnings. However, the links between macroeconomic policies and agriculture go beyond the sector's contribution to foreign exchange earnings. Trade and macroeconomic policies exert their influence on the entire structure of relative prices, essentially through the real exchange rate mechanism. A central premise in this volume is that, in view of the high degree of tradability of agricultural output, the real exchange rate is perhaps the variable that has the greatest influence on the structure of price incentives for agriculture. The theory of real exchange rate determination is therefore particularly relevant in empirical assessments of the effects of sector-specific and economywide policies on agricultural incentives.

Among the many policy influences on agricultural incentives, industrial protection appears the most pervasive. In the case of Africa, for example, Oyejide observes that the agricultural exports of Côte d'Ivoire and Mauritius absorbed a tax amounting to more than 80 percent of the protection for the industrial sector in those countries during the 1970s and early 1980s. The evidence cited by Bautista on Asia and García García on Latin America indicates that agricultural exporters in those regions, along with the producers of unprotected import-competing products, have paid at least half the cost of the heavy protection of domestic industry.

Government expenditures are another policy variable influencing the real exchange rate. Particularly in the cases of Latin America and sub-Saharan Africa, the real exchange rate has often appreciated because of a lack of fiscal discipline. That hurt the relative profitability of producing tradable goods and constrained the growth of output.

Agriculture plays a strikingly similar role in the development strategies of the three regions. One common feature of these strategies was their emphasis on industrialization as the key to economic growth, financed partly through a transfer of resources from agriculture. Second, many countries depended quite heavily on taxes from trade as a source of government revenue, a practice that inevitably imposed a heavy burden on agricultural exports.

One of the most important findings of the three regional surveys is that, by and large, the indirect effects of economywide policies were more powerful than the direct effects of sector-specific policies. The surveys also reveal that a strong link exists between macroeconomic policies and wages (and employment) in agriculture in some countries: in Nigeria, where the policy response to the Dutch disease phenomenon in the 1970s resulted in a labor cost squeeze that led to a significant loss of competitiveness by the agricultural sector, and in Colombia and Chile, where macroeconomic policies during the 1960s and 1970s led to a marked decline in real rural wages and agricultural employment.

Concluding Remarks

The fact that trade and macroeconomic policies in many predominantly agricultural economies show a significant price bias against agriculture implies that long-run economic efficiency and growth are not the only concerns of policy makers in developing countries. Although the country studies in this volume focus on the effects of trade and macroeconomic policies, they do not consider why governments adopted those distortionary policies and why policy makers were unable or unwilling to correct them.

Some countries were reluctant to move to a more neutral (or less distorted) structure of incentives through trade policy reform because they thought the short-run variability of international prices would be transmitted more fully to the domestic price structure under a more open trade regime. Agricultural price stabilization is significant enough to merit a detailed discussion, which is given in Chapter 13. An important point argued by Knudsen and Nash is that long-run average domestic price levels that conform to world price trends do not preclude government efforts to stabilize agricultural prices in the short run.

Policy makers in developing countries are also deeply concerned about the short-run negative fiscal, balance of payments, and growth effects that adjustment to a more open trade regime might entail. This policy issue is discussed in Chapter 15 with particular reference to developing countries that have limited access to commercial credit and need to undertake macroeconomic adjustment to deal with the related problems of external debt servicing, foreign exchange shortages, and depressed economic activity.

The country studies and regional surveys do not examine the political factors bearing on the observed distortion in agricultural prices. It is of course important to recognize the political constraints on the choice of economic policies; in particular, the "determination of agricultural prices is intensely political" (Ahmed and Mellor 1988, 1). Indeed, quite often governments do not adopt superior policies for political reasons. Policy makers do not march solely to the economist's drumbeat. Apart from economic rationality, a key ingredient in effective policy making is political feasibility. It is difficult not to agree with Schultz, however, that policy analysts "lose their potential as educators" if they "merely accommodate governments" and "rationalize what is being done" (Schultz 1978, 9). The experience of many developing countries shows only too well the marked disparity between official declarations of goals oriented toward social welfare on the one hand and the government's revealed preferences on the other.

Instead of taking a fatalistic and deterministic view of the political process, economists can try to improve the knowledge base for policy making and to appraise policy trade-offs, drawing on economic theory and empirical evidence to provide, for example, estimates of the economic effects of current government policy and of any proposed policy changes. As Krueger points out in Chapter 14, the role of knowledge in influencing policy can be significant. Increased public understanding of the benefits of trade and exchange rate liberalization can help generate political pressures that offset the vested interests seeking to maintain industrial protection at the expense of agriculture and the rest of the economy. It can also confer a sense of legitimacy on political decisions affecting economic policies, which may then be easier to implement.

Policy makers are not a homogeneous group. There are likely to be different voices in the policy debate within the government. Except where an individual personality or a powerful ideology dominates, unanimity of opinion on policy choices that stand to produce many gainers and losers among various constituencies is rare. It is not clear that the protagonists would accept any set of economic policies without knowledge of their likely effects on relative prices and associated distribution of net benefits.

The results of positive (as opposed to normative) analysis are therefore an important input into policy making, contributing to informed discussion, both within and outside government, of the relative merits of alternative economic policies. This argument assumes greater force in cases where the indirect effects of government policy are not readily discernible. In the present context, as indicated above and well demonstrated in the country studies, the indirect price, output, and distributional impacts of trade and macroeconomic policies, evaluated from a general equilibrium perspective, often diverge from and invariably outweigh their partial equilibrium direct effects. Policy makers (or at least their advisers) need to know the unintended consequences of policies that have been adopted and to remain alert to the likely direct and indirect repercussions of proposed policy changes.

Notes to Chapter 1

1. In Nigeria, for example, agricultural exports such as cocoa, rubber, cotton, palm oil, palm kernel, and groundnuts faced taxes of 5–60 percent during the 1960s and early 1970s (Oyejide 1986a, 25). In the Philippines, sugar was a government monopoly in both the domestic and foreign markets from 1974 to 1980, and producers received an average of only 77 percent of the world price (Bautista 1987b, 27).

2. It is also possible that a country's income per capita and agricultural share in GDP can be affected significantly by the nominal protection of its major agricultural products. In turn, other more dominant factors (unrelated to agricultural protection) underlie intercountry differences in income per capita and agricultural share.

3. Under the small-country assumption, a country's trade is too small to affect significantly the world prices of its exports and imports.

4. Bond's frequently cited study of agricultural supply response in sub-Saharan Africa has been faulted for using output *per capita* as the dependent variable (Schiff 1987, 385).

II

Country Studies

Trade Policies, Relative Prices, Real Incomes, and Food Consumption in Peru, 1964–1982

From the late 1950s through the late 1970s, Peru pursued policies that protected import-competing nonagricultural activities and depressed the structure of agricultural incentives. At the same time, the government used price controls and subsidies in the markets for food to foster industrialization by lowering the urban cost of living. Recent policies have begun to reverse the distortions against agriculture, but they still appear to be biased in favor of commercial rather than household-based agriculture.

This chapter measures the induced taxation of agriculture that has arisen from these conditions as a result of their independent effects on the real exchange rate. The policies of interest to us are those that affect the structure of relative prices within the Peruvian economy. Relative prices are the signals that influence the way individuals allocate resources to production and consumption. In this analysis, we divide the productive side of the economy into traded and nontraded components of agriculture and the rest of the economy. We divide the consumption side of the economy into real expenditures for food and other consumption for five population groups—the upper and lower halves of the expenditure and income distribution in the city of Lima, the rural Sierra, and other urban and rural populations.

Our central hypothesis is that the effects of the import-substitution policy on the structure of relative prices dominated the effects of the direct agricultural price policies in determining the patterns and levels of agricultural output and expenditures for food.

Trade Policy and the Structure of Relative Prices

Peru's trade or commercial policy of the past four decades has entailed a complex structure of tariffs, quota restrictions, and other protective mechanisms. The government's aim was to promote industrialization and import substitution by protecting the import-competing nonagricultural sectors from international competition.

Such attempts to protect a particular sector through tariffs and other barriers to imports can generate important and perhaps unintended effects on the unprotected sectors through the real exchange rate (see also Sjaastad 1980, and García García 1981). In short, in a small open economy such as Peru's, theory predicts that the economic forces resulting from attempts to protect a particular sector from international competition will increase the share of imported foods and decrease the share of nontradables in the food consumption patterns of the population. Such a phenomenon is widely believed to have taken place in Peru.

Analytical Framework

The analytical framework for assessing the effects of agricultural pricing and trade policies on food consumption is based on assumptions for a small open economy—that is, one that faces given international prices for the goods it trades. We divide the real sectors of the economy into two principal sectors: agriculture and the rest of the economy. Within each of these, there is one subsector whose output is not traded internationally, whereas the other subsectors produce internationally tradable commodities (exports or products that compete with imports).

We used time-series data on prices to estimate the incidence of trade policies on the structure of relative prices under general equilibrium conditions. Similarly, we used time-series data from Peru's national product and income accounts to estimate the supply elasticities for value added in three agricultural subsectors and the manufacturing sector. We traced the effects of changes in relative prices on the expenditure patterns of five population groups by means of econometric estimates of the demand systems for consumption expenditures for the five groups. The three components of the analytical apparatus—incidence of policies on relative prices, supply analysis, and income and expenditure analysis—were integrated by means of a computer simulation model to calculate the effects of alternative trade policies on relative prices, sectoral outputs, and households' real income and expenditure patterns. The apparatus is a model of resource allocation to the real parts of the economy and excludes explicit consideration of monetary aspects. Readers must therefore interpret the conclusions of this study as if these omitted effects were neutral with respect to food consumption, sectoral employment, and the distribution of income.

The most relevant issue here is the existence of at least one sector in the economy that is, in principle, not traded internationally. In Peru, the service sector (which includes construction, transportation, and most important, marketing services for agricultural and food commodities) is that sector. In agriculture, roots, tubers, legumes, and horticultural crops are also considered nontradables.

In the case of mineral exports, it is assumed that performance is governed by sectoral policies and international prices and not by the economic policies for other sectors, particularly agriculture.

The nomenclature and symbols for the analytical framework are defined as follows:

a = agriculture

n = the rest of the economy (nonagriculture)

x = exports (traded subsector in each sector)

m = import-competing goods (traded subsector in each sector)

h = home goods (nontraded subsectors)

Z = production in value added terms

C = consumption in final household expenditure terms

Total value added (gross domestic product, GDP) was disaggregated into the following components:

$$Z = Z_{ah} + Z_{ax} + Z_{am} + Z_{nx} + Z_{nm} + Z_{nh}, \qquad (2.1)$$

where $Z_a = Z_{ah} + Z_{ax} + Z_{am}$ (that is, the value added of the agricultural sector is equal to the sum of the value added of the nontraded, import-competing, and export-producing subsectors, respectively).

Consumption, in the form of final household expenditures, is

$$C = C_{ah} + C_{ax} + C_{am} + C_{nm} + C_{nh}, \qquad (2.2)$$

the sum of aggregate household expenditures on agricultural and non-agricultural products. Final consumption expenditures on agricultural products (for example, food expenditures) include expenditures on manufactured goods (such as processing and packaging) and services (such as marketing).

The Structure of Relative Prices

The household model highlights the effects of price changes on real income. Two sets of prices are relevant:

1. The retail price of food. This price is derived from the wholesale price (farmgate), the price of manufactured foods (used as inputs into the production and processing of food), and the price of nontraded services (such as marketing). It is related to the consumption functions. Symbolically, the retail price index for food (importable) can be expressed as

$$EP^R = \alpha_{am}EP_{am} + \alpha_{nm}EP_{nm} + \alpha_{nh}EP_{nh}, \qquad (2.3)$$

where E denotes logarithmic differentiation ($E = \text{dln}$), superscript R represents retail prices, and α_{am}, α_{nm}, and α_{nh} are the value weights of agricultural products, manufactured goods, and nontraded nonagricultural services, respectively, in the final consumption expenditures for food. The price of home goods and importables from nonagricultural sectors affects the price of food in two ways—as inputs into the production process and as components of the farm-to-retail price spread. A policy that favors manufactured goods over agricultural goods may produce smaller than anticipated reductions in the retail price of food, since the effects of "protecting" industry would offset the effects of cheap food policies (at least in part). Relation (2.3) may be used for agricultural export prices.

2. The relative wholesale price for agricultural commodities and import-competing (protected) nonagricultural commodities. It is related to the value-added functions. The domestic price of the tradable commodities can be expressed as

$$EP_{am} = EP^*_{am} + Et_{am} + EN, \qquad (2.4)$$

where N is the nominal (or official) exchange rate, P^* is the world price (including cost, insurance, and freight) of the particular tradable commodity (free on board for exportables), and t_{um} is a proportional tax or subsidy on that commodity. Relation (2.4) may be used for both agricultural export commodities and manufactured goods.

The pricing structure for the analysis consists of wholesale (farm-gate) and retail prices given in relative terms, with the price of nonagricultural nontradables as the economy's numeraire. The log differentials form of the *wholesale* relative prices is given by

nontraded agriculture

$$E(P_{ah}/P_{nh}) = E(P_{ah}/P_{nh}), \qquad (2.5)$$

exportable agriculture

$$E(P_{ax}/P_{nh}) = E(P^*_{ax}/P_{nh}) + Et_{ax} + E(N/P_{nh}), \qquad (2.6)$$

import-competing agriculture

$$E(P_{am}/P_{nh}) = E(P^*_{am}/P_{nh}) + Et_{am} + E(N/P_{nh}), \qquad (2.7)$$

and import-competing manufactures

$$E(P_{nm}/P_{nh}) = E(P^*_{nm}/P_{nh}) + Et_{nm} + E(N/P_{nh}). \qquad (2.8)$$

The log differentials of the *retail* prices are given by

nontraded agriculture

$$E(P_{ah}/P_{nh})^R = \alpha_{ah}E(P_{ah}/P_{nh}), \qquad (2.9)$$

exportable agriculture

$$E(P_{ax}/P_{nh})^R = \alpha_{ax}E(P_{ax}/P_{nh}) + \alpha_{nm,ax}E(P_{nm}/P_{nh}), \qquad (2.10)$$

import-competing agriculture

$$E(P_{am}/P_{nh})^R = \alpha_{am}E(P_{am}/P_{nh}) + \alpha_{nm,am}E(P_{nm}/P_{nh}), \qquad (2.11)$$

and import-competing manufactures

$$E(P_{nm}/P_{nh})^R = E(P_{nm}/P_{nh}). \qquad (2.12)$$

The structure of the relative prices shows how the retail prices for food can be affected directly by the tax and tariff structure resulting from trade policy and indirectly by the effect on the real exchange rate ($E[N/P_{nh}]$). It is difficult to predict the net results of these effects, however, since some move in opposite directions. Changes in the relative prices will affect the composition and size of household expenditures on food and nonfoods not only directly, but also indirectly through the effect of the price change on household real income and on labor income, as production adjusts to respond to the new structure of relative prices.

The relative price of agricultural home goods (P_{ah}/P_{nh}) is assumed to be determined by conditions of internal equilibrium. The demand function for aggregate household expenditures for nontraded agricultural goods is

$$EC_{ah} = \eta_{ah,y}\, EY + \eta_{ah}E(P_{ah}/P_{nh})^R + \eta_{ah,ax}\, E(P_{ax}/P_{nh})^R$$
$$+ \eta_{ah,am}\, E(P_{am}/P_{nh})^R + \eta_{ah,nm}E(P_{nm}/P_{nh})^R, \quad (2.13)$$

where the η's are the income, own-price, and cross-price elasticities of demand for the nontraded agricultural commodity, respectively. The corresponding supply relationship is given by

$$EZ_{ah} = \epsilon_{ah}E(P_{ah}/P_{nh}) + \epsilon_{ah,ax}E(P_{ax}/P_{nh})$$
$$+ \epsilon_{ah,am}E(P_{am}/P_{nh}) + \epsilon_{ah,nm}E(P_{nm}/P_{nh}), \quad (2.14)$$

where the ϵ's are the supply and cross-supply elasticities for the nontraded agricultural commodity, respectively. The equilibrium price is determined by setting $EC_{ah} = EZ_{ah}$ and solving for $E(P_{ah}/P_{nh})^e$:

$$E(P_{ah}/P_{nh})^e = 1/(\epsilon_{ah} - \eta_{ah})\, [(\eta_{ah,ax} - \epsilon_{ah,ax})\, E(P_{ax}/P_{nh})$$
$$+ (\eta_{ah,am} - \epsilon_{ah,am})\, E(P_{am}/P_{nh})$$
$$+ (\eta_{ah,nm} - \epsilon_{ah,nm})\, E(P_{nm}/P_{nh})$$
$$+ \eta_{ah,y}\, EY]. \quad (2.15)$$

Analysis of Sectoral Value Added

After determining the relative prices and supply functions for each good, we estimated the elasticities of supply for each kind of good. Table 2.1 presents the direct and cross-supply elasticities for the three agricultural commodity groupings and for manufactured goods. The elasticities were estimated as a system of equations using maximum likelihood techniques and a Nerlove (1958) specification for each supply equation. The relative prices of all tradables were treated as exogenous (that is, as

TABLE 2.1   Maximum Likelihood Estimates of Supply and
Cross-Supply Elasticities for the Peruvian Economy,
1950–1982

Sectoral value added	Price			
	Agricultural			
	Home goods	Export-ables	Import-ables	Manu-facturing
Agricultural home goods	0.39	−0.49	0.14	−0.55
Agricultural exportables	−0.20	0.91	−0.30	0.41
Agricultural importables	−0.65	−0.01	0.60	0.44
Manufacturing	−0.27	−0.09	0.22	0.44

SOURCE: Sigma One Corporation, estimates from time-series data.

given by world prices and trade and exchange rate policies); the relative prices of nontraded agricultural goods were treated as endogenous. All prices were relative to the numeraire P_{nh}.

The estimated system of elasticities did not reflect adjustment in the factor markets, particularly the labor market; it was based on exogenous product prices on the assumption that these prices reflected world prices and institutionally determined distortions. The system of supply equations should be considered the result of estimating a set of reduced form equations, because the structure excluded important endogenous relationships. Accordingly, no symmetry conditions were imposed on the parameter estimates. The estimated elasticities represent medium- to short-run adjustments of output in response to changes in relative prices. That is, they were not adjusted for the effects of induced adjustment in the factor markets or of technical innovation. Nevertheless, these elasticities are useful in assessing the direction of changes in output in response to changes in the structure of relative prices, as well as in assessing the approximate magnitudes of the short- to medium-term responses to trade and price policy instruments.

Analysis of Consumer Expenditures

The aggregate consumption expenditure series for the five commodity groups was computed by adding imports or subtracting exports as appropriate and by allocating part of the manufacturing and nontraded, nonagricultural GDP to each subsector so as to equate the output shares from the national accounts data for 1973 to the expenditure shares reported in the ENCA survey (Amat y Leon and Curonisy 1981). The specific computations were as follows. For consumption expenditures:

$$C_{ah} = Z_{ah} + \beta_{ah,nh}Z_{nh} \tag{2.16}$$

$$C_{am} = Z_{am} + Z_{am}^M + \beta_{am,nm}Z_{nm} + \beta_{am,nh}Z_{nh} \qquad (2.17)$$

$$C_{ax} = Z_{ax} - Z_{ax}^X + \beta_{ax,nm}Z_{nm} + \beta_{ax,nh}Z_{nh} \qquad (2.18)$$

where Z_{am}^M and Z_{ax}^X represent food imports and agricultural exports, respectively and the β's represent the contribution of the nonagricultural subsectors (nm, nh) to the agricultural subsectors (ah, am, ax) through the manufacturing and service components. The β's, which are given in Table 2.2, were computed by matching the ENCA expenditure patterns to the national accounts using input-output data for 1973, as reported in Reardon (1984). In the case of manufacturing and services, they are necessary to account for final expenditures. Consequently, the final consumption expenditures for manufacturing and services have to be adjusted downward, to reflect that a portion of the output of these sectors is consumed as part of the "spread" between farmgate and retail food prices.

The expenditure series thus created and the corresponding relative prices were used to estimate econometrically a system of demand equations using a procedure described in Swamy and Binswanger (1983) for transcendental logarithmic demand functions. The following statistical specification was used:

$$\mu_i = a_i + b_{iC} \log (C) + b_2 \log (C)^2 + \Sigma\gamma_{ij} \log P_j, \qquad (2.19)$$

where $\mu_i = C_i/C$; $i,j = ah$, ax, am, nm, and nh, and $C = \Sigma C_i$.

The neoclassical conditions of demand were imposed to yield

1. $\Sigma\gamma_{ij} = 0$ for all i,
2. $\gamma_{ij} = \gamma_{ji}$,

TABLE 2.2   Sectoral Value Added to Food Items by the Manufacturing and Service Sectors, 1973 (percentage of value added in final consumption expenditures for food)

Food items	Nonagricultural sectors	
	Manufacturing	Nontraded (services)
Import-competing items	4	15
Exportables	1	5
Nontradables	0	13

SOURCE: Computations from Amat y Leon and Curonisy (1981), INE (1983), and Reardon (1984).

3. the redundancy for the *nh* equation, and

4. the relativity of prices to P_{nh}.

These conditions either were required (especially, for example condition 3) or were imposed in the estimation. The demand elasticities were estimated from the statistical parameter estimates, as follows:

direct (own) price demand elasticities

$$\eta_{ii} = EC_i/EP_i = \gamma_{ij}/\mu_i + \mu_i - 1 \qquad (2.20)$$

cross-price demand elasticities

$$\eta_{ij} = EC_i/EP_j = \gamma_{ij}/\mu_i + \mu_j \qquad (2.21)$$

income elasticities

$$\eta_{iy} = b_{iC} + 2b_{iC} \text{ Log } C/\mu_i + 1. \qquad (2.22)$$

The translog specification was chosen because it is a flexible demand system (at least locally) and because the formulae for the demand parameters are functions of the estimated coefficients (γ_{ij} and b_{iC}) and of the budget shares (equations (2.20) through (2.22)). This latter feature permits the estimation of demand parameters for different population groups. The budget shares (μ_i) from Table 2.3 and the estimated statistical parameters were used to compute a system of demand elasticities for each of the five population groups, as presented in Table 2.4.

The previous sections presented the methodology to measure the effects of changes in relative prices on consumption expenditures for five population groups. The next sections estimate the distortion in the real exchange rate attributable to trade policies, using the equivalent tariff and the incidence parameter.

The Real Exchange Rate

As stated earlier, the system of protection prevailing in Peru during the 1960s and 1970s consisted of import duties, quantitative restrictions, and export subsidies. Because these duties and subsidies were not uniform, estimation of the "true" tariffs and subsidies (that is, in relation to home goods) requires the estimation of a uniform tariff equivalent (T'). It

TABLE 2.3   Income Distribution and Expenditure Patterns of Five Population Groups in Peru, 1972–1973

Population group	Income distribution		Expenditure patterns (% of total expenditures)				
	Proportion of national consumption by group (%)	Proportion of country's households by population (%)	Agricultural goods			Nonagricultural goods	
			Non-tradable	Exportable	Import-competing	Import-competing	Non-tradable
Lima, upper income	25.5	10.05	12.0	6.0	17.0	38.0	27.0
Lima, lower income	8.5	10.05	15.6	9.9	28.2	20.2	26.1
Sierra, rural	24.0	40.4	30.3	6.3	25.0	18.3	20.1
Non-Lima urban	30.0	25.5	18.6	8.0	27.7	25.4	20.3
Non-Sierra rural	12.0	14.0	20.6	5.7	29.1	20.6	24.0

Sources: Amat y Leon and Curonisy (1981), and national accounts data.

TABLE 2.4   Matrices of Own- and Cross-Price Elasticities for
Consumer Expenditures by Population Group in Peru,
1950–1982

	Income elasticity	ah	ax	am	nm	nh
Lima, upper income						
ah	0.868	−0.764	0.019	0.004	0.407	0.479
ax	0.768	0.039	−0.799	0.196	0.645	0.619
am	0.678	0.003	0.069	−0.678	0.512	0.097
nm	1.274	0.128	0.101	0.228	−0.841	0.387
nh	0.918	0.213	0.138	0.061	0.547	−0.989
Lima, lower half						
ah	0.898	−0.755	0.068	0.154	0.220	0.427
ax	0.859	0.107	−0.815	0.298	0.362	0.478
am	0.806	0.085	0.105	−0.627	0.281	0.162
nm	1.518	0.171	0.177	0.392	−1.221	0.487
nh	0.906	0.250	0.178	0.172	0.370	−0.997
Sierra, rural						
ah	0.948	−0.651	0.047	0.184	0.192	0.265
ax	0.779	0.225	−0.802	0.275	0.434	0.515
am	0.780	0.223	0.069	−0.648	0.271	0.065
nm	1.573	0.319	0.149	0.371	−1.285	0.427
nh	0.996	0.440	0.178	0.089	0.427	−1.201
Other urban						
ah	0.915	−0.739	0.054	0.170	0.270	0.355
ax	0.826	0.125	−0.814	0.297	0.451	0.481
am	0.802	0.114	0.086	−0.631	0.334	0.114
nm	1.413	0.197	0.142	0.365	−1.083	0.395
nh	0.835	0.300	0.176	0.143	0.457	−1.100
Other rural						
ah	0.923	−0.726	0.033	0.194	0.221	0.365
ax	0.757	0.121	−0.795	0.318	0.482	0.609
am	0.811	0.138	0.063	0.621	0.283	0.142
nm	1.508	0.221	0.134	0.398	−1.208	0.459
nh	0.903	0.310	0.143	0.170	0.390	−1.004

NOTE: ah = agricultural home goods; ax = agricultural exportables; am = agricultural importables; nm = nonagricultural import-competing goods; and nh = nonagricultural nontradables.
SOURCE: Sigma One Corporation, estimates from time-series data.

represents a hypothetical uniform tariff expressed as an ad valorem tariff. If the structure of domestic relative prices resulting from the prevailing tariffs, quantity restrictions, and export subsidies were replaced with T', the result would be the same volume of trade, but a different composition of trade, in the absence of adjustments in the nominal exchange rate or the nominal price of home goods. With respect to quantitative restrictions, this tariff estimate represents their tariff and subsidy equivalents (the equivalent uniform tariff would restrict the demand for imports and adjust the supply of exports by the same amount, in terms of the volume of trade, as do the actual trade restrictions).

The procedure for estimating T' is as follows:

$$\frac{P_m}{P_x} = \frac{P_m^*}{P_x^*} \cdot \frac{N}{N} \cdot \frac{(1 + t)}{(1 + s)} = \frac{P_m^*}{P_x^*}(1 + T'), \qquad (2.23)$$

where $(1 + T') = T$ replaces the actual set of trade interventions represented by $(1 + t)$ and $(1 + s)$.

Assuming that T_0 is known in a base period t_0, to estimate T_1 for the next period requires calculating the change in T' by taking the logarithmic derivation of equation (2.23):

$$E(1 + T') = E(P_m/P_x) - E(P_m^*/P_x^*) \qquad (2.24)$$

$$E(1 + T') = \text{Ln}(1 + T_1) - \text{Ln}(1 + T_0). \qquad (2.25)$$

Thus

$$T_1 = (\exp[E\{P_m/P_x\} - E\{P_m^*/P_x^*\}]) \cdot (1 + T_0) - 1. \qquad (2.26)$$

Equation (2.26) is used to calculate T_1, assuming T_0 is known. Beginning with the known value of T_0, the series $T_1, T_2, \ldots, Tn$ can be estimated. $E(1 + T')$ is the variable that explains the changes in the actual volume of trade not explained by changes in the terms of trade (P_m^*/P_x^*) and by other sources of a shift in the demand for imports and supply of exports.

The first step in calculating the expression $E(P_m/P_x)$ of relation (2.26) consists of estimating the import demand or export supply equations and then determining which part of the dependent variable is explained by the variation in the relative price. A reduced form of excess demand for importables (import demand) can be expressed as a function of the two relative prices, (P_m) and (P_h), the level of aggregate real production (national income expressed as Z), and aggregate real expenditures (C):

$$\text{ln}M = a_0 + a_1\text{ln}(P_m/P_x) + a_2\text{ln}(P_h/P_x) + a_3\text{ln}Z + a_4\text{ln}C, \quad (2.27)$$

where M is a quantum index of imports and P_h equals the price of nontradables (for a more detailed presentation, see Sjaastad 1980).

Coefficients a_3 and a_4 should not be treated as output and expenditure elasticities for importables, because M reflects production as well as demand. In that respect, it refers to excess demand (for imports) and not to the demand for importables.

Using the condition of equilibrium in the home goods market and after some substitution, equation (2.27) can be expressed as

$$\ln M = v_0 + v_1 \ln(P_m/P_x) + v_2 \ln Z + v_3 \ln BT + v_4 \ln(M - X), (2.28)$$

where BT equals the trade balance as a fraction of national income, M equals the value of imports in domestic currency at external prices, and X equals that of exports.[1]

It can be established that

$$E(P_m/P_x) = \frac{E(M) - v_2 E(Z) - v_3 E(BT) - v_4 E(M - X)}{v_1}. \quad (2.29)$$

This expression, when replaced in (2.26), permits T' to be defined for a determined period.

We estimated the import demand equations used in this analysis with regression analysis, using annual data for the period 1940–1983. The regression coefficients for relative prices, income, and the import-export ratio were quite stable and significant, while the terms of trade and balance of trade were not.

The evolution of the uniform equivalent tariff (T') for Peru is presented in Table 2.5. It indicates the economy became closed to international trade during the late 1960s and the 1970s.

The Incidence Parameter

In this section, we compute the effects of trade policy on the relative prices of agriculture tradables by estimating the incidence parameter.

TABLE 2.5   Peru's Uniform Equivalent Tariff (T'), 1949–1982

Period	Average annual percentage
1949–1953	5.4
1954–1958	29.9
1959–1963	71.2
1964–1968	133.0
1969–1973	256.0
1974–1978	181.7
1979–1982	91.3

NOTE: The base value of T'_0 for 1948 equal to 6 percent was obtained from Nogues (1991).
SOURCE: Authors' calculations.

Our analysis of the incidence of the trade regime and exchange rate policy for a small open economy is based on a simple three-sector model of importables, exportables, and home goods (Dornbusch 1974; Sjaastad 1980). General equilibrium is implied by equilibrium in the home goods market and assumed equilibrium in the balance of payments and in the monetary sector.

Given the relationship of equation (2.23), if we hold income, capital, labor, and technology constant, we arrive at a new equilibrium when

$$(\eta_m - \epsilon_m)\, E(P_m/P_h) + (\eta_x - \epsilon_x)\, E(P_x/P_h) = 0, \qquad (2.30)$$

where E represents the logarithmic differential, η_m and η_x represent the demand elasticities for home goods with respect to the price of importables and exportables, respectively, and ϵ_m and ϵ_x are the corresponding cross-supply elasticities.

Given world prices, the incidence of a change in the trade barriers on exportables is given by:

$$E(P_h) - E(P_x) = \omega(E[P_m] - E[P_x]) \qquad (2.31)$$

and

$$\omega = (\eta_m - \epsilon_m)/([\eta_m - \epsilon_m] + [\eta_x - \epsilon_x]), \qquad (2.32)$$

with $0 \leq \omega \leq 1$. The incidence parameter, ω, consists essentially of substitution relationships (Sjaastad 1980).

Equation (2.31) leads directly to the statistical specification for estimating ω:

$$\ln(P_h/P_x) = a + \omega\ln(P_m/P_x), \qquad (2.33)$$

which can be estimated using ordinary least squares.

In line with the approach used by García García (1981) for Colombia and Bautista (1985) for the Philippines to capture the effect on agricultural exports, and by disaggregating importables into agricultural and nonagricultural components (such as manufacturing), we estimated the following equations, using monthly data from 1966 to 1983 (sample size is 215) and the Cochrane-Orcutt technique. For agricultural exportables,

$$\ln(P_{nh}/P_{ax}) = -0.11 + 0.07\ln(P_{nx}/P_{ax}) + 0.67\ln(P_m/P_{ax})$$
$$\qquad\quad (-0.73)\quad (2.7)\qquad\qquad\qquad (18.7) \qquad\qquad (2.34)$$

where $\bar{R}^2 = 0.97$, DW $= 1.96$, and RHO $= 0.99$. For agricultural importables,

$$\ln(P_{nh}/P_{am}) = -0.14 + 0.56\ln(P_{nm}/P_{am}) + 0.19\ln(P_x/P_{am})$$
$$\quad\quad\quad (-0.14)\ (15.7) \quad\quad\quad\quad\quad\quad (5.5) \quad\quad\quad\quad\quad (2.35)$$

where $\bar{R}^2 = 0.96$, DW $= 1.95$, RHO $= 0.99$, and where the t-statistics are in parentheses.

These results can be used to compute the effects on the relative prices of agricultural tradables. Total differentiation of equations (2.34) and (2.35) yields

$$E(P_{nh}/P_{ax}) = \omega_{nx}E(P_{nx}/P_{ax}) + \omega_m E(P_m/P_{ax}) \quad\quad (2.36)$$

$$E(P_{nh}/P_{am}) = \omega_{nm} E(P_{nm}/P_{am}) + \omega_x E(P_x/P_{am}). \quad\quad (2.37)$$

Sjaastad (1980) introduced the concept of "true protection," or the increase in the price of tradables relative to the price of home goods caused by an increase in tariffs. This true tariff, or true tax, on agricultural tradables is

$$E(P_{ax}/P_{nh}) = 1 + t_{ax}/1 + d - 1 = t^*_{ax} \quad\quad (2.38)$$

$$E(P_{am}/P_{nh}) = 1 + t_{am}/1 + d - 1 = t^*_{am}. \quad\quad (2.39)$$

If (2.36) is replaced in (2.38) and (2.37) in (2.39),

$$t^*_{ax} = \frac{(\omega 1_{nm} + \omega_x)EP_{am} - \omega_{nm}EP_{nm} - \omega_x EP_x}{1 + (1 - \omega_{nm} - \omega_x)EP_{am} + \omega_{nm}EP_{nm} + \omega_x EP_x} \quad\quad (2.40)$$

$$t^*_{am} = \frac{(1 - \omega_{nx} - \omega_m)EP_{ax} + \omega_{nx}EP_{nx} + \omega_m EP_m}{1 + (1 - \omega_{nx} - \omega_m)EP_{ax} + \omega_{nx}EP_{nx} + \omega_m EP_m} \quad\quad (2.41)$$

where t^*_{am} and t^*_{ax} are the true tariffs for agricultural import and export goods, respectively.

To illustrate the use of these formulas, consider an increase of 10 percent in the tariff on imports of agricultural goods ($EP_{am} = 10$ percent). The estimated values from equations (2.34) and (2.35) imply a true tariff of 7.3 percent on agricultural imports.

The Simulation Exercise

We next developed a computer simulation program to perform comparative static analyses (see the Appendix). The program considers two periods: (1) 1969 to 1973, when there was a rapid increase in the level of industrial protection and a high degree of market intervention, and (2) 1978 to 1982, a period that included an attempt to liberalize the industrial protection strategy. These two periods are compared with the same base period, 1964–1968.

For each period, we developed two policy scenarios, assuming industrial protection: (1) a policy of agricultural price controls and (2) a policy of free trade for agricultural tradables. The trade (or protection) policy is represented by setting the value for T', the uniform tariff equivalent, equal to the change in the policy from the base period. The average equivalent tariffs for the periods 1964–1968, 1969–1973, and 1978–1982 are 133 percent, 256 percent, and 91 percent, respectively. These simulations for the trade regime scenarios therefore assume (1) an increase in T' of 123 percent in 1969–1973 and (2) a reduction in T' of 42 percent in 1978–1982. The agricultural pricing policy is represented by the values of EP^*_{am} and EP^*_{ax}. If these are set at zero, the price control policy is in effect, and if they are set at the observed changes in world prices, the implication is free trade in agricultural commodities.

Through these comparisons we can evaluate the effects of the attempts in the early 1970s to close the Peruvian economy to manufactured imports and to isolate domestic prices from world price movements, in comparison with what might have occurred under the policies of the baseline period, 1964–1968. Even during the baseline period, however, the Peruvian industrial sector received a substantial increase in protection (as shown in Table 2.5).

Industrial Protection, 1969–1973

Aggregate effects. During the period 1969 to 1973, the instruments for industrial protection would have caused the relative price of manufactured goods to rise by just over 18 percent ("true protection") and induced a modest reduction in the retail price of food (Table 2.6). The industrial protection policy would have reduced real producer prices of exportables in agriculture by approximately 35 percent and of import-competing products by approximately 23 percent as a result of the decline in the real exchange rate. Nontradable (traditional) agriculture would have experienced real prices approximately 3 percent lower.

In comparison with the effects of the industrial protection policy on

TABLE 2.6   Effects of Industrial Protection and Agricultural
             Price Controls on Agricultural Production and
             Consumption in Peru, 1969–1973 in Relation to
             1964–1968 (percentage change)

Indicator	Protection with price controls	Protection without price controls
Retail price indexes		
Nontradable foods	−2.9	−2.6
Importable foods	−2.5	−1.6
Manufactured goods	18.2	18.2
Aggregate consumption		
Nontradable foods	3.5	3.2
Importable foods	4.5	3.8
Agricultural production		
Nontradable foods	3.2	2.9
Importable foods	−6.5	−3.8
Exportable products	−17.4	−16.9
Agricultural producer price indexes		
Nontradable foods	−2.9	−2.6
Importable foods	−28.0	−23.2
Exportable products	−37.6	−35.4

NOTE: The effects are changes relative to what would have happened under the same price control and subsidy policy but with the uniform equivalent tariff of the baseline period (1964–1968). All price indexes are relative to the price index for nonagricultural home goods and services.
SOURCE: Authors' calculations.

agricultural producer prices, the effects of the agriculture-specific pricing policies were relatively minor. The price control policies further reduced producer prices approximately 2 to 5 percent for tradable agriculture and less than 0.5 percent on nontradable agriculture. Similarly, the effect of the producer price controls by themselves was barely perceptible at the level of retail prices. However, the combined effect of all the policies made nontraded food considerably more expensive than imported food in relative terms. The main effects came about as a consequence of the industrial protection policy rather than of the agricultural price control policies. The calculations appear to verify our hypothesis that industrial protection policy was dominant in this period.

The taxation of tradable agriculture through the industrial protection policy apparently caused a major shift in resources out of agriculture and a minor shift within agriculture toward the production of nontradables. Whereas the domestic production of nontradable agricultural products increased by about 3 percent, the domestic production of import-competing foodstuffs declined by about 4 percent. Domestic self-sufficiency thus fell. The principal effect of the industrial protection policies was to lower the output of exportable agriculture by more than 15 percent. Overall agricultural output stagnated as a result of the combined trade and agricultural policies.

The industrial protection policy per se and the price control policy induced a small positive increase in aggregate food consumption: between 3 and 4 percent as a result of the indirect effects of the industrial protection policy alone, and an additional 0.7 percent because of the effects of the price control policy on agricultural importables.

The industrial protection policy, all other things being equal, would have severely worsened the balance of agricultural trade. As a result of the indirect taxation of exportable agriculture, the production of export crops would have declined by approximately 17 percent. The production of import-competing agricultural products would also have declined, and their consumption would have increased.

Consumption and distributional effects. The simulated effects on labor incomes were computed as if no adjustments had taken place in the labor market (Table 2.7). As such, they simply illustrate the direction and approximate magnitude of the adjustments in production and consumption necessary to absorb the induced effects of the changes in relative prices arising from the increase in industrial protection and from the interventions in the agricultural product markets.

The most notable result apparent from Table 2.7 is that, in terms of

TABLE 2.7   Effects of Industrial Protection and Agricultural Price Controls on Income Distribution and Consumption in Peru, 1969–1973 in Relation to 1964–1968 (percentage change)

Population group	Protection with price controls			Protection without price controls		
		Food consumption			Food consumption	
	Income	Non-tradable	Import-able	Income	Non-tradable	Import-able
Lima, upper income	−3.7	6.1	7.7	−3.6	6.5	8.3
Lima, lower income	−5.7	0.4	0.9	−5.5	0.6	1.6
Sierra, rural	−1.1	3.7	4.2	−1.3	3.5	4.6
Non-Lima, urban	−2.9	3.8	4.2	−2.7	4.0	4.8
Non-Sierra, rural	−10.7	−4.4	−3.2	−11.2	−4.8	−3.1

NOTE: The effects are changes from the economic comparative static values that would have prevailed in the absence of the policy changes; these effects abstract from the dynamic adjustment effects, growth, weather, and investment. The nontraded commodities are traditional foods, such as potatoes, vegetables, small animal species, and Andean grains; the importable foods are primarily wheat-based products, rice, processed milk, and beef.
SOURCE: Authors' calculations.

food expenditures, the upper half of the income distribution group in Lima benefited the most from all the policies. The poor in Lima benefited very little, and rural consumers were worse off as a result of the industrial protection policies, because the price of nonfood items rose significantly and retail food prices moved very little. This pattern shifted consumption toward food for the population as a whole, and the upper-income households in Lima increased their consumption of food both relatively and absolutely more than any other group.

According to this analysis, the combined effect of the policies was a significant reduction in the incomes of rural, coastal, and jungle dwellers relative to the rest of the population. Apparently, the Lima upper-income and rural Sierra populations benefited relatively more from the lower food prices than did the rest of the population, because the share of food in their budgets was relatively high and, within food, the share of tradable foods (such as wheat, rice, milk, and beef) was high. In terms of the distribution of income, the share of the Lima upper-income and rural Sierra populations in the smaller national income would have increased slightly, whereas that of the other groups would have declined even more. It is important to remember that the rural Sierra population had household incomes equal to about one-fourth those of the Lima upper-income population. After 1973, their relative income was slightly better, but their absolute income was even lower. The trade and agricultural policies punished the rural producers of agricultural tradables the most.

Several facts explain how the richer Lima dwellers were able to capture absolutely and relatively more of the available foods than were the poor in Lima. Principal among them was that the income effects tended to favor the rich as owners of the factors of production in the protected sector and as consumers of importable (rather than non-traded) foods. The absolute gains arose because the per capita incomes of the rich were three times the average for the poor (Table 2.3). The relative gains came from the relatively high income and price elasticities in the demand of upper-income households for importable foods (Table 2.4). It is important to point out that under this simulation, the relatively modest increases in food consumption in the presence of substantial producer price declines can be attributed, in part, to the tendency of marketing margins to increase (as an induced effect of the industrial protection policies).

Trade Liberalization, 1979–1982

After 1978, Peru initiated a policy of freer trade than what had prevailed in the preceding ten years. This post-1978 period is known as "The

Crisis." Because a multiplicity of interacting economic, political, and ecological disruptions affected economic conditions in Peru during this period, it is difficult to ascertain the causes of the problems that have plagued the country since 1978. Some experts attribute them to the move toward trade liberalization and have called for a return to selective protection of the productive sectors, exchange rate and other price controls, and similar efforts that implicitly mean greater isolation of the Peruvian economy from conditions in the world markets. This study does not resolve this debate, but it does provide an assessment of the degree to which trade liberalization, as manifest in one determinant of the real exchange rate, has helped or hindered food consumption, income distribution, and agricultural production.

The scenarios for the analysis of the effects of trade liberalization are based on the changes that would have occurred had the policies pursued after 1978 been applied throughout the post-1968 period. Specifically, the government lowered the uniform equivalent tariff from 133 percent to 91.3 percent. The price scenarios are based on the agricultural prices that prevailed in world markets in 1978–1982. The analysis focuses on the effect of trade liberalization; the price scenarios are used principally to test the central hypothesis.

Aggregate effects.   With a reduction in protection, imported manufactured goods would have driven the price of all manufactured goods down, and consumers would have substituted those goods for foodstuffs (Table 2.8). The price of industrial (manufactured or imported) goods would have dropped approximately 17.4 percent in real terms. In the absence of price controls, the trade liberalization effects and the fall in world prices for foodstuffs would have lowered the retail price of food by 1 to 5 percent. For agriculture, under the free-trade solution, aggregate food expenditures would have risen slightly (about 1 percent). Price controls, in contrast, would have prevented producer prices for food from dropping and would have maintained exportable prices at a level at least 20 percent higher in real terms than they would have been under free trade; the retail price of nontradable foods would have risen. This protection of tradable agriculture would have extracted resources from nontradable agriculture, particularly for the production of tradable foods.

An analysis by Franklin et al. (1983) showed that the producers of tradable foods, primarily rice, captured the subsidy equivalent of the price control policy. By 1983, Peru was spending approximately US$100 million on food subsidies, of which approximately US$49 million apparently went to producers, US$14 million to the richer half of the Lima population, US$13 million to the poorer half of the Lima population, and the balance to the rest of the country. The government considered the

TABLE 2.8   Effects of Trade Liberalization and Agricultural
Price Controls on Agricultural Production and
Consumption in Peru, 1978–1982 in Relation to
1964–1968 (percentage change)

Indicator	Liberalization with price controls	Liberalization without price controls
Retail price indexes		
Nontradable foods	2.5	−1.1
Importable foods	1.5	−4.5
Manufactured goods	−17.4	−17.4
Aggregate consumption		
Nontradable foods	−3.1	0.9
Importable foods	−3.7	1.4
Agricultural production		
Nontradable foods	−3.1	0.9
Importable foods	3.6	−14.2
Exportable products	16.2	8.5
Producer (real) price indexes		
Nontradable foods	2.5	−1.1
Importable foods	22.1	−11.8
Exportable products	33.8	13.3

NOTE: The effects are changes relative to what would have happened under the same price control and subsidy policy but with the uniform equivalent tariff of the baseline period (1964–1968). All price indexes are relative to the price index for nonagricultural home goods and services.
SOURCE: Authors' calculations.

subsidy necessary because it wanted to isolate the food-producing subsector from lower international prices—in 1982 the effective rate of protection for rice was 12 percent. Direct agricultural policies appear to have been more effective during the trade liberalization period than during the industrial protection period, when the deleterious effects of the industrial policy swamped the direct price policies.

Consumption and distributional effects. During this period, Peru attempted to reduce the uniform equivalent tariff and positive nominal protection for producers of tradable agriculture. The income distribution effects of the trade liberalization would have been progressive for the urban populations (Table 2.9). That is, the urban poor would have gained more in relative terms than the urban rich of Lima. Within rural areas, the relatively better off coastal and jungle populations would have gained in comparison with the highland population. The positive protection of tradable agriculture would have accentuated this latter effect, because the production of tradables is concentrated in the coastal and jungle areas,

TABLE 2.9   Effects of Trade Liberalization and Agricultural
Price Controls on Income Distribution and
Consumption in Peru, 1978–1982 in Relation to
1964–1968 (percentage change)

Population group	Liberalization with price controls			Liberalization without price controls		
	In-come	Non-tradable	Import-able	In-come	Non-traded	Import-able
Lima, upper income	3.5	−5.9	−7.3	4.5	−2.4	−2.8
Lima, lower income	5.4	−0.4	−0.9	7.4	3.0	3.9
Sierra, rural	1.1	−3.5	−4.1	2.0	−1.5	−0.4
Non-Lima, urban	2.8	−3.6	−4.0	4.5	−0.5	−0.5
Non-Sierra, rural	0.2	4.2	3.0	6.0	1.6	2.6

NOTE: The effects are changes from the economic comparative static values that would have prevailed in the absence of the policy changes; these effects abstract from the dynamic adjustment effects, growth, weather, and investment. The nontraded commodities are traditional foods, such as potatoes, vegetables, small animal species, and Andean grains; the importable foods are primarily wheat-based products, rice, processed milk, and beef.
SOURCE: Authors' calculations.

while the highland populations not only produce and consume non-tradables but also consume significant amounts of tradable foods. As consumers of tradable foods and producers of nontradables, the rural Sierra population would have been negatively affected by the higher relative prices for tradable foods arising from the price control policies that kept rice, wheat, milk, and other items above world market prices. From a nutritional and distributional point of view, trade liberalization across all sectors would have been generally beneficial.

Summary

Efforts to close the economy to conditions in the world markets during the 1970s distorted the structure of incentives against agriculture as a whole. Average real producer prices for agricultural products declined by more than the induced increases in the domestic price of manufactured goods. At the retail level, the decline in food prices was modest, so that urban consumers and some rural dwellers (particularly in the Sierra) would have increased their consumption of all foods by modest amounts. Upper-income urban dwellers benefited more in relative and absolute terms than did the rest of the country with respect to food consumption. The improvements in food consumption by these groups would have come at the expense of consumption by rural coastal dwellers, since aggregate disappearance data show a slight decline in total food availability in the 1970s in comparison with the 1960s.

The deterioration in incentives for agriculture arose primarily from the decline in the real exchange rate as a result of the rise in the price of nontradables, induced by the protective measures for the industrial sector. As a result of the deterioration in agricultural incentives, exports of the agricultural sector declined, and more and more food imports were required. Midway through the decade, the government used subsidies for tradable foods to isolate the domestic markets from the rapid increases in the international price of cereals. Later, when international prices declined, the domestic producers of cereals (primarily rice) increasingly captured the subsidies. There has been a general misconception about the nature of food subsidies in Peru; they were not directed at consumers, but rather resulted from the deficits of parastatals. During the period of industrial protection, the parastatals tended to absorb the subsidies as part of their operating costs.

The evolution of the uniform equivalent tariff suggests that, during the 1960s and 1970s, the Peruvian economy became more closed, with greater restrictions on trade. The real exchange rate underwent a large and persistent decline after the 1960s that reduced the profitability of producing tradables in comparison with nontradables. Recovery did not begin until the late 1970s, after a series of major devaluations and the institution of a crawling peg regime. The government ended this policy in 1985, and conditions similar to those of the mid-1970s prevailed at the time of this writing.

Declines in the long-run real exchange rate have been particularly harmful to the production of agricultural tradables in developing countries: they have slowed their production and sped up the rise in the domestic consumption of tradables (imported cereals and exportables), reduced the contribution of agriculture to economic growth and the balance of payments, and made developing countries more dependent on imported food.

It is important to recognize that a falling real exchange rate is not necessarily a sign of a devaluation. The external accounts of a country could be in equilibrium at a low real exchange rate because of restrictions on imports or larger inflows of capital, including foreign assistance. One result would be an implicit tax on agriculture, and on exportables in general. This penalty on agriculture is inherent and lasts as long as industry is highly protected. It cannot be eliminated by better management of other areas of economic policy.

For the 1964–1982 period studied in Peru, the changes in relative prices induced by the trade and agricultural policies caused nontradable agricultural products to become more expensive than tradable (imported) foods. As a result, there was a marked shift in the diet away from traditional foods to food products made from tradable or imported foodstuffs. This effect was most obvious among highland dwellers, whose diets changed the most drastically.

The restrictive trade policies, rather than the direct price policies for agriculture, had the greatest impact on food consumption and income distribution. Although price controls may have shielded tradable agriculture from fluctuations in world markets, the deterioration in real personal incomes that arose from the trade restrictions more than offset any benefits for either farmers or consumers. Even urban dwellers observed declines in their real incomes during the 1970s.

Regarding trade liberalization, it is difficult to blame its real effects for the deterioration in food intake by the poor in Lima or elsewhere in the country. In fact, it would appear that freer trade would have neutralized any possible deleterious impact on food consumption that could have arisen from the liberalization, because the world prices for food were dropping during the period of trade liberalization. Had the government allowed the international prices to be transmitted into Peru, its agriculture would have shifted to exportable products and nontradables, with a net positive effect on the balance of agricultural trade, even though more food would have been imported. From a distributional point of view, trade liberalization throughout the economy, including agriculture, would have been rather neutral with respect to the existing distribution of income.

The analysis was completed in 1982. Since then, Peru has experienced a severe shock from the climatic effects of El Niño in 1983, a deterioration in the world prices for its exportables, a return to restrictive trade and exchange rate policies, and increasing political and civil strife. All these events have heightened the poverty of the Peruvian population, which the trade policies of the 1960s and 1970s had done little to alleviate.

Appendix: The Trade Policy Simulation Program

The parameters are as follows:

1. Incidence parameters, ω_{am} and ω_{ax}, were used to measure the implied taxation through the real exchange rate effects on the relative prices of agricultural importables (am) and exportables (ax), respectively.

2. Supply elasticity matrix, S_{ij}, where $i, j = am, ax, ah, nm$. A fifth

sector is *nh*, nontraded nonagriculture (for example, services), whose resource use and production are solved by residual to equate simulated aggregate value added to realized (actual) value added (GDP), a process that preserves consistency with the assumptions under which the ω's were estimated.

3. Relative retail price weights, α_{ij}, gives the proportions of a retail price for a commodity *i* in terms of the wholesale prices of other commodities, for example, where $i = am$, then $j = am, nm$, because $EP^R_{am} = \alpha_{am,am}EP_{am} + \alpha_{am,nm}EP_{nm}$. These weights were solved using matching 1973 national product and income accounts and the 1973 input-output matrix to the ENCA expenditure data, as described earlier.

4. Demand system, $D^k = (\eta_{ij})_k$, where k = the population group identifier, such as the upper half of the income distribution in Lima, the lower half, rural Sierra, and so on, and $(\eta_i)_k$ is the five sets of demand matrices, D, and income elasticities, η^y, that were estimated econometrically with yearly time-series data from 1950 to 1982, and the budget shares of each commodity for each group.

5. Consumption shares for each population group represent the share of aggregate expenditures (in 1972–1973), with δ_k allocated to the five commodity groupings, as derived from the ENCA data, so that the aggregate demand matrix is given on an element-by-element basis as

$$D_{ij} = \Sigma\delta_k \, D^k_{ij} \text{ and } \eta_i = \Sigma\delta_k\eta^k_i,$$

where δ_k represents the share of aggregate expenditures represented by each population group (Table 2.3).

6. Labor market coefficients, λ_i, with the sectoral labor shares $i = am, ax, ah, nm, nh$ computed from the 1973 input-output matrix, as reported by Reardon (1984) (Table A2.1). Thus, the changes in labor income for each group were computed as

$$EL^k = \lambda_i\rho^k_i (S\mathbf{P}'),$$

where ρ^k_i are the coefficients for distributing sectoral wage bills to the population groups. These were also developed from Reardon's work (Table A2.2). S is the matrix of supply elasticities, and $\mathbf{P}'$ is the vector of proportional changes in the relative

TABLE A2.1   Structure of the Peruvian Economy, 1973 (percentage shares, excluding minerals)

Sector	Value added	Labor force	Share of national wage bill	Labor's share in output
Agriculture				
Nontradable (home)	7.62	12.76	7.85	84.3
Exportable	1.22	4.52	2.78	61.0
Import-competing	4.04	7.04	4.33	49.6
Nonagriculture				
Import-competing	32.40	25.08	21.82	37.7
Nontradable	54.72	50.60	63.22	65.8

SOURCE: Derived from national product and income account data (INE), except for the labor cost shares, which were derived from Reardon (1984).

TABLE A2.2   Distributional Coefficients for Assigning Labor Factor Shares of Sectoral Value Added to Personal Income in Peru

| Population group | Agriculture | | | Nonagriculture | |
	Non-traded	Exportables	Importables	Import-competing	Non-traded
Lima, upper half	0.00	0.15	0.00	0.52	0.54
Lima, lower half	0.00	0.00	0.00	0.10	0.10
Sierra, rural	0.70	0.00	0.50	0.04	0.03
Non-Lima, urban	0.00	0.08	0.00	0.34	0.33
Non-Sierra, rural	0.30	0.77	0.50	0.00	0.00

SOURCE: Derived from Reardon (1984).

prices. Table A2.1 also presents the structure of the Peruvian economy in 1973, the year that serves as the "pivotal" point for the comparative static calculations in the simulation program.

The simulation program solves the following equations by Gauss-Siedel iteration:

1. Relative producer prices for agricultural tradables

$$E(P_{am}/P_{nh}) = EP^*_{am} - [\omega_{am}/(\omega - \omega_{am})]\tau$$

$$E(P_{ax}/P_{nh}) = EP^*_{ax} - [\omega_{ax}/(1 - \omega_{ax})]\tau$$

2. Relative retail prices for agricultural tradables

$$E(P^R_{am}/P_{nh}) = \alpha_{am}E(P_{am}/P_{nh}) + \alpha_{am,nm}E(P_{nm}/P_{nh})$$

$$E(P^R_{ax}/P_{nh}) = \alpha_{ax}E(P_{ax}/P_{nh}) + \alpha_{ax,nm}E(P_{nm}/P_{nh})$$

3. Income effects for each population group

$$EY^k = -\mu^k EP + EL^k, \text{ for each group,}$$

where μ^k is the vector of budget shares corresponding to each population group, P is the vector of the price changes computed in the previous steps, and EL^k are the wage bill effects.

4. Equilibrium price for nontradable agriculture

$$EP_{ah} = \frac{(\eta_{ah,} EY + \Sigma_j \eta_{ah,} {}_jEP^R_j - \Sigma_j \epsilon_{ah,} {}_jEP_j)}{(\epsilon_{ah,ah} - \eta_{ah,ah})}$$

5. Consumption effects on a commodity-by-commodity basis for each population group

$$EC^k_i = \eta^k_i EY^k + \Sigma_j D^k_{ij} EP^R_j.$$

Notes to Chapter 2

The authors gratefully acknowledge the collaboration of the Ministry of Agriculture, Instituto Nacional de Estadística, Banco Central de Reserva del Perú, and the Ministerio de Economía y Finanzas of Peru. Francisco Javier León devoted many hours of hard work developing the data and estimations for the incidence parameters for the analysis of commercial policy. Those efforts and his comments on a preliminary draft are appreciated. Jerry Leonard developed the data for the supply and demand analyses.

Partial funding for the study was provided by the U.S. Agency for International Development through the Office of Nutrition of the Bureau for Science and Technology under the Consumption Effects of Agricultural Policies Project and by Sigma One Corporation and the International Food Policy Research Institute.

1. Similarly, the excess supply of exportables (export supply function) could be specified, but only one equation needs to be estimated.

Effects of the Coffee Boom and Government Expenditures on Agricultural Prices in Colombia

Agriculture is the most important sector in Colombia's economy. It generates 25 percent of the country's real gross domestic product (GDP), and in the period 1970–1983 it accounted, on average, for 61.1 percent of real commodity exports. Agricultural output is divided into roughly equal proportions among (1) coffee, (2) other agricultural products, and (3) animal products; these products make up 32 percent, 35 percent, and 33 percent of agricultural output, respectively. Seventy-five percent of agricultural output can be classified as tradable and 63 percent as exportable, but only a small proportion of output is traded externally (García García and Montes Llamas 1988, Appendix 1). Coffee, Colombia's principal export, contributed 44.1 percent of total commodity exports in the period 1970–1983.

When agricultural production is structured in this way, domestic policies or exogenous events that cause the relative prices of exportables to fall also depress the relative prices of agricultural output. As this chapter shows, variations in Colombia's external terms of trade and changes in government expenditures had an adverse effect on its real exchange rate, relative product prices, and real wages in the agricultural sector over the period from 1967 to 1983.[1]

Main Economic Developments, 1967–1983

After 1967 the government of Colombia reduced the bias toward import substitution, and in the next ten years or so the country experienced GDP growth averaging 6.4 percent a year, the highest growth of the postwar period. After 1979, however, growth decelerated, and from 1979 to 1983 GDP rose only 2.1 percent a year. Real agricultural GDP growth also slowed; after averaging 3.9 percent a year from 1967 to 1979, it dropped to 0.5 percent a year from 1980 to 1983.

Although the increase in imports of agricultural commodities is often cited as the main cause of the stagnation since 1979, the principal causes were domestic macroeconomic policies and economic developments after 1975—most notably, the coffee boom of 1975 to 1979, a significant increase in the size of the government sector and the fiscal deficit, and a corresponding deterioration in Colombia's international reserve position after 1982.

Colombia's drug boom (primarily in marijuana and cocaine) also contributed to the deterioration in relative prices of exportable activities.[2] Although the value added of drug activity was large, the resultant increase in domestic expenditures was probably small since most of the foreign exchange revenue seems to have stayed abroad.[3] Not enough information is available to include the drug trade in this discussion, however, and the chapter may therefore overestimate the impact of the coffee boom and government expenditures.

Growth in Output and Evolution of Expenditures

During the period 1967–1974, one aim of Colombia's economic policy was to reduce the anti-export bias of commercial policies, a shift in emphasis that favored agriculture and the exportable industrial sectors.[4] All sectors did well in this period. From 1975 to 1979, however, the coffee boom dominated the economic scene, and growth appeared to be biased toward nontraded sectors such as services, and against manufacturing and non-coffee agriculture.

The government that took office in 1978 initiated an ambitious expansion of the public works program, which it financed through external credit and money creation. As the external borrowing and the money creation that financed the deficit expanded the money supply beyond a rate that was consistent with a politically acceptable rate of inflation, credit to the private sector was severely curtailed and interest rates increased sharply. At the same time interest rates in the international market also rose sharply. The combined effect of the temporary gains in the terms of trade, the application of a restrictive policy to offset the monetary effects of the expansive fiscal policy, and the increase in interest rates in the international capital markets led to a real appreciation of the peso, a crowding out of the private sector, and a reduction in the country's rate of economic growth.

Balance of Payments and International Reserves

Colombia entered the second half of the 1970s with a fairly strong external position, for the moderate capital inflow between 1968 and 1975 had more than compensated for the deficit on its current account. During that period international reserves rose from US$35 million to US$547 million. Between 1976 and 1981, a surplus in the current account, reinforced by the capital inflows, raised reserves to US$5.6 billion by the end of 1981. The year before, however, Colombia's external position had begun to deteriorate, with the appearance of a deficit in the current account, which increased in 1982 and 1983.

Fiscal and Monetary Policies

Fiscal policy. Between 1967 and 1983 the central government passed through three financial phases: in 1967–1975 its actual deficit averaged 1.0 percent of GDP; in 1976–1978 it recorded a surplus of 0.5 percent of GDP; and in 1979–1983 the fiscal deficit increased, reaching 4.3 percent of GDP by 1983. From the perspective of the consolidated public sector, the most dramatic change in the entire period took place between 1978 and 1983, when expenditures rose from 28.1 percent to 39.9 percent of GDP, while revenues increased only from 27 percent to 31 percent of GDP. Thus between 1978 and 1983 the consolidated public sector deficit went from 1.2 to 8.6 percent of GDP.

Monetary policy. Between 1966 and 1982, it is possible to distinguish two subperiods of monetary expansion: in 1966–1971 the money supply (M1) grew at an annual rate of 16 percent, and in 1972–1982 it increased at 24 percent a year. At the same time, the monetary base increased at 24.4 percent a year, while the money supply grew at 21 percent a year. Thus, the money multiplier fell by 3.4 percent a year, from an average level of 2.0 for 1966–1971 to an average level of 1.5 for 1972–1982. The resulting financial disintermediation contributed substantially to a general increase in real interest rates during the period.

Interest Rates, Capital Movements, Devaluation, and Inflation

Nominal interest rates also went up in response to increases in the rate of inflation, the reserve requirements of commercial banks, and the forced investments on the banking system. In addition, rising interest rates in the external markets in the late 1970s and early 1980s pushed domestic interest rates up. Thus, interest rates were low in the period 1967–1977 (except in 1973–1974), and high in the period 1978–1983.

Relative Prices

Since 1970, the relative prices of agricultural products in Colombia have changed substantially. Agricultural prices as a whole improved between 1970 and 1973, fell slightly in 1974, improved in 1975–1977, and have fallen since 1977. Their movement has been closely linked to variations in the country's external terms of trade, which in turn have been dominated by movements in the price of coffee.

The price of noncoffee agricultural products, compared with that of nonagricultural products, rose between 1970 and 1974 and declined thereafter, except in 1977, when a substantial shortfall in agricultural output pushed agricultural prices upward. There was no well-defined trend in the relative price of coffee between 1970 and 1975, but between 1975 and 1977 the price doubled, and then between 1977 and 1983 it declined 60 percent. Tradable and nontradable commodities in agriculture followed a similar pattern: prices rose between 1970 and 1974 and declined after 1974.

Several factors explain this change in the relative price of noncoffee products in agriculture. The price increase was the result of direct export incentives as well as indirect incentives from higher real exchange rates resulting from exchange rate adjustments and some trade liberalization in the late 1960s and early 1970s. Under Colombia's moderate fiscal and monetary policies, the rise in the nominal exchange rate led to a rise in the real exchange rate. The fall in the price of noncoffee tradables is explained by the large increases in the price and volume of coffee exports between 1975 and 1980 and by the large fiscal deficit in 1979–1983.

Real Wages in Agriculture and Industry

Real wages in agriculture in the 1960s grew at only 1.7 percent a year, while in manufacturing they grew at 2.9 percent a year. By 1970 agricultural wages were only 44 percent of manufacturing wages. In the 1970s, however, agriculture's domestic terms of trade improved. That trend and the substantial increase in urban employment pushed real agricultural wages up at 3.9 percent a year. In 1977, at the peak of the coffee boom, rural wages were about 72 percent of manufacturing wages. Thereafter, they fell in relation to industrial wages, reaching 57 percent of the latter in 1983.

A Model and the Empirical Evidence

Conceptual Framework

Colombia can be considered a small, semi-open economy that is a price taker in goods and capital markets. Restrictions and administrative controls hamper trade in commodities and the mobility of capital. International prices and foreign interest rates affect domestic prices, as do domestic policies.

This section presents a framework for analyzing the effects of changes in the external terms of trade and growing government expenditures on the relative price of Colombia's noncoffee tradables, with emphasis on agricultural products. The model used in the analysis is a small open economy that produces three commodities: nontraded commodities (N), coffee (C), and noncoffee tradables (T).

In this model, there are two relative prices.[5] $P_N = P_N/P_T$ and $P_c = P_C/P_T$, where P_N is the price of nontraded commodities, P_C is the price of coffee, and P_T is the price of noncoffee tradables. It is assumed that the supply of each commodity depends positively on its own relative price, on the factors of production used, and on technology (t). It is also assumed that each sector j (where $j = N$, T, and C) uses capital (K), land (LA), and labor (L). That is,

$$Ns = N_s (P_n, P_c, L_N, K_N, LA_N, t), \tag{3.1}$$

$$T_s = T_s (P_n, P_c, L_T, K_T, LA_T, t), \tag{3.2}$$

and

$$C_s = C_s (P_n, P_c, L_C, K_C, LA_C, t). \tag{3.3}$$

In equation (3.1), the supply of nontraded goods will increase when its relative price increases, while in equations (3.2) and (3.3), the supply of noncoffee tradables and coffee will decline as the relative price of nontradables rises. In equation (3.3), the supply of coffee will move upward as the relative price of coffee rises. An increase in the price of coffee will reduce the *combined* supply of nontraded goods and noncoffee tradables, but the effect on the supply of each is unclear, because it depends on the relative factor intensities of the tradable and nontraded sectors.[6] In this analysis, I assumed that an increase in the price of coffee tends to reduce the supply of both tradable and nontraded commodities.

Total aggregate supply (total income) measured in terms of noncoffee tradables is

$$Y = N_sP_n + T_s + C_sP_c. \tag{3.4}$$

To simplify the analysis, I assumed on the demand side that all coffee produced is exported and that changes in the price of coffee do not affect the demand for tradables and nontraded goods, as far as the substitution effect goes.[7] The price of coffee affects the demand for tradable and nontraded goods through changes in income and expenditures, which are positively related to the price of coffee. In other words, the demand for tradables and nontraded goods can be expressed as a function of one relative price (that of nontradables to noncoffee tradables) and of aggregate expenditures. I also assumed that the demand for nontraded goods rises with a decrease in price and an increase in expenditures. The demand for noncoffee tradables increases, however, when the price of nontraded goods and expenditures rise.

The demand for nontraded goods and noncoffee tradables can then be expressed as follows:

$$N_d = N_d (P_n, E),\tag{3.5}$$

$$T_d = T_d (P_n, E),\tag{3.6}$$

where E stands for total expenditures.

Equilibrium in the market for nontraded goods is established when demand equals supply, that is, when

$$N_s = N_d.\tag{3.7}$$

Equilibrium in the traded goods market occurs when there is equilibrium in the nontraded goods sector and the current account equals zero (income equals expenditures). For this equilibrium to exist, it is necessary that

$$T_s + P_c C = T_d.\tag{3.8}$$

Effects of Changes in the Price of Coffee

The equations in the preceding section allow us to calculate the effects of an increase in coffee prices on the real exchange rate. Consider, first, the market for nontraded goods where the level of resources is held constant in the economy. On the supply side, a rise in the price of coffee will draw resources out of the nontraded goods sector and thereby create excess demand for nontraded commodities. On the demand side, an increase in the price of coffee raises the demand for nontraded goods because of its effect on real income and, hence, on expenditures. As a result, an increase in the price of coffee will tend to create excess demand in the nontraded goods market, and prices there will go up.

In the tradable goods market, an increase in the price of coffee draws resources away from noncoffee tradables and thus reduces their supply. This shift creates an excess demand for tradables (the combined output of coffee and noncoffee) and tends to reduce the price of nontraded goods. The increase in the price of coffee has still other effects. On the demand side, a rise in the price of coffee pushes income and hence expenditures up, and in response the demand for noncoffee tradables increases. Therefore, the net effect of the increase in the price of coffee is greater excess demand for noncoffee tradables, which pushes the price of nontraded goods down.

Coffee affects the tradable market in two ways. First, if the price of coffee goes up, the total supply of tradables increases by an amount equal to the increase in the price of coffee. Second, the increase in the price of coffee draws resources toward coffee production and away from the production of noncoffee tradables and nontraded goods. Presumably, this new allocation of resources is better than the old one, so that the overall effect of the increase in the price of coffee is to raise the supply of tradables. The two effects—on price and on quantity—tend to increase the supply of tradables. (The expenditure effect on the demand for coffee does not take place because it is assumed that all coffee output is exported.) In the case of tradables, viewed separately, an increase in the price of coffee increases the excess demand for noncoffee tradables and the excess supply of coffee. The net effect on tradables (coffee and noncoffee) is not clear. It appears likely, however, that the increase in the price of coffee will create an excess supply of tradables, which will drive the price of noncoffee tradables down. This pattern is presumed because coffee draws resources out of both the noncoffee tradable and nontraded sectors; therefore, the increase in coffee output is larger than the decline in the output of noncoffee tradables. At the same time, the increased demand for noncoffee tradables that results from the expenditure effect is smaller than the increase in the value of coffee exports because part of the extra income is spent on nontradables. Therefore, an increase in the price of coffee tends to raise the price of nontradables in relation to the price of noncoffee tradables.

Government Expenditures, Interest Rates, and the Real Exchange Rate

Government expenditures. To analyze the effect of changes in government expenditures on relative prices, we assume that total expenditures

(E) are divided into government (G) and private (E_P) outlays. E_P depends positively on disposable income (Y_d) and negatively on the real interest rate (r). That is,

$$E = E_P + G \qquad (3.9)$$

and

$$E_P = E\,(Y_d,\, r) = E\,(Y - I,\, r), \qquad (3.10)$$

where I is government revenue from taxes.

The government purchases nontradable goods (G_N) and noncoffee tradable goods (G_T).[8] Equilibrium in the market for nontraded goods is established when demand equals supply. That is,

$$N_s = N_d + G_N, \qquad (3.11)$$

where N_d represents the demand of the private sector for nontraded goods.

Equilibrium in the traded goods market occurs when there is equilibrium in the nontraded goods sector and the current account equals zero (income equals expenditures). To have equilibrium in the traded goods market, it is necessary that

$$T_s + P_cC = T_d + G_T, \qquad (3.12)$$

where T_d represents the demand of the private sector for noncoffee tradables.

It is assumed that the government finances its expenditures entirely with taxes. That is,

$$G = G_T + G_N = I. \qquad (3.13)$$

An increase in government expenditures boosts the demand for nontraded goods if the government's propensity to purchase them is higher than the private sector's. In that case, the price of nontradables will rise. This result holds whether viewed from the perspective of the nontraded or traded goods market. From the perspective of the market for tradables, the increase in government demand for tradables is less than the reduction in the private sector's demand for tradables induced by the increase in taxes. As a result, an excess supply of tradable goods develops, and equilibrium in that market requires an increase in the price of nontraded commodities.

When the government finances its expenditures by borrowing abroad and by printing money, the budget constraint of the government is given by

$$G = I + FB + B_G, \qquad (3.14)$$

where FB stands for net foreign borrowing and B_G for money creation.

If the government's propensity to spend on traded and nontraded commodities is independent of the method of financing, and if the government's marginal propensity to spend on nontraded goods is larger than that of the private sector, then an increase in government expenditures will raise the price of nontraded goods, whether they are financed with foreign borrowing or credit from the Central Bank.

The effect of government expenditures on relative prices is smaller if the public believes that taxes will have to be raised to pay for the government's external debt. Similar reasoning applies if Central Bank credit to the government has to be repaid in the future. The public will then discount future taxes and adjust its consumption accordingly. In this case, which is like the one in which all government expenditures are financed with taxes, the effects of the expenditures depend on the relative size of the propensities of the government and the private sector to spend on nontraded commodities.

For most of the period under analysis, the Colombian public sector ran a deficit that it financed with domestic savings, money creation, and foreign loans. As government expenditures increased, pressure on the market for nontraded goods mounted and produced excess demand for nontraded commodities, which pushed their relative prices up. As such, government expenditure should be expected to have a positive effect on the price of nontraded goods.

Interest rates.   In the market for nontraded commodities, an exogenous increase in the interest rate reduces expenditures and the demand for nontraded goods. This creates an excess supply, which drives the price of those goods downward. In contrast, in the market for noncoffee tradables, a higher interest rate reduces expenditures and creates excess supply, so that the price of nontraded goods is driven up. In other words, the final effect of changes in the interest rate on the relative price of nontraded goods can be positive or negative, depending on the relative size of the excess supplies of nontraded and tradable goods.

If, however, the nontraded goods consist mainly of services (so that changes in the interest rate probably have little or no effect on expenditures) and the traded goods consist of commodities (so that the interest rate has a considerable effect), an increase in the interest rate will probably raise the relative prices of nontraded goods. According to a previous classification (García García and Montes Llamas 1988, Appendix 1), the nontraded goods sector contains mainly services, whereas the traded goods sector contains manufactured and agricultural products. Thus, there is a strong presumption that increases in the interest rate will lead to an increase in the relative price of nontraded goods.

Growth of Resources

Relative prices can be affected by the growth of capital and labor and by technological change. In the same way, the stock of capital, the labor force, and technological change vary with changes in relative prices. The analysis of these interactions is beyond the scope of this chapter,[9] but it should be pointed out that the relative price of nontraded goods depends on four variables: the growth of output, the price of coffee relative to noncoffee tradables, the real interest rate, and government expenditures. An increase in government expenditures and in the price of coffee is likely to raise the price of nontraded goods if the former are biased toward nontraded goods and if the latter boosts real income and, hence, expenditures. No strong presumption exists as to the effects of economic growth and changes in interest rates on the relative price of nontraded goods. If the nontraded goods sector is composed mainly of services, an increase in interest rates will tend to increase its relative price.

Empirical Evidence

To examine the effects of changes in the terms of trade and government expenditures on the real exchange rate, I estimated a real exchange rate equation (price of tradables divided by the price of nontradables). The real exchange rate is determined by the external terms of trade, the size of government expenditures relative to GDP, real per capita income, and the real interest rate. I use government expenditures in relation to GDP because the important determinant of government influence on relative prices is how government spending changes in relation to GDP rather than the absolute volume of spending. Real per capita income is used because it serves as a general measure of the extent of capital accumulation over the period and also because it is a better measure of the relative growth of aggregate demand. As the model in the preceding section indicates, an increase in the terms of trade (mainly an increase in the price of coffee) and in government expenditures (when biased toward domestic goods) caused the exchange rate for noncoffee sectors to appreciate. In other words, the price of tradables over noncoffee tradables decreased.

The next step in the analysis was to run ordinary least-squares regressions. I corrected for autocorrelation when it was present and used annual data for the period 1967–1983, which provided 11 degrees of freedom. The estimating equation of the real exchange rate is

$$\log P_n = \pi_0 + \pi_1 r + \pi_2 \log \text{PCGDP} + \pi_3 \log P_c \\ + \pi_4 G \text{ (or } D) + u, \tag{3.15}$$

where $\log$ = natural logarithm, P_n = the price of nontraded goods relative to the price of noncoffee tradables; r = real interest rate, PCGDP = per capita real GDP, P_c = the price of coffee relative to the price of noncoffee tradables, G = consolidated public sector expenditures relative to nominal GDP, D = consolidated public sector deficit relative to nominal GDP, and u = error term.

Relative Prices of Traded and Nontraded Commodities

The estimated equations are presented in Table 3.1. The coefficients are significant, and the signs for the government variables (G or D) and terms of trade suggest that an improvement in the terms of trade and an increase in government expenditures raise the relative price of nontraded goods. The negative effect of government expenditures on the price of noncoffee tradables also suggests that the government's propensity to spend on nontraded commodities is higher than its propensity to spend on traded commodities.

Note that the interest rate has a positive effect on the price of nontraded goods, and therefore policies that push real interest rates up seem likely, in the medium run, to cause a reduction in the real exchange rate, other things remaining constant. This effect also conforms to the presumption that increases in the interest rate will do the same.

Table 3.2 presents estimates based on equation (3.15) for the three sets of relative prices used as dependent variables. These prices were for noncoffee exportables (equations 1 and 2), noncoffee agricultural exportables (equations 3 and 4), and noncoffee agricultural tradables (equations 5 and 6). The results support the argument that improvements in the terms of trade and increases in government expenditures reduce the real exchange rate for the noncoffee tradable sector in general, and for the agricultural sector in particular. For regressions 2–6, the

TABLE 3.1 Determinants of Nontradable Prices Relative to Noncoffee Tradable Prices for Colombia

Equation	Period	Dependent variable[a]	Constant	Log per capita GDP $(T-1)$	Real interest rate $(T-1)$	LPC[b] $(T-1)$	Government variable		$\bar{R}^2$	RHO	D.W.
							$G(T-1)$	$D(-1)$			
1	1969–1983	LPNC	4.28 (33.13)	−0.26 (−6.81)	0.01 (6.46)	0.20 (6.65)	0.43 (3.58)		0.91	0.34 (1.17)	2.27
2	1969–1983	LPNC	4.35 (28.57)	−0.19 (−4.83)	0.01 (3.36)	0.16 (3.77)		0.28 (2.13)	0.82		1.86
3	1968–1983	LPNC	4.35 (25.84)	−0.15 (−4.13)	0.01 (2.59)	0.14 (3.04)		0.36 (2.64)	0.77		1.51

a. LPNC is the log of the price of nontraded goods over the price of coffee.
b. LPC is the log of the price of coffee over the price of noncoffee tradables.
SOURCE: García García and Montes Llamas (1988, Table 11).

TABLE 3.2 Determinants of Prices of Noncoffee Exportables (General and Agricultural) Relative to Nontradables for Colombia

Equation	Period	Dependent variable[a]	Constant	Log per capita GDP (T-1)	Real interest rate (T-1)	LPC (T-1)	LTTBS (T-1)	Government variable G(T-1)	D(T-1)	G	D	R̄²	RHO	D.W.
1	1968–1983	LPXNC	4.95 (23.63)	0.23 (5.40)	-0.01 (-2.59)	-0.18 (-3.42)		-0.48 (-2.37)				0.65		2.21
2	1968–1983	LPXNC	5.48 (7.90)	0.72 (3.17)	-0.02 (-3.18)		-0.61 (-2.30)		-0.68 (-1.66)			0.78		1.73
3	1969–1983	LPXANC	5.36 (9.34)	0.98 (5.61)	-0.02 (-3.83)		-0.67 (-3.38)			-1.16 (-2.97)		0.87	0.16 (0.42)	1.59
4	1968–1983	LPXANC	5.44 (10.35)	0.82 (4.69)	-0.02 (-4.80)		-0.71 (-3.40)				-0.70 (-2.42)	0.82		2.12
5	1969–1983	LPTANC	5.61 (10.95)	0.80 (4.92)	-0.02 (-3.57)		-0.62 (-3.46)			-1.18 (-3.21)		0.85	0.21 (0.45)	1.45
6	1969–1983	LPTANC	5.98 (15.26)	0.74 (5.86)	-0.02 (-5.59)		-0.73 (-4.87)				-0.92 (-4.01)	0.85	-0.47 (-1.51)	2.15

a. LPXNC is the logarithm of the price of noncoffee exportables over the price of nontradables; LPXANC is the logarithm of the price of noncoffee agricultural exports over the price of nontradables; LPTANC is the logarithm of the price of noncoffee agricultural tradables over the price of nontradables; LPC is the logarithm of the price of coffee over the price of noncoffee tradables; LTTBS is the logarithm of the price of exports of goods and services over the price of imports of goods and services. T−1 indicates a time lag of one year. T-statistics are in parentheses.
SOURCE: García García and Montes Llamas (1988, Table 11).

variable representing changes in the terms of trade is measured by the implicit price of exports of goods and services divided by the implicit price of imports of goods and services.

Relative Prices of Agricultural Output and Nontraded Commodities

Equation (3.15) is used to estimate relative prices for broad aggregates of agricultural products for the period 1970–1983. (The years 1967–1969 are excluded because the required information for this level of disaggregation was not available.) The relative prices in agriculture are measured as the ratio of the implicit price of gross output in agriculture to the implicit price of nontraded goods in the nonagricultural sector.

The estimated equations are presented in Table 3.3. The first three are the estimated equations for the relative price for total agriculture. All the variables have the expected sign and, except for real per capita income, are significant at the 99 percent level (real per capita income is not significant because it has a negative effect on the price of nontraded goods within agriculture but a positive effect on that of traded goods). According to the estimated value of the coefficient for the real interest rate, an increase of 1 percentage point in the interest rate produces a 2–3 percentage point decline in the relative prices of agricultural products. Therefore, the internal policies of the late 1970s and early 1980s and the large increase in interest rates in external markets seem to have affected agricultural incentives negatively.

The effects of changes in the terms of trade were positive during the boom but negative in the following period. The reason is that this set of relative prices includes coffee, which accounts for one-third of agricultural output. Thus it appears that the Dutch disease effect of an improvement in the terms of trade (essentially the effect of increases in coffee prices) was felt one period after the improvement took place. It is important to note the high absolute value of the coefficient for the *size* of the public sector expenditure variable, which is larger than one. That is, a 1 percentage point increase in the amount of public sector expenditures reduces the relative price of agricultural output by more than 1 percentage point. This phenomenon was particularly important between 1978 and 1983, when public sector expenditures increased from 29 percent to 39 percent of GDP. A great proportion of the loss in competitiveness of Colombian agriculture in the late 1970s can be traced to the substantial increase in government expenditures during this period.

Equations 4 and 5 of Table 3.3 show the estimates of the relative price of noncoffee agriculture. Real per capita income is again insignificant, but the other variables are significant at least to a 98 percent

TABLE 3.3   Determinants of Relative Prices in Colombia's Agricultural Sector

Equation	Period	Dependent variable[a]	Constant	Log per capita GDP (T-1)	Real interest rate (T-1)	LTTBS (T)	LTTBS (T-1)	Government variable G(T-1)	Government variable G	Government variable D	$\bar{R}^2$	RHO	D.W.
1	1970–1983	LPAG	5.93 (6.24)	0.27 (1.12)	-0.03 (-4.76)	0.51 (3.34)	-0.94 (-3.71)				0.88		2.31
2	1970–1983	LPAG	4.93 (8.88)		-0.02 (-4.28)	0.62 (5.55)	-0.61 (-5.52)	-1.18 (-2.66)			0.92		2.07
3	1971–1983	LPAG	5.14 (9.94)		-0.02 (-6.84)	0.59 (5.06)	-0.69 (-6.72)			-0.76 (-2.57)	0.93	-0.33 (-0.86)	2.23
4	1971–1983	LPAGNC	7.59 (15.28)	0.25 (1.84)	-0.02 (-4.58)		-0.78 (-4.60)			-0.95 (-3.20)	0.90	-0.42 (-1.30)	2.55
5	1971–1983	LPAGNC	7.44 (12.82)	0.27 (1.67)	-0.02 (-2.95)		-0.69 (-3.61)		-1.16 (-2.81)		0.90		1.85
6	1971–1983	LPTAN1	6.53 (9.38)	0.66 (2.82)	-0.02 (-3.21)		-0.73 (-3.27)		-1.09 (-2.17)		0.83	0.17 (0.72)	1.79
7	1971–1983	LPTAN1	6.49 (12.25)	0.68 (4.27)	-0.02 (-4.58)		-0.80 (-4.14)			-1.06 (-3.33)	0.82	-0.39 (-1.09)	2.14
8	1970–1983	LPXAN1	6.10 (8.38)	0.95 (4.37)	-0.03 (-4.62)		-0.88 (-3.45)			-0.89 (-2.49)	0.82		2.31
9	1971–1983	LPXAN1	6.15 (8.62)	0.95 (4.85)	-0.02 (-3.54)		-0.82 (-3.47)		-1.27 (-2.52)		0.84		1.56
10	1971–1983	LPMAG	7.97 (21.17)	0.28 (2.70)	-0.02 (-5.08)		-0.88 (-6.71)			-0.90 (-4.16)	0.91	-0.61 (-2.11)	2.44
11	1970–1983	LPMAG	7.57 (13.68)	0.35 (2.24)	-0.01 (-2.38)		-0.76 (-3.96)		-1.21 (-3.05)		0.87		2.11
12	1970–1983	LPAGFT	6.46 (11.18)	0.63 (3.63)	-0.02 (-4.62)		-0.76 (-3.77)			-0.88 (-3.11)	0.84		2.36
13	1971–1983	LPAGFT	6.30 (8.64)	0.58 (2.16)	-0.02 (-2.93)		-0.64 (-2.81)		-1.15 (-2.22)		0.83	0.30 (0.54)	1.63
14	1970–1983	LPC1	1.60 (1.49)		-0.03 (-5.57)	1.76 (8.22)	-1.09 (-5.21)			-0.32 (-0.57)	0.92		2.08

a. LPAG is the logarithm of the price of broad agriculture relative to nontraded in nonagriculture; LPAGNC is the logarithm of the price of noncoffee agriculture relative to nontraded in nonagriculture; LPTAN1 is the logarithm of the price of noncoffee agricultural tradables relative to nontraded in nonagriculture; LPXAN1 is the logarithm of the price of noncoffee agricultural exportables relative to nontraded in nonagriculture; LPMAG is the logarithm of the price of agricultural importables relative to nontraded in nonagriculture; LPAGFT is the logarithm of the price of agricultural food tradables relative to nontraded in nonagriculture; LPC1 is the logarithm of the price of coffee relative to nontraded in nonagriculture; LPC is the logarithm of the price of coffee over the price of noncoffee tradables; LTTBS is the logarithm of the price of exports of goods and services over the price of imports of goods and services. T−1 indicates a time lag of one year.
SOURCE: García García and Montes Llamas (1988. Table 12).

confidence level. Here, too, real income is not significant because it has an opposite effect on traded and nontraded commodities.

Equations 6 and 7 of Table 3.3 indicate the results for tradable non-coffee agriculture; equations 8 and 9 for agricultural exportables; equations 10 and 11 for agricultural importables; and equations 12 and 13 for tradable food commodities. In this set of equations, all the explanatory variables are significant and have the expected sign, and the results are similar to those reported in Tables 3.1 and 3.2.

Equation 14 in Table 3.3 provides an estimate of the relative price of coffee. Coffee differs slightly from the previous cases because of the effects of the terms of trade and real income. The variables indicated in equation (3.15) explain more than 90 percent of the variation in coffee prices, but real income was insignificant. Therefore, the real interest rate, the contemporaneous and lagged terms of trade, and the size of government expenditures are used as independent variables. The contemporaneous effect of the terms of trade is positive, but the lagged effect is negative. Thus, the Dutch disease effect of the increase in coffee prices begins to emerge only one period after the improvement in the terms of trade. The total effect of the increases in the external price of coffee is positive, however, whereas the effect on the rest of agriculture is negative. One explanation for the negative sign of the interest rate is that when the rate rises, the cost of holding stocks also rises, so that there is an incentive to release them and reduce prices. Put another way, when the interest rate goes up, coffee prices are held down to avoid an excessive accumulation of stocks and the related increase in the cost of holding them.

Real Wages in Agriculture

The earnings of labor in agriculture continue to be the lowest in the country. Because a large, although declining, proportion of the population still lives in rural areas, it is important to understand the factors that contribute to poverty in agriculture. Since poverty can be associated with low real wages, an analysis of the factors that determine the real wage in agriculture is relevant. To my knowledge, no study dealing with the problem of agricultural poverty or income distribution in rural Colombia has approached the problem in this way.

In Colombia, as in many developing countries, urban unemployment coexists with a relatively high real wage in manufacturing and with a competitive and informal urban labor market. Despite relatively high and perhaps rising rates of urban unemployment, labor has continued to flow from agriculture to the urban sector. Because these conditions have persisted since World War II, it seemed appropriate to incorporate elements of the Todaro model in the present analysis of real wage determination in agriculture (Todaro 1969; Harris and Todaro 1970).

People migrate to the city expecting to get higher-paying urban jobs.[10] To some extent, the probability of success will depend on the extent of urban unemployment. Thus, it can be postulated that the higher the rate of urban unemployment, the lower the probability of finding a well-paid job in the urban sector. The lower the probability of getting an urban job, the lower the expected urban wage and the expected gains from migration, and the higher the supply of labor in the rural sector than it would otherwise be. Thus, two factors that affect the level of real wages in agriculture are the rate of urban unemployment and the real urban wage.

Another such factor is the size of the rural population. The larger the rural population, the larger the supply of rural labor and the lower the real wage. Therefore, the real wage rate in agriculture, the size of the rural population, the rate of urban unemployment, and real urban wages all affect the supply side of the agricultural labor market.

On the demand side, the real wage that agricultural producers are willing to pay depends on the price of their output and on the productivity of labor. Thus, for a given productivity, the higher the relative price of agricultural products, the larger the number of workers agricultural producers are willing to hire. For a given relative price of agricultural output, the higher the productivity of labor in agriculture, the greater the volume of labor services producers are willing to purchase and the higher the price they are willing to pay for them. Finally, for a given relative price of agricultural output and a given productivity of agricultural labor, the lower the real wage paid in agriculture, the more labor agricultural producers are willing to employ.

Symbolically, these variables can be presented as follows:

L^S = supply of agricultural labor

L^D = demand for agricultural labor

W_a = real wage in agriculture

W_u = real urban wage (the wage at which migrants are likely to find employment)

U = urban rate of unemployment

PA/PNA = price of agricultural output (PA) in relation to the price of output in the nonagricultural sector (PNA)

N_r = size of the rural population

K_a = capital stock in agriculture

The capital stock and the state of technology in agriculture determine the marginal physical product of labor in agriculture. The supply of labor in agriculture is given by

$$L^S = L^S (W_a, N_r, U, W_u),$$ (3.16)

and the demand for agricultural labor is given by

$$L^D = L^D (W_a, PA/PNA, K_a).$$ (3.17)

At equilibrium,

$$L^S (W_a, N_r, U, W_u) - L^D (W_a, PA/PNA, K_a) = 0.$$ (3.18)

From equation (3.18), we can derive W_a as a function of U, W_u, PA/PNA, N_r, and K_a to obtain

$$W_a = W_a (PA/PNA, N_r, K_a, U, W_u).$$ (3.19)

Thus, the real wage in agriculture is a positive function of the relative price of agricultural output, of the capital stock in agriculture, and of the urban real wage, whereas it is a negative function of the size of the rural population and of the urban unemployment rate.

The data used to estimate the real wage equation in the agricultural sector are presented in García García and Montes Llamas (1988, Appendix 1). Two rates of unemployment are used. One measures unemployment for Colombia's four major cities (Bogotá, Medellín, Cali, and Barranquilla) on the basis of data from a National Household Survey carried out by the Departamento Administrativo Nacional de Estadística (DANE). Because there is no value for 1973, it is assumed to be the same as for 1972; the regressions can also be run leaving that year out. The other urban unemployment rate is based on information on agricultural employment, total employment, and the economically active population from the Corporación Centro Regional de Población (CCRP). To derive the rate of urban unemployment in this case, we assume that the economically active population in agriculture was equal to the number of people employed in agriculture. We then define the urban rate of unemployment as one minus the ratio of the difference between total employment and agricultural employment to the difference between the economically active population and agricultural employment.

The wage in construction was taken as the real urban wage rate. The average wage of laborers in this category was derived from information on total labor remuneration from the national accounts and from a series on employment in the construction industry, as supplied by the CCRP. Wages for blue-collar workers in manufacturing were also used as a proxy for the opportunity cost of labor in agriculture. This variable, however, is not significant and, as argued by Harberger (1971), does not seem to be relevant to capturing the true opportunity cost of labor in the urban sector.

We can use two sets of figures for capital stock. The first approximates capital stock by the ratio of real value added in agriculture to total employment in agriculture, in accordance with the idea that the higher the capital stock is, the higher the productivity of labor. The second set is taken from Elías's study for the International Food Policy Research Institute (1985).

The equation for estimating real agricultural wages is

$$\log W_a = a + \alpha \log(PA/PNA) + \beta \log K_a + \tau \log W_u \\ + \sigma U + \lambda \log N_r + u,$$ (3.20)

where log stands for the logarithmic value of the variable, and u is a random term. The signs for the coefficients α, β, and τ were expected to be positive, while those for σ and λ were expected to be negative.

The results of the estimation, presented in Table 3.4, support the hypothesis about the determination of real agricultural wages. The coefficients have the expected sign and are statistically significant, and there are no problems of autocorrelation. One important result concerns the role of relative agricultural prices: macroeconomic policies that depress agricultural prices reduce the real agricultural wage and thus work against the economic welfare of the rural population.

Conclusions

The profitability of producing noncoffee tradables in Colombia was subject to substantial negative pressure between 1975 and 1983. This pressure arose mainly from the decrease in the real exchange rate (relative price of noncoffee tradables over nontradables), induced by the improvement in the terms of trade and then by the growing government expenditure.

The determinants of the relative prices in agriculture delineated in this discussion strongly suggest that improvements in the terms of trade and the substantial increase in the amount of government expenditures were significant factors in reducing agricultural incentives between 1975

TABLE 3.4   Real Agricultural Wage Equations for Colombia

Equation	Period	Constant	Log (PA/PNA)[a] (T)	Log (Kₐ)[b] (T−1)	Log (VAWorker)[c] (T)	Log (RWCONS)[d] (T−1)	Log (rural population) (T)	(T−1)	Unemployment rate CCRP[e] (T)	DANE[f] (T)	$\bar{R}^2$	D.W.
1	1968–1983	34.49 (4.10)	0.54 (16.43)		1.46 (13.11)	0.27 (6.16)	−4.25 (−4.30)		−0.94 (−2.81)		0.99	2.29
2	1968–1983	27.80 (3.06)	0.54 (13.95)		1.41 (11.12)	0.24 (5.03)	−3.48 (−3.26)			−0.38 −(1.78)	0.99	2.30
3	1968–1983	230.61 (3.04)	0.48 (5.48)	2.87 (3.88)		0.45 (2.70)		−27.96 (−3.07)	−2.91 (−2.48)		0.96	2.04
4	1968–1983	222.59 (2.47)	0.52 (4.81)	2.62 (3.25)		0.35 (2.19)	−26.82 (−2.50)			−1.65 (−2.29)	0.95	2.04
5	1968–1972, 1974–1983	23.88 (3.05)	0.52 (14.09)		1.39 (11.49)	0.23 (4.97)		−3.04 (−3.29)		−0.48 (−2.02)	0.99	2.52
6	1968–1972, 1974–1983	233.09 (2.51)	0.52 (4.69)	2.72 (3.26)		0.36 (2.18)	−28.07 (−2.53)			−1.92 (−2.35)	0.95	2.23

NOTE: The t-statistics are in parentheses.
a. Log(PA/PNA) stands for logarithm of PA/PNA.
b. Log(K)a stands for logarithm of capital stock in agriculture.
c. Log(VAWorker) stands for logarithm of real value added per worker in the agricultural sector.
d. Log(RWCONS) stands for logarithm of real wage in the construction sector.
e. Unemployment rate CCRP corresponds to the information on unemployment derived from CCRP.
f. Unemployment rate DANE corresponds to the information on unemployment derived from DANE.
SOURCE: García García and Montes Llamas (1988).

and 1983. Improved terms of trade from an increase in the international price of coffee are not necessarily good for other sectors of the economy unless the gain is adequately offset by policies that reduce the expenditure effect of the coffee boom.

The government in Colombia neglected to take such action, and the repercussions caused a great deal of harm to the economy. The impact of government expenditures on relative prices is very strong, as seen in Table 3.3. The effect is larger for exportables, coffee included, than for importables.

The regressions in the present analysis did not include a nominal variable. They also omitted the rate of devaluation as a determinant of relative prices because it was insignificant.

The results of the empirical analysis on the determinants of real agricultural wages indicate that higher capital stock, higher prices for agricultural products, and a higher urban wage tended to increase real wages in agriculture in Colombia, while high rates of unemployment in the urban sector had a negative influence. These findings have several important implications for policy making, especially in addressing poverty in rural areas.

First, policies that artificially depress agricultural prices tend to reduce real agricultural income and heighten rural poverty. Since Colombia's agricultural sector produces mainly exportable commodities, import-substitution policies designed to promote industrialization reduce the prices of agricultural commodities in relation to prices in the rest of the economy; this in turn reduces real agricultural wages. The same is true for policies that reduce the price of food or that subsidize imports of food products to increase the real income of the urban population.

Second, in view of the fact that farmers respond to prices, when policies lower agricultural prices artificially, they discourage the accumulation of capital. In doing so, they also reduce real wages below the level they would otherwise reach.

Third, policies that establish minimum urban wages are likely to increase poverty in agriculture. The reason is that minimum wages tend to raise urban unemployment, reduce the expected real income of the migrant, and push the supply of rural labor above what it would otherwise be, so that rural wages are driven down.

Notes to Chapter 3

1. I first made some of the points in this chapter in an unpublished manuscript (García García 1983). This chapter has benefited from some subsequent analyses; see, in particular, Thomas et al. (1985, especially Chapters 1–4 and the appendix by Sebastian Edwards) and Edwards (1984, 1986b).

2. The estimates of the size of the illegal economy in Colombia cover only part of the period studied in this paper. For an early estimate, see Junguito and Caballero (1978). A more recent estimate can be found in Gomez (1988). Gomez estimates that during the period 1981–1985, net income from the drug traffic ranged from 6.4 percent of GDP in 1982 to 2.6 percent in 1985.

3. In 1982, when the estimated value of the drug activity was at its height (at US$2.5 billion), the sale of dollars to the Central Bank from illegal activities was estimated to have been about US$23 million. In 1979, those sales were estimated at US$312 million, or 20 percent of the total increase in international reserves in that year. See Gomez (1988, Tables 7 and 17).

4. Although import substitution was on the minds of economic authorities at the time they introduced the exchange control system, the evolution of policy can be categorized as an intended reduction in the anti-export bias. The increase in the real exchange rate helped lessen that bias and thereby produced an important change in the domestic terms of trade.

5. The model presented in this section is based on Dornbusch (1980, Chapters 6, 7, 10, and 11), Rodriguez (1982), Frenkel and Mussa (1985), and Corden and Neary (1982).

6. For an exposition on the possible impact of an increase in the price of the main exports on the output of nonbooming sectors, see Corden and Neary (1982).

7. This assumption is reasonable, since about 85 percent of coffee output is exported, and the own-price elasticity of demand for coffee is very low.

8. The assumption that the government purchases only noncoffee tradables and nontraded commodities might appear somewhat unrealistic because the government is an important purchaser of coffee, through the National Coffee Fund. Since the fund exports its coffee, however, the government is acting as an export agent of domestic producers.

9. See Mundlak (1985a). For a discussion of these interactions in Argentina, see Cavallo and Mundlak (1982), and Mundlak, Cavallo, and Domenech (1989).

10. The issue of labor migration and its determinants in Colombia has received considerable attention. See, among others, McGreevy (1968); Schultz (1969, 1971); Colombia's Ministerio del Trabajo, Servicio Nacional de Empleo (1979); Colombia's Departamento Administrativo Nacional de Estadística (1977); Ordóñez (1977); Reyes (1975); Fields (1979); and Ribe (1981).

The Oil Boom, Macroeconomic Policies, and Nigerian Agriculture: Analysis of a "Dutch Disease" Phenomenon

Trade and exchange rate policies, as well as other instruments of macroeconomic policy, generate relative price changes that affect agricultural incentives and growth. These usually unintended effects may be stronger than, or contrary to, more favorable agricultural policies and interventions. Sharp changes in the terms of trade may also influence incentives, as illustrated by the oil boom in Nigeria during the 1970s and early 1980s.

This chapter examines the negative impact on agriculture of the oil boom and the associated macroeconomic developments and policies. Even before the oil boom, Nigeria's trade policy provided large incentives for manufacturing at the expense of other sectors, particularly agriculture.[1] Under that policy, Nigeria launched an import-substitution industrialization program in the 1960s, which it continued throughout the 1970s. The oil boom provided even greater impetus for sustaining an overvalued domestic currency through the trade and exchange rate regime and related macroeconomic policy environment. In combination, these factors put a squeeze on non-oil tradables, particularly agriculture.

Before the oil boom, agriculture had enjoyed a unique position in the Nigerian economy: it was the dominant source of employment and foreign exchange revenue from exports. At that time, Nigeria was a major exporter of agricultural produce, including cocoa, groundnuts, cotton, palm oil, palm kernel, rubber, and timber. Since then, both the volume and range of agricultural exports have declined sharply. The output of agricultural export crops declined more than 20 percent between 1970 and 1982, while the average annual rate of growth of real output for food crops fell to about 2 percent during the 1970s. As a result, the increased income generated by the oil boom caused more than a tenfold increase in the food import bill.

The adverse effects of Nigeria's policies on agriculture have not yet received adequate attention in the government's structural adjustment programs. This chapter draws out the implications of these policies through an analysis of the "Dutch disease" model, the associated macroeconomic policies, and their influence on the real exchange rate. The discussion then moves to the structural changes generated by the oil boom, the subsequent macroeconomic policy responses, the empirical evidence on the effects of sector-specific policies on agriculture, the negative impact of the trade and exchange rate regime, and the relationship between the real exchange rate and agricultural performance.

The "Dutch Disease" Phenomenon and Its Implications

The export boom generated by the sharp increases in the price and quantity of oil had a marked influence on the structure of the Nigerian economy. It led to a significant appreciation of the real exchange rate, which caused competitiveness, output, and employment in the non-oil tradable sectors, particularly agriculture, to decline. This phenomenon, called the Dutch disease, has attracted considerable attention (see, for example, Gregory 1976; Corden and Neary 1982; Harberger 1983; Edwards and Aoki 1983; Siebert 1984; and Neary and van Wijnbergen 1986).

The Dutch disease phenomenon has both short- and long-run effects. In the long run, a resource-based export boom affects production, employment, wages, and profitability. The boom works through two distinct channels: spending and the movement of resources (Corden and Neary 1982).

The spending effect emanates from the higher real income generated by the oil boom. To the extent that both traded (T) and nontraded, or home (H), goods are normal goods, the increased real income will generate a higher demand for the goods. Since the additional income is spent on both traded and home goods, relative prices will change. The excess demand for home goods forces the relative price of these goods up, whereas the increased demand for traded goods pushes up the volume of imports. The higher relative price of home goods amounts to a real appreciation of the exchange rate that draws resources out of traded goods and into home goods. Because the home sector expands at the expense of traditional tradables (such as agriculture and manufacturing), their profitability is squeezed: the factors of production, particularly labor, are diverted from those traded sectors, and their output also declines.

The resource movement effect is manifested in changes in the factor markets. Simple versions of the Dutch disease model treat labor as the only mobile factor, and the impact appears as changes in the wage rate. Initially, the oil boom gives rise to a higher wage rate in the oil industry, which induces labor to move out of both the home and non-oil traded production. Since the spending effect will tend to raise the price of home goods relative to traded goods, the wage rate in the former is likely to rise as well, so that labor will also move out of non-oil traded goods into home goods. The non-oil traded production is squeezed further, and production and employment decline even more.

In the short run, the oil boom adds a slowly clearing monetary sector to the basic three-good Dutch disease model (Harberger 1983; Edwards and Aoki 1983). When money is added to the basic system, the resource boom affects its supply and demand. On the supply side, the boom may generate a balance of payments surplus, which leads to an increase in the money supply, if it is monetized by the Central Bank. On the demand side, the increased income generated by the resource boom causes an increase in the demand for money. Thus, two tendencies coexist, and there will be either an excess demand for, or an excess supply of, money. This situation implies, by Walras's law, an excess supply of, or excess demand for, both home and traded goods. In the case of excess demand, that for home goods will create inflationary pressures, which will tend to reinforce the effect because of the boom-induced increase in income. As a result, the real exchange rate will decline in the short run by a larger amount than in the long run, and the nominal price of home goods will be higher than its eventual long-run equilibrium level. Hence, the loss of competitiveness of the traded sectors, as measured by the relative prices of traded and home goods, will be larger in the short run than in the long run. The opposite result occurs in the case of an excess supply of goods.

Figure 4.1 shows both the short-run monetary and long-run real results. Consider a small open economy with a fixed nominal exchange rate (assumed to be equal to one) that produces three types of goods: oil (O), non-oil tradables (T), and nontradables or home (H) goods. Suppose that excess demand for home goods depends on relative prices and income, that the factors used in producing oil are sector-specific, and that gross substitutability exists between home and traded goods. At equilibrium, the excess demand for home goods will equal zero, that is,

$$H = h(P_T/P_H, Y) = 0 \qquad (4.1)$$

FIGURE 4.1   Short-Run Monetary Effects and Long-Run Real Effects of a Boom in Resource Exports

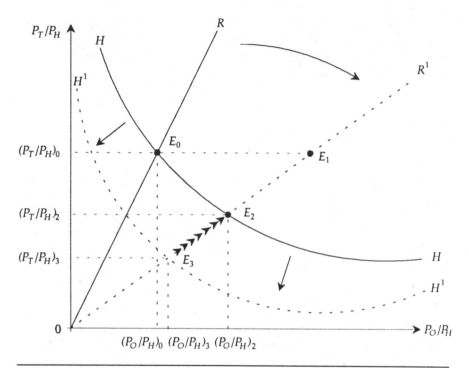

NOTE: O = oil, T = non-oil tradable goods, H = nontradable or home goods, P = prices, and E = equilibrium.
SOURCE: Adapted from Edwards and Aoki (1983).

where P_T/P_H is the relative price of non-oil tradables to home goods and Y is real income in terms of home goods. In Figure 4.1, the negatively sloped HH schedule shows the contribution of relative prices, P_T/P_H and P_O/P_H, that is compatible with equilibrium in the home goods market (P_O is the nominal price of oil, P_T is the nominal price of non-oil tradables, and P_H is the nominal price of home goods). The ray, OR, from the origin measures the price of non-oil tradables relative to oil (P_T/P_O).

The original point of equilibrium in this system occurs at E_0, where OR intersects the HH schedule; the relative prices at equilibrium are $(P_T/P_H)_0$ and $(P_O/P_H)_0$. Now, if an exogenous increase occurs in P_O, the ray OR rotates clockwise (as the relative price P_T/P_O is depressed) to

OR^1. A new equilibrium at E_1 cannot be sustained, as it would imply a constant P_T/P_H ratio. Since the slope of HH is negative, an excess demand for home goods exists at E_1. Elimination of that excess demand calls for an increase in the nominal price of home goods, P_H. As a result, P_T/P_H will fall so that a new equilibrium with the associated relative prices $(P_T/P_H)_2$ and $(P_O/P_H)_2$ is established at E_2. In short, the increase in the price of oil causes a decrease in the price of tradables in relation to home goods and this causes an appreciation in the real exchange rate. The reduction in the relative price of traded goods will draw resources out of non-oil tradables into nontradables.

Note that the shape of the schedule plays an important role in deriving this result. The rate of appreciation of the real exchange rate, or the extent of the loss of competitiveness, depends on the slope of the curve. If all the income generated by the oil boom was spent on home goods, HH would become a vertical line, and the negative effect of the boom on the real exchange rate would be at its maximum. If all additional income was spent on traded goods, however, HH would become horizontal, and the real exchange rate would not be affected by the boom. Hence, the degree of the appreciation reflects the distribution of the additional real income (in terms of spending) between home and traded goods.

Figure 4.1 also illustrates the monetary effects of a resource boom. It is assumed that, when monetized, the balance of payments generated by the boom creates an excess supply of money. This excess supply is, in turn, transformed into excess demand for home and traded goods. The resource boom then has two consequences: (1) the HH curve shifts downward to H^1H^1, as a result of the balance of payments surplus, which leads to an excess supply of money and, hence, to excess demand for home goods in the short run; and (2) the OR ray rotates to OR^1, as the increase in P_O reduces the P_T/P_O ratio. When the HH curve moves to H^1H^1, a short-run equilibrium occurs at E_3, while the final equilibrium occurs, as before, at E_2. Under the dynamics of the adjustment process, the HH schedule shifts back to its original position as the excess supply of money is eliminated. Since the real exchange rate at E_3 is lower than its value at E_2, the loss of competitiveness is greater in the short run than in the long run.

An oil boom brings both opportunities and challenges. Policy makers concerned with the macroeconomic management of the economy may respond to these opportunities and challenges in various ways. Since an oil boom is usually accompanied by an increase in the net amount of funds received from abroad, for example, expenditures are able to increase in relation to income. If part of the rise in expenditures is devoted to home goods, excess demand is likely to emerge, and equilibrium will be difficult to restore unless there is an appreciation of the real exchange rate or an increase in the price of home goods in relation to traded goods. Similarly, large capital outflows can induce an increase in the real exchange rate, or inflows a decline. Creating those outflows may be one way to ameliorate the negative impact of the resource boom. Hence, a policy of foreign exchange sterilization (which means accumulating foreign assets, investing overseas, and retiring foreign debts) may help protect the non-oil tradables sector.

An oil boom provides an almost irresistible opportunity for increased government spending, particularly when the greater oil revenues accrue primarily and directly to the government. The effect of increased government spending on the real exchange rate depends on the size of the government sector, the source of financing, and the area in which the resources are spent (home as opposed to traded goods). If a high share of government spending is devoted to increasing the supply of public utilities so that the cost of their services falls, the price of domestic goods may be expected to drop, all other things being equal, and the real exchange rate will rise. Since the government is also a consumer of home and traded goods, however, any expansion in government spending will lower the real exchange rate if it boosts public sector demand for home goods without displacing private sector demand.

Increasing government expenditures through deficit financing also has implications for the real exchange rate. In general, deficit financing through foreign borrowing causes the real exchange rate to appreciate, assuming that part of it goes toward home goods and that private sector expenditures are not reduced. Deficit financing through the creation of domestic credit under a fixed nominal exchange rate has a similar effect.

Structural Change and Macroeconomic Developments

The Nigerian economy underwent massive structural changes in the years between 1960 and 1984, particularly during the oil boom of the 1970s. These changes have had substantial consequences for agriculture. The sharp drop in the share of agriculture in GDP represents one of the most important changes in the macroeconomic structure over the entire period.

In the early 1960s, agriculture accounted for almost 60 percent of total GDP. During the oil boom period, this share fell to less than 25 percent. Its decline in relation to non-oil GDP was slightly less sharp, but no less significant. For instance, agriculture's share in non-oil GDP, which averaged 60 percent during 1960–1965, fell to 30 percent, its lowest average level between 1978 and 1981, before recovering slightly to just over 31 percent following the oil slump from 1981 to 1984. Correspondingly, the nontraded sectors (infrastructure and services) increased their share of non-oil GDP markedly, from an average of 34 percent in the period 1960–1965 to about 61 percent between 1973 and 1981. This share remained close to 60 percent through 1984, in spite of the slump in the oil market beginning in 1981.

Sectoral employment and export shares underwent a similar pattern of structural change, although it was less pronounced in the former than in the latter. Agriculture's share of total employment fell from about 75 percent to 59 percent between 1970 and 1982, while that of infrastructure and services rose from 10 percent to 23 percent. The share of the oil and mining sectors in total employment remained at less than 0.5 percent.

Export shares experienced much larger changes: agriculture declined from more than 70 percent in 1970 to less than 3 percent in 1982, while the oil sector's share rose from 15 percent to almost 98 percent over the same period.

A crude measure of the effects of the structural change is derived by computing a set of hypothetical sectoral values for 1982, using actual 1970 shares, and then comparing them with actual 1982 sectoral shares. The result shows sectoral gains and losses in values and percentages.

Table 4.1 presents the results with respect to output, exports, and employment. The two non-oil tradable sectors, agriculture and manufacturing, suffered relative losses as a result of the sectoral shifts that accompanied the oil boom. Agriculture's loss, however, was clearly more pronounced: an almost 55 percent drop in output, an almost 97 percent loss in exports, and slightly more than a 27 percent loss in employment. Although the loss in exports by the manufacturing sector—just under 100 percent—was just as bad as agriculture's (in relative terms), its loss of output was more modest—just over 21 percent—and it actually posted a gain in employment of slightly more than 15 percent.

When the total (actual) change in output and employment is examined (by combining the structural shift effect with the overall economic growth effect), the picture changes somewhat. Although both non-oil tradable sectors suffered large losses because of the structural shifts, the relative gains flowing from the overall economic growth generated by the oil boom more than compensated for the losses. For the oil and nontraded sectors, the gains from both were cumulative.

The infrastructure and service sectors accounted for more than 48 percent of the total increase in output, well above the 26 percent share of the oil sector and the 20 percent and 6 percent shares of agriculture and manufactures, respectively. As in the case of output, those who gained the most in terms of employment were the nontradable sectors,

TABLE 4.1   Effects of Sectoral Shifts on Output, Exports, and
             Employment in Nigeria, 1970–1982

Sector	Output		Exports		Employment	
	₦ million	%	₦ million	%	Thousand	%
Agriculture	−12,477.8	−54.5	−5,900.4	−96.6	−5,440	−27.1
Manufacturing	−707.4	−21.1	−1,037.6	−99.6	918	15.3
Oil and mining	6,875.4	143.4	6,739.4	533.3	68	100.0
Infrastructure and services	6,309.7	39.7	0.0	0.0	4,454	57.2

NOTE: + = gain; − = loss.
SOURCE: Oyejide (1986a, 38–39).

which accrued about 70 percent of the total increase, compared with 27 percent for the manufacturing sector. The oil and agriculture sectors each accounted for less than 2 percent of the increase.[2]

The oil boom and the resulting structural changes were accompanied by other important macroeconomic developments. Since the oil revenues accrued largely and directly to the government, and there was no deliberate policy of sterilizing foreign exchange, public sector expenditures expanded rapidly between 1970 and 1980. During the first half of this period, federal capital expenditures rose fortyfold, while state capital expenditures grew by a factor of 16. Overall government spending increased faster than GDP. As a result, total expenditures as a proportion of GDP jumped sharply: starting at 6 percent in 1960, the ratio reached 15 percent in 1970 and then doubled again within the next five years. It remained around 30 percent up to 1980 before the fall in oil revenue forced it down to just over 20 percent between 1981 and 1984.

In spite of the increased revenues generated by the oil boom, budget deficits reemerged in 1975 (at 7 percent of GDP) and continued through 1984. In fact, the budget deficit as a proportion of GDP reached almost 9 percent in 1981 and peaked at 11 percent in 1983. Correspondingly, the current account was negative during most of the 1970–1984 period. Essentially, the oil boom produced only brief surpluses when the price of oil rose. Thus, the first oil shock (in 1973–1974) resulted in current account surpluses in 1974 and 1975, which soon gave way to increasingly large deficits through 1978. Similarly, the second oil shock, in 1979, generated current account surpluses through 1980 and deficits thereafter.

The budget and current account deficits of the 1970–1984 period resulted in a massive buildup of internal and external debt. Total internal debt grew from just over ₦ 1 billion in 1970 to about ₦ 8 billion in 1980 and more than ₦ 25 billion in 1984. Approximately 75 percent of this debt was owed to the banking system, and the corresponding debt-service obligation was equivalent to 20 percent of government revenue in 1984.

Similarly, external debt (outstanding and disbursed) rose from less than US$0.5 billion in 1970 to US$4.4 billion in 1980 and almost US$12 million in 1984. The debt-service ratio (as a percentage of export earnings) rose from 4.2 percent in 1970 to 25.6 percent in 1984, while debt as a proportion of GDP increased from 0.7 percent to 5 percent in the same interval.

A marked shift occurred in the source of external debt. The share of official (bilateral and multilateral) creditors declined from 60 percent in 1970 to 23 percent in 1980 and 15 percent in 1984. The share of the financial markets shot up from only 3 percent in 1970 to 76 percent in 1980 and 83 percent in 1984. As a result, the concessional element of external debt fell from 30 percent in 1970 to 3 percent in 1984, while the element with variable interest rates rose from less than 1 percent to more than 70 percent in the same period.

Policy-Induced Incentives, the Real Exchange Rate, and Agricultural Performance

Agricultural performance is influenced by many price and nonprice factors. Sector-specific policies influence agricultural incentives, as do economywide measures implemented through trade, exchange rate, and related macroeconomic policy changes. The Dutch disease phenomenon also generates sectoral shifts through changes in relative prices and the real exchange rate, and corresponding changes in the structure of incentives.

These three categories of factors have incentive and disincentive effects on agriculture that sometimes reinforce one another but that may also pull resources in opposite directions, depending on the circumstances.

Sector-Specific Policies

There is substantial evidence that Nigeria's agricultural pricing and marketing policy up to about 1970 was not directed toward creating or improving producer incentives (see, for example, Helleiner 1964; Oyejide 1985). Rather, its goal was to withdraw resources from agriculture to finance government spending and the development of such sectors as manufacturing, infrastructure, and social services.

Agricultural policy changed radically in the 1970s. The oil boom provided the government with increased revenue and thus reduced the need to extract resources from agriculture. This was also a period of rising domestic food prices, which increasingly focused government attention on agriculture's poor performance. Thus in 1973 the government made an initial effort to reform the agricultural marketing board system and at the same time abolished all crop (export and sales) taxes. In a further reorganization in 1977, the state governments and their marketing boards lost the power to fix producer crop prices. Instead, price fixing authority was vested in the federal government under new centralized boards. The boards were precluded from generating trade surpluses. A system of guaranteed minimum prices was instituted to support food crops that were not subject to government control through the marketing board system. In addition, the government offered generous input (particularly fertilizer) subsidies.

At first sight, the agricultural sector appears to have benefited from the more favorable sector-specific policies implemented between 1970 and 1984. Nominal producer prices rose two- or threefold over the period.[3] As Table 4.2 shows, however, the real price trends tell a different story. Real producer crop prices (that is, nominal prices deflated by the consumer price index) either declined sharply (palm kernel, for example, dropped 36 percent) or remained roughly constant over the period. Although nominal producer prices rose substantially during the 1970s and early 1980s, the rates of increase were insufficient to compensate for the general effect of inflation. Thus, they could not have generated many incentives. The guaranteed minimum prices for food crops were also ineffective, since they were never more than about 50 percent of the corresponding domestic retail prices.

Price spreads (that is, the difference between producer crop prices and corresponding unit export values) reflect a similar picture. From 1960 to 1969, the ratio of producer prices to unit export values was low (Table 4.3), particularly for cotton (20 percent), palm kernel (51 percent), groundnut (58 percent), and palm oil (59 percent).[4] The reason for this was the apparent decision of the regional and state governments to use their marketing boards as fiscal agents. The reforms of the 1970s, however, allowed producer prices to move closer to their unit export values for all crops (the producer price for palm oil was even 28 percent higher than its unit export value). From 1977 to 1984, the producer prices of all crops except cocoa were well in excess of, or about equal to, their unit export values—in nominal terms. In real terms—that is, when the unit export values are adjusted for domestic currency overvaluation (Oyejide 1986b)—the implicit taxation of export crops was higher over the 1970–1984 period than the nominal ratios indicate. Except for palm oil (during 1970–1976) and groundnuts (during 1977–1984), exports crops were not subsidized in real terms.

Trade and Exchange Rate Policies

Trade and exchange rate policies influence the level and structure of an economy's production incentives. These in turn determine the intersec-

TABLE 4.2   Nominal and Real Producer Prices in Nigeria, 1970–1984 (naira per tonne)

Year	Cocoa		Groundnut		Seed cotton		Palm oil		Palm kernel		Rubber	
	Nominal	Real	Nominal	Real	Nominal	Real	Nominal	Real	Nominal	Real	Nominal	Real
1970	297	297	63	63	102	102	76	76	61	61	n.a.	n.a.
1971	256	256	67	58	102	88	76	65	61	53	n.a.	n.a.
1972	354	297	75	63	123	103	84	71	61	53	n.a.	n.a.
1973	487	390	81	65	132	106	204	163	130	104	n.a.	n.a.
1974	660	468	145	103	156	111	265	138	150	106	n.a.	n.a.
1975	660	351	250	133	308	164	265	141	150	80	n.a.	n.a.
1976	660	284	250	108	308	133	295	127	150	65	n.a.	n.a.
1977	1,030	383	250	93	330	123	355	132	150	56	365	136
1978	1,030	328	275	88	330	105	355	113	150	48	365	116
1979	1,200	343	290	83	330	94	450	129	180	51	420	120
1980	1,300	338	350	91	400	104	495	129	200	52	485	126
1981	1,300	279	420	90	465	100	495	106	200	43	600	129
1982	1,300	259	450	90	510	102	495	99	230	46	700	139
1983	1,400	227	450	73	560	91	495	80	230	37	700	113
1984	1,500	174	650	75	700	81	600	70	400	45	750	87

n.a. = not available.
SOURCE: Oyejide (1986b, 42, 45).

TABLE 4.3	Average Producer Price as a Percentage of Average Unit Export Value (Nominal and Adjusted) in Nigeria, 1960–1984		
Export	1960–1969	1970–1976	1977–1984
Cocoa			
Nominal	65.2	67.9	72.0
Adjusted	68.4	61.2	49.2
Groundnut			
Nominal	57.6	73.1	160.0
Adjusted	60.3	65.8	109.2
Cotton			
Nominal	20.1	41.4	105.6
Adjusted	21.1	37.4	72.1
Palm oil			
Nominal	58.5	128.4	124.3
Adjusted	61.4	116.0	85.4
Palm kernel			
Nominal	50.9	86.5	94.8
Adjusted	53.5	77.9	64.7
Rubber			
Nominal	n.a.	n.a.	96.8

n.a. = not available.
Source: Oyejide (1986b, 41, 47).

toral flow of resources. Dornbusch (1974) and Sjaastad (1980) have established that the effects of these policies often differ substantially from those intended by policy makers when viewed from the perspective of their impact on relative prices rather than on nominal prices. They argue that protecting any one sector penalizes other sector(s) and that the degree of damage to other sectors depends on the substitution relationships in production and consumption.

Note that ω is an incidence parameter that measures the extent to which an import duty intended to protect some import-competing activities (for example, manufacturing) may be shifted in part or transformed completely into a tax on producers of exportables (for example, agricultural exports). In more general terms, the ω parameter measures the combined effects of changes in trade and exchange rate policies and shows how the consequent changes in relative prices affect the different sectors.

The model provides a simple technique for estimating the ω parameter:

$$\ln (P_h/P_x) = \text{constant} + \omega \ln (P_m/P_x) + \text{error term} \qquad (4.2)$$

In light of equation (4.2), the estimated numerical value of ω reflects the proportional change in the price of home goods in relation to the price of exportables as a function of the proportional change in the price of importables in relation to the price of exportables.

Table 4.4 presents the estimated numerical values of ω for several categories of Nigeria's exports (Oyejide 1986a). The results indicate that the incidence of trade and exchange rate policies on these exports ranged from 51 to 90 percent. These high values may be explained in part by the fact that the calculations employed annual data and therefore may not adequately reflect the variations in relative prices between years. Alternatively, the ω values may be high because Nigeria's home goods and importables were fairly close substitutes, or because its exports, being primarily resource-based (oil) or agricultural, had a fairly inelastic supply. Hence, they were likely to absorb a high proportion of the tariff incidence in the form of reduced rents on the natural resource or land.

Whatever the reason, high ω values imply that a tariff on imports falls almost entirely on the producers of exportable goods. It may be inferred, therefore, that Nigeria's trade and exchange rate policies, which are designed primarily to protect import-competing manufacturing activities, have substantially reduced the relative incentive to produce export goods.

A case could be made for using an export subsidy to compensate for the adverse effects of industrial protection on Nigeria's exportable (primarily agricultural) producers. Given an average import duty of 50 percent during the 1970–1984 period and an average ω value of 0.83 for all agricultural exports, a 42 percent export subsidy would have been necessary to offset the negative impact of industrial protection. In fact, although the trade policy shifted from explicit taxation to (nominal) protection for domestic production of agricultural crops beginning in the 1970s, the actual levels of nominal protection fell far short of what was needed to neutralize the adverse effects of the industrial protection.

The Real Exchange Rate and Agricultural Performance

General macroeconomic management policies affect agriculture through changes in the real exchange rate, which plays a critical role in the profitability of both export-oriented and import-competing agriculture.

TABLE 4.4   Omega Estimates for Selected Nigerian Exports

Export category	Range of omega values
Total	0.55–0.90
Agriculture	0.82–0.84
Oil	0.51–0.69
Cocoa	0.83–0.86
Groundnut	0.61–0.82
Palm kernel	0.66–0.79

SOURCE: Oyejide (1986a, 50).

The real exchange rate measures the real terms of trade between traded and nontraded goods. Hence, it can be viewed as the ratio of the prices of tradables to the prices of nontradables. When the rate drops, the prices of tradable goods fall in relation to the prices of nontradables, and vice versa. To the extent that intersectoral resource flows are sensitive to changes in relative prices, changes in the real exchange rate can be expected to affect intersectoral profitability and thereby induce a movement of resources between different sectors of the economy. More specifically, a reduction in the real exchange rate would divert resources away from tradables to nontradables, while an increase would have the opposite effect.

Changes in the real exchange rate may be brought about by policy changes in various areas—trade, fiscal and monetary matters, capital movements and the nominal exchange rate, and wages—as well as by autonomous shifts in the terms of trade. The Dutch disease phenomenon usually starts with an autonomous and drastic change in the terms of trade. Subsequent policy behavior and responses could, however, cause changes in many of the other policy variables that influence the real exchange rate. In the case of Nigeria, the oil boom, together with the associated macroeconomic developments and policies, were probably the dominant factors governing the behavior of the real exchange rate between 1970 and 1984.

FIGURE 4.2   Exchange Rate Indexes for Nigeria, 1960–1984
(1970 = 100)

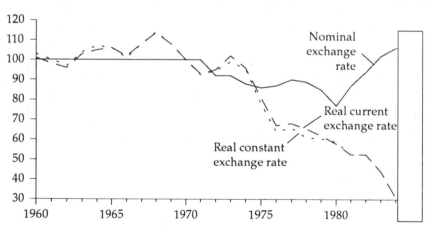

SOURCE: Computed from data in Central Bank of Nigeria, *Annual Reports*, and International Monetary Fund, *International Financial Statistics*.

FIGURE 4.3   Real Exchange Rate and Agricultural Performance
               Indexes in Nigeria, 1960–1984 (1970 = 100)

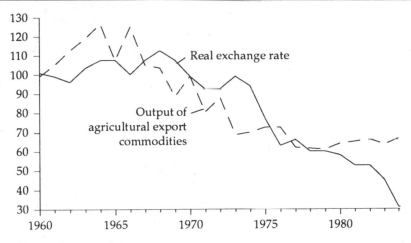

SOURCE: Real exchange rate index is from Figure 4.2; index of agricultural export output was computed from data in Central Bank of Nigeria, *Annual Reports*.

As Figure 4.2 illustrates, Nigeria's oil boom triggered a sharp decline (or a significant appreciation) in the index of the real exchange rate, even though the nominal exchange rate policy was apparently pointed in the opposite direction. This decline indicates a reduction in the relative prices of traditional agricultural exports and import-competing agricultural products. Unlike the manufacturing sector, agriculture has not traditionally been shielded against the negative impact of the relative price changes implicit in a falling real exchange rate.

Figure 4.3 makes clear that agricultural performance, as measured by the index of output of agricultural export commodities, shows the same sharp downward trend and moves fairly closely in line with the index of the real exchange rate.[5] This means that agriculture's performance is quite sensitive to changes in the real exchange rate and that the appreciation in the rate caused by the oil boom and associated macroeconomic policies has had a marked negative impact on agriculture.

Concluding Comments

Starting in 1986, Nigeria embarked on the most ambitious policy reform and structural adjustment program in its history. Since then, the government has instituted many radical changes, including the abolition of the agricultural commodity boards and the establishment of a second-tier foreign exchange market in which the nominal external value of the naira is largely market-determined. Among the immediate results have been a fourfold increase in the domestic price of cocoa and a 400 percent nominal devaluation of the naira. Other measures have been directed at shrinking the budget deficits and controlling foreign borrowing more tightly. Still on the drawing board is a comprehensive review of the tariff structure.

If successfully carried out, the adjustment program should reestablish a favorable macroeconomic environment in which some of the damages to agriculture caused by the oil boom and related policy errors can be corrected. Two outstanding issues still need to be tackled, however. First, current policy discussions in Nigeria have not clarified the extent to which agriculture would be explicitly integrated with the other sectors in the ongoing process of tariff restructuring—this is a vital issue in view of the fact that Nigeria's agricultural exports usually bear the brunt of industrial protection. Second, there is the question of the efficacy of the price incentives for sustained and rapid agricultural response in the absence of supportive structural factors (Delgado and Mellor 1984).

Even after the macroeconomic environment has been put right, more needs to be done in critical nonprice areas if Nigerian agriculture is to be fully revived and revitalized.

Notes to Chapter 4

1. The implicit taxation of agriculture that was associated with Nigeria's import substitution industrialization policy predated and continued through the oil boom of the 1970s. The conditions before the boom are not explicitly discussed in this chapter, but an analysis is available in Oyejide (1985).

2. Although the analysis of relative shares shows that the agricultural sector suffered significant declines with respect to output, exports, and employment, in absolute terms, agricultural output actually increased from ₦ 1.7 billion in 1970 to ₦ 10.4 billion in 1982; agricultural employment also grew from ₦ 19.9 million in 1970 to ₦ 20.1 million in 1982; but agricultural exports fell from ₦ 238 million to ₦ 199 million between 1970 and 1982 (see Oyejide 1986a). Thus, agricultural exports declined in both relative and absolute terms.

3. Nominal producer prices refer to buying prices announced annually by the Marketing/Commodity Board. The prices actually received by farmers may be lower in certain cases. See Oyejide (1985) for details.

4. Producer prices are as defined in note 3, while unit export values are f.o.b. export prices per unit of output.

5. The agricultural output index was constructed at 1970 prices.

Agricultural Pricing and the Exchange Rate in Zaire

This chapter considers the direct and indirect effects of trade, exchange rate, and other policies on the farm sector in Zaire between 1960 and 1982. Because this study uses official time-series data, it is restricted to the formal sector of the economy. Data on unofficial trade and marketing activities were unavailable.

Agriculture in Zaire

The agricultural sector in Zaire is made up of traditional farms and modern plantations. Traditional agriculture concentrates on food crops for both home consumption and the domestic market and is practiced mainly by peasant farmers, who rely on household labor, hand tools, and the seeds from previous crops as the principal means of production. In general, land is abundant, and access is not a constraint. The cultivated area per household rarely exceeds 1 hectare in the forested zones and 2 hectares in the savannah region (Tshibaka 1986).

In contrast, the plantations are mainly in the hands of large foreign-owned corporations and produce primarily export crops. Output depends on both paid labor and capital. Because plantation agriculture makes use of machinery, processing plants, and intermediate producer goods, its share of capital is much higher than that in peasant farming.

About 75 percent of the population lives in rural areas, and at least 80 percent of the labor force is engaged in agriculture. Nevertheless, agriculture has accounted for only about 40 percent of GDP since 1960, the year Zaire gained its independence (Banque Nationale du Zaire [Congo], various years).

The share of the farm sector in foreign exchange earnings amounted to 38.9 percent in 1959 but then fell to 16.0 percent during the 1971–1981 period (Banque Nationale du Zaire [Congo], various years). Mining has been responsible for the overwhelming share of export earnings, which has been the key variable used by Zairian policy makers to rank the importance of different sectors in promoting overall economic growth.

Agricultural Output, Exports, and Imports

Agriculture in Zaire has gone through three distinct periods since independence. In the first period, from 1960 to 1965, output declined, mainly because of the violent political strife that resulted in the destruction of the pre-independence economic infrastructure (see Table 5.1). The second period, from 1966 to 1970, was one of rapid recovery, during which the total output of staple food crops grew at an annual average rate of 4.0 percent and that of major export crops at 8.9 percent.[1] Then, from 1971 to 1982, the growth rate of staple food crops dropped to 1.6 percent and that of major export crops fell to 0.8 percent.

Of Zaire's main crops, coffee grew at an average annual rate of 3.3 percent during the crisis period, rose to about 7.1 percent during the recovery, and then fell to 2.4 percent in the subsequent period. Cotton, once an export crop, is now produced solely by peasant farmers, although the government—working through the Société de Textiles Cotonnière (SOTEXCO) created in 1976—pushed farmers to produce more cotton to meet the demand of the newly established textile plants. Production increased about 6.7 percent a year between 1976 and 1982, but output growth dropped from 23.4 percent in 1966–1970 to 0.7 percent in 1971–1982.

After a substantial increase during the recovery period, agricultural exports fell sharply during the period from 1971 to 1982. Cotton disappeared completely from the export list in 1977. Further evidence of the poor performance of agriculture is seen in the rising volume of food imports during the last two periods, which jumped from 2.1 percent a year to 7.2 percent (Banque Nationale du Zaire [Congo], various years; FAO, Trade yearbook tapes, various years).

These food imports became increasingly difficult to finance from agricultural exports. The food import bill, which represented 43 percent

TABLE 5.1   Growth of Zaire's Agricultural Output and Exports by
              Crop, 1961–1982 (percentage)

Crop	1961–1965 Output	1961–1965 Export	1966–1970 Output	1966–1970 Export	1971–1982 Output	1971–1982 Export
Staple food crops	1.8	0.0	4.0	0.0	1.6	0.0
Cereals[a]	−3.7	0.0	9.1	0.0	2.8	0.0
Nongrain food[b]	2.7	0.0	2.2	0.0	1.9	0.0
Pulses (groundnut)	−1.5	0.0	8.4	0.0	1.7	0.0
Major export crops	−9.4		8.9		0.8	0.0
Palm oil	−13.5	−17.0	12.8	49.6	−1.1	−25.8
Coffee beans[c]	3.3	−9.7	7.1	8.7	2.4	8.2
Palm kernel	−10.9	−7.2	12.5	10.5	−5.2	−9.2
Natural rubber	−12.2	−11.8	10.3	10.5	−1.4	−4.5
Cotton	−21.2	−27.1	23.2	0.0	0.7	0.0
Cocoa beans	−8.6	−8.6	9.0	5.9	−1.2	−2.3

a. Cereals include maize, rice, sorghum, and millet.
b. Nongrain food includes cassava, sweet potatoes, bananas, and plantains.
c. Export growth refers to robusta coffee only, whereas output growth refers to both robusta and arabica.
SOURCES: Derived from data in FAO (1978) and *FAO Production Yearbook* (various years).

of crop export earnings during the period from 1966 to 1970, claimed nearly 70 percent of agricultural export earnings in the following decade.

Food Supply

As Table 5.2 shows, the growth rate of the total supply of staple foods has been declining since the late 1960s. Moreover, it has lagged far behind the rate of population growth. As a result, the population's average caloric intake remains only 80 to 90 percent of the minimum requirement and malnutrition has been spreading rapidly (World Bank 1980, 24–25).

Economic Policies

Macroeconomic and Trade Policies

Zaire's most important trade policy instrument during the period under study was imports and exports, along with quantitative restrictions. Its macroeconomic policy instruments consisted mainly of a currency devaluation (28 percent in 1961 and 201.8 percent in 1967), a restriction of credit accorded to the private sector, and limits on salary increases. The last round of reforms, in 1967, had favorable results: between 1966 and 1970, undeflated export earnings from agriculture and mining rose at

TABLE 5.2   Annual Average Growth Rate of Staple Food Supply in Zaire, 1961–1981 (percentage)

Period	Staple food crops	Cereal imports	Total staple food crops
1961–1965	1.8	35.0	2.3
1966–1970	4.0	11.2	4.1
1971–1975	2.4	5.2	2.0
1976–1981	1.1	14.8	1.6
1971–1981	1.6	10.4	1.8

Sources: Derived from data in *FAO Production Yearbook* (various years); International Food Policy Research Institute (1981); and Zaire, Institut National des Statistiques (various years).

annual rates of 9.4 percent and 22.0 percent, respectively (FAO, Trade yearbook tapes, various years; IMF 1984, 625). The foreign exchange reserve also rose (Banque Nationale du Congo 1968); gross domestic output increased at an annual rate of 6.4 percent, total output of staple food crops at 4.0 percent, and major export crops at 8.9 percent.

In the first half of the 1970s, the current account deficit rose at an average annual rate of 60.0 percent, the real value of the domestic currency in terms of foreign exchange deteriorated, and the difference between the parallel market and official exchange rates grew at an average rate of 70.8 percent a year. By 1978, the share of taxes on international trade and transactions in government revenue had dropped to 28.5 percent, after hitting 52.6 percent in 1970. This decline was largely due to a growing weakness in tax administration and an increase in tax evasion (Banque Nationale du Zaire, various years). Between 1970 and 1977, the ratio of import taxes to import value declined from 25 percent to 20 percent and that of export taxes to export value from 34 percent to 14 percent (Table 5.3).

In 1978, the government made adjustments in key policy areas in order to stimulate production, exports, diversification, employment of local resources, savings, investment, and repatriation of capital. As a first step, it devalued the zaire in relation to the special drawing rights (SDRs) of the International Monetary Fund (IMF)—by 50 percent in late 1978 and by another 25 percent the following summer. In addition, it reorganized the customs service and public enterprises and made an effort to improve tax collection, the allocation of foreign exchange, the administration of the government payroll, and investment selection.

On the whole, these measures proved to be insufficient, too late, and uncoordinated. Output in 1978 was about 17 percent below 1974 levels, and import volume was down by about 50 percent. The budget deficit was equivalent to 9 percent of GDP, and the inflation rate from December 1977 to December 1978 averaged close to 100 percent.

TABLE 5.3   Import and Export Tax Performance Indicators for Zaire, 1970 and 1974–1977

Tax	1970	1974	1975	1976	1977
Import taxes[a]	0.250	0.226	0.209	0.217	0.206
Export taxes[b]	0.343	0.318	0.222	0.135	0.143
GECAMINES[c]	0.428	0.432	0.264	0.117	0.046
Others[d]	n.a.	0.087	0.146	0.137	0.184

n.a. = not applicable.
a. Ratio of import taxes to import value, based on merchandise imports financed with domestic resources.
b. Ratio of export taxes to export value, based on merchandise exports (f.o.b.).
c. Ratio of export taxes paid by GECAMINES (the national copper mining company) to GECAMINES' export earnings.
d. Ratio of export taxes other than GECAMINES to export earnings generated by others.
SOURCES: Unpublished data provided by the Banque du Zaire and Department of Planning, Zaire.

In September 1983, Zaire began a substantial liberalization and simplification of the exchange rate and trade system. As part of this move, it drastically overhauled customs duties, decontrolled most prices (including agricultural producer prices), and revised interest rates. These changes had a favorable impact on the economy.

Although the situation remained difficult in 1983, GDP expanded by more than 1 percent in real terms as a result of some recovery in mining production, particularly in diamonds and petroleum. The devaluation, together with the restraint in expenditures, helped reduce the budgetary deficit to about 4 percent of marketed GDP. These policy changes, and their implementation, helped shape the structure of incentives for both the farm and nonfarm sectors.

Price Control and Marketing Arrangements

Except in areas devoted to government projects, where farmers are compelled to sell their products at official prices, the bulk of marketed food is sold in the domestic parallel markets. Official producer prices for agricultural products have consistently been far below those in either the domestic parallel markets or the world market. In Turumbu in the Zairian Basin, a rice-producing zone with few overland links to urban areas, the 1981 average farmgate price for paddy rice was Z 3,609 per metric ton, compared with the official price of Z 800 per metric ton, while that for maize was Z 1,170 per metric ton, in contrast to the official rate of Z 650 per metric ton (Tshiunza 1982).

The impact of government price controls on agricultural incentives varies greatly from one crop to another, depending on marketing channels. Cotton, for example, is produced exclusively by peasant farmers and has no parallel domestic market outlet. The impact of any government policy directly or indirectly designed for cotton will be fully transmitted to producers.

Palm oil has a large parallel domestic market, which handles the output from both the peasant farms and the plantations. Smuggling of palm oil to neighboring countries is probably limited. Consequently, the effects of government policies are partly transmitted to producers.

Peasant farmers who produce coffee and cocoa beans sell the bulk of their output to licensed exporters and processors at the official prices. These exporters, some of whom are also large producers, avoid government controls by smuggling or underreporting (World Bank 1980), but the extent of these activities is hard to determine. A cross-examination of trade and output data from Zairian officials and international sources indicates it is fairly limited.

A far more serious problem concerns the repatriation of foreign exchange. Because most crop exporters have a high degree of leverage, they are able to withhold a substantial amount of their foreign exchange earnings outside the country to avoid taxation, the overvalued exchange rate of the domestic currency, and the high domestic inflation (World Bank 1980).

This practice limits the availability of foreign exchange and hurts not only agriculture but also the rest of the economy. The policy reform initiated in September 1983 partly corrected this situation: since then, crop producers have been free to set their prices (Banque Nationale du Zaire, various years).

Other Government Policies

The average share of agriculture in the government's budget has been small compared with the size of the farming population and its contribution to overall output (less than 10 percent during the postindependence period). As a result, the basic infrastructure for agriculture has deteriorated. Furthermore, efforts to spread output-enhancing technologies among farmers and to improve the human resources serving the farm sector (training, research, and extension) have been limited.

The state-controlled development bank, Société Financière de Développement (SOFIDE), created in 1970, has given little attention to agriculture in its credit policy guidelines. Both the environment and the terms under which SOFIDE extends loans exclude most, if not all, peasant farmers, as well as many large farmers (SOFIDE 1984, 19). The State Agricultural Credit Bank, Banque du Crédit Agricole, created in 1983, seems to have adopted the same policy line (Banque du Crédit Agricole 1985).

Measures of Agricultural Price Interventions

This study takes Zaire to be a small, open economy in which prices, the trade regime, and exchange rate policies affect the structure of farm incentives and hence agricultural output. The agricultural sector in Zaire produces nontradable, exportable, and importable commodities. Nontradable crops—which include mainly cassava, sweet potatoes, and plantains—form the largest share of total food production. They constitute the principal subsistence crops where they are produced, and they are also a primary source of cash income for peasant farmers (particularly cassava in Bas-Zaire and Bandundu). Zaire's traditional export crops include coffee, tea, rubber, palm oil, and cotton. Importable crops are mainly cereals such as maize and rice.

The price of nontradable farm products is determined primarily by domestic demand and supply. Since these products are substitutes for importable crops in both production and consumption, their supply and demand schedules are also affected by importable farm products. Exportable crops are generally handled through official and parallel channels. Cotton, however, is marketed only through official channels. The government continues to fix the producer price of cotton, an exception to the liberalization measures of September 1983. Hence cotton growers continue to bear the full impact of trade, exchange rate, and price policies. Coffee and palm oil are sold in both the official and parallel markets. To assess the effective impact of the trade, exchange rate, and price policies, one needs to compute the weighted average prices paid to palm oil and coffee producers since the share of the output of each crop sold in each market outlet is not known. The prices paid to farmers in the local parallel markets are the most relevant for analysis. All producers have access to the local parallel markets, whereas official and parallel export markets are limited to a small number of producers who have a high degree of leverage. The Zaire government does not provide a subsidy to crop exporters.

Most importable food commodities such as rice and maize are sold in the domestic parallel market, although until September 1983 a small fraction was sold through officially controlled marketing channels (paddy and maize were sold to mill owners). Data on imports are available only for crops coming in through official channels; they probably underestimate the volume because underreporting and smuggling are highly likely. Northern Zambia and the southern part of Shaba Province in Zaire, for example, have long conducted a parallel trade in maize and wheat, flour, sugar, dairy products, eggs, chickens, and other items.

It should be emphasized that most food imports, including those moving through official channels, are sold in the domestic parallel market. The price paid to farmers in this market is therefore the most relevant.[2]

The structure of relative prices between traded and nontraded commodities is represented by

$$P_x/P_h = (E_o/P_h)P_x^*(1-t_x)(1-d_x) \tag{5.1}$$

$$P_m/P_h = (E_o/P_h)P_m^*(1 + t_m)(1 + d_m) \tag{5.2}$$

and

$$P_m/P_x = (P_m^*/P_x^*)(1 + t_m)(1 + d_m)/(1-t_x)(1-d_x). \tag{5.3}$$

Expressions (5.1) and (5.2) show that the real exchange rate (E_o/P_h) plays a crucial role in both export-oriented and import-competing farm and nonfarm activities. It provides a measure of the relative prices of importables and exportables to home goods in the economy (for the theoretical details, see Dornbusch 1974; Sjaastad 1980; and Sjaastad and Clements 1981). Expression (5.3) implies that the domestic price of importables relative to exportables is a function of world prices, the trade regime, and price policy measures.

In the absence of data on individual policy variables (t_x, t_m, d_x, and d_m) for Zaire, the analysis concentrates on the effect of exchange rates on the movement of domestic prices in absolute and relative terms over time.

Exchange Rate Policy and Domestic Price Movements

As Table 5.4 indicates, the real exchange rate followed a downward trend between 1966 and 1982. From 1966 to 1970, it increased at an average annual rate of 4.8 percent, in response to the less restrictive trade and exchange rate policies of this period. Direct intervention of the IMF in the second half of the 1970s accelerated the decline, to an average annual rate of 8.3 percent. From 1980 to 1982, however, the real exchange rate improved significantly, increasing at a rate of 5.3 percent per year.

This overall decline suggests that nontradables were increasingly protected, in comparison with tradables, and that exportables were becoming cheaper than home goods for domestic consumers and less profitable for producers.

If the real exchange rate and the domestic price of exportables both continue to decline, the domestic market will reach an equilibrium as

TABLE 5.4   Average Domestic Relative Prices and Real Exchange
Rates in Zaire, 1966–1982

Period	Relative price of exportables (P_x/P_h)	Relative price of importables (P_m/P_h)	Real exchange rate $([FPI]E_o/P_h)$
1966–1970	264.6	59.9	120.6
1971–1974	130.2	70.8	108.1
1975–1979	96.9	132.1	87.2
1980–1982	83.5	118.6	84.6

NOTE: P_x stands for the index of the domestic price of exportables; P_m for the index of the domestic price of importables; P_h for the index of the domestic price of nontradables; E_o for the index of the official exchange rate (defined as the number of domestic currency units per US$1.00); and FPI for the consumer price index for Zaire's principal trading partners (the United States, the European Community, and Japan). In this study housing is a proxy for home goods, since a large share of the cost of housing is made up of home goods such as labor and building materials (sand, gravel, power, and water).
SOURCES: Computed from basic data provided by the government of Zaire, particularly the Institut National des Statistiques, Banque Nationale du Zaire, and the Département de l'Agriculture. Other basic data were obtained from the World Bank (1984a) and IMF (1985b).

soon as enough production resources have been shifted to other activities to reduce output. In such a case, the commodities would no longer be exportable, but nontradable. If equilibrium is not maintained and excess demand occurs in the domestic market, the once exportable crop could become importable.

In the medium and long run, however, factors other than the relative domestic price of a given commodity will govern any change in the quantity produced. For instance, if the domestic demand for a commodity rises significantly as a result of a rapidly growing population while its supply remains inelastic with respect to its own price, and technological changes in its production are negligible, an increase in its domestic relative price would not ensure that the commodity remained on the export list. The country might eventually find itself a net importer of that commodity.

A fall in the real exchange rate makes importables cheaper for domestic consumers than home goods and less profitable for producers. The demand for importables then increases and the domestic price goes up. Thus, even though the real exchange rate may fall over time, the domestic price of importables in relation to home goods may continue to rise (see Figure 5.1).

In other words, the real exchange rate played a central role in the trade reversal of some exportable commodities. Zaire moved from being self-sufficient in maize and rice on the eve of independence to being a net importer of these commodities. The country is no longer an exporter of groundnut oil and cotton but an importer, and it has moved from

FIGURE 5.1   Domestic Relative Prices and the Real Exchange Rate
in Zaire, 1966–1982

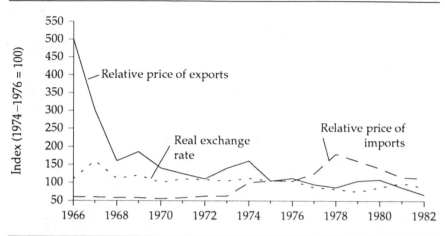

SOURCES: Computed from basic data provided by the government of Zaire, particularly the Institut National des Statistiques, Banque Nationale du Zaire, and the Département de l'Agriculture. Other basic data were obtained from the World Bank (1984a) and International Monetary Fund (1985b).

being the second largest palm oil exporter in the world to a position of self-sufficiency. If no substantial policy changes are made, Zaire will find itself on the list of palm oil importers in the near future.

Table 5.5 shows that farming in Zaire and economic activity in general declined along with the real exchange rate during the period from 1966 to 1982. This would seem to suggest that, to achieve acceptable growth in the economy, the government needs to manage the real exchange rate through suitable fiscal, monetary, income, and other economic policies. The aim would be to maintain the real exchange rate at a level that promotes competitiveness of the farm and other tradable good sectors of the economy.

Price Intervention and Farm Protection

The extent to which agricultural producer prices differ from world prices provides an indication of the level of agricultural protection in Zaire. A crude measure of this price differential is the implicit rate of taxation or subsidy (Scobie 1981), represented by the wedge between the average price received by local producers and the relevant world price (c.i.f. for imports and f.o.b. for exports), after an exchange rate adjustment based

TABLE 5.5   Rate of Change in the Real Exchange Rate and Growth Rates of Farm and Gross Domestic Output in Zaire, 1966–1982 (percentage)

Rate	Recovery period, 1966–1970	Postrecovery period, 1971–1982
Rate of change in real exchange rate	0.8	−0.6
Growth rate		
Major staple food crops[a]	4.0	1.6
Major export crops[b]	8.9	0.8
Gross domestic output	6.4	0.4

a. The major staple food crops are maize, rice, sorghum, millet, groundnuts, cassava, sweet potatoes, bananas, and plantains.
b. Major export crops are coffee, palm oil, palm kernels, natural rubber, cotton, and cocoa beans.
SOURCES: Derived from IMF (1985b); World Bank (1984a); and FAO Production Yearbook (various years).

on purchasing power parity.[3] Although the effective rate of protection would have been a more reliable measure, it could not be computed because of inadequate data.[4]

Table 5.6 presents estimates of the implicit rates of protection for six crops under government control during the entire study period, three of them import-competing products. Of the three main food crops, rice was protected, whereas maize and groundnuts were discriminated against. Groundnut producers bore the highest burden of direct taxation.

For export crops, palm oil production was subsidized at an average annual rate of 51.1 percent from 1971 to 1974 and about 32.5 percent from 1975 to 1979, but was taxed at only 16.3 percent between 1980 and 1982. Coffee and cotton were taxed during the entire period at average annual rates of 55.1 percent and 87.7 percent, respectively.

The patterns of direct taxation clearly indicate that the government followed three distinct policy approaches during the 1971–1982 period. From 1971 to 1974, before the IMF intervention, it taxed cotton, groundnuts, coffee, and maize, but not rice and palm oil. In the aggregate, exportable crops (coffee, palm oil, and cotton) were taxed slightly more but less often than importable crops.

The direct IMF intervention in the economy in 1975–1979 coincided with a reversal in government policy. Authorities now accorded rice a high level of protection, maintained the direct taxes on maize, and greatly reduced the tax burden on groundnuts. In addition, they increased the tax rates for coffee and cotton and lowered the subsidy for palm oil. Export crops as a group were discriminated against even more during this period.

TABLE 5.6   Implicit Rates of Protection of Farm Products in Zaire, Five-Year Averages, 1971–1982 (percentage)

Traded commodity	1971–1974	1975–1979	1980–1982
Import-competing goods			
Maize[a]	−2.3	1.1	−27.3
Rice[a]	11.7	65.3	52.3
Groundnuts	−55.9	−39.4	−22.1
Exportables			
Coffee	−40.6	−54.8	−58.2
Palm oil	51.1	32.5	−16.3
Cotton	−82.7	−86.9	−93.6

NOTE: All the numbers were multiplied by −1. Positive numbers are implicit rates of subsidy. Negative numbers are implicit rates of taxation.
a. Maize and rice prices are not available for 1979.
SOURCES: Computed from basic data provided by the government of Zaire, particularly the Institut National des Statistiques, Banque Nationale du Zaïre, and the Département de l'Agriculture. Other basic data were obtained from the World Bank (1984a), and IMF (1985b).

Between 1980 and 1982, after the IMF intervention, the government raised the taxes on export crops and began taxing food crops in place of subsidizing them.

The government discriminated against export crops more than food crops during the period from 1971 to 1982. In 1971–1982—in contrast to 1966–1970, when both crops grew rapidly—importable food crops increased at a slower pace, and export crops fell (Figure 5.2). A few crops registered impressive growth between 1965 and 1969 as a result of renewed economic activity in the Haut-Zaire and Kivu regions, the two export crop-producing zones most affected by the civil war of 1963–1965.

The Incidence of Trade and Exchange Rate Policies on Relative Agricultural Prices

Estimating the Incidence Parameter and the Extent of Taxation

The model for estimating the incidence of commercial and exchange rate policies on the structure of relative prices assumes that real income, productive capacity (measured by given stocks of capital, labor, and technology), and international prices are constant (Tshibaka 1986), and that the balance of trade is in equilibrium. Since historical data invalidate these assumptions for Zaire and it is necessary to include these variables in the regression equations, this analysis took into account real income (Y), as measured by gross domestic product, and the balance of trade

FIGURE 5.2   Output Indexes for Major Traded Farm Crops in Zaire,
1963–1981 (1974–1976 = 100)

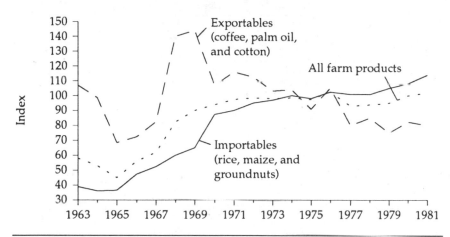

SOURCES: Computed from basic data provided by the government of Zaire, particularly the Institut National des Statistiques, Banque Nationale du Zaire, and the Département de l'Agriculture. Other basic data were obtained from the World Bank (1984a) and International Monetary Fund (1985b).

(*BOT*) as explanatory variables. Government capital expenditures (*GIE*) and trend (*T*) were included in the model separately as proxies for change in the productive capacity of the economy (change in capital stock and technology).

The analysis drew on annual data for the years 1970–1982. Ordinary least-squares techniques performed on a small sample of data gave error terms that were significantly autocorrelated. The estimation method described by Gallant and Goebel, which Harvey called the two-step full transform method, was used to correct for first autocorrelation (Gallant and Goebel 1976; Harvey 1981, 182–202). This method proved more efficient than the traditional Cochrane-Orcutt Iteration technique in estimating from small samples. The regression equations are presented in Table 5.7.

Estimates of the incidence parameters were computed for total exports (*x*), agricultural exports (*xa*), and nonagricultural exports (*nxa*). Two variables, the price indexes for housing and cassava, were used as proxies for home goods.

The regression equations using the price index for cassava produced unacceptable results, possibly because cassava, a nontradable crop, acted statistically like an importable crop in both production and consumption.

Table 5.7   Regression Results for Total, Agricultural, and
Nonagricultural Exports in Zaire, 1970–1981

	Dependent variables		
Variable	All exports $(\ln P_h/P_x)$	Agricultural exports $(\ln P_h/P_{xa})$	Nonagricultural exports $(\ln P_h/P_{nxa})$
Constant	9.08	7.85	7.98
	$(3.49)^a$	$(2.65)^b$	$(2.60)^b$
$\ln P_m/p_x$	0.52		
	$(5.02)^a$		
$\ln P_m/P_{xa}$		0.41	
		$(3.37)^b$	
$\ln P_{nxa}/P_{xa}$		0.74	
		$(4.61)^a$	
$\ln P_m/P_{nxa}$			0.72
			$(2.23)^b$
$\ln P_{xa}/P_{nxa}$			0.17
			(0.83)
$\ln Y$	−2.07	−1.86	−1.67
	$(-3.46)^a$	$(-2.74)^b$	$(-2.45)^b$
$\ln GIE$	0.87	0.14	
	(0.87)	(1.31)	
BOT	−0.00	0.004	0.001
	(−0.45)	(1.77)	(0.37)
T			−0.03
			(−1.02)
Adjusted R^2	0.90	0.93	0.95

Notes: P_h = the index of the price of home goods, P_m = the index of the price of imports, and P_x = the index of the price of exports. P_{xa} = the index of the price of agricultural exports; P_{nxa} = the index of the price of nonagricultural exports. These are mostly minerals, copper being the leading commodity. Y = real gross domestic product, GIE = real government capital expenditures, and BOT = the balance of trade. Numbers in parentheses are t-values.
a. Significant at the 1 percent level.
b. Significant at the 5 percent level.
Sources: Computed from basic data provided by the government of Zaire, particularly the Institut National des Statistiques, Banque Nationale du Zaire, and the Département de l'Agriculture. Other basic data were obtained from the World Bank (1984a), and IMF (1985b).

As a substitute in consumption, the domestic price of cassava was in-directly affected by the impact of world market conditions on the do-mestic market for importable crops. That is, when the world price of grain rose, the domestic demand for grains declined, whereas the demand for cassava—a substitute crop—rose.

The explanatory variables included in the equations account for at least 90 percent of the total variations in the dependent variables. The regression coefficients for BOT, GIE, and T are not significant. The es-timated coefficients for Y are significant and negative, the implication being that positive growth in real income leads, other things being equal, to a decrease in the domestic price of home goods compared with that of exportables. The explanation is not obvious, however. The regression coefficient for the price of nonagricultural exports relative to agricultural exports is positive and significant. The implication here is that the domestic price of home goods is positively and significantly affected by changes in the prices of nonagricultural exports compared with agricultural exports.

The estimated numerical values for the incidence parameters are significant for all the categories of tradables and home goods listed in Table 5.7. For total exports, the incidence parameter is about 0.52. This means that a price distortion (from tariffs, quantitative restrictions, domestic pricing and marketing policies, and so forth) that leads to an increase in the domestic price of importables falls partly as a tax on producers of exportables. To illustrate, assume that the domestic price of importables has risen 10 percent as a result of a change in trade policies. That increase represents a tax on exportables of about 5.2 percent. As such, exportables in Zaire bear no less than 50 percent of the burden associated with the protection of importables. In addition, if exportables are directly taxed—say, at 15 percent—then the total tax rate would be 20.0 percent. It is difficult to compute the rate of total taxation of exportables in Zaire because the official import tariffs and export taxes do not reflect the smuggling, underreporting, and underinvoicing that go on. The pervasiveness of these practices, however, indicates the restrictiveness of the trade regime.

The disaggregation of exportables yields incidence parameters of 0.407 for agricultural exports and 0.721 for nonagricultural exports. A comparison of these estimates suggests that nonagricultural exports, primarily mining, bear the largest share of the burden associated with the protection of importables.

Implications for Farm Output

The above analysis clearly suggests that the trade, exchange rate, and price policies adopted in Zaire during the period under study had far-reaching negative effects on the production incentives for exportable goods. These policies would also have tended to reduce substantially the production of exportables in relation to home goods.

From 1971 to 1982, Zaire's trade, exchange rate, and other price-distorting policies were by and large inward-looking (see Table 5.1). The rate of output growth for importable crops (cereals) in this period was 3.5 times higher than that of exportable crops, whereas it had been only 1.1 times higher between 1966 and 1970. The rate for nontradable food crops such as cassava, sweet potatoes, bananas, and plantains was only one-fourth that of export crops during 1966–1970 but was 2.4 times higher during 1971–1982. The rates for all three groups of commodities, however, were significantly lower in 1971–1982 than in 1966–1970.

Farm output in general declined because most of the resources diverted from exportable crops came from agriculture. As export crops contracted, there was also a reduction in the foreign exchange receipts needed to maintain, improve, and expand the productive capacity of the farm sector, as well as the economy as a whole. The country became more dependent on mining exports, mainly copper. The limited foreign exchange earnings flowed mainly into urban areas, where they were used to maintain and expand the production of import-competing manufactures and to provide socioeconomic services to the urban population, at the expense of the rural and farming communities. The farm sector was therefore unable to meet its import requirements, and its growth rate began to slow down. Furthermore, Zaire lacked sufficient foreign exchange to invest extensively in the hard and soft infrastructure that it needed to expand food and export production.

By discriminating against export activities, the country's economic policies prevented the population from achieving food self-sufficiency. Despite the protection for importable and nontradable food crops, the country's food supply deteriorated significantly between 1971 and 1982.

Conclusions

The trade, exchange rate, and other economic policies pursued in Zaire between 1960 and 1982 have had adverse effects on the entire economy, particularly on agriculture. A comparison of domestic producer and world prices shows that the policies consistently discriminated against importable food crops as a group and against exportable crops. The degree of discrimination varied by crop but was greater generally for exportables than for importables.

The government kept domestic producer prices of food commodities well below world prices to depress real wages as an incentive to promote import-substituting industries. In addition, it used some of the tax revenue from agricultural and nonagricultural exports (mostly mining) to expand the productive capacity in urban areas and to provide cheap credit to industry. By promoting industrialization through import-substitution, however, it jeopardized not only the development of agricultural and mineral exports, but also that of industrial exports. Within industry, resources moved away from exports to import-competing goods. In agriculture, resources moved out of agricultural exports to-ward the production of import-competing and home goods, in both the agricultural and industrial sectors. The resources used in mining, which in Zaire is almost exclusively an export industry, also moved into the production of industrial import-competing and home goods.

These resource movements reduced export activity, with the result that the country was unable to earn enough foreign exchange to expand economic activity. The growth of the farm sector and the economy as a whole decelerated. Within the farm sector, the growth in food produc-tion declined from 4.0 percent in 1966–1970 (when trade and exchange rate policies were less restrictive) to 1.6 percent in 1971–1982, while export production dropped from 8.9 to 0.8 percent.

Clearly, restrictive trade and exchange rate policies do not increase the country's food self-sufficiency. This study indicates that policy mak-ers should strive for a uniform across-the-board treatment for all trad-ables. Also, the real exchange rate is a critical variable that developing countries need to monitor and manage properly through fiscal, mone-tary, income, and other policies if they are to avoid distorting relative production incentives between tradable and nontradable goods.

Notes to Chapter 5

1. The rate of growth of export crops seems particularly impressive because it was at such a low level in 1965, following the civil war.

2. The prices paid to domestic producers of both importable and exportable crops can be related to world prices by Cassel's law, or the law of one price, as follows:

$$P_x = P_x^* E_o \,(1\!-\!t_x)(1\!-\!d_x) = P_x^* E_o t_{x\prime} \tag{5.4}$$

where

P_x = the price paid to the exportable crop producer in domestic currency

P_x^* = exportable crop world price in foreign exchange

E_o = official exchange rate expressed as a number of units of do-mestic currency per one unit of foreign exchange

t_x = export tax

d_x = domestic parallel market price distortion

t_x = price-distorting policy adjustment factor for exports

and

$$P_m = P_m{}^*E_o (1 + t_m)(1 + d_m) = P_m{}^*E_o t_m, \tag{5.5}$$

where

P_m = the price paid to importable crop producers in domestic currency

$P_m{}^*$ = importable crop world price in foreign exchange

t_m = import tariff rate

d_m = domestic parallel market price distortion

T_m = price-distorting policy adjustment factor for imports

3. The producer wedge for an individual product is given by

$$\Delta P = (P^*E_o\text{FPI/CPI}) - (P/\text{CPI}) \tag{5.6}$$

where

ΔP = producer price wedge in local currency

P^* = world price of the product in foreign currency

P = local producer price

E_o = official exchange rate

FPI = the consumer price index of Zaire's principal trading partners (the United States, the European Community, and Japan)

CPI = the domestic consumer price index

The implicit rate of taxation or subsidy would be

$$\Delta P/(P^*E_o\text{FPI/CPI}) = 1 - (P/P^*E_o\text{FPI}). \tag{5.7}$$

4. The effective rate of protection is defined as value added at domestic prices less value added at world prices divided by value added at world prices.

Industrial Protection, Foreign Borrowing, and Agricultural Incentives in the Philippines

Agriculture plays a dominant role in the Philippine economy. Although it has declined in importance since the early 1950s, it still accounts directly for about one-half of total employment and one-fourth of gross domestic product. It also earns some 40 percent of total export receipts (from raw and simply processed agricultural products), while accounting for less than 10 percent of the total import bill. This chapter provides a quantitative analysis of the effects of trade and exchange rate policies on relative incentives in the Philippine economy, with special attention to the agricultural sector. The discussion covers the evolution of the foreign trade regime since the early 1950s, the impact of trade and exchange rate policies on production incentives for tradable goods, and the effects of the trade regime on the relative incentives between home goods and various classes of tradable goods. It also examines the sources of policy-induced distortion in the real exchange rate and their effects on the domestic prices of agricultural products in relation to home goods and nonagricultural products, and the implicit transfer of resources out of agriculture and the other economic repercussions that arise from the relative price effects of trade and exchange rate policies.

Postwar Trade and Exchange Rate Policies

To cope with the severe balance of payments problem that developed soon after the end of World War II, the Philippine government instituted

111

a comprehensive program of import and exchange controls in 1949–
1950. A key aspect of the program was the rationing of foreign exchange
among various claimants while maintaining the prewar exchange rate of
2 pesos to the U.S. dollar. The immediate effect was a sharp rise in the
prices of imported goods that in turn prompted the government to
liberalize imports of "essential" consumer goods, raw materials, and
capital equipment relative to so-called nonessential goods.

Together with the highly overvalued currency, the criterion of es-
sentiality governing the system of direct trade controls created a strong
bias toward the domestic production of substitutes for finished industrial consumer goods and in effect penalized primary producers (who
were in agriculture and mining), export-oriented industries, and the
producers of intermediate and capital goods (categories that are not
mutually exclusive). The chronic trade deficits of the 1950s, particularly
in the second half of the decade, were a reflection of the country's
increasing dependence of domestic industries on imports and its inability to stimulate new exports.

Over the course of the decade, as balance of payments difficulties
persisted, charges of corruption and criticism of the administration of
the controls mounted. There was also increasing pressure from exporters for a more favorable exchange rate. In addition, the public had begun
accusing importers of reaping windfall gains. Toward the end of the
1950s, there was little room left for nonessential imports, as producer
goods accounted for nearly 90 percent of the annual import bill.

The worsening trade deficit prompted the authorities, beginning in
April 1960, to gradually dismantle the control system and rationalize the
foreign exchange rate. By June 1962, they had removed most of the
controls on foreign exchange and the licensing of imports; in addition,
the exchange rate, which had been allowed to float in the free market six
months earlier, had stabilized at 3.90 pesos per dollar.

Despite these policy reforms, the incentive structure continued to
favor import-substituting consumer goods industries. A discriminatory
system of sales taxes and a highly distorted and protective tariff system
created a bias against exporting. The tariff escalation in the system—
according to which import duties on semifinished products were higher
than on raw materials and higher still on finished products—discriminated against backward integration and encouraged assembly and pack-
ing operations, both of which were heavily dependent on imported
materials and capital equipment.

From the beginning of 1966, when President Ferdinand Marcos assumed power, to mid-1967, the government pursued expansionary
monetary and fiscal policies. It undertook a massive program of capital
formation, emphasizing investments in infrastructure and the develop-

ment of services, with financing from both internal and external borrowing.

In late 1969, a foreign exchange crisis developed, precipitated by the need to service the short-term credit that was financing the trade deficits and expansionary policies of the immediately preceding years. The government responded by floating the Philippine peso in February 1970 and eliminating some of the exchange controls in effect since 1967. By December 1970, the nominal exchange rate had settled at 6.4 pesos to the U.S. dollar, which translated into a devaluation of 61.4 percent over the year.

As part of the devaluation package, 80 percent of the foreign exchange earnings from some traditional exports (including copra, sugar, logs, and copper concentrates) were to be surrendered to the Central Bank at the old exchange rate of 3.90 pesos per dollar, while the remaining 20 percent could be sold at the free market rate. This system was replaced in May 1970 by a temporary stabilization tax on traditional exports (at rates ranging from 4 to 10 percent ad valorem), a measure that was made a permanent part of the customs and tariff code in 1973. In February 1974, the government levied an additional tax on the premium derived from export price increases initiated in 1973. Thus, the significant gains from the devaluation and the world commodity boom in the early 1970s were partly siphoned off from the producers of traditional exports.

The de facto devaluation was followed by the enactment of the Export Incentives Act of 1970, which signaled a policy shift toward a more outward-looking industrial development strategy. Among other incentives under this act, enterprises registered with the Board of Investments (BOI) qualified for various kinds of tax exemptions (including export taxes), were allowed to deduct their export revenue from taxable income for five years, and could receive a tax credit equivalent to all sales, specific, and import taxes on raw materials used in export production. These tax benefits came on top of the fiscal incentives made available to producers of exports under the Investment Incentives Act of 1967. The average rate of tax subsidy for BOI-registered firms as a proportion of input value in the mid-1970s has been estimated at 15 percent (Tan 1979).

In addition, export producers, particularly those in labor-intensive manufactures, received various forms of support related to financing and infrastructure. For example, the government established export processing zones and marketing services and simplified export procedures and documentation. This served to compensate in part for the still pervasive bias against exporting in the incentive system. The primary source of this bias was the highly protective tariff system.

One important and controversial aspect of Philippine economic policy in the 1970s was the government's management of the nominal exchange rate. In the period between the floating of the peso in February 1970 and the 1983 foreign exchange crisis, the authorities maintained a flexible exchange rate, allowing the domestic currency to depreciate in nominal terms. The annual rate of depreciation varied slightly from year to year, exceeding 5 percent (but staying within 10 percent) only in 1972, 1975, and 1982.

In view of the large deficits in the current account during the 1970s and the fact that inflation was surpassing rates being registered by the country's trading partners, it is surprising that the peso did not depreciate much more rapidly. The explanation lies in the capital account. The Philippines, having received relatively large foreign loans in the 1970s, faced no threat of a depletion of its international reserves, and hence there was no immediate pressure to devalue. Indeed, the extent of foreign borrowing after 1974 was such that the Central Bank reserves even increased significantly through the end of the decade.

The current account deficits of the 1970s were related to the external shocks that buffeted the economy after the oil crisis of 1973–1974. In response, Philippine policy makers expanded foreign borrowing sharply. In deciding to sustain the growth momentum initiated in the early 1970s, they pursued a countercyclical strategy through expansionary fiscal and monetary policies. From 1974 to 1980, government spending and the money supply rose an average 22 percent and 18 percent a year, respectively, which were much higher than the trend rates.

Another notable aspect of the policy environment in the 1970s was the increased role of government in regulating the economy. It held a monopoly over the foreign trade in food grains and used direct price controls to reduce the instability in the domestic prices of the major food crops. In an effort to promote self-sufficiency in rice, the government instituted the so-called Masagana 99 program, which provided farmers with noncollateral, low-interest loans to purchase fertilizer and seeds, which were made available at subsidized prices. From 1973 to 1977, government investment in irrigation (in constant pesos) expanded tenfold over that of the 1966–1970 period (Barker 1984), and large subsidies went into irrigation water (David 1983).

Government intervention—via export taxes, premium duties, and an export quota—was particularly heavy in the markets for coconut and sugar, the country's dominant export crops. In addition, beginning in 1970, state corporations took over the domestic and foreign trade in sugar. From 1974 to 1980, producers received on average only 77 percent of the world price (Nelson and Agcaoili 1983). It has been estimated that, as a result of the government monopoly, sugar producers suffered a net loss of 11–14 billion pesos between 1974 and 1983 (Canlas et al. 1984). Moreover, this system led to additional markups and a substantially increased marketing margin.

In the case of coconut, the government imposed a production levy, established a dominant coconut milling company, and initiated a program of replanting. The levy has since evolved into a variety of special levies used to finance other programs to promote production.

By the late 1970s, Philippine policy makers were acutely aware that the country needed to improve the international competitiveness of its domestic industry, which was more heavily protected from foreign competition than industries in the other market economies of Southeast Asia (Bautista 1981). In 1981, with technical and financial support from the World Bank, the Philippines initiated a program of industrial structural adjustment. It included measures designed to liberalize the foreign trade regime significantly, through tariff reform and a relaxation of import licensing; rationalize fiscal incentives; revitalize certain consumer goods industries, through technical and credit assistance; and promote backward integration, through the establishment of eleven so-called major industrial projects (that were to produce intermediate and capital goods). Unfortunately, the foreign exchange crisis beginning in August 1983 overtook the program, and some of its components, particularly the phasing out of import licenses, were superseded by policy actions introduced to deal with short-term contingencies.

What remained relatively intact was the tariff liberalization scheme. The government reduced to 50 percent the peak tariff rates of 100 percent and 70 percent (this reduction did not apply to fourteen strategic industries that had their own sectoral plans), and it raised low tariffs to at least 10 percent by 1985. Overall, the average tariff rate dropped from 43 percent in 1980 to 28 percent in 1985. The effective tariff protection for manufacturing declined from 70 percent to 31 percent (Bautista 1981). Protection for import-substituting industries also subsided, but it rose significantly for export industries. Nevertheless, the bias in favor of the former remained.

The rapid growth in the country's external debt that led to the foreign exchange crisis could have been avoided with a more prudent macroeconomic policy. As already pointed out, the government borrowed heavily abroad and pursued expansionary fiscal and monetary policies in the face of the large current account deficits since the 1973–1974 oil crisis in order to sustain the growth momentum initiated in the early 1970s. Unfortunately, the investments did not pay off. Government financial institutions bankrolled many projects of doubtful economic viability.[1] Nonfinancial government corporations also suffered huge deficits, averaging about 12 billion pesos in 1981–1982. By 1982, foreign borrowing had reached a record 8.5 percent of gross national product (GNP), while the government deficit was an unprecedented 4.3 percent of GNP.

The current account deficit of US$2.7 billion incurred in 1983 (representing 8.0 percent of GNP) had to be financed from international reserves, which slumped to less than one month of imports by mid-October. This foreign exchange crisis prompted the Philippine government to declare a moratorium on the payment of debt principal. At that time, total debt outstanding amounted to about US$26 billion.

Beginning in October 1983, the government imposed foreign exchange and import controls, signaling an emergency retreat from the trade liberalization, with the new controls on foreign exchange and imports superseding the scheduled lifting of import bans in 1983. The tariff rate revisions implemented through 1985, although made redundant by the exchange and import controls, were not substantially affected. To discourage imports and reduce capital outflow, the government devalued the peso three times between June 1983 and June 1984, bringing it to 18 pesos, and then in October 1984 declared a free float. In 1984–1985, as the foreign exchange crisis took its toll and the government launched a contradictory stabilization policy prescribed by the International Monetary Fund, real GNP declined by about 10 percent.

In late 1984 the government launched a comprehensive program for agriculture, which it considered critical to future stable growth. A specific objective was "to increase agriculture's contribution to the balance-of-payments through expanded exports and import substitution" (Galang 1985). The principal objective of the program was to improve agricultural productivity and promote "a stronger and more diversified farming system."

The new government of Corazon Aquino went still further, quickly announcing, in mid-1986, the adoption of employment-oriented agricultural and rural growth as the centerpiece of an Agenda for a People-Powered Development. The government sharply increased public spending on rural infrastructure and improved agricultural prices to raise farm productivity and rural incomes. By working through intermediate and final demand, these measures were expected to stimulate the demand not only for food and other agricultural products, but also for industrial goods and services.

Effects on Relative Incentives among Tradable Goods

At the most aggregate level, the extent to which the trade regime discriminates in favor of, or against, the production of exportables in comparison with importables can be represented in the following measure of the overall trade bias (OTB):

$$\text{OTB} = \frac{P_x/P_m}{P_x^*/P_m^*} = \frac{1 - t_x}{1 + t_m}, \tag{6.1}$$

where P_x and P_m are the domestic prices of exportables and importables, respectively, P_x^* and P_m^* are their respective foreign (border) prices, and t_x and t_m are the implicit export tax and tariff rates, respectively. A proportionate change in this relative price ratio can be interpreted to represent the change in the domestic price ratio attributable to the implicit trade taxes. If, on the one hand, OTB < 1, there is an antitrade bias in the country's commercial policy: the production of importables is being promoted over exportables, a condition that tends to reduce foreign trade. If, on the other hand, OTB > 1, the implication is a pro-trade bias: there is price discrimination in favor of export production and against import substitution, so that the possibilities for trade are greater. If OTB = 1, the trade regime is neutral, encouraging neither exporting nor import substitution.

The estimated annual values of the trade bias from 1950 to 1980 are plotted in Figure 6.1.[2] They are consistently less than one, and therefore Philippine trade policy throughout the entire period appears to have favored producers of import-competing goods rather than export producers. The bias against trade decreased, however. The intensity of the bias (represented by the deviation of the OTB value from one) was highest in the 1950s, as might be expected in that period of comprehensive import and foreign exchange controls. The policy reform in the early 1960s appears to have benefited export production, as reflected in the increasing levels of the overall trade bias. It seems the government provided further encouragement to exporting in the 1970s, when it made fiscal and other incentives available to export producers, but these measures did not fully offset the significant price bias in favor of import-competing production. After 1975, the trade bias was reversed, as export subsidies declined. The average values for the trade bias—which came to 0.388 for the period from 1950 to 1961, 0.600 for 1962 to 1969, and 0.763 for 1970 to 1980—broadly reflect the extent of the price discrimination against export producers in the aggregate in the country's foreign trade regime.

At the same time, the bias conceals possible differences in the effects on various classes of export and import-competing products. In the Philippine context, this consideration is important in view of the nature of the trade and exchange rate policies of the postwar period. These

FIGURE 6.1   Time Profile of the Overall Trade Bias in the
Philippines, 1950–1980

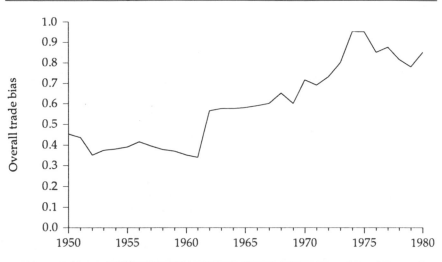

SOURCE: Author's calculations.

policies distinguish between "essential" and "nonessential" imports of consumer goods and between "traditional" and "new" exports. The two principal food crops, rice and corn—which competed with imports throughout most of the postwar period—are in the category of essential consumer goods (EC), while the major export crops such as sugar and coconut are classified as traditional exports (TX). Imports of most industrial consumer goods, especially light manufactures, are in the nonessential (NEC) category, and their domestic production was promoted through direct trade controls in the 1950s and subsequently through high tariffs. Since 1970, the government has encouraged the expansion of new exports (NX), which consist largely of manufactured goods and, to a limited extent, nontraditional agricultural and mining products.

One useful indicator of the sectoral incentives provided by the foreign trade regime is the effective exchange rate for various types of external transactions, that is, the number of units of domestic currency actually paid by importers or received by exporters per unit of foreign exchange, including trade-related taxes and subsidies. Invoking the law of one price for the small open economy, the long-term effects of differential changes in the effective exchange rate among various classes of tradables on their relative domestic prices is equiproportional. That is, other things remaining the same, a 10 percent increase in the ratio of the

TABLE 6.1   Average Effective Exchange Rates (EERs), by Product
Category, for the Philippines, 1950–1980 (pesos per
U.S. dollar)

Product category	1950–1959	1960–1969	1970–1980
Traditional exports	2.000	3.459	6.602
	(0.549)	(0.327)	(0.259)
New exports	2.294	3.704	8.018
	(0.629)	(0.351)	(0.315)
Essential consumer good			
(EC) imports	2.064	3.906	8.136
	(0.566)	(0.370)	(0.320)
Nonessential consumer good			
(NEC) imports	3.645	10.563	25.459

NOTE: The numbers in parentheses indicate the ratios of the EER for a given product category to the
EER for NEC imports.
SOURCE: Calculated from Baldwin (1975) for 1950–1971 and Senga (1983) for 1972–1980.

effective exchange rate for imports to that for exports should ultimately
lead to a 10 percent rise in the domestic price of import goods in relation
to export goods, which encourages a shift in production toward import-
competing goods.

Table 6.1 gives the average effective exchange rate for the above-
mentioned categories of tradable goods. It is evident from the markedly
higher values for nonessential imports that the trade regime indeed
favored industrial import substitution. Because these values do not capture the additional protective effect of the quantitative import restrictions, those for the control period of the 1950s even understate the
implicit protection accorded to import-competing production, in particular, to nonessential consumer goods.

The annual movements in the effective exchange rate between 1950
and 1980 indicate that the ratio between traditional (agricultural) exports
and nonessential imports and between traditional and new (industrial)
exports were consistently less than one over this period. In other words,
there was a continuing relative discrimination in the trade regime
against exports of primary products. Moreover, the bias in favor of
import-substituting production rose over the entire period. During the
1970s, when the government was promoting an outward-looking development strategy, the trade policy bias against exports of agricultural
products worsened. Relative to new industrial exports, the effective
exchange rate ratio was highest in the 1960s and lowest in the 1970s, the
latter reflecting the export taxes on primary products introduced in 1970,
as well as the fiscal and financial benefits under the Export Incentives
Act that favored labor-intensive manufacturing enterprises.

TABLE 6.2   Average Values of EER_i/EER_j in the Philippines, 1950–1980

	1950–1959	1960–1969	1970–1980
Coconut (TX)	0.976	0.966	1.070
Sugar (TX)	1.030	1.036	0.963
Pineapples (TX)	1.118	0.907	1.031
Tobacco (TX)	0.829	0.654	0.548
Abaca (TX)	1.008[a]	1.013	1.013
Rice (EC)	n.a.	1.078	0.890
Corn (EC)	n.a.	0.754	1.093

n.a. = not available.
NOTE: EER_i/EER_j denotes the ratio of the effective exchange rate for commodity category i (coconut, . . ., corn) to that for commodity category j (= TX, EC), which includes i, where TX and EC denote traditional exports and essential consumer goods, respectively.
a. Based on data for 1950 and 1955 only.
SOURCE: Calculated from Baldwin (1975) and Senga (1983) estimates of EER_j and from Central Bank data.

The differential price effects of Philippine trade and exchange rate policies on agricultural tradables are evident in the following categories of major agricultural commodities: traditional exports (coconut, sugar, pineapple, tobacco, and abaca) and import-competing goods (rice and corn). An effective exchange rate for commodity i, EER_i, representing the number of units of domestic currency (pesos) per U.S. dollar received by exporters or paid by importers of i, can be defined as follows:

$$EER_i = P_i/P_i^*, \qquad (6.2)$$

where P_i and P_i^* are the domestic and border prices of commodity i, respectively.

The ratio of EER_i to EER_j, the latter denoting the effective exchange rate for the commodity category j (= TX, EC), which includes i, indicates the extent to which the price effect of the trade regime is more (or less) favorable to commodity i in comparison with the other commodities included in category j. Table 6.2 gives the subperiod averages of the annual values of EER_i/EER_j. Among the traditional export commodities, tobacco had the lowest values for the effective exchange rate ratio, an indication of relative price discrimination, which became more severe over time. This bias undoubtedly contributed to the declining profitability of tobacco production. Pineapples appear to have been the most favored product in the 1950s, sugar in the 1960s, and coconut in the 1970s.

In comparison with other import-competing essential consumer goods, rice benefited from domestic price policies in the 1960s. It did not do so in the next decade, despite the government's well-publicized efforts to promote rice self-sufficiency. The trade regime apparently discriminated against corn in the 1960s but favored it in the 1970s.

Effects on Incentives for Tradable and Home Goods

In a simple model of a small economy that produces three goods—exportables, importables, and home goods—trade policy directly affects the domestic price of each tradable good in relation to the other, and through general equilibrium interactions also the domestic price of exportables (importables) in relation to home goods (Sjaastad 1980). It can be shown that general equilibrium with trade balance implies the following comparative static relationship:[3]

$$\dot{P}_x - \dot{P}_h = \omega(\dot{P}_x - \dot{P}_m), \tag{6.3}$$

where P_m = domestic price of importable goods, P_x = domestic price of exportable goods, P_h = domestic price of home goods, ω = incidence parameter, and the dot (.) over a variable denotes proportionate change. The incidence parameter, ω, will be greater the higher (lower) the degree of substitutability in consumption and production between home goods and importables (exportables). For any given change in P_x and P_m (for example, as a result of trade taxes), ω determines uniquely the induced change in the domestic price of exportables in relation to home goods.

When distinguishing between agricultural and nonagricultural export goods, the analogous equations are, respectively,

$$\dot{P}_{ax} - \dot{P}_h = \omega_m (\dot{P}_{ax} - \dot{P}_m) + \omega_{nx} (\dot{P}_{ax} - \dot{P}_{nx}) \tag{6.4}$$

and

$$\dot{P}_{nx} - \dot{P}_h = \omega_m(\dot{P}_{ax} - \dot{P}_m) - (1 - \omega_{nx}) (\dot{P}_{ax} - \dot{P}_{nx}), \tag{6.5}$$

where P_{ax} and P_{nx} are the domestic prices of agricultural and nonagricultural export products, respectively. In equations (6.4) and (6.5), the domestic prices of agricultural and nonagricultural export products in relation to home goods depend on the structure of domestic prices among the three classes of tradable goods and the incidence parameters ω_m and ω_{nx}. The effects of trade restrictions on the relative prices of the three classes of tradable goods (in relation to home goods) can be shown explicitly as follows:

$$\dot{P}_{ax} - \dot{P}_h = \omega_m (\dot{T}_{ax} - \dot{T}_m) + \omega_{nx} (\dot{T}_{ax} - \dot{T}_{nx}), \qquad (6.6)$$

$$\dot{P}_{nx} - \dot{P}_h = \omega_m (\dot{T}_{ax} - \dot{T}_m) - (1 - \omega_{nx}) (\dot{T}_{ax} - \dot{T}_{nx}), \qquad (6.7)$$

and

$$\dot{P}_m - \dot{P}_h = \omega_{nx} (\dot{T}_{ax} - \dot{T}_{nx}) - (1 - \omega_m) (\dot{T}_{ax} - \dot{T}_m), \qquad (6.8)$$

where $T_m = 1 + t_m$, $T_{ax} = 1 - t_{ax}$, and $T_{nx} = 1 - t_{nx}$ denote the "power" of the import tariffs and export taxes.

With respect to the Philippine data, P_{ax} and P_{nx} are defined as the domestic prices of traditional agricultural export products and other export goods, respectively, and P_m is the Central Bank wholesale price index for imported commodities. To represent the price of home goods, we calculate a weighted average of the Central Bank wholesale price index of "locally produced commodities for home consumption" and the two consumer price index components for housing and services. Econometric estimation yields the following values of the incidence parameters: $\omega_m = 0.659$ and $\omega_{nx} = 0.412$.

Based on the estimated values of the incidence parameters, the extent to which the trade regime affected the relative prices of tradable goods in relation to home goods from 1950 to 1980 can be quantified. Using an unbiased trade regime as a reference, we can derive the following expressions for the natural logarithm of the relative price ratios RPR_{ax}, RPR_{nx}, and RPR_{mh} from equations (6.6) to (6.8):

$$\log RPR_{axh} = \begin{aligned} &- \omega_m (\log T_m - \log T_{ax}) \\ &- \omega_{nx} (\log T_{nx} - \log T_{ax}) \end{aligned} \qquad (6.9)$$

$$\log RPR_{nxh} = \begin{aligned} &(1 - \omega_{nx}) (\log T_{nx} - \log T_{ax}) \\ &- \omega_m (\log T_m - \log T_{ax}) \end{aligned} \qquad (6.10)$$

$$\log RPR_{mh} = \begin{aligned} &(1 - \omega_m) (\log T_m - \log T_{ax}) \\ &- \omega_{nx} (\log T_{nx} - \log T_{ax}) \end{aligned} \qquad (6.11)$$

where $RPR_{axh} = (P_{ax}/P_h)/(P_{ax}/P_h)^*$, $RPR_{nxh} = (P_{nx}/P_h)/(P_{nx}/P_h)^*$ and $RPR_{mh} = (P_m/P_h)/(P_m/P_h)^*$ are the relative price ratios between each category of tradable good (m = importables, ax = traditional agricultural export products, and nx = other export goods) and home goods; the asterisk (*) denotes the relative price under an unbiased trade regime, that is, when the implicit tariff and export tax rates are zero ($T_m, T_x = 1$). Note that an RPR value of unity implies a neutral price effect.

FIGURE 6.2   Trade Policy–induced Relative Prices of Tradable Goods
Compared with Home Goods in the Philippines,
1950–1980

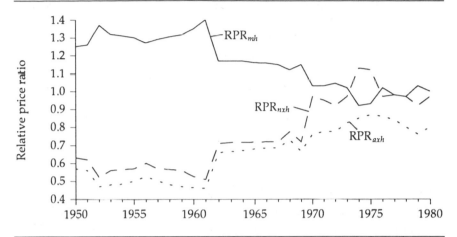

NOTE: RPR_{mh}, RPR_{nxh}, and RPR_{axh} represent the domestic price effects on importables, nontraditional (industrial) exports, and agricultural exports, respectively, relative to home goods. A value of 1.0 implies a neutral price effect.
SOURCE: Author's calculations.

As the time profiles in Figure 6.2 show, the calculated values of the relative price ratios generally indicate significant disincentives in the production of traditional agricultural exports ($RPR_{axh} < 1$) and, to a lesser extent, the nontraditional manufactured export products, compared with home goods. At the same time, domestic production of import-competing goods appears to have been favored over home goods until the early 1970s, after which there is a slight bias toward the production of home goods.

The marked improvement in RPR_{nxh} values is evident from the following subperiod averages: 0.574 during 1950–1961; 0.737 during 1962–1969; and 0.997 during 1970–1980. Traditional agricultural exports appear to have been more heavily penalized than new exports throughout the period. Although there have been some increases in the RPR_{axh} values over the years, the average value of 0.819 during the 1970–1980 period reflects a strong bias against traditional agricultural exports at a time when the government was officially promoting a general expansion in export capacity.

The Real Exchange Rate and Agricultural Prices

Agricultural output in the Philippines has a high degree of tradability, given the dominance of export and import-competing products. Overvaluation of the domestic currency—or, to use the standard terminology, an overvalued exchange rate—acts as a tax on tradable goods, depressing their prices (in domestic currency) in relation to home goods. This distortion in the incentive structure penalizes agriculture and makes the production of home goods more attractive. Because there is a greater component of home goods production in the nonagricultural sector than in agriculture, the effect of exchange rate overvaluation on domestic relative prices encourages a shift in resources toward nonagricultural production.

Two Sources of Policy-Induced Exchange Rate Distortion

Domestic policies can influence the real exchange rate through a restrictive trade regime and a sustained trade imbalance. Consider, first, the comparative static effect of trade restrictions on the real exchange rate. With foreign prices remaining the same,

$$\dot{r} = \dot{R} - \dot{P}_h = -[\omega_m \dot{T}_m + \omega_{nx} \dot{T}_{nx} + (1 - \omega_m - \omega_{nx}) \dot{T}_{ax}], \quad (6.12)$$

where r and R denote the real and nominal exchange rates, respectively. Again, with reference to an unbiased trade regime, equation (6.12) implies

$$\log (r^a/r) = \omega_m \log (1 + t_m) + \omega_{nx} \log (1 - t_{nx})$$
$$+ (1 - \omega_m - \omega_{nx}) \log (1 - t_{ax}), \quad (6.13)$$

where r^a is the real exchange rate associated with an unbiased or free-trade policy ($t_m, t_{ax}, t_{nx} = 0$). A measure of the distortion in the real exchange rate attributable to trade policy is given by the ratio r^a/r, which can be evaluated using equation (6.13), given the incidence parameters and implicit tariff and export tax rates.

It is clear from the expression for $\log (r^a/r)$ that trade restrictions in the form of tariffs and quotas on imports ($t_m > 0$), as well as subsidies on exports ($t_{ax}, t_{nx} < 0$), raise r^a/r and hence lower the real exchange rate in relation to its free trade value. The calculated annual values of r^a/r from 1950 to 1980 are plotted in Figure 6.3. They are consistently greater than one, the implication being that the trade policy sustained an overvalued exchange rate throughout the period; however, the trend declines over the years. The real exchange rate deviated most from the unbiased value

FIGURE 6.3   Index of Exchange Rate Distortions Attributable to
Trade Restrictions in the Philippines, 1950–1980

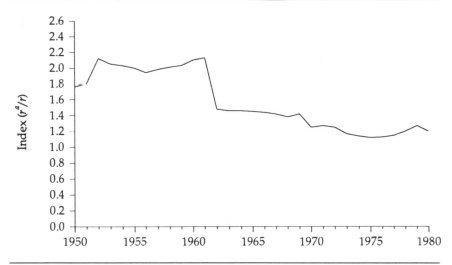

SOURCE: Author's calculations.

during the 1950s, the period in which the government imposed import
and foreign exchange controls and the index averaged 2.00. After decontrol and the devaluation of the peso in the early 1960s, the real
exchange rate distortion diminished, and the average value of the index
dropped to 1.44 for the 1962–1969 period. The nominal exchange rate
flexibility and less restrictive trade policies of the 1970s brought the
average value of r^a/r to 1.20.

Note that the trade liberalization measures implemented in 1970
seem to have helped lower the degree of overvaluation of the exchange
rate through 1975, after which it rose again, reaching a peak of 1.29 by
1979. By then the Philippine peso (based on 1978–1980 average values)
was overvalued by 22–24 percent because of the trade restrictions.

As already indicated, a distortion in the real exchange rate can also
arise from an unsustainable imbalance in the external accounts. For
instance, a trade deficit in any given year can be accommodated by
drawing down international reserves or by foreign borrowing and other
forms of capital movement influenced by macroeconomic policies. The
exchange rate then becomes overvalued in comparison with what it
would have been without them. The question is, what is a "sustainable"
deficit? Just because foreign borrowing is not excessive and international
reserves are adequate does not necessarily signify sustainability. For

present purposes, we can simply estimate the degree to which the exchange rate is distorted by accommodation of the observed trade surplus or deficit in a given year.

Deficits have been the rule rather than the exception in Philippine trade transactions over the years. For the most part, the trade deficits in the 1950s and 1960s were financed by drawing down reserves, a practice that led to drastic reductions in international reserves and balance of payments crises. In the 1970s, the government accommodated the massive deficits incurred after the first oil shock of 1974 through external financing, which led in turn to massive external debt, rising debt-service payments, and the foreign exchange crisis that began in late 1983.

The extent to which the exchange rate was distorted in a given year as a result of trade imbalances can be estimated by the following equation:

$$\log (r^b/r) = T_d/(\epsilon_x X - \eta_m M),\qquad(6.14)$$

where r^b is the real exchange rate under balanced trade; T_d, X, and M are the trade deficit, exports, and imports, respectively, in U.S. dollars; and ϵ_x and η_m are the price elasticities of export supply and import demand, respectively. As is well-known, equation (6.14) applies to the small-country case, in which foreign export demand and import supply are assumed to be perfectly elastic. According to earlier estimates of export supply and import demand functions for the Philippines (Bautista 1977), $\epsilon_x = 2.90$ and $\eta_m = -1.43$.

The calculated annual values of r^b/r for the period 1950–1984 are plotted in Figure 6.4. Had there been a trade balance throughout the period, while other conditions such as trade policy and the external terms of trade remained the same, the real exchange rate would have been 3.8 percent higher in the 1950s on average, 2.1 percent higher from 1960 to 1974, and as much as 8.0 percent higher in the most recent period, 1975–1984.

The effects of trade restrictions and trade deficits on the real exchange rate are additive. In any given year there could be an equilibrium exchange rate under the existing tariffs and export taxes that is x percent below the equilibrium exchange rate under unrestricted trade. Further, in that year, accommodation of the observed trade deficit through foreign borrowing or use of reserves could defend an exchange rate that is y percent below the equilibrium exchange rate. The combined effect of these two independent influences on the real exchange rate would be $(x + y)$ percent. Using the earlier notations, $x = (r^a/r) - 1$ and $y = (r^b/r) - 1$, so that an index of the *combined* exchange rate effect is given by

$$r^c/r = 1 + x + y = r^a/r + r^b/r - 1,\qquad(6.15)$$

FIGURE 6.4   Index of Exchange Rate Distortions Attributable to
Trade Imbalances in the Philippines, 1950–1984

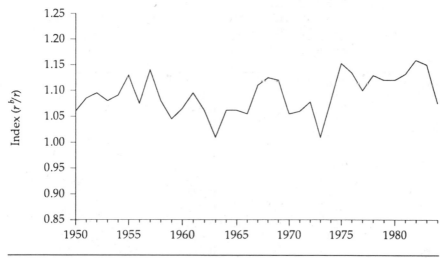

SOURCE: Author's calculations.

where r^c denotes the "undistorted" real exchange rate associated with unbiased trade policy *and* balanced trade. The calculations for this index are shown in Table 6.3, with the annual values from 1950 to 1980 given in the last column.

The first point to note is the consistent overvaluation of the Philippine peso (in relation to the hypothetical exchange rate, r^c) throughout the period. The degree of overvaluation differs significantly over time, however. In the 1950s, the distortionary effects of the trade imbalance, particularly of the heavily protective trade regime of direct controls on imports and foreign exchange, resulted in a highly overvalued exchange rate, with the index averaging 2.03 during the 1950–1961 period.

Although the decontrol program and nominal exchange rate adjustment in the early 1960s greatly reduced the overvaluation, the high and uneven tariff rates that replaced the system of import and exchange controls amounted to a stringent penalty on the production of tradable goods. The average value of r^c for the period from 1962 to 1969 is 1.47.

The first half of the 1970s appears to have been the least unfavorable period for the producers of tradable goods from the viewpoint of policy-induced price competitiveness: from 1970 to 1974 the overall index of exchange rate effects declined to an average of about 1.22. This result is attributable to two favorable developments. The Philippine peso depre-

TABLE 6.3   Exchange Rate Distortions Attributable to Trade Restrictions and Trade Imbalances in the Philippines, 1950–1980

| Year | Proportionate exchange rate effects attributable to | | Index of combined exchange rate effects |
	Trade restrictions (x)	Trade imbalances (y)	r^c/r $(= 1 + x + y)$
1950	0.764	0.008	1.772
1951	0.804	0.032	1.836
1952	1.116	0.048	2.164
1953	1.049	0.030	2.079
1954	1.035	0.043	2.078
1955	0.995	0.078	2.073
1956	0.916	0.026	1.942
1957	0.980	0.089	2.069
1958	1.017	0.030	2.047
1959	1.040	−0.003	2.037
1960	1.099	0.018	2.117
1961	1.137	0.049	2.186
1962	0.490	0.013	1.503
1963	0.466	−0.036	1.430
1964	0.467	0.012	1.479
1965	0.457	0.012	1.469
1966	0.451	0.007	1.458
1967	0.434	0.063	1.497
1968	0.351	0.074	1.425
1969	0.434	0.070	1.504
1970	0.245	0.006	1.251
1971	0.272	0.010	1.282
1972	0.244	0.025	1.269
1973	0.167	−0.037	1.130
1974	0.138	0.034	1.172
1975	0.125	0.106	1.231
1976	0.132	0.087	1.219
1977	0.155	0.053	1.208
1978	0.212	0.081	1.293
1979	0.287	0.072	1.359
1980	0.215	0.072	1.287

SOURCE: Author's calculations.

ciated markedly in nominal terms after the government adopted the floating exchange rate system beginning in February 1970. In addition, it introduced selective subsidies for export production under the Export Incentives Act of 1970, which compensated in part for the still pervasive bias against exporting attributable to the tariffs and indirect taxes.

With the massive trade deficits and increasing trade restrictions in the latter part of the decade, the overvaluation worsened, and the competitiveness index rose from an average of 1.15 in 1973–1974 to 1.32 in 1979–1980.

It seems reasonable to infer from the above findings that the degree of distortion in the real exchange rate bears a significant, negative relationship to the country's ability to prevent a foreign exchange crisis. Sooner or later, a highly overvalued exchange rate is bound to lead to a severe balance of payments problem, as demonstrated by the foreign exchange crisis of the late 1950s and late 1960s. The government policy response in both cases proved adequate for only a short time, with the real exchange rate sliding back to unsustainable levels after three or four years. These circumstances eventually led to another balance of payments crisis.

As discussed, the government adopted trade liberalization measures in the early 1980s as part of a wider program of policy reform and industrial restructuring designed to improve the international competitiveness of domestic producers. In particular, the tariff reform was expected to reduce significantly the degree of real exchange rate distortion attributable to trade restrictions. From the viewpoint of price competitiveness in the production of tradable goods, however, the large trade deficits financed by foreign borrowing through 1983 had offsetting effects on the real exchange rate (see Figure 6.4).

Although political developments undoubtedly precipitated the foreign exchange crisis that began in August 1983, some underlying economic factors, as reflected in the severity of the real exchange rate overvaluation since the mid-1970s, would have inevitably caused another balance of payments crisis. The policy mistake was to opt for expansionary macroeconomic policies, in disregard of a balance of payments that was being battered, during 1975–1983, by the adverse external terms of trade. Because sociopolitical conditions were not conducive to efficient economic growth—especially since the government tended to confer economic gains on so-called crony capitalists—the economy must have incurred both static and dynamic losses from the pursuit of what were being touted as countercyclical policies.

Effects on Relative Agricultural Prices

Implicit tariffs and export taxes or subsidies and the external terms of trade are also thought to have a direct effect on the relative prices of agricultural products, P_a/P_h and P_a/P_{na}. Preliminary regressions in this study, however, consistently indicate a lack of significance for the estimated coefficient of the terms of trade variable, a result suggesting that

TABLE 6.4   Estimated Equations: Relative Agricultural Prices as
Dependent Variables in the Philippines, 1950–1980

	Dependent variable	
	$\text{Log } P_a/P_h$ (1)	$\text{Log } P_a/P_{na}$ (2)
Constant	−.404	−.373
Log r	.398	.329
	(9.22)	(6.18)
Log T_{ax}	.336	.446
	(1.68)	(2.33)
Log T_{nx}		−.112
		(−.93)
Log T_m		−.418
		(−2.37)
$\overline{R}^2$	.884	.779

NOTE: Estimation by TSLS using annual data for 1950–1980. The numbers in parentheses are the t values. P_a/P_h and P_a/P_{na} denote the domestic prices of agricultural products in relation to home goods and to nonagricultural products, respectively. Blank cell indicates variable not included in regression equation.
SOURCE: Author's calculations.

only its indirect effect through the real exchange rate needs to be considered.[4] Table 6.4 reports the regression results based on specifications that exclude the terms of trade variable. Since the export tax and tariff variables also affect the real exchange rate, it seemed appropriate to use two-stage least squares (TSLS) estimation, with the terms-of-trade index and a trade deficit variable as additional instrument variables. Introduction of a few alternative lag structures did not appear to improve the statistical fit, a result that suggests the absence of lagged effects (that is, beyond one year) on domestic relative prices because of changes in the explanatory variables.

The first column of the Table 6.4 shows a coefficient estimate of 0.398 for the exchange rate variable, implying that a 10 percent increase in the real exchange rate (or a real depreciation of 10 percent) will boost the price of agricultural products compared with home goods by slightly less than 4 percent. The same (10 percent) increase in the real exchange rate will lead to a 3.3 percent rise in domestic agricultural prices in relation to the prices of nonagricultural products, according to the coefficient estimate under column 2. This effect is understandably smaller, given that nonagricultural output also includes tradable goods—although to a lesser extent than does agricultural output.

The estimated elasticity of P_a/P_h with respect to the export tax variable ($T_{ax} = 1 - t_{ax}$) is more than 0.3, while that of P_a/P_{na} is more than 0.4. The sign in either case is positive, as expected, since a rise in the agricultural export tax rate (t_{ax}) that lowers T_{ax} should lead to a lower price for agricultural products, other things remaining the same. The elasticity estimates suggest that the average agricultural export tax rate of 6.8 percent in the 1970s directly lowered P_a/P_h by about 2.0 percent and P_a/P_{na} by about 2.6 percent.

Nonagricultural tradables have been subject to import taxes, aimed especially at nonessential consumer goods. They have also benefited from subsidies for nontraditional export production. The elasticity estimate for T_{nx} ($= 1 - t_{nx}$), where t_{nx} is the negative of the export subsidy rate, has the correct sign but is statistically insignificant, presumably because of the small share of nontraditional export products in nonagricultural output. For T_m ($= 1 + t_m$), the elasticity estimate of -0.42, which is significant at the 5 percent level, indicates that a reduction in the implicit tariff rate from 68 percent to 20 percent, as occurred in the 1970s led directly to an increase in P_a/P_{na} of about 12 percent.

Together with the estimates of real exchange rate misalignment caused by the trade restrictions and trade imbalances, as derived earlier, the relative price response of agricultural products to changes in the real exchange rate and in the trade tax variables can be used to evaluate their effects on relative agricultural prices compared with home goods and nonagricultural products.

Table 6.5 presents the results of the calculations distinguishing between the two sources of exchange rate distortion during the four stages in the evolution of the country's trade and exchange rate policies. The direct and indirect effects of the trade restrictions on relative agricultural prices are included in the entries along the first four rows. From 1950 to 1961, the direct effect of the prevailing import and foreign exchange controls (associated with very high values of the implicit tariff rate) was the dominant influence on P_a/P_{na}, which fell by more than 100 percent. The indirect effect through the real exchange rate, as indicated by the induced decline in P_a/P_h, was about 40 percent. The separate influence of the trade deficits on relative agricultural prices during the period was less significant. The two sources of exchange rate distortion jointly lowered the domestic agricultural price by 41 percent in relation to home goods and by 104 percent in relation to nonagricultural products.

Even after implementation of the decontrol measures and nominal exchange rate adjustment in the early 1960s, trade restrictions continued to be the most important (negative) influence on domestic agricultural prices, as the protective tariff system retained the qualitative biases in the incentive structure against agriculture through the late 1970s. However, the distortionary effect of trade policy on relative agricultural prices continued to subside. Even so, the policy-induced incentive bias against agricultural production remained high from 1975 to 1980, reducing P_a/P_h by 12 percent and P_a/P_{na} by 20 percent, in part because large

TABLE 6.5   Average Proportionate Effects of Exchange Rate
Distortions on Relative Agricultural Prices in the
Philippines, 1950–1980

Period	P_a/P_h	P_a/P_{na}
Effects of trade restrictions		
1950–1961	−.396	−1.026
1962–1969	−.176	−.438
1970–1974	−.111	−.215
1975–1980	−.089	−.174
Effects of trade imbalances		
1950–1961	−.015	−.012
1962–1969	−.011	−.009
1970–1974	−.003	−.003
1975–1980	−.031	−.026
Effects from both sources		
1950–1961	−.411	−1.038
1962–1969	−.187	−.447
1970–1974	−.114	−.218
1975–1980	−.120	−.200

NOTE: P_a/P_h and P_a/P_{na} denote the domestic prices of agricultural products in relation to home goods and to nonagricultural products, respectively.
SOURCE: Author's calculations.

trade deficits in those years helped defend the overvalued exchange
rate.

Concluding Remarks

The results of this study provide empirical support for the view that the
highly distorted trade and exchange rate policies pursued in the Philippines since the early 1950s have had a substantial, negative impact on
the incentives for agricultural production. Thus a policy shift toward a
more neutral trade regime can be expected to affect the domestic price
structure favoring the agricultural sector. Trade liberalization will have
further repercussions on the national economy, since relative price
changes presumably influence the patterns of sectoral production, consumption, and trade, as well as income distribution.[5]
    It bears emphasizing that the real exchange rate is an important
determinant of domestic agricultural prices in relation to the prices of
both home goods and nonagricultural products. If the agricultural sector
is to contribute significantly to the country's economic recovery and
long-term growth, as hoped for in the government's medium-term development plan, the authorities need to improve not only sector-specific

policies, but also trade and macroeconomic policies that influence the real exchange rate. To get the right agricultural prices, they must also focus attention on the system of industrial protection, monetary policy, government expenditures, nominal exchange rate policy, and other aspects of macroeconomic management that have a potentially strong influence on the incentives for agricultural production because of their effects on the real exchange rate.

The price bias against agriculture attributable to trade and exchange rate policies translates into an effective resource transfer out of the agricultural sector that is quite large in comparison with the amount transferred into agriculture through government spending. In 1980, the latter amount totaled about 3.5 billion pesos (Intal and Power 1986), as calculated from the national government's budgetary allocations for current operating expenditures and capital outlays. By comparison, even when considering only export crops, the resource outflow in 1980 amounted to 6.6 billion pesos—of which 2.3 billion pesos were attributable to the export taxes and 4.3 billion pesos to the policy-induced overvaluation of the exchange rate.

In fact, the overvalued exchange rate is penalizing the production of all tradable goods, not only actual exports. As already pointed out, the high degree of tradability of agricultural output makes agricultural incentives particularly dependent on real exchange rate movements. It follows that the implicit resource transfer out of agriculture caused by the peso overvaluation has been much larger than is indicated when only export crops are considered.

The need to extract agricultural surplus to finance capital formation in the rest of the economy during development is a widely accepted proposition in development economics. The problem, however, is that the transferred resources may be used inefficiently in the nonagricultural sectors. In the Philippine case, as in most other developing countries where the industrial sector has been highly protected, distortions in the product and factor markets have led to the inefficient use of investment resources for manufacturing, and an inability to compete in the international markets (Bautista, Power, and associates 1979). Unless such policy-induced distortions are corrected, the opportunities for rapid growth in agricultural productivity are exploited, and the capital requirements for technological change and rural infrastructure development are met, transfers of agricultural resources are unlikely to help accelerate development.

Increased rural incomes as a result of improvements in agricultural prices and farm productivity can stimulate a more rapid expansion of output and employment within and outside the agricultural sector (Mellor 1976). A liberalized trade regime that encourages export production and efficient import substitution in agriculture, as well as in the rest of the economy, will facilitate such agriculture- and employment-based development, given the biases in the Philippine trade and exchange rate policies examined in this study.

Notes to Chapter 6

1. In many cases, financially troubled firms were bailed out by converting government loans into equity. In mid-1983, for example, the government's Development Bank of Philippines owned or managed seventy-three large, once-private firms. Other public corporations, such as the National Development Company and the Philippine National Bank, also took over many firms threatened by failure in which government exposure was substantial.

2. The OTB values were derived from the weighted average of Baldwin's (1975) estimates of the effective exchange rate for various categories of imports and exports in the base year (1971), the Central Bank indexes of wholesale and trade unit values of imported and export goods, and the annual effective exchange rate for exports estimated by Baldwin from 1950 to 1971 and by Senga (1983) from 1972 to 1980. For details, see Bautista (1987b).

3. See Bautista (1987b) for the derivation of the equations in this section and the estimation of the incidence parameters using Philippine data.

4. This result is presumably caused by the markedly increasing share of manufactured products in total exports since the early 1970s and the sharp changes in the foreign price of oil imports since 1974.

5. In a multisectoral, general equilibrium analysis using 1978 benchmark data, removal of the export taxes and reduction of the sectoral tariff rates to a uniform 10 percent would have the following comparative static effects: total exports and total imports would increase by 8.1 percent and 7.7 percent, respectively; agricultural value added by 6.2 percent; and national income by 2.8 percent, with the distribution in income gains significantly favoring rural over urban households. See Bautista (1986b).

Effects of Exchange Rate and Trade Policies on Agricultural Prices in Pakistan

Agricultural price policies play an important role in determining prices, but a sectoral policy focus can miss important linkages between economywide policies (trade and macroeconomic policies) and the agricultural sector. By changing the relative prices of importables, exportables, and home goods, trade and exchange rate policies can have a profound indirect effect on agriculture. This link is particularly important to recognize in a country such as Pakistan, where the share of agriculture in gross domestic product (GDP) is high and a large percentage of the labor force is employed in agriculture. Agricultural growth is thus crucial for overall economic development and for improving the welfare of the poor. As the Pakistan government seeks new sources of revenue to ease its budgetary problems, it is giving serious consideration to the idea of increasing explicit taxation of its large agricultural sector. Although not an analysis of fiscal policy, this study demonstrates that the actual level of indirect taxation of agriculture through appreciation of the real exchange rate is already considerable and should be given closer attention in the policy debate.

This study follows the analytical approach developed by Krueger, Schiff, and Valdés (1988) and by Hurtado, Muchnik, and Valdés (1990). Hamid, Nabi, and Nasim (1990) first applied the approach to Pakistan, and their work provides a valuable foundation for the empirical analysis employed here.[1]

The discussion opens with an explanation of the nominal exchange rate and trade policies in Pakistan and the effective exchange rates for imports and exports between 1960 and 1987. Regression analysis is then used to calculate the equilibrium real exchange rates. The final section presents calculations of the nominal and effective rates of protection for agricultural commodities in Pakistan (the direct trade effects) and compares these with measures of the total effective rates of protection, which incorporate the total effects of trade and exchange rate policies on the prices of output and value added.

Exchange Rate and Trade Policies in Pakistan

For most years since its independence in 1947, Pakistan has had a fixed official exchange rate. Until January 1982, when the government adopted a managed float, the exchange rate was revised only three times in thirty-five years—in 1955, 1972, and 1973.

For much of the 1960s and 1970s, Pakistan relied primarily on trade policies to help sustain its current accounts position. The trade policy instruments included import tariffs, quotas, export taxes, and export bonuses. These trade policies served two other purposes as well. Trade taxes accounted for 38 percent of government revenues between 1976 and 1980, and the protection that the tariffs and quotas afforded domestic industry was an integral part of the government's strategy—which was to promote development through import substitution.[2]

Average import tariffs or export tax rates calculated using actual tax revenues and trade values may be good measures of tm and tx in the absence of import or export quotas. To take into account the effects of binding quantitative restrictions, however, the implicit import tariff or export tax, calculated from the ratio of domestic to world prices of the import goods, is a more accurate measure of the direct effect of trade policies.

In practice, calculating the implicit import tariff or export tax when quotas are binding and tax rates are not uniform across commodities requires detailed data on the world and domestic prices of all traded goods. In this study, estimates of the implicit tariffs (taxes) for individual categories of imports (exports) from Naqvi and Kemal (1983a) were aggregated using import (export) value shares as weights to calculate the average implicit tariff (export tax).

Two aspects of Pakistan's trade policy in particular are noteworthy. First, the quantitative restrictions on imports have had a significant effect on the domestic prices of imports. The implicit tariff on imports in 1981 was 54.8 percent, while the average import tax (calculated as total import revenues divided by the total value of imports) was only 29.7 percent (data from Pakistan Economic Survey 1987–1988). Thus, import taxes captured only 54 percent of the economic rent accruing to the holders of import licenses. Second, there was a large variance in the implicit tariffs by commodity group, a dispersion that was even more pronounced for effective rates of protection (see Naqvi and Kemal 1983b). The large variance in implicit tariffs suggests that the quantitative restrictions may have had unintended effects on the structure of the relative incentives for import-competing sectors.

Figure 7.1 shows the pattern of $1 + tm$ and $1 - tx$ over time.[3] From the early 1960s to 1971, the implicit tariff on imports rose from 130 percent to 220 percent. At the same time, the export subsidy (implicit in the system of multiple exchange rates) was between 60 percent and 80 percent in most years. Thus, while the official exchange rate was held fixed at 4.76 rupees per U.S. dollar, the effective exchange rate for imports rose from 11.2 to 15.4 rupees per dollar, and the effective exchange rate for exports varied from about 7.5 to 9.5 rupees per dollar (Figure 7.2 and Table A7.2).

The 1972 devaluation of the nominal exchange rate from 4.76 to 11.00 rupees per dollar brought about a greatly simplified exchange rate system that ended the bonus export scheme and lowered the level of many nominal import tariffs. As a result, the implicit import tariff and the implicit export subsidy were both greatly reduced. The effective exchange rates for imports and exports increased by 5 percent and 20 percent, respectively, much less than the official exchange rate following a 121 percent devaluation (Figure 7.2).[4]

The implicit import tariff declined further in 1974 and 1975, but from the mid-1970s to 1987 it remained at about 0.60. Export taxes and subsidies were also brought down beginning in the mid-1970s, and they did not increase greatly even when the official exchange rate depreciated sharply in the 1980s. As a result, the effective exchange rate for exports approximated the official exchange rate during this period, and unlike the 1972 devaluation, the 73 percent depreciation of the official exchange rate (relative to the U.S. dollar) resulted in an approximately equal 61 percent depreciation of the effective exchange rate for exports between 1981 and 1987.

The depreciation of the 1980s also differed from the devaluation of 1972 in that it was not accompanied by a reduction in implicit import tariffs. This result appears counterintuitive since, other things being equal, the implicit import tariff is reduced by a nominal devaluation because the devaluation increases the world price of imports expressed

138   PAUL DOROSH

FIGURE 7.1   Pakistan's Overall Trade Policy Bias, 1960–1987

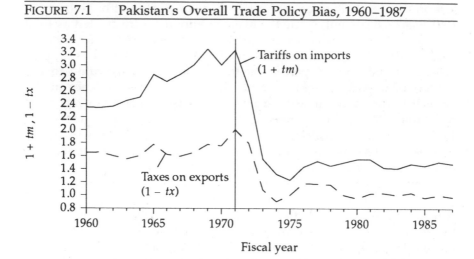

NOTES: The vertical line indicates the devaluation and unification of exchange rates. 1971: Secession from East Pakistan and creation of Bangladesh. 1971–1977: Bhutto government. 1977–1988: Zia regime.
SOURCE: Derived from basic data in Pakistan, Ministry of Finance, *Economic Survey* (various years).

in rupees while leaving the domestic price unchanged, assuming the tariff is still binding (see equation (7.3) in note 3). The fact that the implicit tariff did not change significantly (and even increased slightly) indicates that the quotas were reduced (or that the demand for the restricted import goods increased).

The Real Exchange Rate

The above analysis of the effective exchange rates ignores changes in the domestic price of nontraded goods and in world prices. Although the effective exchange rates for imports and exports determine the nominal prices of traded goods in the domestic economy, another measure of price incentives, the real exchange rate, is needed to reflect changes in the domestic price of traded goods in relation to the price of home goods.[5]

Figure 7.3 shows real exchange rate indexes over time. The large nominal devaluation of the rupee (more than 100 percent) combined with the changes in trade policies resulted in a much smaller deprecia-

FIGURE 7.2   Devaluation Episodes and Evolution of Effective
              Exchange Rates in Pakistan, 1960–1987

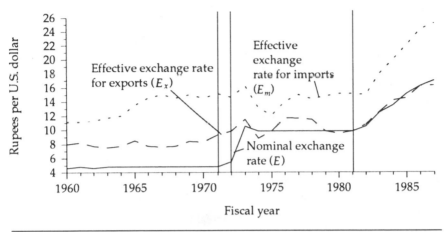

NOTES: The vertical lines indicate nominal devaluations. 1971: Secession from East Pakistan and creation of Bangladesh. 1971–1977: Bhutto government. 1977–1988: Zia regime.
SOURCE: Derived from basic data in Pakistan, Ministry of Finance, *Economic Survey* (various years).

tion of the real exchange rate (about 20 percent) between 1971 and 1973. The 73 percent nominal devaluation, however, resulted in a 43 percent depreciation of the effective real exchange rate for exports between 1981 and 1987.

Determinants of the Real Exchange Rate

Even when the nominal exchange rate remains fixed for long periods, the effective real exchange rate can adjust to bring about equilibrium in the markets for traded and home goods. These adjustments come about through changes in world prices, the prices of home goods, the implicit import tariffs, and export taxes. Thus, factors such as world prices and government trade policies that influence supply and demand in these markets affect the real effective exchange rate.

Import tariffs and export taxes influence the real exchange rate by changing the domestic demand for and supply of both tradable and nontradable goods (Dornbusch 1974; Sjaastad 1980; and García García 1981). For example, an increase in import tariffs raises the domestic price of importables in relation to the domestic prices of exportables and home goods, and as a result, the demand for these goods rises. To restore

FIGURE 7.3   Pakistan's Real Effective Exchange Rate Indexes,
              1960–1987

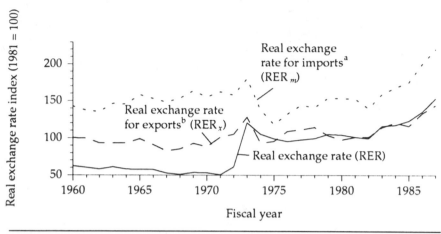

a. $RER_m = RER (1 + tm)$.
b. $RER_x = RER (1 - tx)$.
SOURCE: Derived from basic data in Pakistan, Ministry of Finance, *Economic Survey* (various years).

equilibrium in the home goods market, the price of home goods must rise in relation to the price of exportables and the new after-tariff price of importables. Thus, the real exchange rate appreciates. An export subsidy has an analogous effect—it shifts domestic demand away from exportable goods to importables and home goods.

The extent to which an increase in the domestic price of imports causes an increase in the demand for home goods (and an increase in their price) is measured by the incidence parameter, defined as the percentage change in the real exchange rate for exportables (P_x/P_h) for a given percentage change in the domestic price of importables in relation to exportables (P_m/P_x) (Sjaastad 1980). This incidence parameter (ω) is determined in part by the degree of substitutability between home goods and import goods in production and consumption. For example, if home goods are close substitutes for import goods in terms of demand, then an import tariff that raises the price of import goods will cause a large shift in demand toward home goods and a sizable increase in their price.[6]

The external terms of trade (expressed as the ratio of the world price of export goods to the world price of import goods) affects the relative prices of tradables to nontradables in two ways. As with trade policy, there is a direct effect on prices. A worsening of the terms of trade through an increase in the world price of importables raises the domestic price of importables, increases the demand for home goods, and leads to an appreciation of the real exchange rate—just as an increase in the import tariff does. There is also an income effect. A higher world price for importables reduces the purchasing power of export earnings and real income. The effect on the relative demand for tradables and home goods (and on their relative prices) depends on the income elasticities of the demand for these goods. In general, a worsening of the terms of trade (that is, a reduction in income) might be expected to cause a decrease in demand for home goods and a depreciation in the real exchange rate. A priori, the net effect on the real exchange rate is indeterminate, although it is usually expected that the income effect will predominate, with a worsening of the terms of trade requiring a real exchange rate depreciation to restore external balance (see Edwards 1988).

In the case of Pakistan, workers' remittances (largely from Pakistani workers in the Middle East) are an important part of foreign exchange earnings. Remittances and other private unrequited transfers are spent partly on home goods, which thus go up in price and cause an appreciation of the real exchange rate. In the 1980s workers' remittances declined, and the government decided to depreciate the rupee in relation to the currencies of its trading partners.

Likewise, foreign grants and long-term borrowing can lead to an appreciation of the real exchange rate. Because this inflow of foreign exchange accrues to the government rather than the private sector (as do workers' remittances), the composition of spending on home goods versus tradables is likely to differ, as is the magnitude of the effect on the real exchange rate.[7]

Regression Results

A number of studies have estimated real exchange rate regressions for Latin American countries using either the domestic price ratio of exportables to home goods (P_x/P_h) or a real exchange rate constructed from the wholesale prices of the major trading partners as the dependent variable (see Valdés 1986). Following the study of Chile by Hurtado, Muchnik, and Valdés (1990), I expressed the real exchange rate as a function of trade policy (LTRPOL), terms of trade (LTT), and other variables (RREMIT and RAID). Because export subsidies and taxes have been significant in Pakistan (but negligible in Chile), the real effective exchange rate for exports was used instead of an average real exchange rate index.[8]

Equation (7.10) uses quarterly data from the second quarter of 1972 to the first quarter of 1987 for the regression on the logarithm of the real effective exchange rate for exports:

$$logRER_x = \begin{array}{c} 2.81 \\ (26.28) \end{array} - \begin{array}{c} 0.41log[(1 + tm)/(1 - tx)] \\ (3.25) \end{array} + \begin{array}{c} 0.07log(P_x^w/P_m^w) \\ (0.61) \end{array}$$

$$\begin{array}{cc} - \, 170.5RREMIT & - \, 259.2RAID \\ (-1.70) & (-5.10) \end{array} \qquad (7.10)$$

$R^2 = 0.81$,
RHO $= 0.85$,
D.W. $= 1.63$,

where C = the unit constant, LTRPOL = $log([1 + tm]/[1 - tx])$, LTT = $log(P_x^w/P_m^w)$, RREMIT = (private transfers in dollars divided by P_t^w)/ real GDP index, RAID = (sum of aid loans and grants to Pakistan measured in dollars divided by P_t^w)/real GDP index, and the t-values are in parentheses.

I estimated the equation using two-stage least squares to correct for the endogeneity of some of the explanatory variables. Terms of trade, an index of national income in developed countries, the deflated dollar price of oil, and a constant were used as instruments. In addition, because of the autocorrelation of the residuals, I also used the lagged values of instruments listed above and the lagged real exchange rate as instruments.

The coefficient on the trade policy variable (equal to $-\omega$) in equation (7.10) indicates that a 1 percent increase in the ratio of 1 plus the implicit import tariff to 1 minus the implicit export tax will produce a 0.41 percent appreciation of the real effective exchange rate.[9] The positive (but statistically insignificant) coefficient on the terms of trade indicates that an improvement in the terms of trade will cause a depreciation of the real effective exchange rate. The signs for the private unrequited transfers and foreign aid variables (RREMIT and RAID) are negative, as expected.

In another regression, I used a larger sample of quarterly data from the first quarter of 1960 to the first quarter of 1987 and introduced a dummy variable (DBANG = 1 for quarters prior to the first quarter of 1972, 0 otherwise) to help capture the effects of the secession of East Pakistan in December 1971. The coefficients of TRPOL, LTT, and RAID were also allowed to vary between periods. The estimated value of

TABLE 7.1   Calculation of the Equilibrium Real Exchange Rate for
Pakistan, 1960–1987 (omega approach, annual average)

Year	RER$_x$ (1)^a	Equivalent tariff (2)^b	$(1+T)^{-\omega}$ (3)^c	Equilibrium RER$_x$ (4)^d
1960–1971	98.37	1.62	1.22	119.41
1972–1977	106.03	1.35	1.13	120.10
1978–1982	98.66	1.45	1.16	114.62
1983–1987	107.44	1.48	1.17	126.16

a. Real exchange rate index for exports (1981 = 100).
b. Equivalent tariff = 1 + T = (1 + tm)/(1 − tx).
c. Misalignment in the real exchange rate (ω = −0.410).
d. Equilibrium real exchange rate index (column 1 · column 3).
SOURCE: Author's calculations.

ω for the 1972–1987 period is −0.68; for the earlier period, ω takes the value of −0.27.[10]

The high values for the autocorrelation coefficient (RHO) in both regressions indicate that errors unexplained by the included variables have persistent effects—perhaps because the real exchange rate takes time to adjust to changes in the explanatory variables and other shocks. One quarter is likely too short a time for complete adjustments in the real exchange rate to take place, especially when nominal exchange rates are fixed and overall domestic inflation is low. Further research might estimate a system of equations rather than a single reduced-form equation to capture the adjustment and the effects of other variables on the real exchange rate in Pakistan.

Equilibrium Real Exchange Rates

The ω parameter estimated using the real exchange rate equations above can be used to estimate the equilibrium exchange rate under alternative trade policies.[11] Table 7.1 presents the calculations of the percentage change in the real exchange rate for exports under the assumption that the implicit import tariff and the implicit export tax were reduced to zero ([1 + tm]/[1 − tx] = 1). For example, in the period before 1972, removing all the trade tariffs and taxes reduces (1 + tm)/(1 − tx) from 1.62 to 1.00, a reduction of 38.3 percent (0.62/1.62), and results in a depreciation of the real exchange rate of 22 percent.

As shown in Figure 7.4, the gap between the official exchange rate (which applied to some agricultural products) and the calculated equilibrium exchange rate is even larger. Under the Bhutto government (1972–1977), (1 + tm)/(1 − tx) averaged only 1.35, so that the removal

FIGURE 7.4   Pakistan's Nominal Exchange Rates, 1960–1987

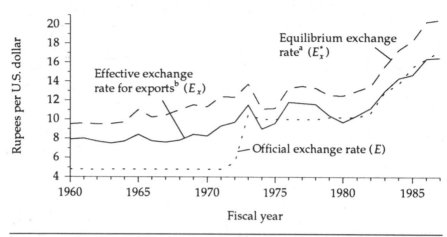

a. $E^*_x = E^*$.
b. $E_x = E(1 - tx)$.
SOURCE: Derived from basic data in Pakistan, Ministry of Finance, *Economic Survey* (various years).

of all trade barriers would have resulted in a smaller depreciation (13 percent) of the real exchange rate. The implicit tariffs have changed little in the 1980s, despite a large depreciation of the nominal (and real) exchange rates. Thus, the overvaluation of the rupee caused by trade policy has persisted.

Agricultural Prices

In Pakistan, the government has used a number of policy instruments, including export taxes, government monopolies on trade, producer support prices, and input subsidies, to influence the prices of agricultural output and the costs of production. The bias toward import substitution in industrial trade policy and the resulting appreciation of the real exchange rate discussed in the previous section have also indirectly affected the prices of agricultural commodities in relation to nonagricultural goods.

Following the framework set forth in Krueger, Schiff, and Valdés (1988), I quantified the effects of agricultural trade and price policies (direct effects) in terms of the nominal and effective rates of protection for leading agricultural commodities, calculated using historical nominal exchange rates in determining border prices. The indirect effects of overall trade policy and appreciation of the real exchange rate were then included in measures of the total effects on prices and value added by using the free-trade equilibrium real exchange rates of the previous section.[12]

Direct Effects on Output Prices: Nominal Rates of Protection

Agricultural trade and price policies (including trade taxes, quotas, government monopolies on trade and marketing, and processing subsidies) have a direct effect on output prices. Nominal rates of protection measure these direct effects on output prices by comparing actual domestic prices with the free trade prices that would prevail in the absence of government interventions:

$$\text{NRP}i = (Pi - Pi')/Pi' = Pi/Pi' - 1, \tag{7.11}$$

where NRPi is the nominal rate of protection on good i, Pi is the domestic price of good i, and Pi' is the border or world price of good i adjusted for transport and other marketing costs.

Indirect and Total Effects

Nominal rates of protection calculated using the official exchange rate measure only the direct effects of trade policy. Notice, however, that exchange rates as well as trade policies affect border prices and the opportunity costs of production and consumption. To capture the indirect effects of misalignment of the exchange rate, the indirect effect of trade of nonagriculture and exchange rate policies on farm prices can be measured as[13]

$$(Pi' - Pi^*)/Pi^* = Pi'/Pi^* - 1 = \frac{Pi'}{\dfrac{E^*Pi'}{Eo}} - 1 = \frac{Eo}{E^*} - 1 \tag{7.13}$$

where Pi' and Pi^* are the border price of commodity evaluated at the official and equilibrium exchange rates, respectively, and E^*/Eo measures the exchange rate adjustment. This indirect effect is, of course, common to all tradable farm products.

The above measures of indirect effect assume that the price of non-agricultural goods and services remain unchanged. As Valdés (1986) has argued, however, long-term investments in agriculture are a function of the relative prices of agricultural to nonagricultural goods (the domestic terms of trade of agriculture). Thus, the ratio of the output price of a commodity to the price of nonagricultural goods is the appropriate measure of the incentives. Because trade and exchange rate policies affect the prices of nonagricultural goods as well as agricultural goods, the total effect of policy on the ratio of the commodity price to the price of nonagricultural goods is

$$([Pi/Pna] - [Pi^*/Pna^*])/(Pi^*/Pna^*) = (Pi/Pna)/(Pi^*/Pna^*) - 1, \quad (7.14)$$

where Pna is the price index of nonagriculture and Pna^* is the price index of nonagriculture with free trade and an equilibrium exchange rate.[14] This measure combines the effect of the sectoral and economywide price interventions on agricultural prices and represents the measure of price incentives used in this study; it represents the nominal rates of protection adjusted by sectoral and economywide policies. A synthesis of the estimated nominal rates of protection to production of the various products from 1961 to 1987 is reported in Table 7.2.

As Table 7.2 shows, high direct taxation of exportables (−15 percent on average) was reinforced by indirect taxation (adding up to a total of −38 percent). In contrast, the average for the direct and total protection to import-competing products is positive, although the indirect effects reduce this protection from 48 to 7 percent in the period from 1972 to 1987. However, this positive average for importables masks the difference between the high protection of sugar and milk and considerable taxation of wheat and vegetable oil.[15]

The same relationship can be used to measure the effective rate of protection in agriculture, in relation to the effective rate in the nonagricultural sector, as explained in the following section.

Effective Rates of Protection

Government trade and exchange rate policies influence the prices of the tradable inputs that go into agricultural production as well as the prices of output. The direct effects on the value added in production (the value of output less the value of nonfactor inputs) were measured by the effective rate of protection, defined as:

$$ERPi = (VAi - VAi')/VAi' = VAi/VAi' - 1.[16] \quad (7.17)$$

TABLE 7.2   Direct and Total Nominal Protection Rates to Producers
of Agricultural Commodities in Pakistan, 1961–1987
(average annual percentage)

| | Importables | | | | Exportables | |
Year	Total effect	Direct effect	Total effect	Direct effect	Total effect	Direct effect
	Wheat		Maize		Basmati	
1961–1965	8	−49	23	−41	−37	−76
1966–1971	28	−46	37	−41	−14	−72
1972–1977	−38	−56	−30	−52	−50	−67
1978–1982	−34	−48	0	−20	−48	−60
1983–1987	−19	−33	−1	−18	−57	−65
1961–1971	19	−48	30	−41	−20	−73
1972–1987	−31	−46	−12	−31	−52	−65
	Vegetable oil		Milk		Ordinary rice	
1961–1965	4	−40			16	−53
1966–1971	42	−21			18	−60
1972–1977	−18	−37	51	18	−34	−61
1978–1982	−36	−46	78	51	−38	−53
1983–1981	−26	−35	82	53	7	−17
1961–1971	24	−30			17	−57
1972–1987	−26	−40	61	35	−23	−44
	Sugarcane		Sugar (ex-mill)		Cotton	
1961–1965	538	20	97	3	34	−46
1966–1971	−287	63	154	26	76	−41
1972–1977	−22	−50	21	43	10	38
1978–1982	30	−7	9	−11	5	−20
1983–1987	628	210	69	43	25	−3
1961–1971	88	43	128	16	57	−43
1972–1987	197	45	17	−6	6	−21
	Total importables		Total exportables			
1961–1971	21	−11	28	−54		
1972–1987	48	7	−15	−38		

NOTE: Total importables (exportables) is a weighted average of nominal rates of protection of importables (exportables). The weights are the relative value shares of production of the selected products
(wheat, 33 percent; maize, 2 percent; sugar, 15 percent; vegetable oil, 2 percent; milk, 48 percent;
basmati, 19 percent; ordinary rice, 36 percent; and cotton; 45 percent). As noted in the text, the indirect
effect is common to all tradable farm products; numerically, however, the implicit indirect effect may
vary among commodities.
SOURCE: Author's calculations.

The total effects (including indirect effects of exchange rate policy) can be measured as

$$ERPT = ([VAi/Vna]/[VAi^*/Vna^*]) - 1, \qquad (7.19)$$

where VAi is the value added for agricultural product i and Vna represents the value added in the nonagricultural sector.

The adjustment of Vna to Vna^* was beyond the scope of this study, and Pna and Pna^* were used as proxies. The costs of the inputs used to calculate the value added by crop were based on data on the cost of production for a single year. The time series of input costs assumed constant yields and constant input-output relations. The prices of inputs were estimated using price indexes for fertilizer, nonagricultural goods and services, or nontraded goods.

In calculating the direct effects of policy on value added, I used the border prices of fertilizer (assuming free trade in agricultural inputs but no change in exchange rates). In calculating the total effects of policy on value added, I included the effects of changes in the exchange rate in the estimations of input costs. The price index of nonagricultural goods and services under free trade with equilibrium exchange rates (Pna^*) was used in estimating the changes in the prices of some inputs, including irrigation, tractor services, and plant protection. In calculating the effective rates of protection for sugarcane, cotton, and rice, I assumed the domestic processing costs were unchanged. To the extent that processing was inefficient, the costs of production at world prices were overestimated and the effective rates of protection underestimated.

Table 7.3 presents the results of the calculations of value added and effective rates of protection for wheat, basmati rice, ordinary rice, cotton, sugar cane, and maize. Because the value added at world prices is small in some years, the calculated effective rates of protection can be extremely large. In general, the pattern of effective rates of protection is similar to that of the direct and total effects of output prices, since the costs of the traded inputs were small for most of the commodities considered.

Price Instability

Pakistan's government intervenes in agricultural markets not only to influence the average level of prices, but also to provide greater year-to-year price stability for both producers and consumers. Table 7.4 presents the coefficients of variation for real agricultural (nominal) prices deflated with an index of nonagricultural prices (Pna or Pna^*).

TABLE 7.3   Measures of Direct and Total Effective Rates of Protection to Agricultural Producers in Pakistan, 1961–1987 (average annual percentage)

	Importables		Exportables	
Year	Direct effect	Total effect	Direct effect	Total effect
	Wheat		Basmati	
1961–1965	1	−60	−61	−88
1966–1971	36	−55	−39	−86
1972–1977	−44	−62	−64	−78
1978–1982	−42	−56	−61	−72
1983–1987	−25	−42	−72	−78
1961–1971	20	−57	−44	−86
1972–1987	−37	−54	−65	−76
	Sugarcane		Ordinary rice	
1961–1965	1,751	108	16	−65
1966–1971	510	393	29	69
1972–1977	−18	−52	−38	−69
1978–1982	97	18	−49	−63
1983–1987	−435	121	12	−22
1961–1971	1,074	263	26	−68
1972–1987	−112	24	−26	−53
	Maize		Cotton	
1961–1965	87	−28	34	−61
1966–1971	141	−19	142	−55
1972–1977	17	−26	−11	−44
1978–1982	92	41	16	−18
1983–1987	−10	−30	117	27
1961–1971	117	−23	93	−58
1972–1987	32	−6	38	−14
	Total importables		Total exportables	
1961–1971	351	44	43	−67
1972–1987	−57	−28	−3	−43

NOTE: Total importables (exportables) is a weighted average of importables (exportables). The weights are the relative value shares of production of the selected products (wheat, 65 percent; sugarcane, 31 percent; maize, 4 percent; basmati, 19 percent; ordinary rice, 36 percent, cotton, 15 percent.)
SOURCE: Author's calculations.

Agricultural trade and price policies have resulted in greater price stability for producers of wheat, basmati and ordinary rice, cotton, sugar, maize, and milk. Only for vegetable oil and fertilizer are coefficients of variation of border prices calculated using equilibrium exchange rates approximately the same as or lower than coefficients of

TABLE 7.4   Coefficient of Variation of Producer Prices in Pakistan, 1961–1987

	P_p/P_{na}	P'_p/P_{na}	P^*_p/P^*_{na}
Wheat (import parity)	0.11	0.57	0.42
Wheat (export parity)	0.11	0.48	0.29
Basmati (unmilled)[a]	0.12	0.46	0.22
Basmati[a]	0.09	0.39	0.21
Ordinary rice (unmilled)	0.12	0.67	0.44
Ordinary rice	0.12	0.63	0.42
Cotton	0.14	0.39	0.28
Vegetable oil	0.26	0.27	0.22
Sugar (ex-mill)	0.13	0.71	0.57
Sugarcane	0.17	1.17	0.80
Maize	0.15	0.54	0.40
Milk[b]	0.07	0.42	0.30
Fertilizers	0.26	0.36	0.27

NOTE: P_p/P_{na} is the actual relative price to producers. P'_p/P_{na} is the border price for a farm product relative to actual prices of nonagricultural products. P^*_p/P^*_{na} is the ratio of the border price of a farm product to the price of nonagricultural products with both prices measured using the equilibrium exchange rate.
a. Prices for 1960–1961 to 1962–1963 are not included.
b. Border prices for 1960–1961 to 1970–1971 are not included.
SOURCE: Author's calculations.

variation of actual domestic prices. For producers of wheat, rice, cotton, and maize, increased price stability has been accompanied by lower average prices (see Chapter 13 for a detailed analysis of the stabilization issue).

Conclusions

The indirect effects of exchange rate policies have been a dominant factor in determining the overall effects of government policy interventions on agricultural price incentives. Trade policies designed to protect industry caused the real exchange rate to appreciate by about 20 percent in the 1960s and about 15 percent in the mid-1970s. Despite adopting a managed float, Pakistan's quantitative restrictions on imports in 1987 carried a high implicit import tariff (47 percent) and thus caused the real exchange rate to appreciate about 19 percent.

Appreciation of the real exchange rate has reduced and sometimes reversed the protection that agricultural trade policies have provided for some commodities. The overvaluation of the rupee in the 1960s outweighed the protection provided by direct trade policies for wheat, ordinary rice, and cotton and increased the taxation of basmati rice. The direct effect of trade policies outweighed other effects for wheat, basmati rice, and ordinary rice in the 1970s and early 1980s because the appreciation of the real exchange rate caused less distortion than in the 1960s. For cotton, trade policies had only small direct effects on domestic prices, but domestic prices have remained significantly lower than equilibrium free-trade prices because of the indirect effects of exchange rate appreciation and overall trade policy.

Thus, the principal agricultural products (wheat, basmati and ordinary rice, cotton, and sugar) were consistently taxed from the 1960s to the early 1980s. Although it is difficult to quantify the real effects of this implicit taxation of agriculture within the scope of this chapter, the general implications are clear.[17] Lower prices to farmers discouraged agricultural production and reduced farm incomes. As a result, the volume of exports declined while imports of agricultural products increased. In turn, rural employment opportunities dwindled and labor incomes contracted. Incentives for rural-to-urban migration increased, and incentives for investment in agricultural capital were reduced.

Government intervention in agricultural markets had positive effects as well, however. The domestic prices of all major agricultural commodities except oilseeds and fertilizer were less variable than world prices evaluated at the free-trade equilibrium exchange rate. The large dairy sector also benefited greatly from protection from milk imports, as did some of the other sectors of the economy. In particular, the import-competing industries enjoyed protection behind the high implicit import tariffs, and all consumers faced lower and more stable prices for food products, but higher prices for nonfood goods and services.

Whatever the general equilibrium effects of lower agricultural prices on the real side of Pakistan's economy, the indirect effects of the trade and exchange rate policies on agricultural producer prices have been large and have persisted for more than two decades. The indirect effects taxed producers and subsidized consumers of most food crops and cotton. Milk was the only major commodity for which the indirect effects (appreciation of the real exchange rate) did not outweigh the high levels of direct protection in the last decade. In the case of Pakistan, therefore, these indirect effects are too large to be ignored and should be taken into account in the analysis of agricultural pricing policy and taxation.

Appendix: Methodology for Calculating Effective Rates of Protection

The estimates of the costs of production used to calculate the value added for wheat, cotton, basmati rice, and ordinary rice were based on data from the

Pakistan Agricultural Prices Commission for the average costs of all farmers in the Punjab in the 1982–1983 crop year (APCOM 1986). The cost of sugarcane production was based on data for 1975 from Ilahi (1978).

To construct a time series of the costs of production, I assumed constant technology and yields. Changes in the costs of production therefore derive from changes in input prices only. Time series of input costs are based on price indexes of fertilizer in nonagricultural goods and services, $P_{na}(t)$.

In calculating the cost of production under free trade and no change in exchange rates, I assumed the prices of all inputs changed except for goods with essentially no tradable component (manure). The new fertilizer price series was constructed using an estimate of the border price of fertilizer. The time series of other input costs were estimated using $P'_{na}(t)$, the index of the free-trade prices of nonagricultural goods and services.

The cost-of-production figures under free trade with equilibrium exchange rates were constructed in a similar manner.

Price indexes for nonagricultural goods and services (P_{na}, P'_{na} and P^*_{na}) were constructed using price indexes of imports, exports, and nontraded goods. P_{na} was defined as

$$P_{na} = w1 \cdot P_{mna} + w2 \cdot P_{xna} + (1 - w1 - w2) \cdot P_{nt}$$

where P_{mna} and P_{xna} are the price indexes of nonagricultural imports and exports, respectively, and P_{nt} is the price index of nonagricultural nontradables. Weights $w1$ ($= 0.05$) and $w2$ ($= 0.20$), the shares of nonagricultural importables and exportables in nonagricultural value added, were estimated using 1980–1981 data for GDP and value added (Ministry of Finance, Economic Survey 1987–1988). The nonagricultural export sector was estimated as value added in textiles, wearing apparel, cotton ginning, and sports equipment. The remainder of the value added in manufacturing was assigned to the nonagricultural import sector.

P_{mna} and P_{xna} are weighted averages of the domestic prices of the nonagricultural import and export goods used in the construction of P_m and P_x (Table A7.1). The Pakistan consumer price index (CPI) is used as a proxy for the index of nonagricultural nontradables (P_{nt}).

P'_{na} and P^*_{na} were constructed using estimates of the world prices of imports ($P_{mna}\$$) and exports ($P_{xna}\$$), measured in dollars and converted to rupees using the official and equilibrium nominal exchange rates, respectively.

TABLE A7.1   Equivalent Tariff Calculations for Pakistan, 1980–1981

Exports	Value (Mn Rs)	NRP[a] (%)	Imports	Value (Mn Rs)	NRP[a] (%)
Raw cotton	5,203.4	−24	Capital goods		
Cotton yarn	2,048.7	52	Iron, steel bars	76	116
Cotton cloth	2,389.6	61	Plates, sheets	1,512	116
Irri rice	2,730.6	−46	Hoop, strip iron	26	116
Basmati rice	2,871	−46	Rails, track	58	116
Fish	559.2	30	Iron, steel wire	50	106
Tanned leather	891.9	79	Tubes, pipes	281	58
Carpets, rugs	2,242.8	0[b]			
POL[c] products	1,675.2	53	Machinery		
Sports goods	312.3	106	Power generation	560	12
Raw wool	80.2	0[b]	Agricultural	1,048	14
Other	8,273.6	0[b]	Textile, leather	739	32
			Specialized	828	12
Total	29,278.5	2.7[d]	Electric power	742	12
			Motor vehicles	2,345	140
			Other	6,617	72[e]
			Consumer goods		
			Wheat	633	−41
			Other food	2,983	73[e]
			Petroleum products	1,774	53
			Medicines, drugs	936	11
			Printed matter	100	−9
			Other	1,340	73[e]
			Raw materials		
			Crude petroleum	9,840	53
			Petroleum products	3,585	53
			Edible oil	2,625	−11
			Chemicals	1,212	51
			Dyeing, tanning material	462	51
			Fertilizers	3,537	0
			Other chemicals	550	51
			Pig iron	120	116
			Ingots	383	116
			Other nonferrous metals	5	65
			Iron, steel forgings	20	116
			Copper	184	65
			Aluminum	234	65
			Others	8,130	72[e]
			Total	53,535	55.04[d]

a. Nominal rate of protection.
b. Assumed to equal zero.
c. Pakistan Oil Fields Limited.
d. Weighted average of the nominal rates of protection using trade weights.
e. Assumed to equal the average level of protection for the subsector.
SOURCE: World Bank (1987a); Naqvi and Kemal (1983a).

TABLE A7.2   Tariffs and Effective Exchange Rates in Pakistan, 1960–1987

Year	$1 + tm$ (1)	$1 - tx$ (2)	Equivalent tariff (3)	E (4)	Ex (5)	Em (6)
1960	2.34	1.65	1.42	4.78	7.89	11.19
1961	2.34	1.69	1.38	4.79	8.10	11.18
1962	2.36	1.62	1.45	4.77	7.74	11.25
1963	2.45	1.56	1.57	4.79	7.48	11.74
1964	2.52	1.62	1.55	4.79	7.77	12.06
1965	2.85	1.77	1.61	4.80	8.49	13.70
1966	2.73	1.64	1.67	4.79	7.84	13.07
1967	2.86	1.59	1.79	4.80	7.65	13.73
1968	3.01	1.66	1.81	4.79	7.95	14.40
1969	3.14	1.77	1.78	4.80	8.50	15.09
1970	3.02	1.73	1.74	4.79	8.30	14.45
1971	3.22	2.00	1.62	4.78	9.54	15.42
1972	2.65	1.78	1.48	5.56	9.92	14.73
1973	1.53	1.08	1.41	10.56	11.45	16.11
1974	1.33	0.90	1.47	9.90	8.93	13.15
1975	1.24	0.99	1.25	9.90	9.77	12.24
1976	1.44	1.19	1.21	9.90	11.75	14.28
1977	1.53	1.18	1.30	9.90	11.68	15.13
1978	1.46	1.17	1.24	9.90	11.58	14.41
1979	1.51	1.01	1.49	9.90	10.00	14.91
1980	1.55	0.96	1.62	9.90	9.49	15.35
1981	1.55	1.03	1.51	9.90	10.17	15.33
1982	1.44	1.04	1.38	10.55	11.01	15.17
1983	1.42	1.01	1.41	12.70	12.81	18.04
1984	1.47	1.05	1.40	13.48	14.21	19.85
1985	1.46	0.95	1.53	15.16	14.46	22.07
1986	1.52	1.00	1.51	16.13	16.18	24.47
1987	1.47	0.95	1.54	17.17	16.35	25.23

NOTE: (1) $1 + tm = Pmt/(Et \cdot Pmt^*)$. Pmt = weighted average of domestic wholesale price of importables = $\sum wi \cdot Pmi,t$. The weights for 1972–1987 (the 1960–1971 weights are in parentheses): manufacturing 0.55 (0.80), fuel 0.30 (0.04), fertilizer 0.05 (0.03), wheat 0.05 (0.10), and vegetable ghee 0.05 (0.03). Pmt^* = dollar price index of imports. (2) $1 - tx = Pxt/(Et \cdot Pxt^*)$. $Pxt = \sum wi \cdot Pxi,t$. The weights for 1972–1987 (the 1960—1971 weights are in parentheses): raw cotton 0.31 (0.44), cotton yarn 0.12 (0.18), cotton textiles 0.14 (0.19), basmati rice 0.33 (0.19), and petroleum 0.10 (0.00). (3) = (1)/(2). (5) = effective exchange rate for exports = (4) · (2). (6) = effective exchange rate for imports = (4) · (1).
SOURCE: Author's calculations based on IMF (1985a); IMF, *International Financial Statistics*, various years; and Pakistan, Ministry of Finance (various years).

Notes to Chapter 7

1. Alberto Valdés provided valuable guidance and support throughout the project. Romeo Bautista, A. R. Kemal, Anjum Nasim, Thomas C. Pinckney, and Jorge Quiroz also offered helpful comments. Special thanks go to Marcelle Thomas for her work as a research assistant and to Norma Bonifazi, who typed

the manuscript. The research for this paper was funded as part of USAID contract 391-0491-C-00-5033-00.

2. The effects of trade policies on the actual price of foreign exchange for exports (imports) can be given as the effective exchange rate for exports (imports), defined as

$$Ex = E \cdot (1 - tx) \tag{7.1}$$

and

$$Em = E \cdot (1 + tm), \tag{7.2}$$

where E is the official nominal exchange rate (E, Ex, and Em are expressed in rupees per unit of foreign currency), tx is the implicit export tax, and tm is the implicit import tariff.

3. Time series for tm and tx were constructed using price indexes for import and export goods based on the following equations:

$$1 + tm = P_m^d / EP_m^w \tag{7.3}$$

and

$$1 - tx = P_x^d / EP_x^w \tag{7.4}$$

where w indicates world prices. The indexes of the world prices of imports and exports (P_m^w and P_x^w) that I used were the import and export unit values, based on actual quantities and values of Pakistan's trade. The domestic price indices (P_m^d and P_x^d) were constructed using the domestic prices of major imports and exports. The two sets of weights used for the periods before and after 1971 were based on the value shares in total imports and exports. The $1 + tm$ and $1 - tx$ series were then multiplied by a constant to set the 1980–1981 values of tm and tx equal to the implicit import tariff and export tax values above. This methodology is similar to that of Diaz-Alejandro (1982). Sjaastad (1980) presents an alternate methodology based on the residuals of an estimated import demand function.

4. Changes in the effective exchange rates were calculated for the period between fiscal 1971 and 1973.

5. The real exchange rate is defined as the relative price of tradables to home goods. In this study, the actual real exchange rate was measured as

$$RER = E \cdot P_t^w / P_h, \tag{7.5}$$

where P_t^w and P_h are the world price of traded goods and the domestic price of home goods, respectively, and where the numerator represents a policy for the price of tradable goods. A weighted average of the wholesale price indexes of Pakistan's major trading partners is used to represent P_t^w:

$$\ln(P_t^w) = \text{sum } (w_i \cdot \text{WPI}_i/E_i) \tag{7.6}$$

where w_i, WPI_i and E_i are the weight, wholesale price index, and exchange rate (expressed in units of the country's own currency per dollar) of country i, respectively. The weights used are based on the average share of trade (exports plus imports of nonpetroleum products) of Pakistan's leading trading partners from 1972 to 1986. The weights are: United States 0.278, Japan 0.277, United Kingdom 0.160, the Federal Republic of Germany 0.146, Italy 0.080, and France 0.059 (these six countries accounted for almost half of Pakistan's trade in this period). An index of consumer prices in Pakistan was used as a proxy for the price of home goods, on the argument that home goods weigh heavily in this price index.

The effective real exchange rate indexes for imports and exports are defined as

$$\text{RER}_x = \text{RER} \cdot (1 - tx) \text{ , } (1981 = 100) \tag{7.7}$$

and

$$\text{RER}_m = \text{RER}x \cdot (1 + tm)/(1 - tx). \tag{7.8}$$

6. Bautista (1987b) derives an expression for ω as a function of the price elasticities of demand and supply for home goods:

$$\omega = em - nm/(em - nm + ex - nx), \tag{7.9}$$

where em and ex are the demand elasticities for home goods with respect to the relative prices of importables and exportables, respectively, and nm and nx are the corresponding supply elasticities.

7. Valdés (1986) discusses other determinants of the real exchange rate that are important in the Latin American context.

8. That is an index of $\text{RER}x = E(P_t^w/P_h)(1 - tx)$, where the numerator $E(P_t^w/P_h)$ represents a price index of the Pakistan trading partners that includes both exportables and importables.

9. The coefficient of LTRPOL differs slightly from the ω coefficient estimated in studies of other countries for which export taxes or subsidies were relatively small, since the dependent variable, log $\text{RER}x$, is not identical to the real exchange rate used in these studies. For example, Hurtado, Muchnik, and Valdés (1990) estimated a regression of the form

$$\log \text{RER} = a1 + b1 \cdot \log(1 + tm) + b2 \cdot \log(1 - tx) + b3 \cdot \log(X),$$

where X represents other variables in the equation. (Note that the term $b2 \cdot \log(1 - tx)$ was omitted in their regression because $\log(1 - tx)$ was approximately equal to zero in all years.)

The regression used in this study is of the form

$$\log RER_x = A1 + B1 \cdot \log(1 + tm) - B1 \cdot \log(1 - tx) + B3 \cdot \log(X).$$

The two regressions can be shown to be equivalent if $b1$ is constrained to equal $-b2 - 1$.

10. This procedure was carried out by using dummy variables DTRPOL, DLTT, and DRAID where

DTRPOL	=	LTRPOL	for 1960.1 to 1972.1
	=	0	for 1972.2 to 1987.1
DLTT	=	LTT	for 1960.1 to 1972.1
	=	0	for 1972.2 to 1987.1
DRAID	=	RAID	for 1960.1 to 1972.1
	=	0	for 1972.2 to 1987.1.

In the case of private transfers (RREMIT), comparable data were not available for most of the period before 1971 (the transfers were very small compared with those of the 1970s), so that no dummy variable for transfers was included. (DLTT and DLTT lagged one period were added as instrumental variables.)

Only the coefficients on DTRPOL and DRAID are significantly different from zero, an indication that there is no significant difference in the coefficients of the other explanatory variables in the two periods. For inflows of aid, the coefficients are approximately equal in absolute magnitudes but opposite in sign, an indication that aid flows were not a significant factor in explaining the real exchange rate in Pakistan before 1971. One reason may be that total aid flows (and not just the flows to West Pakistan) are the appropriate variable for that period

A full set of regressions is found in Dorosh and Valdés (1990).

11. The estimate from equation (7.7) was used for the calculations because the dummy variables used in the regressions over the entire sample period may not have adequately captured the massive structural changes in the economy resulting from the secession of Bangladesh. Equilibrium exchange rates calculated for the period before 1972 thus were calculated using an out-of-sample estimate of ω.

12. The Krueger, Schiff, and Valdés (1988) framework was also used by Hamid, Nabi, and Nasim (1990) in their estimations of the effects of policies on agricultural prices.

13. Strictly speaking, if the formula adjusts for P_{na}^*, the measure of the estimate rate adjustment becomes

$$\frac{P_{na}^* E_o}{P_{na} E^*} - 1. \tag{7.12}$$

14. Note that the formula for the nominal rate of protection can also be written in this form, but since the calculation of direct effects assumes no changes in overall trade policy or exchange rates,

$$P'_{na} = P_{na} \tag{7.15}$$

and

$$\text{NRP}i = (Pi/P_{na} - Pi'/P'_{na})/(Pi'/P'_{na}) = (Pi - Pi')/Pi'. \tag{7.16}$$

The methodology is described in the appendix.

15. The historical value of production of milk is high (Rs. 40,253 million in 1986–1987) compared with that of cereals (Rs. 28,502 million for wheat, and Rs. 2,692 million for basmati rice in the same period). This is reflected in the fact that the average protection on importables is positive in spite of the high taxation on cereals.

16. Or, equivalently, $\text{ERP}i = ([VAi/Vna] - [VAi'/Vna])/(VAi'/Vna)$

$$= (VAi - VAi')/VAi'. \tag{7.18}$$

17. See Hamid, Nabi, and Nasim (1990) and Dorosh and Valdés (1990) for quantitative estimates of the effects of these price changes on real output, consumption, and trade.

Yair Mundlak, Domingo Cavallo, and
Roberto Domenech

8

Agriculture and Growth:
The Experience of Argentina,
1913–1984

Economic growth generates significant changes in the sectoral composition of an economy. In the early stages of growth, an economy is
largely rural, while in mature economies, agriculture's role becomes far
smaller. Since a large portion of the world's population still lives in rural
areas, it is important to understand the dynamics of this shift. The
process can be placed in a broader perspective, because growth in mature economies generates other sectoral changes of great importance,
such as a shift toward services. The process is similar in many respects
to the process of industrialization.

Growth is generated by an accumulation of physical and human
capital and technological change. The rate of technological change and
its factor bias depend on the pace of capital accumulation. An increase
in the capital-labor ratio generates incentives for innovations aimed at
producing labor-saving techniques (Mundlak 1988). The appearance of
new, more productive labor-saving techniques affects the rates of intersectoral mobility.

Overall growth raises the possibilities for consumption. The utility
functions of consumers are not homothetic, and the income elasticity for
food is considerably smaller than one. Moreover, the price elasticity of
demand for food is low. Thus, an equiproportionate increase in output
will cause an excess supply in the income-elastic sector[1] and its relative

price will decline. The lower the price elasticity, the further the price will decline in response to a given amount of excess supply. As a result, the value of the output distributed to the factors of production in agriculture will decline, and their rates of return will fall relative to those obtained in nonagriculture. Resources will then move away from agriculture.

This simplified statement of the process omits many pertinent details. Because it applies to a closed economy, on the face of it, the behavior of open economies, such as that of Argentina, should be different. Since the world as a whole is a closed economy and the process is common to all countries, it generates global excess supply. That excess supply causes world agricultural prices to decline and affects exporting countries. Indeed, over the period 1900–1984 the world prices of the main agricultural products, deflated by U.S. wholesale prices, fell at an average annual rate of at least 0.5 percent a year (Binswanger et al. 1985). Thus, the necessary adjustment in factor allocation does not skip exporting countries.

Argentina's economy experienced a significant decline in the pace of agricultural growth after the 1930s. Was it the exclusive effect of a worldwide deterioration in the terms of trade for agricultural products, or was it mainly due to domestic economic policies? If policies played a role in reducing agricultural growth, was this phenomenon helpful to overall growth, or did it damage Argentina's performance? These are the main questions this chapter addresses. It examines the relationship between agriculture and overall economic growth in Argentina during the period 1913 to 1984 and looks, in particular, at the influences of economic policies on the sectoral composition of output and on the process of growth.

Historical Background

Until the Great Depression of the 1930s, agriculture was the backbone of the Argentine economy. Between 1860 and 1930, exploitation of the rich land of the pampas fostered economic growth, and Argentina grew more rapidly than the United States, Canada, Australia, and Brazil, which were all similarly endowed with rich land and received large inflows of capital and of European immigrants. As Table 8.1 shows, during the first three decades of this century, Argentina outgrew the other four countries in population, total income, and per capita income.

In the 1930s, however, Argentina's economic vitality began to deteriorate (Table 8.1), particularly in agriculture. A comparison of crop yields in Argentina and in the United States (plotted in Figure 8.1) during this period provides a clear picture of the dramatic changes that were taking place. From 1913 to 1930 and 1975 to 1984, U.S. agriculture tripled its yields, whereas Argentina could not even double them.

Macroeconomic and Trade Policies

Economic policies are classified here into two main groups: macroeconomic and trade. Macroeconomic policy includes decisions concerning the size of government expenditures, the way they are financed, and the rate of growth of the money supply.

TABLE 8.1   Comparative Growth in Population and Income in Selected Countries, 1900–1984 (average annual percentage rate)

	Argentina	Australia	Brazil	Canada	United States
1900–1904 to 1925–1929					
Population	2.8	1.8	2.1	2.2	1.1
Income	4.6	2.6	3.3	3.4	2.9
Per capita income	1.8	0.8	1.2	1.2	1.3
1925–1929 to 1980–1984					
Population	1.8	1.7	2.5	1.5	1.3
Income	2.8	3.9	5.5	3.9	3.1
Per capita income	1.0	2.2	3.0	2.4	1.8

SOURCE: Cavallo (1986).

FIGURE 8.1   Crop Yields in Argentina and the United States, 1913–1984 (1913 = 100)

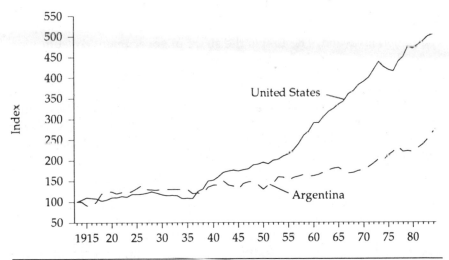

NOTE: This figure is based on a Divisia index of yields in fourteen crops in Argentina and the United States.
SOURCE: Mundlak, Cavallo, and Domenech (1989).

FIGURE 8.2   Government Expenditures in Argentina, 1913–1984
(percentage of total income)

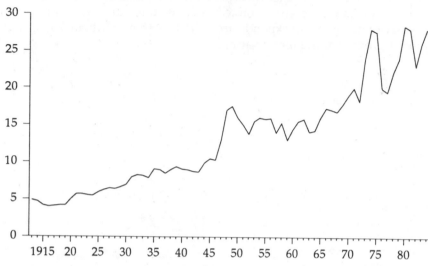

SOURCE: Mundlak, Cavallo, and Domenech (1989).

We constructed three relevant macroeconomic policy indicators for the period analyzed. The first is the share of government consumption in total income, which provides a measure of the size of government expenditures. As can be seen in Figure 8.2, government expenditures show a clear, long-term upward trend. (The actual values are plotted in solid lines; the dotted lines are discussed later.) Several significant ups and downs after the mid-1940s suggest a drastic increase in expenditures to levels that the government could not sustain. Therefore, the high levels were partly reversed after a few years.

Macroeconomic policies are also reflected in the fiscal deficit. Figure 8.3 plots the fiscal deficit, financed by borrowing, as a proportion of national income. After 1930, the deficit was much larger than previous levels, exceeding 10 percent of total income during some subperiods.

Figure 8.4 shows the rate of growth of the money supply over and above the rate of growth of output valued at foreign prices, that is, the rate of devaluation adjusted for real growth and foreign inflation. Note that monetary policy was very unstable after 1930, with large expansions in some years, followed by large contractions.

FIGURE 8.3   Fiscal Deficit by Source of Financing in Argentina
1913–1984 (percentage of total income)

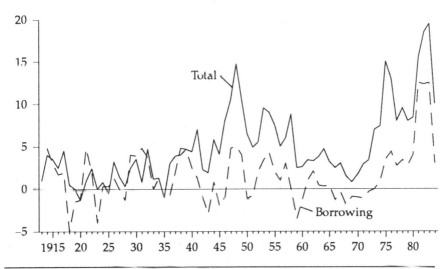

NOTE: This is the total fiscal deficit financed by borrowing and monetary expansion as a proportion of total income. Negative values are surpluses.
SOURCE: Derived from Instituto de Estudios Económicos sobre la Realidad Argentina y Latinoamericana (1986).

Trade policy encompasses taxes on exports and tariffs on imports, as well as quantitative restrictions on both sides of foreign trade. The shadowed area in Figure 8.5 indicates the wedge between domestic and foreign prices caused by the taxation on foreign trade. This wedge increased significantly after the Great Depression. The government adjusted taxes on imports so as to take into account the differential exchange rates for imports and exports.

In practice, whenever the official exchange rate for imports is set at a lower level than that for exports, there is an implicit subsidy for imports that has a counterbalancing effect on that of taxes. This was especially the situation between 1975 and 1976, when the rate for imports was considerably lower than that for exports.

The wedge became thinner in subsequent decades, but this by itself is not an indication of declining distortion. Taxes on exports and tariffs on imports were estimated by dividing actual tax revenues by the value of exports and imports, respectively, and as such do not reflect the effect of quantitative restrictions. Taxes were the most important, but not the

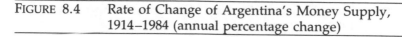

FIGURE 8.4   Rate of Change of Argentina's Money Supply,
1914–1984 (annual percentage change)

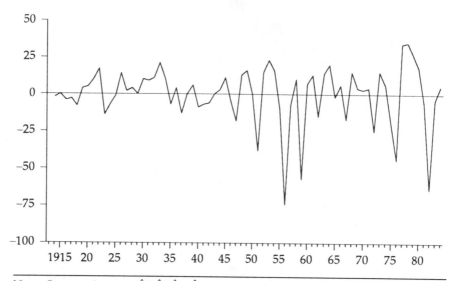

NOTE: Computed as $\hat{\mu} = \hat{M} - \hat{E} - \hat{P}^* - \hat{Y}$, where M is the M3 stock of money supply, E is the nominal exchange rate, P^* is the foreign price of Argentine imports and exports, Y is real output, and the hat above each variable indicates the rate of growth.
SOURCE: Derived from Instituto de Estudios Económicos sobre la Realidad Argentina y Latinoamericana (1986).

only, restriction on exports, whereas on the import side quantitative restrictions became dominant after the 1940s. Although there is no direct measurement of quantitative restrictions, they usually became more stringent whenever the exchange rate in the black market departed from the official rate. The black market premium is represented in Figure 8.6.

Analytic Framework

The analytic framework evolved from the idea that in dealing with economic dynamics, it is not meaningful to begin by assuming a long-term equilibrium and to infer from it current movements in the economy. On the contrary, such movements are largely determined by the state of the economy. Whether the economy will eventually reach the presently perceived point of long-term equilibrium depends largely on the economic signals that develop.

FIGURE 8.5   Indicators of Argentina's Trade Policy, 1913–1984
(1913 = 100)

NOTE: The average tax on exports is $1-t_x$ and the average tax on imports is $(1+t_m)$ (E^m/E), where t_x is the proportion of taxes collected on exports over the value of exports, t_m is the proportion of taxes collected on imports over the value of imports, E_m is the nominal exchange rate for imports, and E is the nominal exchange rate for exports.
SOURCE: Derived from Instituto de Estudios Económicos sobre la Realidad Argentina y Latinoamericana (1986).

This particular formulation, which was used to calculate sectoral growth in a previous study of the period 1947–1972 (Cavallo and Mundlak 1982), made it possible to evaluate the consequences of significant economic policies implemented in Argentina. As already mentioned, these policies mainly involved taxes on agriculture imposed either directly, through export taxes, or indirectly, through the protection of nonagriculture. The country maintained a large and highly inefficient public sector and, not independently, a highly overvalued peso. The present study shows that these policies caused agricultural growth to lag behind that observed in other countries producing grain and livestock, such as the United States.

That 1982 study also suggested that policies that harmed the performance of agriculture, especially those that were reflected in currency overvaluation, had a negative effect on overall growth. The present study looks at both issues in more detail over a longer period, from 1913 to 1984.[2]

FIGURE 8.6   Degree of Financial Openness in Argentina, 1913–1984

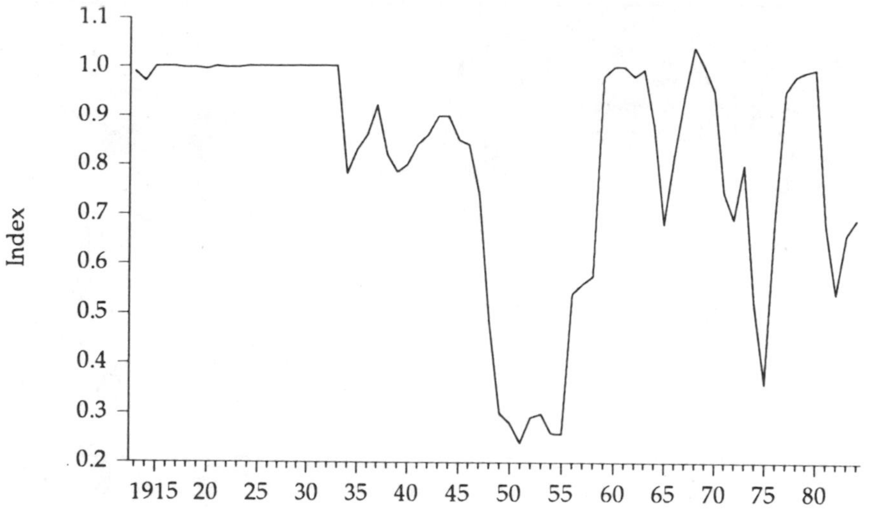

Note: This is the ratio E/E^b, where E is the official rate of exchange for exports and E^b is the rate of exchange in the black market.
Source: Mundlak, Cavallo, and Domenech (1989).

Sectoral Disaggregation

The analysis distinguishes three sectors: agriculture, nonagriculture excluding government, and government. Agriculture produces the bulk of exportable goods, while nonagriculture excluding government produces import substitutes. Economic policies have different effects on agriculture and nonagriculture because of two basic sectoral characteristics. First, agriculture is more capital-intensive than nonagriculture. The shares of capital in sectoral income are plotted in Figure 8.7 for each sector. As summarized in Table 8.2, the share of capital over the study period averaged 60 percent in agriculture and 42 percent in nonagriculture. Note, however, that toward the end of the period the difference became much smaller.

Second, agriculture is more internationally tradable than nonagriculture, as can be seen in Figure 8.8, which indicates the implicit shares of tradable commodities in sectoral output. Whereas agriculture had an average tradable component of 67 percent of sectoral output, nonagriculture averaged only 47 percent (Table 8.3).

FIGURE 8.7   Sectoral Shares of Capital in Argentina, 1913–1984
(percentage)

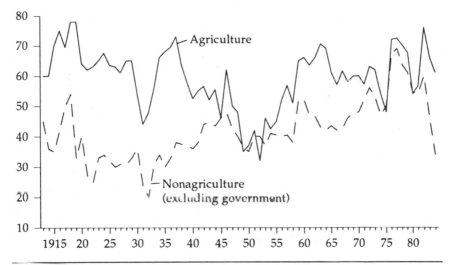

NOTE: This is the share of output that accrues to capital in each sector, computed as one
minus sectoral labor income.
SOURCE: Mundlak, Cavallo, and Domenech (1989).

TABLE 8.2   Sectoral Shares of Capital in Argentina, 1913–1984
(percentage)

Sector	Average share	Standard deviation	Maximum share	Minimum share
Agriculture	60	10	78	31
Nonagriculture excluding government	42	10	69	19

NOTE: Computed as one minus the ratio of the sector's labor income to sector's total income.
SOURCE: Mundlak, Cavallo, and Domenech (1989).

An Overview of the Model

Here we will consider the main characteristics of the model. The details
appear in Mundlak, Cavallo, and Domenech (1989).

The price of government services is taken as exogenous. The prices
of agriculture and nonagriculture in relation to the prices of government
are determined by the relative price of the traded component of each
sector and some macroeconomic policy indicators that influence the
price of the nontraded component. The prices of traded goods are

FIGURE 8.8   Sectoral Degree of Tradability in Argentina, 1913–1984 (percentage)

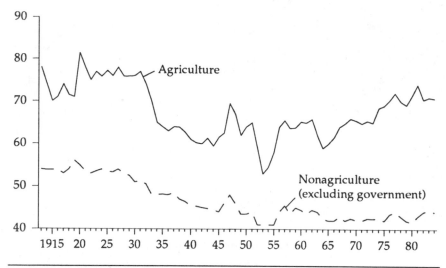

NOTE: This is the traded share in sectoral output.
SOURCE: Mundlak, Cavallo, and Domenech (1989).

TABLE 8.3   Sectoral Degree of Tradability in Argentina, 1913–1984 (percentage)

Sector	Average level	Standard deviation	Maximum level	Minimum level
Agriculture	67	6	81	53
Nonagriculture excluding government	47	4	56	42

SOURCE: Mundlak, Cavallo, and Domenech (1989).

determined by foreign prices and the taxes on foreign trade (both of which are taken to be exogenous) and the real rate of exchange (which is explained by the foreign terms of trade, commercial policy, and some macroeconomic policy indicators). The way each of the determining factors influences the real rate of exchange depends on the degree of commercial and financial openness of the economy.

The intersectoral allocation of resources and technology is given at any moment. The price of land, the price of livestock in relation to crops, and conditions in the credit market as they relate to agriculture determine the area under cultivation, a resource that is specific to the agriculture sector. Total employment is determined by wages and is allocated to agriculture by a function that explains the rate of labor migration from this sector. In turn, wage differentials, urban unemployment, and the price of land determine the migration rate. Labor that is not allocated to either agriculture or government is absorbed by nonagriculture. The additions of net investment determine the stock of physical capital. Investment, in turn, is assigned to agriculture by a function that is determined by the differential rate of return and the sectoral share of capital. Investment not assigned to agriculture or government goes to nonagriculture.

Since the intersectoral allocation of resources and technology is predetermined, sectoral outputs are also predetermined. The sectoral production functions depend on state variables. Some of the state variables are common to both sectors: the sectoral rates of return, the price of government services, the volatility of sectoral prices, and the degree of openness of the economy. Climatic conditions are a state variable for agriculture and fiscal deficits and public expenditures for nonagriculture.

The use of total output is determined by the demand for its components. Personal income and wealth determine the demand for private consumption, while the expected rate of return on capital, the acceleration in growth, and government actions regarding both public investment and the method chosen to finance the fiscal deficit define the demand for investment goods. Consumption and investment by the government are exogenous, and net exports are calculated as a residual.

Equations were estimated with the model for the real exchange rate, relative sectoral prices, cultivated land, total employment, labor migration, investment allocation, sectoral production and factor shares, consumption, private investment, and total trade. The estimated model closely reproduces not only the trends of Argentine growth in the period 1916–1984, but also the main cycles of the endogenous variables. The key to this simple explanation of the Argentine economy suggested by economic theory lies in the formulation of resource allocation and of changes in productivity. In explaining the response of the economy to economic forces, it is essential to take the state of the economy explicitly into account.

Supply Response

The model was used to compute the price elasticities for all the endogenous variables, assuming a permanent 10 percent increase in agricultural prices starting in 1950. This increase was matched by the necessary

TABLE 8.4   Price Elasticities of Output, Labor, Capital, and Land in Agriculture in Argentina

Period	Output	Labor	Physical capital	Land
1	0.19	0.00	0.05	0.03
2	0.24	0.06	0.12	0.06
3	0.31	0.14	0.19	0.08
4	0.38	0.19	0.24	0.11
5	0.43	0.21	0.30	0.14
10	0.51	0.26	0.65	0.27
15	0.73	0.15	1.07	0.41
20	0.99	0.02	1.45	0.56

NOTE: The elasticities are computed by imposing a 10 percent increase in the price of agriculture, compensated by a decline in the price of government services, in order to keep the general price level constant. The price of land is increased in the same proportion as the agricultural price.
SOURCE: Authors' calculations.

adjustment in the price of government services so as to keep the economy's price level at its historical levels. On average, the price of government services fell by 9 percent, the price of land rose by the same proportion as the price of agriculture, and government wages fell by the same proportion as the price of government services.

The computed elasticities of some of the endogenous variables are reported in Tables 8.4 and 8.5 for selected years. The results clearly indicate that agriculture responded to prices, although some time was required. By the fourth year after the price increase, output had moved up by 38 percent of the price change, implying an elasticity of 0.38. With time the elasticity converged to a value of 1. The response mainly resulted from a rapid process of capital accumulation.

Significantly, the effects of the changes in agricultural prices also had a positive effect on nonagricultural output—as a result of the more rapid capital accumulation that took place as a consequence of the response of aggregate investment to the rate of return. The rate of return rose because of the improvement in agricultural and nonagricultural prices relative to the price of government services (see Table 8.5). Note, also, that the economy's total output responded to the increase in agricultural prices, when it was offset by a decline in the price of government services, with an elasticity of 0.96 after twenty years.

Of course, the response would have been different if the 10 percent increase in agricultural prices had been matched by a proportional reduction in the price of nonagriculture (excluding government), rather than being offset by a reduction in the price of government services. The resulting reduction in the price of nonagriculture needed to offset the

TABLE 8.5   Price Elasticities of Output, Labor, and Capital in
Private Nonagriculture and in the Aggregate Economy
in Argentina

	Private nonagriculture			Aggregate economy		
Period	Output	Labor	Capital	Output	Labor	Capital
1	0.42	0.00	0.09	0.33	0.00	0.06
2	0.72	0.43	0.24	0.55	0.26	0.15
3	0.75	0.35	0.37	0.60	0.22	0.23
4	0.79	0.38	0.49	0.63	0.24	0.31
5	0.74	0.29	0.60	0.61	0.19	0.39
10	0.64	0.06	1.01	0.56	0.02	0.72
15	0.83	0.02	1.24	0.73	−0.05	0.95
20	1.08	0.06	1.34	0.96	−0.07	1.08

NOTE: The elasticities are computed by imposing a 10 percent increase in the price of agriculture, compensated by a decline in the price of government services, in order to keep the general price level constant. The price of land is increased in the same proportion as the agricultural price.
SOURCE: Authors' calculations.

increase in the price of agriculture was, on average, 2 percent. The results are not reported here because they support the results discussed above, namely, agriculture responded to the price incentives. Not surprisingly, the response of nonagriculture was negative. Consequently, the effect of this change in relative prices on aggregate output was also negative, although very close to zero.

The striking implication that emerges from these results is that transferring resources from nonagriculture to agriculture did not have a positive effect on aggregate output. In contrast, when resources were taken away from the government sector, the overall effect was positive and significant.

Simulating the Effects of Policy
Changes on Sectoral Growth

We used the model to simulate the effects of a program of trade liberalization and macroeconomic policy management. We did so by simulating the economy with the new relative prices that result from the alternative commercial and macroeconomic policies and by comparing the results with those obtained for the base run of the model.

Before presenting the simulation results, we outline the trade and macroeconomic policies assumed under the trade liberalization and macroeconomic policy management.

Macroeconomic Policies

We assumed that public expenditures as a proportion of income were at their actual levels except in the two periods during which drastic increases took place. Thus, we assumed that public expenditures grew smoothly from 1946 to 1953 and that from 1974 to 1984 they remained at the 1973 level.

The imposed values for the fiscal deficits financed by borrowing as a proportion of income are obtained by subtracting the amount by which public expenditures are reduced from their actual levels. In the case of the rate of monetary expansion over and above nominal devaluation, foreign inflation, and real growth, we assumed that this control variable is stabilized during the period 1930–1984, with an average value of −0.008 in those years.

Trade Policies

The simulation is based on the modification of trade policy beginning in 1930. It involved the elimination of taxes on exports, a uniform tariff of 10 percent on imports, and no restrictions on international financial transactions, that is, no premium in the black market for foreign exchange.

Results

Figures 8.9 to 8.12 compare the base-run values and simulated values of the degree of commercial openness, the real rate of exchange, the relative price of agriculture, and the relative price of nonagriculture excluding government. Relative prices responded strongly to the policy changes, as quantified in Table 8.6, which indicates the percentage increases in the simulated values in relation to the actual values.

These results imply that if the Argentine economy had been more integrated into the world economy after 1929, the volume of trade would have been almost 70 percent higher than its actual level. Moreover, relative prices would have been more in line with international prices. That is to say, price incentives would favor agriculture and nonagriculture at the expense of government. For the period 1930–1984, the price of agriculture would have been, on average, 40 percent higher, and the price of nonagriculture excluding government would have been almost 20 percent higher. In the two cases, the sectoral prices are relative to the price of government services. Of course, a greater supply of agricultural and nonagricultural goods (excluding government) could have weakened the increase in relative prices.

Table 8.7 summarizes the results of the simulation. The figures

FIGURE 8.9   Simulated Values for the Degree of Commercial
              Openness in Argentina, 1913–1984

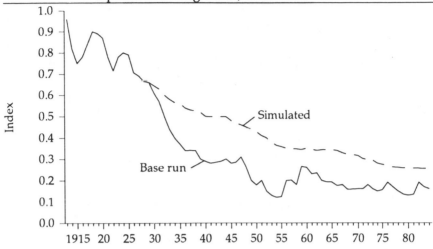

SOURCE: Mundlak, Cavallo, and Domenech (1989).

FIGURE 8.10   Simulated Values for the Real Exchange Rate in
               Argentina, 1913–1984

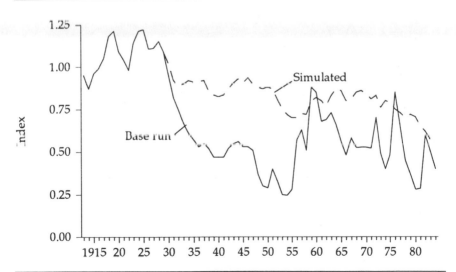

SOURCE: Mundlak, Cavallo, and Domenech (1989).

FIGURE 8.11   Simulated Values for the Relative Price of Agriculture
               in Argentina, 1913–1984

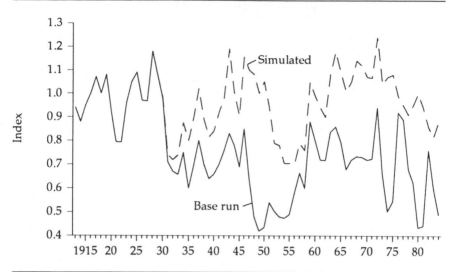

SOURCE: Mundlak, Cavallo, and Domenech (1989).

FIGURE 8.12   Simulated Values for the Relative Price of
               Nonagriculture in Argentina, 1913–1984

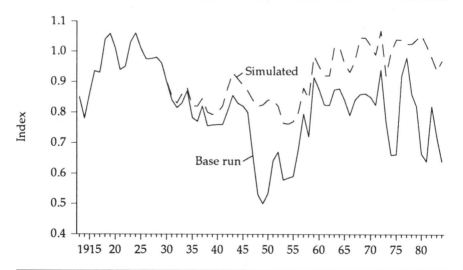

SOURCE: Mundlak, Cavallo, and Domenech (1989).

TABLE 8.6   Response of Relative Prices to Trade Liberalization in
Argentina, 1930–1984

| Variable | Average value for 1930–1984 | | Percentage increase $100[(2)/(1)-1]$ |
	Base run (1)	Simulated (2)	
Degree of commercial openness	.24	.40	67
Real rate of exchange	.54	.82	52
Relative price of agriculture	.68	.95	40
Relative price of nonagriculture	.77	.91	18

SOURCE: Mundlak, Cavallo, and Domenech (1989).

speak for themselves: a freer trade regime combined with monetary and fiscal discipline would have yielded substantially better economic performance, especially in the case of agriculture. According to these results, if the Argentine economy had operated under a more open trade regime after the Great Depression, in 1984 agriculture would have generated an output 115 percent higher than its actual level. This increase in production would have resulted from both the accumulation of capital and the increase in employment. Moreover, nonagriculture would also have performed better than it did under a more closed trade regime. In this case, the increased output is explained mainly by capital accumulation, but the higher degree of commercial openness also had a positive effect on factor productivity in nonagriculture.

Notes to Chapter 8

1. The basic determinant of the process is income elasticity, an empirical quantity. Many studies report income elasticities for food. As income increases, food is purchased with an increasing component of nonagricultural inputs, and therefore the income elasticity for the agricultural product is smaller than that reported for food. For details, see Mundlak (1985b).

2. The discussion is based on a comprehensive study of sectoral growth in Argentina (see Mundlak, Cavallo, and Domenech 1989).

TABLE 8.7   Effects of Alternative Economic Policies with Redistribution for Argentina, 1930–1984 (percentage of base-run value)

Endogenous variable	Average annual response		Response in 1984	
	Changes in monetary, exchange, and fiscal policies	All policy changes	Changes in monetary, exchange, and fiscal policies	All policy changes
Relative prices				
Price of land	9	29	32	46
Degree of openness	4	77	1	57
Real exchange rate	12	70	72	59
Agriculture (P_1/P_3)	12	45	72	81
Nonagriculture (P_2/P_3)	11	20	56	53
Agricultural sector				
Labor	5	31	0	64
Physical capital	5	26	20	59
Cultivated land	7	22	2	37
Output	12	42	41	115
Wages	3	18	18	26
Rate of return	15	47	104	140
Nonagricultural sector (excluding government)				
Labor	2	−1	7	−8
Capital	5	20	33	50
Output	8	23	47	65
Wages	2	5	6	6
Rate of return	10	23	74	106
Government sector				
Labor	−4	−15	−24	−35
Wages	−5	−2	−11	6
Aggregate economy				
Labor	2	2	1	−3
Total capital	5	19	23	41
Output	8	24	40	63
Private consumption	10	27	46	70
Private investment	12	32	92	112
Exports	12	124	53	187
Imports	13	118	24	114
Wages	0	3	4	3

NOTE: Results reported in this table assume a tax-subsidy mechanism to transfer income from nonwage to wage earners.
SOURCE: Authors' calculations.

Chilean Agriculture in a Changing Economic Environment

On the whole, the share of agriculture in total output declines during the process of economic growth. The main reason for this is the low income elasticity for food. A small open economy can overcome the demand constraint on the growth of agricultural production, however, by expanding its net exports. Chile serves as a good example; its share of agriculture in total output averaged 9.46 percent in the period 1986–1990, compared with an average value of 9.66 percent in the period 1960–1964 (Figure 9.1). The relative long-term constancy of this share in Chile is a sharp departure from the experience of most countries. (The option of maintaining a constant share is not open to all countries at once because that would be inconsistent with income-inelastic demand.)

In the short term, however, the share of agriculture in total output in Chile was not stable, it fluctuated over the thirty-year period and reached its lowest level of 7 percent in 1973, the last year of the Allende government. The time path of the agricultural share in total output is determined by the differential growth rates of agriculture and nonagriculture, and these varied considerably over time in Chile as elsewhere. In this paper we examine the causes for this variability, with reference to the changing policies within the broader issue of the determinants of sectoral growth.

FIGURE 9.1   Share of Agriculture in Total Output and Total
Employment in Chile, 1960–1990

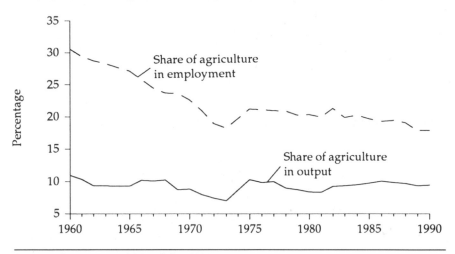

SOURCE: Coeymans and Mundlak (1992).

Economic growth is achieved through the accumulation of physical and human capital and changes in the available technology. By and large, the theoretical growth literature concentrates on the long-run aspects of the growth process and takes no account of the prevailing economic environment. Does this provide us with a good guideline for empirical analysis? In reviewing the Chilean experience in Figure 9.2, we note that over the period 1936–1970 per capita income grew at a fairly steady rate of 1.6 percent per year. This growth was interrupted as a result of the shocks to the economy introduced initially by the Allende government (1970–1973) and the difficulties of returning to normality, by whatever definition of normality one wishes to use, and by the recessions of 1975 and 1982 triggered mainly by unfavorable external conditions. Basically, there are two periods of catching up: 1976 to 1981, which was followed by a deep recession in 1982, and the period of continuous growth beginning in 1983. Both the fall and the subsequent rise of output are results of exogenous events and policies. These policies, in part specific to agriculture and in part general, affected the economic environment and thereby affected growth performance. The economic environment affects sectoral growth through its effects on factor productivity and resource allocation.

The challenge for empirical analysis is to relate the changes in the

FIGURE 9.2   Per Capita Gross Domestic Product in Chile, 1909–1990

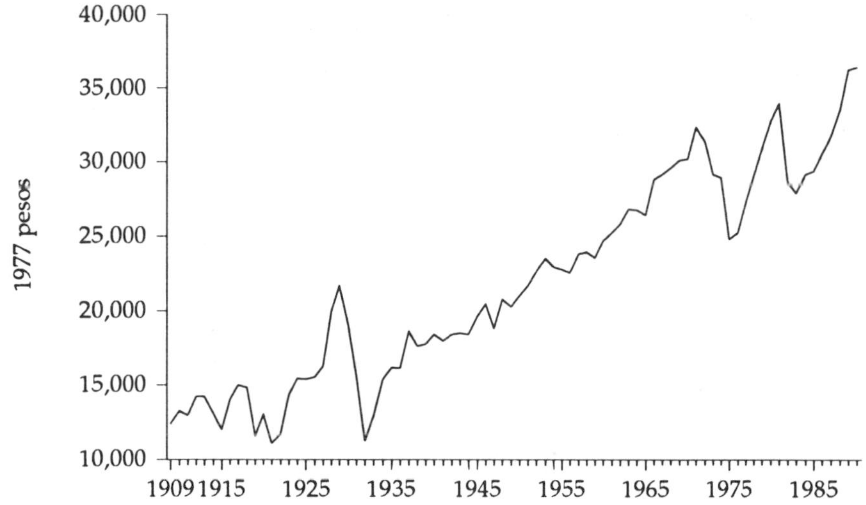

SOURCE: Coeymans and Mundlak (1992).

economic environment to the performance of the economy. This is not a simple matter because there is no obvious dominant relationship between any of the natural variables, such as prices and output. The analysis and the results presented here are based on a detailed study, Coeymans and Mundlak (1992), which will be outlined below. We then present some empirical results for key equations used in a dynamic simulation of the economy intended to evaluate the response of agriculture, and more generally the composition of the economy, to changes in prices and investment. The discussion then concludes with a summary view of the dynamics of Chilean agriculture. To place all this within an appropriate context, we briefly review some of the pertinent economic policies in the study period and beyond.

Review of Policies

The study period covers four very different administrations in Chile: Alessandri (1958–1964), Frei (1964–1970), Allende (1970–1973)—who tried to implement a socialist regime—and the military regime of Pinochet (1973–1990). Their widely different economic policies, combined with changing, and at times volatile, external events—particularly the terms of trade and international rates of interest—strongly affected the performance of the economy. The outcome is well illustrated in Figure 9.2, which shows the per capita gross domestic product (GDP) in the period within a historical perspective.

To provide background on the prevailing economic environment, we briefly review some of the important events that affected agriculture directly or indirectly, through the effect on the economy. The section on general economic policies draws on Coeymans and Mundlak (1992), and the description of the agricultural programs draws on Hachette and Rozas (1992) as well as on Valdés, Muchnik, and Hurtado (1990).

The period 1960–1990 can be divided into two major periods: 1960–1973, with civilian governments, and 1973–1990, with a military government. The first period can be further divided into the pre-Allende and the Allende (1970–1973) subperiods. The prevailing economic thinking in the 1960s saw an important role for the government in regulating the economy. This resulted in broad economywide intervention, including in agriculture. These policies were greatly intensified under the Allende government.

The military government that took control in September 1973 wasted no time in implementing drastic changes in the economic policies, shifting to a market orientation. The first subperiod, 1973–1982, was marked by measures designed to stabilize and liberalize the economy, leading to a recovery that was terminated by a recession in 1982–1983. In the remaining subperiod, 1984–1990, the economy emerged from the recession and started a remarkable growth process that has continued to the present under the new government.

The sections below describe some of the main events in the macroeconomic environment.

Fiscal Deficits and Inflation

The fiscal deficit was relatively low in the 1960s and was further reduced at the end of that decade, but a huge increase under Allende led to inflation on the order of 700 percent. The deficit was reduced beginning in 1974, and inflation has declined since 1975, almost reaching international levels in the early 1990s.

Exchange Rate Policies

The exchange rate was fixed until 1962, and from 1964 to 1970 a passive crawling peg was used. The Allende regime adopted exchange rate controls and multiple exchange rates. When the military government took power in 1973, it relied on a mixture of a passive crawling peg and sudden changes until 1977, when it adopted an active crawling peg.

From 1979 to 1982 the government returned to a fixed exchange rate, which it abandoned in mid-1982.

Trade Policies

A foreign exchange crisis at the end of 1961 led to import controls. Controls declined after 1965, and a modest liberalization of trade took place at the end of the 1960s, but it was reversed under the Allende administration. Trade interventions took the form of export and import prohibitions, import quotas, tariffs, and multiple exchange rates. In 1973 the highest exchange rate was fifty times higher than the lowest one. A massive trade liberalization began in 1975, and almost all trade controls were significantly reduced or eliminated. Quantitative import restrictions were abolished. Tariffs ranging from 5 percent to 750 percent were gradually adjusted to a uniform 10 percent in June 1979. Capital goods, which had been legally exempted from custom duties, were subject to the same uniform tariff. The principle of a uniform exchange rate for trade was maintained. As a result of this and other policies, exports have grown at a high rate since the mid-1970s.

Agricultural Policies

The price policies of the 1960s were guided by the objective of maintaining low food prices in order to suppress demand for higher urban wages. Price policies, consisting mainly of price controls, concentrated on products with an important weight in the consumer price index. To partly offset the negative effects of low prices on farmers, some inputs were subsidized. The controls intensified in the early 1970s under the Allende administration and resulted in black markets and queuing for basic commodities. The growing degree of intervention considerably increased the number and size of public agencies needed to administer the programs.

By the end of 1973, the majority of price controls were eliminated, with the exception of the prices for wheat, maize, rice paddy, and sunflower, which were fixed until 1977 with the intervention of a procurement agency. The subsidies on agricultural inputs were eliminated in 1974. To reduce the effects of price increases on low-income families, some subsidies were temporarily granted. Price bands were operational during 1977–1978 on wheat, oilseeds, and sugar. The price bands were dismantled in 1979, and for the first time, after a long period of intervention, agricultural prices were largely free of intervention. The change in policy reduced the demand for public agencies dealing with agriculture. Consequently their scope and number were drastically reduced; some were privatized, and the others were eliminated.

The severe recession of 1982–1983 resulted in some policy modifications. After direct intervention in some agricultural prices in 1982 and 1983, the government introduced price bands for wheat, oilseeds, and sugar. Also, there was intervention in prices for some other agricultural products. Tariffs were subject to some contradictory adjustments, and nontariff barriers were raised. The uniform tariff was raised to 20 percent in March 1983 and to 35 percent in September 1984 and reduced back to 30 percent in March 1985, to 20 percent in June 1985, and to 15 percent in January 1988. Nevertheless, the rates remained uniform and without exceptions. At the same time export promotion policies were intensified, and for the first time agricultural exports were not discriminated against relative to the exports of other sectors.

The military government followed essentially nondiscriminatory credit, debt, and investment policies in the liberalization of the economy. Among the measures that affected the agricultural sector were the elimination of quantitative limits on commercial lending operations, the progressive raising and ultimate elimination of the legal ceiling on interest rates, the progressive fading of special credit lines to the private sector, the implementation of subsidies to stimulate investment in forestry, and the establishment of the same treatment for national and foreign investors.

Land Reform

An important measure affecting agriculture is the land reform introduced in 1965 by the incoming Frei administration (1964–1969). Until 1969, the criterion used for expropriation of land was inefficiency in farm operation. As the reform progressed under the Allende administration (1969–1973), the procedures followed had less to do with efficiency considerations and more with the sole objective of land redistribution. The landowners in the commercial farm sector began to lose interest in improving productivity and instead tried to minimize their losses due to expropriation. This increasingly aggressive expropriation policy led to unrest among farm workers, who wished to expropriate the farms on which they worked, disregarding the efficiency criterion that might have existed at the time. The process eventually led to near paralysis of the commercial farm sector in 1973. Over the period 1965–1973 about 48 percent of the country's agricultural land was expropriated.

When the military government came to power it was generally recognized that the land reform process fell short of fulfilling the expectations of the previous period. Only a small fraction of rural poor people had access to land. Thus expropriations were stopped altogether at the end of 1973, and expropriated land was distributed. In contrast to the previous governments, the military administration favored individually owned family farms. The government returned illegally expropriated lands to their owners, but it took more than three years to do so.

All these changes led to the liberalization of land, labor, and capital markets, but the pace was slower than that achieved in the product market. The performance of the land market was improved, however, by the strengthening of property rights, the correction of problems in the legal system, and the liberalization of land leasing and land partition. It has been argued that the resulting division of land created an active land market that was conducive to the entry of small entrepreneurs into the rapidly growing fruit production industry.

The taxation of agriculture was based on imputed income of unimproved land. The income was largely underestimated in the first period, but farm investment nevertheless remained relatively low, essentially because of an environment characterized by insecure property rights and confusing signals given out by government rules. In the second period, agricultural taxation continued to be based on the imputed income of unimproved land, but values were corrected upward.

An Overview of the Model

The Impact of Policies

The economic environment is affected by the collection of all policies, as well as by exogenous variables such as those coming from the world markets or induced by weather. Clearly, when so much is happening, it is difficult to relate changes in the variables of interest to any particular policy. The task in building a framework for analysis is to formulate the main forces that affect the performance of the economy and to evaluate the effect of the policies in question. An efficient and practical way to summarize the effect of the various forces is to examine their effect on the economic incentives and constraints to producers' decisions. The following gives an overview of such a framework. It is extracted from a more comprehensive study that analyzes in detail a five-sector model consisting of agriculture, mining, manufacturing, services, and government (Coeymans and Mundlak 1992).

Factor markets.   Lack of instantaneous factor mobility results in uneven rates of return across sectors. The intersectoral differences in income returns determine the pace of labor and investment allocation across sectors. Off-farm labor migration also depends on the employment conditions in nonagriculture. This migration and the natural growth of the labor force determine the labor supply to agriculture and nonagriculture. The labor demand is determined by the production function, and the agricultural wage is determined so as to equate supply and demand.

In nonagriculture the prevailing sectoral wages are determined autonomously, through negotiation of government wage guidelines, in a way that resulted in urban unemployment. The sectoral real wages in nonagriculture were negatively affected by unemployment and by the acceleration of inflation, which is taken here as exogenous.

Total investment is allocated among sectors according to the expected differentials in the sectoral rates of return, taking into account institutional forces prevailing in the economy. The rates of return are determined endogenously, conditional on prices, technology, and resource allocation.

Technology. A distinction is made between available and implemented technology. The implementation of available technology is determined by economic variables and as such it is endogenous. Technology changes affect factor demand and thereby factor prices, resource allocation, and hence, output.

Intermediate inputs. In addition to primary inputs—labor, capital, and land—each sector uses products of other sectors as intermediate inputs. The relationships between the output of the various sectors is summarized by an input-output table that is allowed to vary every year.

Prices. The explicit inclusion of intermediate inputs calls for a distinction between sectoral prices of gross output and those of value added. Prices of gross output, deflated by the price of the consumption good (*PC*), are determined by the prices of traded components (export and import) and the sectoral wages. The weights for each of these components reflect their importance in total output, so that the effects of foreign prices and of commercial policies depend on the degree of tradability of sectoral outputs.

Profits of each sector are calculated as the difference between sectoral value added on the one hand and wages, depreciation, and indirect taxes on the other. Sectoral rates of return are equal to profits, net of taxes, divided by the value of capital stocks.

An Overview of the Empirical Analysis

In what follows we review the important empirical equations for agriculture. Similar equations are obtained for nonagriculture but are not discussed here, although they affect the working of the model; for details see Coeymans and Mundlak (1992).

Agricultural Supply of Labor

Assuming a constant participation rate in the labor force, the agricultural supply of labor at time t is obtained by adjusting the labor force of $t - 1$ by the natural growth rate and subtracting from it the off-farm migration. The empirical migration equation is

$$m = -0.052 + 0.051 \ln RL_{t-1} + 0.116 \ln d_{t-1}$$
$$\quad\ (1.5) \qquad (2.2) \qquad\qquad\qquad (3.3)$$

$$+ \ 0.238 \ln (1 - UN_t) + 0.050 \ln P_{1Ct-1} + 0.056\ D72$$
$$\quad (2.6) \qquad\qquad\qquad (1.2) \qquad\qquad (3.2)$$

$$R^2 = 0.72,\ D.W. = 1.9,$$

where, m is the ratio of off-farm migration to the agricultural labor force, d is a measure of the income differential between agriculture and nonagriculture, UN is the rate of unemployment in nonagriculture, RL is the ratio of the labor force in nonagriculture to that of agriculture, and P_{1C} is the real agricultural price deflated by PC. Numbers in parentheses throughout the paper are the absolute values of the t ratios. The reported R^2 corresponds to a dynamic simulation of the block of equations pertaining to agriculture.

The result indicates that an increase in the income gap between nonagriculture and agriculture increases the migration rate, whereas unemployment in nonagriculture has an opposite effect.

The agricultural labor force is presented in Figure 9.3. The results of the estimated migration equation explain the variability in this labor force, which declined from 707,000 workers in 1960 to 515,000 in 1973, a fall of 27 percent. The average annual migration rate for the period 1960–1973 was 3.86 percent.

The situation changes drastically after 1973. The average migration rate for the post-1974 period was 0.39 percent. This rate was smaller than the natural rate of population growth, and as a result agricultural employment increased. The fall in the migration rate was the result of the shrinking of the income differential and of a large increase in nonagricultural unemployment. Unemployment in nonagriculture increased from an average rate of 7.8 percent during the period 1960–1973 to 15.8 percent during the period 1974–1982 (Figure 9.4). The outcome of all this was an increase in agricultural employment from 515,000 workers in 1973 to 591,000 in 1982, an increase of 14.7 percent.

FIGURE 9.3   Labor Force in Agriculture in Chile, 1960–1982

SOURCE: Coeymans and Mundlak (1992).

Figure 9.5 presents real wages in agriculture. Their path is different from that of wages in nonagriculture. This is particularly the case in the 1960s when agricultural employment was declining and wages were on an upward trend.

Technology

The relationships between the output of the various sectors are summarized by an input-output table. Thus, agricultural output is defined as a sum of the intermediate inputs and value added:

$$X_1 = \sum_i A_{1j} X_j + V_1,$$

where X_1 is gross agricultural output in 1977 prices, A_{1j} = input-output coefficients, $j = 1,...,5$ is the sector index ($j = 1$ for agriculture), and V_1 is real agricultural value added to be determined as a function of primary inputs.

The production function is analyzed using the choice-of-technique approach, which differentiates between available and implemented technology. Producers are assumed to choose the techniques of production

FIGURE 9.4   Unemployment in Nonagriculture in Chile, 1960–1982

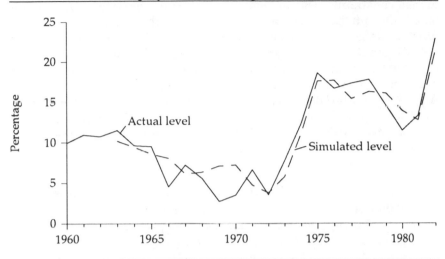

SOURCE: Coeymans and Mundlak (1992).

FIGURE 9.5   Real Wages in Agriculture in Chile, 1960–1982

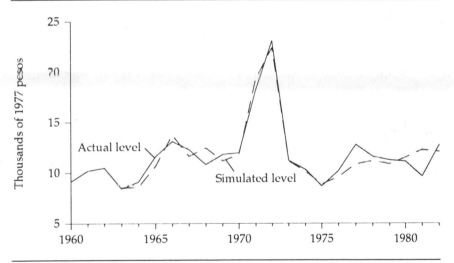

SOURCE: Coeymans and Mundlak (1992).

so as to maximize profits, given the economic environment and subject to their constraints. The implemented techniques are determined simultaneously with the level of inputs and therefore the aggregate production function, as is commonly used, is not uniquely defined. In general, the best we can do is to approximate the aggregate production function by a function that includes, in addition to the inputs, the state variables that determine the choice of techniques. A similar system was estimated for Argentina by Mundlak, Cavallo, and Domenech (1989).

The empirical function has the form of a Cobb-Douglas function with one major difference: the coefficients depend on the state variables. The state variables represent the incentives and constraints. Specifically, in the case of agriculture we use the following variables:

1. *The rate of return to capital.* This variable represents the profitability of agriculture. It is a summary measure that reflects not only the product prices, but also the prices of intermediate goods and the various explicit as well as implicit taxes and subsidies. In the analysis we use the expected value, as determined from autoregression on past values.

2. *Technology.* Technology, broadly defined, is captured by the historical maximum of the average labor productivity (a three-year moving average), referred to as PEAK. For details see Coeymans and Mundlak (1992).

3. *Agrarian reform.* This variable is represented by the proportion of land expropriated in a given year, UAR, as well as by the stock of the expropriated land. The latter was not significant and is not included here. The criterion for expropriation was changed in 1969, and we therefore include a dummy variable for this period, D6973, as well as a dummy variable for the last year of the Allende period, D73.

$$\ln V = 20.82 + 14.44\,r - 1.94\,\text{PEAK} + 0.0055\,\text{UAR} - 1.11\,\text{D73}$$
$$\quad\;\;(2.4)\quad\;(2.7)\quad\;\;(2.3)\qquad\qquad(4.8)\qquad\qquad(3.5)$$

$$+0.191 + S\ln k + \ln L\,; \qquad\qquad R^2 = 0.95;\; D.W. = 2.07;$$
$$\;\;(7.7)$$

$$S = -1.73 - 1.04\,r + 0.24\,\text{PEAK} - 0.00034\,\text{UAR} - 0.00014\,\text{UAR D6973}$$
$$\quad\;(2.5)\quad\;(2.5)\quad\;\;(3.6)\qquad\quad(3.4)\qquad\qquad(3.4)$$

$$-0.0665\,\text{D73} - 0.1907\,\text{D82}\,; \qquad R^2 = 0.84;\; D.W. = 2.02;$$
$$\;\;(2.7)\qquad\qquad(7.7)$$

where k is the ratio of capital (including land) to labor in agriculture.

The output elasticities vary throughout the sample. Their mean values are: 1.14 for the PEAK, 1.26 for the rate of return, and 0.67 for the capital elasticity. Except for 1982, where a distortion was included, the elasticities of capital are equal to the capital shares.

The estimated coefficient of the expected rate of return in the share equation is negative, showing that the set of techniques became more labor intensive when the expected rate of return increased. This result is consistent with the large expansion in the agricultural labor demand—reflected in higher wages and employment—observed during the post-sample years when a sizable real devaluation led to important increases in agricultural profitability.

The estimated positive coefficient of the PEAK in the share equation reveals that in the long run there is a tendency to incorporate labor-saving techniques. Physical, as well as human, capital is a carrier of innovations. Therefore, the availability of comprehensive capital represented by the peak is the most important constraint on the adoption of new techniques. The higher the capital availability, the more capital intensive will be the implemented techniques.

The elasticity with respect to the agrarian reform variable is positive for the first period of the reform (1965–1968) and negative during the second period (1969–1973). The effect of the agrarian reform on the capital share is negative, so that the share of labor in total income increased with the reform. The uncertainty with respect to property rights in commercial or private agriculture led farmers to implement techniques that were less capital intensive as a way of preventing capital from being expropriated. This explanation also applies to the coefficient of the dummy for 1973 in the share equation. The elasticity of the dummy for 1973 was negative [1]

Prices

Agricultural commodities are in principal largely tradable, and their prices are strongly influenced by world prices. The link between the world and domestic prices, however, can be completely distorted by domestic policies. This was indeed the case during the first part of the sample period. The price and trade liberalization processes that started in 1974–1975 in the economy at large were not immediately applied to agriculture. They were implemented only gradually, and as indicated above, in 1977 the government was still intervening in the determination of prices of wheat, sugar beets, and oilseeds. The liberalization of agriculture reached its high point by 1981, but interestingly, a new wave of direct intervention, although much more moderate than the one that had previously prevailed, started after the sample period.

In view of this record, we can expect the role of world prices in influencing domestic prices to vary over the period in accordance with the changing policies. To take this into account, we conduct the

Table 9.1   Agricultural Price Equation for Chile, 1975–1982

	1975–1982	1976–1982	1977–1982
Constant	−0.136	−0.128	−0.112
	(4.3)	(4.7)	(4.7)
P_{1T}	0.251	0.409	0.677
	(1.9)	(3.0)	(3.7)
Adjusted R^2	0.28	0.56	0.72
D.W.	1.08	1.52	1.78

Source: Coeymons and Mundlak (1992).

empirical analysis by subperiods. This reduces the number of observations considerably, and therefore it is necessary to keep the number of parameters to minimum. We thus aggregate the exportables and importables, using their relative weights in trade, to obtain a price index of the traded component, P_{1T}. This price is deflated by PC. We then regress the log of the domestic prices on the log of the price of tradables. The elasticity of the tradable price was not significantly different from zero for the period 1962–1974 nor was it significant for the whole sample period of 1962–1982. As Table 9.1 shows, however, the results are different for the period of liberalization.

The value of the elasticity changes from 0.25 when computed for the period 1975–1982 to 0.68 for the period 1977–1982. Thus the importance of the tradable price increases as we drop the years of strong intervention. Of course, the exercise of eliminating observations cannot go much farther because of the small sample size.

What is then the relevant value of the elasticity of the tradable price? This is a legitimate question considering the fragile nature of the results. The answer is somewhat indirect in that we refer to a similar study for Argentina for a much longer period, 1913–1984, by Mundlak, Cavallo, and Domenech (1989, 41). To be exact, the large sample for Argentina facilitated a more elaborate analysis that, among other things, allowed the elasticity of the tradable price to vary with the degree of openness. The average value of this elasticity for the period as a whole was 0.67. This result provides support for the value of 0.68 that we obtain for the six years 1977–1982 as a measure of tradability for the period with relatively little intervention.

Investment

The share of agriculture in total investment was estimated within a larger system that includes the equations for the other sectors of the economy. The system imposes the homogeneity property in the rates of return, which implies that an equal increase in all rates leaves the investment allocation unchanged. We report here only the equation for agriculture:

$$\theta = 0.182 + 0.403\ R_1^e - 0.091\ R_3^e - 0.312\ R_5^e - 1.063\ I/K + 0.373\theta_{t-1}$$
$$\quad\ (5.6)\quad\ (2.3)\qquad\quad (1.3)\qquad\quad (*)\qquad\quad (2.5)\qquad\quad (2.9)$$

$$R^2 = 0.56,\ D.W. = 1.92$$

where I is overall investment, K is the overall capital stock, R_1^e, R_3^e, and R_5^e are the expected rates of return in agriculture, manufacturing, and services respectively, and * indicates that the coefficient was obtained by using a restriction on the model. The equation shows that there is substitution between agriculture and manufacturing and between agriculture and services. The rate of return of mining, however, does not affect agriculture.

The Working of the Model

The foregoing equations are part of the larger five-sector model. By way of summary, it is useful to review the working of the model in response to a change in relative prices, holding total resources and, to a large extent, technology constant. In the simulation we change product prices. This change immediately affects the price of intermediate inputs, and as a result the price of value added changes in accordance with the input-output relationships. This in turn changes the ratios of wages and rates of return to value-added prices. The changes in the rates of return affect sectoral allocation of investment, and thereby the sectoral capital stocks. The changes in the rates of return, and investment in the case of manufacturing, also affect sectoral productivity.

The change in the sectoral wage-price ratios changes the sectoral employment in nonagriculture and, consequently, the sectoral capital-labor ratios. Unemployment in nonagriculture is determined as the difference between total demand and supply of labor at the going wages. Unemployment affects nonagricultural wages. In agriculture, the wage rate clears the labor market. The farm and off-farm income differentials and unemployment levels affect off-farm migration and, consequently, the labor supply in agriculture and nonagriculture. The changes in sectoral capital-labor ratios affect the marginal productivity of capital and rates of return and thus the investment in the next period. Although the model is largely recursive, several variables are determined simultaneously.

Changes in Relative Prices

Much of the ideological basis for agricultural policies, particularly in Latin America, rests on the assumption that agricultural output is unaffected by prices, or simply that it is supply inelastic. This conclusion was derived initially from casual observations and later on from simple-minded regression analysis in which outputs were regressed against prices. To say that agricultural output is supply inelastic is to say either that farmers are indifferent to income or that they have no way to take advantage of changing opportunities. It is probably the latter that led to the view that agricultural supply is inelastic. Such a view cannot be treated as a legitimate ideological position and should be evaluated within the appropriate framework, as we now proceed to do.

To isolate the price effect, we evaluate the response of the economy to an exogenous change in price conditional on the historical values of overall supplies of labor and capital. The results of such an exercise indicate mainly the substitution effect among sectors and as such underestimate the full impact of the price change.

Our interest is in the change in relative prices; therefore, in order to maintain the price level at its historical value, the increase in the agricultural price is compensated for by a decrease in the price of services. The increase in the agricultural price can be interpreted as an elimination of tax on agriculture.

The impact on the economy of a 1 percent change in the agricultural price is summarized in Table 9.2 for selected years. The response is measured relative to a base run obtained by solving the model by a dynamic simulation using the historical values for the exogenous variables. We now review the main results.

Output

There is a substantial increase in agricultural output, capital, and labor that builds up with time. Output increases by 0.58 percent in the fifth year and by 1.01 percent after ten years. This amounts to a ten-year supply elasticity of unity. Thus, if for example the average price distortion in Chilean agriculture were 20 percent, its correction would imply an increase in sectoral output of approximately 20 percent. The initial response is weaker, and it takes ten years to reach this level. This response is substantial even though it represents only the substitution effect in that it is evaluated conditional on fixed resources and technology.

Where does the agricultural expansion come from? It comes at the expense of manufacturing and services output. Although the declines in manufacturing and services outputs are important, they are relatively

TABLE 9.2   Effect of a 1 Percent Increase in Chile's Agricultural
Price in Selected Years, 1963–1982 (percentage)

Year	1963	1967	1972	1977	1982
Product price					
Agriculture	1.000	1.000	1.000	1.000	1.000
Mining	0.000	0.000	0.000	0.000	0.000
Manufacturing	0.000	0.004	0.056	0.076	0.099
Services	−0.209	−0.214	−0.289	−0.315	−0.347
Value-added price					
Agriculture	1.726	1.726	1.745	1.753	1.760
Mining	0.045	0.044	0.037	0.034	0.031
Manufacturing	−0.269	−0.257	−0.080	−0.014	0.063
Services	−0.280	−0.288	−0.399	−0.438	−0.486
Rate of return					
Agriculture	0.242	0.228	0.207	0.182	0.088
Mining	0.018	−0.012	−0.091	−0.056	−0.063
Manufacturing	−0.148	−0.189	−0.287	−0.134	0.224
Services	−0.093	−0.101	−0.232	−0.150	−0.250
Wages					
Agriculture	1.718	2.126	1.730	1.310	0.912
Mining	−0.011	0.170	0.508	0.658	0.809
Manufacturing	−0.015	0.223	0.724	0.936	1.154
Services	−0.014	0.209	0.621	0.807	0.991
Labor share	0.147	0.373	0.705	0.791	1.099
Output					
Agriculture	0.004	0.576	1.011	1.046	1.180
Mining	0.000	0.064	0.240	0.298	0.363
Manufacturing	−0.032	−0.204	−0.528	−0.484	−0.585
Services	−0.018	−0.050	−0.274	−0.239	−0.375
Total	−0.017	−0.016	−0.205	−0.113	−0.183
Capital stock					
Agriculture	0.000	0.331	0.771	0.904	1.072
Mining	0.000	0.184	0.416	0.422	0.470
Manufacturing	0.000	0.105	−0.230	−0.289	−0.309
Services	0.000	−0.067	−0.171	−0.222	−0.280
Labor					
Agriculture	0.012	0.658	1.395	1.900	2.270
Mining	0.000	0.064	0.240	0.298	0.363
Manufacturing	−0.093	−0.313	−0.719	−0.722	−0.858
Services	−0.043	−0.020	−0.240	−0.200	−0.359
Total	−0.032	0.106	0.004	0.171	0.118
Unemployment	0.040	−0.112	0.009	−0.111	−0.024

NOTE: The figures are percentage changes from the base run except for rates of return and unemployment, where they are percentage-point deviations from the base run.
SOURCE: Coeymans and Mundlak (1992).

small when compared with the change in agriculture. This difference simply reflects the relative size of the sectors in question.

Capital

The allocation of investment flows and the paths of capital stocks depend on the sectoral rates of return, which approximate the realized value marginal productivity of capital. As such, they depend on the implemented technology, the capital-labor ratio, the value-added price, and the price of the capital stock. In this simulation, the agricultural rate of return increases with respect to the historical levels by about 0.2 percentage points, whereas the rates of return in manufacturing and services decline. These changes are sufficient to produce an expansion of capital in agriculture at the expense of manufacturing and services.

Labor

The expansion of agricultural output is achieved largely by the expansion in employment, which grows by 0.66 and 1.4 percent in five and ten years, respectively. The corresponding changes in the capital stock are 0.33 and 0.77 percent, respectively. Hence, agriculture becomes more labor intensive, and on the whole nonagriculture becomes more capital intensive. The declining sectors that provide the labor and capital are manufacturing and services.

It appears that labor is more mobile than capital because capital is more sector specific. Consequently, capital is allocated across sectors mainly through the allocation of investment, and this takes time to accumulate.

The rise in agricultural price increases the demand for labor in agriculture, and since the short-run labor supply is fairly inelastic, the agricultural wages rise by 1.7–2.1 percent during the first ten years. This rise reduces the wage differential between agriculture and nonagriculture, causing a decline in the rate of off-farm migration and a rise in the agricultural labor force relative to the base run.

The reduction in the off-farm migration reduces the labor supply in nonagriculture relative to the base run. This reduction should have reduced unemployment, but this is hardly the case. The weak response of unemployment is an outcome of the strong response of wages to unemployment. Thus, as soon as unemployment declines, wages rise and cause a reduction in the quantity demanded of labor. The increase in total employment would have been larger had wages not been so responsive to unemployment. This result reflects the behavior of the labor market in Chile during the study period. Finally, the price change initially produces a considerable effect on the wage differential between agriculture and nonagriculture, but the eventual increase in wages is similar in all sectors because of factor mobility.

Income Distribution

The effect of the price change on labor and capital income is measured in terms of the share of total wages in total income. The table shows that the labor share rises considerably with time, reflecting the rise in wages discussed above. The rise in agricultural wages favored mostly agricultural workers, who are the lowest-paid workers in the economy. This result shows that policies biased against agriculture intended to help workers and low-income people may have the opposite results.

The Real Exchange Rate

The real exchange rate (RER) is endogenously determined by macroeconomic and trade policies and by other variables affecting the domestic price level, such as institutional constraints. In the long run it is also affected by technical change in the production of tradable and nontradable goods and by changes in tastes and in sectoral composition that affect the demand for these two goods. There is no doubt that the macroeconomic and trade policies dominated in the study period. This is clear from Figure 9.6. In general, the values of the RER in the 1960s were relatively low and declining. Large devaluations, not sufficiently supplemented by other measures, raised the RER to unsustainable levels in 1974 and 1975. The more balanced and restrained policies of the 1980s raised it to unprecedented levels, a situation that was conducive to the development of exports in general and of agricultural exports in particular.

To evaluate the importance of the RER, we simulate the economy with a 1 percent change in the RER without discussing the underlying policies needed to achieve such a real devaluation. The change in the RER affects sectoral prices through the sectoral price equations that take into account the degree of sectoral tradability. The results are summarized in Table 9.3.

Prices

The response of sectoral prices to the change in the RER depends on two important attributes: the degree of tradability and the degree of openness. The price of mining products, the most tradable goods, increases by 0.8 percent and that of agricultural products by 0.7 percent. The price equations for these two products were not responsive to the degree of

FIGURE 9.6   Real Exchange Rate Index in Chile, 1960–1990

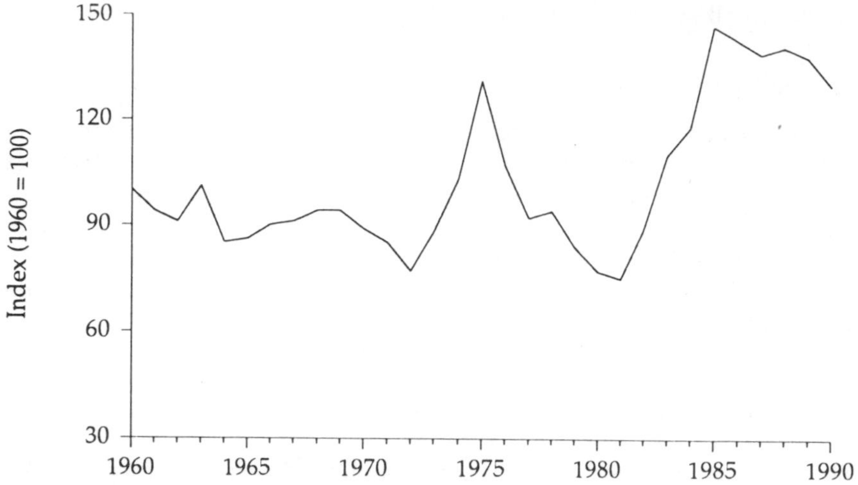

SOURCE: Coeymans and Mundlak (1992).

openness. This is not the case for the price of manufactured products, which increases with the degree of openness from 0.2 percent in the first year to 0.4 percent at end of the period. During the sample period manufacturing was less tradable than mining and agriculture and therefore its price was less responsive to the change in the RER. The change in the real price of services needed to keep the PC constant is higher than that observed in the previous simulation.

The cost structure of each sector and the changes in sectoral product prices determine the changes in the value-added prices. The value-added prices of agriculture and mining increase more than that of manufacturing, but the relative differences diminish with time.

Inputs

The changes in value-added prices have an immediate effect on the rates of return: the rates in the more tradable sectors increase, and those in services decline. The percentage changes of the rates in the first year are 1.5 for agriculture, 2.7 for mining, 0.6 for manufacturing, and -1.8 for services.[2] The allocation of investment responds to these changes in the rates of return, and this is reflected in the sectoral growth of the capital stocks. In ten years capital grows by 0.65 percent in agriculture, 1.3 percent in mining, and 0.08 percent in manufacturing, whereas capital in services declines by 0.36 percent.

TABLE 9.3   Effect of a 1 Percent Increase in Chile's Real Exchange
Rate in Selected Years, 1963–1982 (percentage)

Year	1963	1967	1972	1977	1982
Product price					
Agriculture	0.677	0.677	0.677	0.677	0.677
Mining	0.838	0.838	0.838	0.838	0.838
Manufacturing	0.226	0.242	0.265	0.368	0.396
Services	−0.469	−0.494	−0.524	−0.666	−0.707
Value-added price					
Agriculture	1.230	1.235	1.244	1.277	1.286
Mining	1.422	1.420	1.417	1.403	1.399
Manufacturing	0.377	0.433	0.513	0.865	0.960
Services	−0.683	−0.720	−0.765	−0.975	−1.035
Rate of return					
Agriculture	0.174	0.163	0.159	0.146	0.072
Mining	0.483	0.476	0.280	0.174	0.215
Manufacturing	0.213	0.182	0.147	0.152	0.291
Services	−0.233	−0.223	−0.294	−0.220	−0.356
Wages					
Agriculture	1.224	1.521	1.190	0.879	0.487
Mining	0.008	0.057	0.248	0.344	0.415
Manufacturing	−0.012	0.072	0.353	0.486	0.591
Services	−0.011	0.070	0.304	0.421	0.507
Labor share	0.073	0.223	0.504	0.561	0.888
Output					
Agriculture	0.003	0.455	0.828	0.863	0.994
Mining	0.000	0.208	0.750	0.841	0.904
Manufacturing	0.049	0.097	0.165	0.203	0.488
Services	−0.048	−0.287	−0.568	−0.532	−0.783
Total	−0.012	−0.070	−0.147	−0.096	−0.168
Capital stock					
Agriculture	0.000	0.323	0.654	0.732	0.878
Mining	0.000	0.595	1.254	1.197	1.186
Manufacturing	0.000	0.037	0.083	0.120	0.328
Services	0.000	−0.157	−0.359	−0.433	−0.533
Labor					
Agriculture	0.009	0.520	1.152	1.594	1.985
Mining	0.000	0.208	0.750	0.841	0.904
Manufacturing	0.142	0.183	0.195	0.297	0.562
Services	−0.116	−0.239	−0.522	−0.531	−0.736
Total	−0.025	0.054	0.007	0.117	0.076
Unemployment	0.031	−0.052	0.003	−0.065	0.005

NOTE: The figures are percentage changes from the base run except for rates of return and unemployment, where they are percentage-point deviations from the base run.
SOURCE: Coeymans and Mundlak (1992).

The immediate response in wages was strongest in agriculture: 1.2 percent in the first year and over 1.5 percent in the subsequent four years. This response reflects the increase in demand and the fact that the labor supply is largely predetermined in the short run. With time, the agricultural labor supply increases, because of a rise in the labor force associated with population growth and a decline in the off-farm migration, to a level of 2 percent at the end of the period, thereby reducing the wage increase to a level of 0.5 percent.

This simulated response of wages to a real devaluation resembles the observed pattern in the post-study years, when a high real rate of exchange has prevailed. Although there are no official data on agricultural wages for the post-sample period, there is the general view that in recent years agricultural wages have increased more than wages in other sectors. This increase in wages eventually becomes a deterrent for further expansion of output and exports. This behavior of the labor market should be taken into consideration when attempting to extrapolate output and exports for longer periods.

We conclude, therefore, that the policy produces a substantial reallocation of employment from nonagriculture to agriculture. As in the previous exercises, the overall labor share increases, indicating that the increase in the real exchange rate is capital saving.

Output

The strongest output response is observed in agriculture, even though its value-added price increases less than that of mining. The strength of the response can be quantified by computing the implicit supply elasticities as a ratio of the percentage change in value added to the percentage change in its price. The results for 1972 are services, 0.74; agriculture, 0.67; mining, 0.53; and manufacturing, 0.32. The values for 1982 are somewhat higher, but they maintain the same sectoral rankings.

Summary of Results

The foregoing experiments, as well as others not reported here for lack of space, indicate that the sectoral composition of the simulated economy is strongly influenced by changes in the relative prices. Because the response takes time to build up, there are two pertinent aspects of the price response: magnitude and speed. For instance, in the case of the response of agriculture to changes in its terms of trade, the implicit supply elasticity is 0.3 after three years and 1.0 after ten years. The weak response of agriculture in the short run explains the pessimism of the structuralists with respect to the effect of price policy on agricultural output.

The supply response evaluated in our simulations assumes away uncertainty in that the contemplated price change is taken to be permanent. The reason for the gradual response is that changes in the structure of the economy are carried out by resource allocation, and this process is time consuming. This sluggishness in resource mobility is a reflection of the supply of labor and capital and is not specific to changes instigated by price changes. A similar pattern is expected to exist when responding to other changes in the economic environment. This means that there are no shortcuts for changing the structure of the economy.

Adjustment in the sectoral composition of the capital stock is carried out through investment, and therefore it requires more time to respond to price changes than that of labor. The slow speed of factors' response to prices seems to be insufficient to eliminate differences in relative factor prices across sectors during the time span of the simulations.

Because the simulations were conditional on total factor supply and technology, changes in relative prices have shown no important effect on overall output of the economy. This is an interesting result in view of the high rate of unemployment that prevailed during much of the period. The lack of a significant improvement in sectoral employment in response to price improvement reflects the behavior of the labor market at the time that translated an increase in labor demand into wages rather than employment. A rise in the terms of trade in favor of agriculture leads to an increase in the labor demand in agriculture, and therefore to a decline in the labor supply in nonagriculture and to higher wages in all sectors of the economy, with agricultural workers gaining the most. Consequently, policies biased against agriculture that are intended to favor workers and low-income people seem to be producing the opposite results.

A change in the real exchange rate affects sectoral prices according to their degree of tradability, with mining being the most, and services the least, tradable. The strength of the effect is directly related to the degree of openness. The supply response is strongest in mining and agriculture, which are the most tradable sectors. The resources needed for the expansion of these sectors are provided by services, the least tradable sector. The long run effect on agriculture is to reduce the off-farm migration and thereby increase employment in agriculture at the expense of nonagriculture and the wage rates in all sectors. This leads to an increase in the share of wages in total income.

Growth and Sectoral Composition

The foregoing discussion indicates that changing the relative prices while holding resources constant has a strong effect on the composition of the economy but not on growth. The reason is that resources and technology in these experiments are held constant. We can examine the growth attributes of the model by allowing capital to change while holding product prices at their historical level.

The role of capital in growth is an important topic on which there is no clear and conclusive view. Current theoretical discussion views human capital as the engine of growth (see Lucas 1988).[3] The empirical implication of this view is not immediate. The framework for this theoretical discussion has two pertinent aspects for our discussion. First, it evaluates the economy in a steady-state position, and second, it does not distinguish between implemented and available technology; whatever is known is immediately used. The empirical implications of these two assumptions are rather limited. In terms of our analysis, it is not helpful to think of Chile in the sample period as an economy in a steady state, and it is definitely misleading to assume that there was no gap between available and implemented technology.

The growth performance of the economy was summarized in Figure 9.2. This performance is related to the investment behavior summarized in Figure 9.7, which presents the investment-output ratio for the period 1960–1990. In the 1960s this ratio fluctuated in the range of about 18 to 23 percent. With a few exceptions, it was considerably lower for the 1970s and most of the 1980s. This ratio reflects the prevailing economic environment, but this aspect is not discussed here.

We evaluate the net effect of capital by simulating the response of the

FIGURE 9.7   Investment-Output Ratio in Chile, 1960–1990

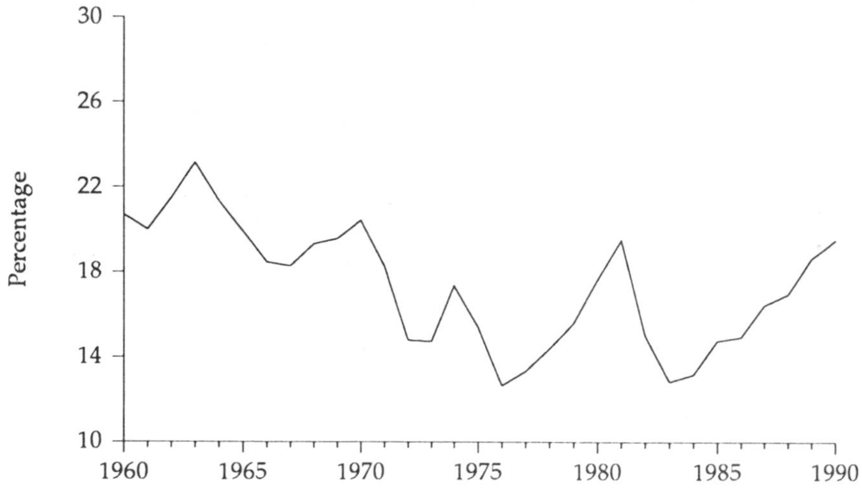

SOURCE: Coeymans and Mundlak (1992).

TABLE 9.4   Effect of a 1 Percent Increase in Chile's Investment Ratio on the Composition of the Economy in Selected Years, 1967–1982 (percentage)

	1967	1972	1977	1982
	Total economy			
Capital	1.70	4.22	6.70	10.38
Output	2.11	7.71	9.94	19.84
Employment	1.20	4.57	5.98	11.22
Unemployment	−1.48	−5.84	−6.30	−10.98
	Sectors			
Rate of return				
Agriculture	0.06	0.64	0.51	0.87
Mining	−0.12	−0.08	−0.04	0.12
Manufacturing	0.45	0.85	0.36	1.38
Services	0.21	1.30	0.81	2.84
Output				
Agriculture	1.23	5.76	8.23	18.64
Mining	0.41	1.70	4.94	8.78
Manufacturing	3.10	7.94	9.60	17.69
Government	2.11	7.71	9.94	19.84
Services	2.03	8.59	11.11	22.63
Labor				
Agriculture	−0.87	−3.43	−6.00	−10.40
Mining	0.41	1.70	4.94	8.78
Manufacturing	3.00	7.56	9.79	17.82
Government	2.11	7.71	9.94	19.84
Services	1.56	5.98	8.74	15.74
Capital				
Agriculture	1.50	3.40	6.10	8.77
Mining	1.21	3.04	5.96	8.42
Manufacturing	2.29	5.12	7.43	11.91
Services	1.66	4.37	6.84	10.91

SOURCE: Coeymans and Mundlak (1992).

economy to an increase of the historical investment-output ratio by one percentage point. Thus, for example, when the historical ratio was 0.18, it is now set at 0.19. This increase is imposed, beginning in 1963, for the whole period. The changes in the main aggregate variables are summarized in the top section of Table 9.4. This simulation is obtained by holding the nonagricultural wages at their historical values, and therefore it exaggerates somewhat the effect on output and employment. The reason for this is beyond the scope of this paper. In any case the results are indicative and useful for examining the effect of growth on the sectoral composition of the economy.

The changes in the composition of the economy are summarized in the second panel of Table 9.4. The increase of overall capital is spread to all sectors. The capital-labor ratio increases in agriculture, varies little in manufacturing and declines in mining and services. The decline in the capital-labor ratio, with an increase in capital stock, reflects a strong positive employment response in nonagriculture, where the real wages are held constant, and a decline in agricultural employment, where wages are allowed to rise. When the production function is held constant, an increase in the capital-labor ratio results in a decline in the rate of return. This simulation, however, shows an increase in the rates of return for all sectors except mining. The reason is that in the present framework the implemented technology is not constant; it changes with the increase in the capital-labor ratio. Changes in the rates of return affect the sectoral competitive position for new investment, which in turn affects the sectoral pattern of growth in the capital stock. Manufacturing responds most strongly to the changes in investment, but the sectoral differences are not large. The increase in the capital stock, in investment, and in the rate of return change the implemented technology so that output and the demand for labor increase. Consequently, unemployment declines, and this in turn increases the off-farm migration and decreases the agricultural labor force. The effect of the decline in unemployment on migration is strong enough to overcome the increase in agricultural income as measured by the average labor productivity. The decline in agricultural labor and the rise in its capital stock increase the capital-labor ratio in agriculture, whereas this ratio declines for most other sectors, as can be seen by comparing the proportionate increments in capital and in employment. Finally, except for mining, output increases considerably more than capital.

Conclusions

What, then, are the events that affected agriculture? There is no simple answer to this question. The foregoing analysis indicates that agriculture, like the other sectors, is price responsive and that sectoral growth is favorably affected by overall investment. But this is not the whole story, and we now turn to some pertinent details.

The macroeconomic policies affected the price level over the period, its rate of change (or rate of inflation), and the acceleration of inflation. These price changes in turn affected the real exchange rate, the real wages, the real interest rate, and the level of confidence in the economy and the direction it was taking. As the macroeconomic policies affected the real economy, they affected the trade balance, which had implications for trade policies and decisions on the nominal exchange rate.

The wages in the nonagricultural sectors were determined through a bargaining process in which the inflation rate was an important input. Most important, the wages were not market clearing. In fact, during the period of stabilization the real wages were set at relatively high levels, which generated considerable unemployment. Such unemployment discouraged off-farm migration, increased the agricultural labor force, and thereby contributed to an increase in the agricultural output.

The real exchange rate, as used in this study, is the ratio of the nominal exchange rate, adjusted for foreign inflation, divided by the consumption deflator. Thus, an increase in the domestic price level relative to world inflation that is not accompanied by devaluation reduces the real exchange rate. The RER affects the sectoral prices according to their degree of tradability, as well as the degree of openness generated by the domestic policies. Thus, agriculture is a tradable sector, with a degree of tradability of around 0.6, but it is not responsive to the variations in the RER under price controls that shield it from world prices. This was the case from the 1960s until about 1977, when the intervention was reduced. From that year on, agricultural prices were responsive to changes in the RER, which increased sharply in the first half of the 1980s and stayed at a high level for the remainder of the 1980s. This change in the RER probably contributed to the expansion in agricultural output in the 1980s. The increase in the productivity of tradables, as well as in overall expenditures, however, has prompted a downward trend in the RER starting in 1985 that has continued through 1992. This decline, if it continues, will affect agriculture as well as other tradable products.

Prices affected output through their effect on the rates of return and wages, which in turn affected resource allocation and productivity. In both cases, it is the price of value added that matters, and this is positively related to the own-product price and negatively related to the product prices of the intermediate inputs to agriculture. Thus, the protection of manufacturing reduces the value-added price of agriculture. The same effect is obtained by the increase in the price of services. Because services is the least tradable sector, its price is positively affected by the foreign terms of trade and inflow of capital.

The increase in value-added price increases the rate of return to capital in agriculture and thereby agricultural investment and output. The rate of return also had a direct effect on productivity. These are important channels through which an increase in the RER, and through it macroeconomic policies, affected agricultural output.

There is another aspect to the stability, or lack of it, that is generated by the macroeconomic policies, which is related to the level of investment. As we saw, the investment-output ratio declined from its peak to its trough by almost one half. This decline had a huge cost in terms of overall growth that affected all sectors. The recovery in the 1980s returned the investment-output ratio to the level of the 1960s and thereby led to the expansion of output in the economy in general and in agriculture in particular.

Agriculture was also strongly affected by the land reform. The direct effect on productivity, as measured through the effect on the production function, was marginal. The uncertainty generated by the process, however, reduced investment in agriculture and thereby discouraged production.

The foregoing discussion provides a framework for understanding the recovery of agriculture since 1983. In this period the macroeconomic policies stabilized the economy, investment was growing, the RER was at a historically high level, the land reform was undone, property rights were established, and a viable land market developed. This is the supply story. We now turn to the demand side.

The growth in agricultural output was accompanied by a considerable growth in exports, largely of fruits. Total agricultural exports were at a level of US$25 million from 1960 to 1973. They started to grow in 1974, from a value of US$55 million, to 1982, with a few interruptions. They gained impetus beginning in 1984 and reached US$981 million in 1990. The share of exports in agricultural output grew from 2 percent in 1973 to 11 percent in 1990. The reasons for the rapid export growth require a special study. It is interesting, however, to note that the growth started with the liberalization of the economy, including agriculture, and with the return of land titles, gaining impetus with the increase in the RER. This growth in exports provided an outlet for the growing agricultural production. The question is, what would have happened to agriculture had this development of exports not taken place? This is a hypothetical question about which we can only speculate based on the experiences of other countries. The growing output would have had to be sold domestically, which would have depressed domestic prices and slowed agricultural growth.

Policy Implications

The general policy implications are clear. It is important to maintain a stable economy and to let the markets direct resource allocation. This is the general advice for a healthy economic environment. Of more immediate interest for us are the specific lessons with respect to agriculture. We saw that the supply response of agriculture builds up gradually.

This is presumably the reason why some policy makers do not believe in its existence. In that they commit several errors. First, their perception of no supply response is based on variations in actual prices that are seen by producers as transitory and as such do not justify a response. The simulation presented above deals only with price changes that can be perceived as permanent. When dealing with policy, we should consider only price changes of a permanent nature. Second, the slow response is related to the behavior of labor and capital whose sectoral allocation is based on intertemporal considerations and whose adjustment is subject to costs. In general, policies that tax agriculture are not transitory; they are long-lasting, and therefore, if based on the wrong view as to how the economy is working, they cause a distortion that builds up with time. Finally, the results, whether we like them or not, reflect the working of the system. The message is that there are no shortcuts.

To sum up, the output response in agriculture to changes in the economic environment is sizable, but it requires time to materialize. This distinction between magnitude and speed is extremely important in that it highlights the importance of maintaining consistent economic policies.

Notes to Chapter 9

1. The coefficient of D82 was restricted to be equal in the two equations. This implies that its elasticity is zero.

2. The changes in the rates of return reported in the table are in percentage points. When these are divided by their base-run values, we obtain the percentage change.

3. In this discussion it becomes important to qualify the type of capital under consideration. Thus, when we use the word capital without further qualification, we refer to physical capital.

III

REGIONAL SURVEYS

Development Strategies, Industrial Policies, and Agricultural Incentives in Asia

This chapter is about the experiences of nine nonsocialist economies in Asia that have a large agricultural share in gross domestic product (GDP) (at least 20 percent in the early 1970s): the Republic of Korea, Malaysia, Thailand, the Philippines, Indonesia, Sri Lanka, Pakistan, India, and Bangladesh. These nine countries differ significantly in their per capita income and economic growth (Table 10.1). The discussion focuses on three central questions: how the growth and trade strategies adopted in these countries have affected relative incentives for agricultural production; how the real exchange rate, acting in an intermediary role, has transmitted the indirect effect of trade and macroeconomic policies to agricultural incentives and what total (direct and indirect) effects government price intervention policies have had on specific agricultural products; and what further repercussions these policies have had on agricultural output, distribution of incomes, and intersectoral resource transfer in these nine countries.

Development Policies and Agricultural Incentives

Except for Thailand, these nine countries were formerly under colonial rule, and their economies before independence were closely integrated

Table 10.1   Selected Economic Indicators for Nine Asian Countries, 1965–1985

Country	GNP per capita		Agricultural share in GNP (%)		Average annual growth rate (%), 1965–1985	
	U.S. dollars, 1985	Average annual growth rate (%), 1965–1985	1965	1985	Agriculture	GDP
East Asia						
Republic of Korea	2,150	6.6	38	14	3.8	9.1
Malaysia	2,000	4.4	30	21[a]	4.4[b]	6.8
Thailand	800	4.0	35	17	4.5	6.8
Philippines	580	2.3	26	27	3.9	4.3
Indonesia	530	4.8	59	24	4.0	6.8
South Asia						
Sri Lanka	380	2.9	28	27	3.0	4.3
Pakistan	380	2.6	40	25	3.0	5.4
India	270	1.7	47	31	2.8	4.2
Bangladesh	150	0.4	53	50	1.8	2.7

a. For 1983
b. For 1970–1985.
SOURCE: World Bank (1982, 1986b, 1987b).

with those of the colonizing powers. After independence, development policy concentrated on rapid industrialization with a view to diversifying the economy so as to avoid relying exclusively on primary production and, more generally, to redirect the country's production capacity away from the goals of the former colonial powers and toward establishing a basis for modernizing the economy (Bautista 1983). The colonial pattern of production and trade, in which income derived from agricultural plantations and large mines flowed mostly out of the country, was rejected in favor of a domestic market–oriented, industry-based approach to economic development.

The need for economic independence led, at least initially, to an industrialization strategy based on import substitution involving the promotion of domestic industries through high tariff walls, quantitative import restrictions, or both.[1] This strategy benefited mainly the producers of final consumption goods and in effect discriminated against other manufacturing industries and the agricultural sector. The developing countries of Asia differed in the comprehensiveness, intensity, and duration of their import-substitution policies, with some eventually shifting to a more "outward-looking approach" to industrial development. This accounts in part for the differences in the present state of their industrial development, and in their past economic performance.

The Republic of Korea, for example, promoted exports through trade liberalization policies and other major policy reforms enacted between 1962 and 1965, at a point relatively early in the country's industrialization. This marked a turning point in Korea's manufacturing and export growth (Westphal and Kim 1981). Malaysia kept tariff protection for domestic industry low, even in the early years of its industrial development, did not impose exchange controls, and rarely adopted quantitative restrictions. This liberal trade policy "was important in the continuing expansion of Malaysia's primary exports and contributed to the rise of a significant export manufacturing sector" (Lim 1981, 189). In Thailand, the industrialization strategy became more balanced between import substitution and export promotion in the first half of the 1970s (Akrasanee 1981).

Although the trade and industrial policies of the other six Asian countries also became less inward-looking, especially after the early 1970s, their foreign trade regime remained highly biased toward import-substituting industries. In the Philippines, which has the longest history of import-substituting industrialization in the region, trade and industrial policies became more outward-oriented in the first half of the 1970s. Later in the decade, however, they reverted to a strong anti-export bias (Bautista 1987b). Although Bangladesh provided significant incentives for nontraditional exports after the early 1970s, the trade regime continued to favor import-competing industrial production (Stern, Mallon, and Hutcheson 1988). In Indonesia, after the easy stage of import substitution was completed around 1975, policy makers "chose to push the process of industrialization into the second phase of import substitution by promoting upstream industries" (Wie 1987, 89). In the case of India, whose restrictive trade regime and licensing policies in the industrial sector "led to economic inefficiencies and impaired her economic performance" (Bhagwati and Srinivasan 1975, 245), the development of heavy industries was promoted first, starting in the early 1950s, with lower-stream industries being forced to rely on inferior domestically produced inputs and capital equipment.

In 1977 the Sri Lankan government introduced a new policy package aimed at liberalizing many aspects of the national economy, including the trade regime and industrial protection. Although the "original objective of achieving neutrality in the overall industrial incentive structure" (Athukorala 1986, 78) has not been met, the policy reform represented a substantial departure from the previously very strong bias toward import-competing production. Finally, in the case of Pakistan, there has been slow but fairly steady progress in trade liberalization since 1960; nevertheless, import quotas and high tariffs persist, particularly for industrial consumer goods (Guisinger and Scully 1988).

To compensate for the observed discrimination of trade and exchange rate policies against agricultural production and export industries, these Asian countries have been inclined to provide subsidies for agricultural inputs (fertilizer, credit, and irrigation) and industrial exports (especially labor-intensive manufactures). These selective subsidies have fallen far short of fully offsetting the pervasive biases attributable to the trade restrictions.

Trade restrictions affect production incentives in two ways: they produce a differential direct effect on the domestic prices of tradable goods, and they have an impact on the real exchange rate, which in turn affects the domestic prices of tradable goods in relation to home goods. For example, import duties and quotas raise the domestic price of import-competing products in relation to exportables and therefore encourage a shift away from export production. The same policy instruments reduce the demand for imports, which lowers the price of foreign exchange so that the domestic prices of tradable goods fall in relation to home goods and hence indirectly bias the production incentives against both import-competing and export goods. Protection for industrial import substitutes then penalizes the domestic production of agricultural goods in the following ways: (1) the rise in the domestic price of the protected industrial output reduces the relative price of agricultural products; (2) the cost of industrial inputs (fertilizer, pesticides, and farm equipment) for agricultural production increases; and (3) the induced appreciation in the real exchange rate renders agricultural exports and import-competing products less profitable than nontradable (or home) goods.

Other government policies not specifically directed at the agricultural sector have also affected relative production incentives in Asian developing countries. Since the early 1970s, as already mentioned, many of these countries have followed the Korean example of actively promoting nontraditional (mostly manufactured) exports. At the same time, traditional (mostly agricultural) exports have frequently been subject to export duties, which in some Asian countries are a major source of government revenue. Producers of nontraditional exports not only have been free of export taxes, but they have also benefited from such subsidies as low-interest credit, labor training subsidies, import duty drawbacks, and export credit insurance, all of which serve to offset in part the general policy bias against exports. Some of these incentives are effective only to the extent that the exporter uses imported inputs. In other words, they impose a penalty on the use of domestically produced inputs—as is evident from the high import content of the leading nontraditional export products, such as garments and consumer electronics, and the importance of export processing zones to the industrial performance of some countries (particularly Malaysia and the Philippines)—and inhibit the development of intersectoral links within the domestic economy.

A country's monetary and fiscal policies, foreign borrowing, and nominal exchange rate management may have a critical effect on the real exchange rate and hence the profitability of the production of agricultural tradables. In the Philippines, for example, the government borrowed heavily abroad and pursued expansionary macroeconomic policies in the face of the large current account deficits after the 1973–1974 oil price shock; this action contributed to the worsening overvaluation of the real exchange rate during the second half of the 1970s and early 1980s (Bautista 1987b). For oil-rich Indonesia, the increased inflow of oil revenues in the mid-1970s led to the "Dutch disease" syndrome and squeezed profitability in the non-oil tradable goods sectors both by directly bidding resources away from them and by causing an appreciation of the real exchange rate (in response to the increase in the money supply and the rate of inflation while the nominal exchange rate remained fixed).

In addition, agricultural sector-specific policies may directly affect production incentives for farmers. These can offset or reinforce the indirect penalty stemming from industrial and macroeconomic policies. At one time or another, Asian governments have directly suppressed the producer prices for specific farm products by imposing export taxes, setting up agricultural marketing boards, or directly controlling domestic prices. An important objective of Malaysia's agricultural pricing policy, for example, has been to set levels of taxation on the rubber and palm oil sectors to finance public investment within and outside those sectors (Jenkins and Lai 1989). Some countries have used subsidies for agricultural inputs to compensate for the low prices of farm output, as mentioned earlier.

Differential Effects on the Prices of Tradable Goods

As the foregoing discussion makes clear, it is difficult to fully under-stand the effects of the Asian policies on agricultural incentives unless we distinguish between traditional (agricultural) and new (industrial) exports in representing the relative price effects (with respect to im-portables) and also take into account the rates of protection for specific agricultural products, along with the indirect price effects of trade and macroeconomic policies, as transmitted through the real exchange rate.

Table 10.2 gives some indication of the disparities in the extent to which the production of importables and exportables (the latter divided into agricultural and manufactured goods) was taxed or subsidized (in relation to the border prices at prevailing exchange rates) in Bangladesh and the Philippines from 1970 to 1980. The estimates of the implicit tax rates are based on import tariffs, export taxes, and other trade-related taxes and subsidies, but not the scarcity premiums from the quantitative import restrictions. Hence, they understate the differential price effects on imported goods subject to import licensing.[2] Nonetheless, sector-specific policies indeed favored the production of import-competing goods, which benefited from the high import tax rates averaging more than 20 percent in both countries during this decade. Meanwhile, agri-cultural exports were taxed at average rates of 2.3 percent in Bangladesh and 5.8 percent in the Philippines. While industrial export production was subsidized, the rates were generally much lower than the import tax rates.

A less severe distortion in relative production incentives has been observed for Malaysia, which did not heavily protect import-competing industries. The average implicit tax rate for imports from 1979 to 1980 was only 9.7 percent (Jenkins and Lai 1989), while that for agricultural exports was 4.5 percent. In sharp contrast, trade taxes in Sri Lanka for the same period were very large, averaging 80.6 percent for imports and 40.0 percent for exports (Bhalla 1988).

A number of studies have been done on the price effects of sector-specific policies for particular agricultural products in Asian developing countries.[3] Of particular interest for present purposes are the findings of a recently completed World Bank research project on the political econ-

Table 10.2   Implicit Tax Rates in Bangladesh and the Philippines, 1970–1980 (percentage)

Period	Imports		Agriculture exports		Manufactured exports	
	Bangladesh	Philippines	Bangladesh	Philippines	Bangladesh	Philippines
1970–1972	n.a.	30.1	n.a.	9.5	n.a.	−11.6
1973–1975	19.5	9.5	0.6	4.7	n.a.	−19.2
1976–1978	29.7	16.9	3.2	4.2	n.a.	−12.4
1979–1980	25.8	27.6	3.4	4.1	−4.0	−15.8

n.a. = not available.
NOTE: Positive rates are taxes; negative rates are subsidies.
SOURCE: Basic data from Stern, Mallon, and Hutcheson (1985) and Bautista (1987a).

Table 10.3   Direct Nominal Protection Rates in Six Asian Countries, 1975–1984 (percentage)

Country and commodity[a]	1975–1979	1980–1984
Republic of Korea		
Rice (F)	91	86
Malaysia		
Rice (F)	38	68
Rubber (X)	−25	−18
Phillippines		
Corn (F)	18	26
Copra (X)	−11	−26
Thailand		
Rice (X)	−28	−15
Sri Lanka		
Rice (F)	18	11
Rubber (X)	−29	−31
Pakistan		
Wheat (F)	−13	−21
Cotton (X)	−12	−7

a. F and X denote food and export crops, respectively.
SOURCE: Krueger, Schiff, and Valdés (1988, 262, 263).

omy of agricultural pricing policies, which provide quantification of the degree of intervention affecting agriculture arising out of both direct and indirect policies on a comparable basis for eighteen developing countries (Krueger, Schiff, and Valdés 1988).

Table 10.3 contains estimates of the nominal protection rate, which represents the deviation of the domestic price from the border price at the official exchange rate,[4] for some of the most important import-competing food (F) and export (X) crops in the six Asian countries included in the World Bank study. They indicate a general price disprotection against export crops as a result of direct government interventions during the 1975–1984 period. In contrast, import-competing agricultural food products were accorded positive protection in most cases (wheat in Pakistan is an important exception). Average nominal protection rates for rice exceeded 85 percent in Korea and approached 70 percent during the 1980s in Malaysia. Among the export crops, rubber in Malaysia and Sri Lanka was the most severely penalized by the direct pricing policies, with disprotection rates for the period averaging −22 percent and −30 percent, respectively.

The nominal rate of protection for some major crops in the remaining countries of the group has been estimated as follows: (1) −19 percent and 0 percent for rice and wheat, respectively, in India during the late 1970s (Binswanger and Scandizzo 1983) and −37 percent and −28 percent, respectively, during the period from 1980 to 1985 (Gulati 1987); (2) –24 percent for wheat and −17 percent for rice in Bangladesh in the late 1970s (Binswanger and Scandizzo 1983); and (3) −16.7 percent and −18.7 percent for rice and corn, respectively, in Indonesia from 1974 to 1979, and 2.8 percent and −8.2 percent, respectively, from 1980 to 1986 (Rosegrant, Kasryno, Gonzales, Rasahan, and Saefudin 1987).

The Real Exchange Rate and Relative Incentives

Restrictions on foreign trade distort the real exchange rate relative to its free trade value. Tariffs and quantitative restrictions act as a tax on imported goods, reducing import demand and lowering the price of foreign exchange. Export subsidies have a similar effect on the exchange rate since they tend to increase export supply. Export taxes have the opposite effect. In short, import taxes and export subsidies lead to an overvaluation of the real exchange rate, while export taxes lead to an undervaluation.

Apart from trade restrictions, an imbalance in the external accounts can lead to real exchange rate overvaluation or undervaluation. The unsustainable component of a current account deficit made possible by, say, heavy foreign borrowing serves to defend an overvalued exchange rate. Also, a temporary boom in one tradable good sector (for example, oil) places upward pressure on the real exchange rate, to the detriment of other tradable good sectors (non-oil). Trade and macroeconomic policies that shape the foreign trade regime and the various accounts in the balance of payments are therefore basic determinants of the real exchange rate.

The price competitiveness of importables and exportables in comparison with home goods is aggregatively reflected in the real exchange rate. Overvaluation of the domestic currency (or undervaluation of foreign exchange) artificially lowers the price of imported goods—a disincentive to import-competing production. It also penalizes export production because lower prices of foreign exchange are received by exporters. The agricultural sector is particularly vulnerable to misalignment of the real exchange rate, given the high degree of tradability of agricultural output. For instance, the severe overvaluation of the Philippine peso during the second half of the 1970s effectively lowered the domestic price index of agricultural products in relation to home goods by an annual average of 19 percent (Bautista 1987b, 61). Regression analysis that takes into account other influences on relative agricultural prices indicates that a 10 percent depreciation of the real exchange rate was associated with a 3.3 percent improvement in the agricultural terms of trade (that is, in relation to nonagricultural products).

Table 10.4   Divergence of the Equilibrium Exchange Rate from the Actual Exchange Rate in Six Asian Countries, 1975–1984 (percentage)

Country	1975–1979	1980–1984
Republic of Korea	8.1	6.1
Malaysia	0.4	6.0[a]
Philippines	32.1	33.5[b]
Thailand	24.1	25.5
Sri Lanka	11.2	14.3
Pakistan	21.8	19.6

a. For the period 1980–1983.
b. For the period 1980–1982
SOURCE: Moon and Kang (1989), Jenkins and Lai (1989), Intal and Power (1990), Siamwalla and Setboonsarng (1989), Bhalla (1988), and Hamid, Nabi, and Nasim (1990).

The real exchange rate of the Indonesian rupiah was highly over-valued in the 1960s, especially during the first half of the decade, in comparison with 1971, a year in which the purchasing power parity level can be reasonably assumed (Dorosh 1986, Table 3.4). It also appreciated in the aftermath of the 1973–1974 oil boom—the average degree of over-valuation reached 37.7 percent by 1978. This overvaluation effectively reduced the domestic prices of corn and cassava, two important agri-cultural tradables in Indonesia, by 23.3 percent and 36.0 percent, re-spectively (Dorosh 1986, Table 4.12).

Table 10.4 contains average estimates of the extent of the real ex-change rate overvaluation during 1975–1979 and 1980–1984 in the six Asian countries included in the World Bank study. They range from 0.4 percent for Malaysia in the second half of the 1970s to 33.5 percent for the Philippines in the early 1980s. The relatively slight exchange rate overvaluation observed for Sri Lanka can be attributed to its high export taxes (which tended to offset the distortionary effect of import tariffs). In the case of Malaysia, the obvious explanation is its atypically low level of industrial protection. During the 1970s, the degree of exchange rate distortion decreased markedly in Korea and Pakistan, but increased sharply for the Philippines, which had incurred massive trade deficits in the second half of the decade.

These real exchange rate distortions led to *negative* "indirect" price effects on the major crops which, in combination with the "direct" rates of protection rates given in Table 10.3, yielded the "total" protection rates attributable to government interventions shown in Table 10.5. Food products in Korea and Malaysia, which had the highest GNP per capita among the Asian countries included in Table 10.5 benefited from high total rates of protection. The other countries appear generally to

Table 10.5   Total Protection Rates for Six Asian Countries,
               1975–1984 (percentage)

Country and commodity[a]	1975–1979	1980–1984
Republic of Korea		
Rice (F)	73	74
Malaysia		
Rice (F)	34	58
Rubber (X)	−29	−28
Philippines		
Corn (F)	−9	−2
Copra (X)	−38	−54
Thailand		
Rice (X)	−43	−34
Sri Lanka		
Rice (F)	−17	−20
Rubber (X)	−64	−62
Pakistan		
Wheat (F)	−61	−56
Cotton (X)	−60	−42

a. F and X denote food and export crops, respectively.
SOURCE: Krueger, Schiff, and Valdés (1988, 262, 263).

have maintained high levels of total disprotection not only for export crops, but also for food crops. In some cases (corn in the Philippines and rice in Sri Lanka), the positive direct protection accorded the latter products was swamped by the negative indirect price effects arising from the overvaluation of the real exchange rate.

The quantitative importance of the indirect price effects of trade and macroeconomic policies in other Asian countries, transmitted through real exchange rate overvaluation, has also been recognized in other studies. Binswanger and Scandizzo (1983) obtained the following comparative estimated values of the "nominal protection coefficient" (NPC = 1 + NPR) and the "adjusted net protection coefficient" (ADNPC) (the latter measure is based on shadow exchange rates instead of official exchange rates):

		NPC	ADNPC
India:	Rice	0.81	0.65
	Wheat	1.00	0.80
Bangladesh:	Rice	0.83	0.69
	Wheat	0.76	0.63

In Indonesia, the appreciation of the real exchange rate caused by the Dutch disease associated with the huge oil export revenues during the mid-1970s had a strong impact on the relative domestic prices of non-oil tradable goods. The sharp decline in the (purchasing power parity-adjusted) real exchange rate index of the Indonesian rupiah—from 100 in 1972 to 63 in 1976—not only led to a substantial squeeze on the profitability of the import-competing sectors (Warr 1984, 54), but also "discouraged traditional labor-intensive agricultural exports . . . because of a lack of international competitiveness" (Paauw 1981, 157). During the first half of the 1980s, however, Indonesian policies (which brought about a large government surplus, tight monetary control, and the March 1983 devaluation) succeeded in countering the downward pressure on the real exchange rate arising out of the growing receipts from oil exports.

Effects on Output, Income Distribution, and Intersectoral Resource Transfer

The relative price effects of sector-specific, trade, and macroeconomic policies have had further repercussions on output and income, as indicated by partial equilibrium (mostly supply-based) estimates of the long-run effects on output of government price interventions in the six Asian countries included in the World Bank study (derived from the estimated total price effects and relevant own-price and cross-price elasticities drawn from existing studies). In general, the long-run effects on output have been negative, the exceptions being rice in Malaysia during 1975–1979 and 1980–1983 and in Korea during 1975–1979 and 1980–1984. The largest proportionate losses in output appear to have involved export crops: rubber in Malaysia, copra in the Philippines, rice in Thailand, and rubber in Sri Lanka.

The impact of government intervention on income distribution has been measured in terms of the differential income effect on small and large farms, on the type of crops grown, and on the patterns of consumption expenditures. Direct interventions that reduce prices have a negative effect on the incomes of both small and large farmers. However, because large farmers market more of their produce, they are hurt relatively more by the lower prices. In Pakistan, for example, small farmers in the Punjab received 16 percent less income in 1980 than they would have without the direct interventions, whereas large farmers received 19 percent less. Indirect interventions affecting the real exchange rate tended to magnify the effect, so that small farmers received 45 percent less income, whereas large farmers received 50 percent less (Hamid, Nabi, and Nasim 1990). Where there is positive agricultural protection, larger producers, who market a greater share of their output, benefit more. In Korea, the direct price supports from 1980 to 1984 brought income gains of 58 percent and 16 percent to large and small farmers, respectively (Moon and Kang 1989). The negative indirect price effects in the 1970s were harder on the large farmers, but as the exchange rate of the Korean won was brought into close alignment with its equilibrium rate over the decade, their relative disadvantage became less marked. Even so, the income disparity between small and large producers tended to increase.

The income from export crops tended to decline more than that from food crops. In the Philippines, sugar and copra producers suffered proportionately larger income losses than did rice and corn growers (Intal and Power 1990). Similarly in Malaysia, rice farmers were not hurt nearly as much as were producers of rubber and palm oil (Jenkins and Lai 1989). In Sri Lanka, the real income of the Tamils, who make up the majority of tea estate workers, has declined substantially over the past two decades (Bhalla 1988).

Government price interventions also produce regional income effects, depending on the primary crops in the region. In the Philippines, the hardest hit regions were coconut-dependent Eastern Visayas (the poorest region in the Philippines), Western Visayas (the primary sugar region) and the other major coconut producing regions, that is, Northern Mindanao, Western Mindanao, Southern Mindanao, and Bicol. Not surprisingly, the growth of the Communist insurgency movement was most rapid in these regions during the 1970s and early 1980s, a trend that represented a shift away from the predominantly rice-growing Central Luzon region (Intal and Power 1990, 15?)

Agricultural price policies affect both rich and poor consumers, but the effects may differ significantly in degree. If consumer prices are kept artificially high through the protection accorded domestic producers, the effect on the real income of urban food consumers is negative. Nevertheless, poorer consumers suffer more, as they spend a greater proportion of their income on food. In Korea, low-income consumers lost 6.1 percent of their real income because of government price interventions in the early 1980s, whereas high-income consumers lost only 2.8 percent (Moon and Kang 1989). The indirect price effects arising from exchange rate overvaluation have the opposite effect on income distribution. As more affluent consumers purchase more nonagricultural goods that are highly protected, they suffer more than poorer consumers. In the Philippines, the real income of wealthy urban consumers was reduced by 4.4 percent because of the overvaluation of the peso in the 1960s, whereas that of low-income consumers declined by only 1.8 percent (Intal and Power 1990).[5]

As already mentioned, the effects of government price interventions on food and export crops differ in degree if not in direction. In view of the official concern that Asian developing countries frequently express about rural welfare, it is of policy interest to consider how agricultural income from both food and export crop products might be affected if the incentive biases against them were eliminated, allowing for intercrop substitution as relative prices change. Calculations based on a supply-oriented model of the agricultural sector, with the food-export crop trade-off in production as a key component, suggest that in the absence of policy-induced distortions in domestic prices, agricultural income in the Philippines would have been as much as 31 percent higher during the 1970s (Bautista 1986a).

Substitution possibilities exist not only in production, but also in other areas of the national economy: production structures, consumption patterns, foreign trade, and the distribution of income are inextricably intertwined. These possibilities need to be examined simultaneously and their interactions analyzed within an integrated macroeconomic framework in order to capture fully the economywide repercussions of agricultural pricing policies. Accordingly, some studies have made use of computable general equilibrium (CGE) models that provide an integrated macroeconomic framework emphasizing agricultural activities and their links to the other production sectors and distinguishing between rural and urban households in their income-generation and consumption patterns.

These models differ with respect to the underlying assumptions that determine the time frame of the analysis and, relatedly, the extent to which the domestic price structure influences factor allocation and productivity across sectors. For example, the fixity of total capital and its sectoral allocation assumed in Bautista (1986b) implies short-run adjustments (within one or two years), whereas the neoclassical assumption of equalizing rental rates to capital across sectors requires a much longer period. Dynamic CGE models invariably use one year as the time unit, a period in which static equilibrium is attained and the short-run effects are evaluated; the economy "lurches" from one static equilibrium to the next "as the model continually attempts to adjust to intertemporal disequilibria" (Adelman and Robinson 1978, 9). The dynamic effects of policy changes have been assessed with the aid of model simulation runs for periods of several years (for example, seven years in a study by Amranand and Grais 1984, and nine years in one by Adelman and Robinson 1978). Such runs allow time for factor supply changes (new investments and growth of labor force) and the reallocation of resources among sectors.

A dynamic twenty-nine-sector CGE model has been used to simulate the effects of various policy measures in Korea, mostly rural-oriented reforms aimed at improving income distribution (Adelman and Robinson 1978). According to the results of these simulations, the economy adjusts to policy interventions largely through price changes, and "among the price effects, the most significant impact on the size distribution of income is due to changes in the agricultural terms of trade" (Adelman and Robinson 1978, 185). Simulations based on a CGE model with seven production sectors indicate that in India, "where 47 percent of the rural population are net buyers of food" (de Janvry and Subbarao 1986, 93), agricultural price supports reduce the purchasing power of both the rural and urban poor significantly, while medium-scale and large farmers gain in both nominal and real terms.

Using a ten-sector CGE model with benchmark data for 1978, Bautista (1986b) found that trade liberalization in the Philippines would raise rural income more than it would urban income and that agricultural production would benefit more than nonagricultural production. When Amranand and Grais (1984) investigated the economywide effects of removing the export tax on rice in Thailand using a twenty-commodity CGE model based on alternative values of the price elasticity of world demand for Thai rice (1.0, 3.0, and 10.0), they found the income effects would vary by type of household: the income of crop farmers would increase by 1.44–2.05 percent, while that of other households would decrease; "casual workers would suffer most as their real income would decline by 0.64–0.89 percent, followed by rubber farmers, nonagricultural own-account households, blue-collar and white-collar households, respectively" (Amranand and Grais 1984, 165).

The price bias against agriculture that many Asian developing countries have fostered through government intervention causes resources to move out of the agricultural sector. Offsetting this resource flow is the amount transferred into agriculture by government spending. According to calculations of the net resource transfers out of agriculture, the annual average of agricultural value added amounted to about 25 percent in the Philippines during the 1970–1982 period (Intal and Power 1990), whereas in Malaysia the corresponding figure was only 5 percent (Jenkins and Lai 1989). Korea registered a net transfer out of agriculture in excess of 20 percent of agricultural value added in 1962–1969 and a net transfer into agriculture of 4 percent in 1970–1974, 26 percent in 1975–1979, and 34 percent in 1980–1984 (Moon and Kang 1989).

Implications for Development Strategy and Policy

Increased specialization in agricultural products—according to Ricardo's model of trade, income distribution, and growth—leads to a redistribution of income from capitalists to landowners and an accompanying shift in expenditures from investment to luxury consumption. The case for taxing primary production and exports continues to be made in the context of present-day resource-rich developing countries on the assumption that most of the income earned by the plantations and mines "leaks out" of the country in the form of profit remittances by multinational corporations and consumption of imported luxury goods by the local elite.

As Findlay (1984, 25) has pointed out, that argument no longer applies to the Asian countries, where "the owners of agricultural land are typically the cultivators themselves." Instead of having large farms owned by absentee landlords, many Asian countries have a predominance of small landholdings, averaging one hectare or less, in the hands of rural households. Indeed, owing to the industrial import-substitution policies adopted in the 1950s and 1960s, the composition of the elite has shifted from landlords to urban-based industrialists and businessmen.

Although the extraction of agricultural surplus to finance industrial capital formation is frequently assumed to be a concomitant to structural transformation during development, the efficiency with which the transferred resources are used outside agriculture is open to question. In virtually every Asian developing country where the industrial sector has been highly protected, policy-induced distortions in the product and factor markets have led to the inefficient use of investment resources for manufacturing. At the same time, the opportunities for rapid growth in productivity in agriculture cannot be discounted if the capital requirements for rural infrastructure (among other needed investments) are met. An additional consideration is the stimulus to nonagricultural production to be induced by increased rural incomes deriving from rising agricultural prices and productivity. This link to rural growth is at the heart of recent proposals to adopt an agriculture-based development strategy.[6]

The effectiveness of such a strategy depends on the extent to which the real income of rural households expands initially as a result of agricultural growth. As a first-round effect, this rise in income will help increase the demand for food as well as for labor-intensive industrial products and services that make up a large part of the consumption of rural households. In addition, such a demand stimulus will set in motion a sequence of employment and income multiplier effects on the rural, regional, and national economies. Therefore, beyond directly promoting agricultural growth, it is vital for an agriculture-based development strategy to strengthen the multiplier or linkage effects on the rest of the economy. This approach contrasts sharply with the enclave-type development strategy associated with specialization in primary products in the simple Ricardian model.

Whether supply will be able to match the increased demand for food and other labor-intensive goods that results from a rising rural income depends on the availability of production inputs and their prices. For instance, if a restrictive foreign trade regime or an underdeveloped domestic transport system makes intermediate inputs into agricultural and nonagricultural production artificially scarce or expensive, the full benefits from increased final demand in terms of output growth and labor absorption will not be realized. It will also be critical to improve the rural infrastructure, not only to help generate and distribute advanced agricultural technologies, but also to develop and integrate rural markets.

Despite comparably rapid agricultural growth in the Philippines and Taiwan during the 1960s (about 4.3 percent a year on average), Taiwan generated a much greater impetus for nonagricultural activities that led to more rapid GDP growth. This outcome has been attributed to (1) strong rural growth and labor absorption in Taiwanese agriculture, which in turn were determined by the interrelated influence of smaller landholdings, less mechanization, and more labor-using farm machinery, and (2) more favorable government policies with respect to rural infrastructure, interest rates, tariffs, the exchange rate, and fuel prices (Ranis and Stewart 1987).

The more that the consumption pattern is skewed toward food and other labor-intensive products, the greater effect that a given increase in rural income will have on total employment and the more broadly based output growth is likely to be. The households of less affluent, small agricultural and nonagricultural producers are most likely to fit this pattern; the families of the more prosperous owners of large farms and industrial enterprises generally spend more on capital-intensive goods, whether locally produced or imported. It is therefore important for improvements in price incentives, production technologies, and infrastructure facilities to reach the small producers in dispersed areas.

To reiterate, the real exchange rate is an important determinant of incentives for agricultural production. Therefore, to "get prices right" for agriculture, policy makers must carefully examine the conduct of trade and macroeconomic policies, not just sector-specific pricing policies, to determine their effects on the real exchange rate. Most Asian developing countries will need to prevent the real exchange rate from becoming overvalued, so as not to impair the price competitiveness of agricultural tradable goods. This means that they may have to liberalize the import restrictions unduly protective of domestic industry and make every effort to maintain a sustainable external account. In the long run, an improved exchange rate policy encourages not only export production, but also efficient import substitution in agriculture and in the rest of the economy.

Notes to Chapter 10

1. Sri Lanka deviated from this general pattern—its first decade of independence was characterized by free trade and a heavy dependence on exports of tree crops. It was only in the late 1950s that the government began to actively promote industrial development via import substitution.

2. Note, too, that the tax rates for imports represent the average for "all imports." Nonfood consumer imports have been taxed more heavily than have imports of food and producer goods.

3. See Binswanger and Scandizzo (1983), for example, for estimates of the nominal protection coefficient—the ratio of domestic to foreign prices at the same point in the marketing chain—for two to six of the leading crops from Bangladesh, Pakistan, India, Korea, Thailand, and the Philippines.

4. Some adjustments were made for transport costs, storage costs, and differences in quality. This measure does not include the protection or penalty from the pricing of intermediate inputs. Because of data limitations, not all the country studies in the World Bank project produced estimates of the "effective protection rate," which would have indicated the extent to which domestic agricultural value added was protected. It would appear, however, that the structure of protection is not significantly affected by taking into account the cost of intermediate inputs because of the latter's relatively small share in the value of agricultural output.

5. Since most households both consume and produce, what really matters are the *net* effects on them as consumers *and* producers. Unfortunately, the studies cited above have not evaluated those effects.

6. See Mellor (1976) for an early statement.

The Effects of Trade
and Macroeconomic Policies
on Agricultural Incentives
in Latin America

This chapter reviews the research on the effects of trade and macro-economic policies on agricultural incentives and the performance of agriculture in Latin America.[1] Two policies have had a particularly important influence: industrial protection and government expenditures. General equilibrium models have been used to analyze the relationship between trade and macroeconomic policies and agricultural incentives.

The first section looks at the studies that emphasize the effect of trade policy on agricultural incentives, the next section at those that address the impact of macroeconomic policies on agricultural incentives and economic growth. The effect of trade and macroeconomic policies on the real income of rural labor is dealt with in the third section. The last section presents some conclusions.

Trade Policy and Agricultural Incentives

Most Latin American countries are exporters of agricultural products. Very few are net importers. Policies that have led to a real appreciation of domestic currencies have discouraged the production of exportables. At the same time, countries that are net importers and in which agricultural imports have been relatively free of import restrictions have

227

found that a real appreciation of the currency has stimulated imports and reduced the incentive to produce import-competing agricultural products (as has been the case in Mexico).

Developments in the external sector and in the agricultural sector are linked through the real exchange rate (units of domestic currency per unit of foreign currency × foreign price index/domestic price index or price index of traded commodities/price index of nontraded commodities). The studies that examine the impact of trade policy on agricultural incentives using a general equilibrium framework compare the effects of direct interventions—those specific to a particular product—with the effects of indirect (economywide) interventions. Economists have used the traded-nontraded goods model and the elasticity approach to exchange rate and balance of payments for the analysis.

The Traded-Nontraded Goods Model

This model has been used to determine the incidence of commercial policy, ω, defined as the percentage change in the price of exportables in relation to the price of nontraded goods, on the relative price of agricultural commodities.

In most Latin American countries, the agricultural sector can be categorized as exportable. For present purposes, this classification pertains also to countries that are net importers of agricultural products because they give priority to agricultural imports for food or industrial raw materials. Therefore, appreciation of the domestic currency in real terms discourages the production of both agricultural exportables and importables. It is also assumed here that the industrial sector is import-competing. Finally, the services sector can be associated in most countries with the nontraded goods sector, except in the case of Mexico because of tourism, an exportable commodity.

The model.   The model has three sectors: importables, exportables, and nontraded (see Corden 1971; Dornbusch 1974 and 1980, Chap. 6). For a small open economy, the international price of importables and exportables is given by the world market, while the price of nontraded goods is determined by domestic demand and supply.

A value of one for ω means that a tariff increase causes the same percentage increase in the price of nontraded goods and importables. Thus, all prices but those of exports rise by the same amount as the increase in the tariff, or the prices of exportables fall in relation to prices in the rest of the economy. As a result, resources move out of export activities. Because the prices of import-competing commodities and nontraded goods have risen proportionately, however, resources will not necessarily move into import-competing activities, the objective of protection. In fact, the net increase in protection for import-competing activities is nil. That is, the economic authorities cannot control the "true" amount of protection that results.

Empirical evidence.   Most studies estimating the incidence of commercial policy with the traded/nontraded goods model have used the model to measure the impact of policy on the export sector. In a review of studies on Chile, Uruguay, Argentina, El Salvador, Australia, Brazil, and Colombia, Clements and Sjaastad (1984) noted that the estimates of ω, the incidence of commercial policy, ranged from a low of 53 percent for Chile to a high of 95 percent for Colombia. Agriculture was the main export in all countries except Chile, whose main export sector is mining, but even there an important part of the agricultural sector—fruits—was an exportable. For a long time, however, Chile imported agricultural products, mainly because of an overvalued currency that made imports cheaper.

García García (1981) estimated the incidence of commercial policy and measured overall protection and the overvaluation resulting from this policy for Colombia for the period 1953–1978. To determine the net incentive provided to produce a given product, he compared the overvaluation with the amount of protection or subsidization resulting from direct interventions in that product's market (see Krueger, Schiff, and Valdés 1988 for the distinction between direct and indirect interventions).

García García found that during most of the 1970s the incidence of protection in Colombia (the value of ω) was up to 95 percent and protection to import-competing activities thus strongly discouraged the exportable sector, including agriculture, since 60 percent of its output is exportable. García García also found that, on average, the tariffs and quantitative restrictions raised the domestic price of imports by 53–70 percent in the period from 1956 to 1967 and by about 20 percent from 1967 to 1978.[2] He estimated that this implicit import tax plus the specific interventions led to an overall net tax on coffee agriculture of 68–85 percent in 1956–1967 and 36 percent in 1967–1978, on noncoffee export agriculture of 20–37 percent in 1956–1967 and 4 percent in 1967–1978, and on industrial exports of around 10–27 percent in 1956–1967 and 10 percent in 1967–1978.

García García also compared the extent of overvaluation of the peso (to simplify, he assumed it to be, on average, 70 percent in 1956–1967 and 30 percent in 1967–1978) with the nominal rate of protection (or taxation) for selected products. The net result of all policy interventions between 1956 and 1978 was protection for the production of milk and wheat and taxation of the production of cotton and coffee. Rice, corn, and sugar were protected in the 1950s and 1960s but taxed in the 1970s.

Valdés and Leon (1987) estimated the effect of protection in Peru on exportables in general, on agricultural and nonagricultural exportables, and on agricultural importables. They found the incidence of commercial policy to be around 0.7 for all exportables and 0.46 and 0.26 for agricultural importables and exportables, respectively. That is, commercial policy in Peru discriminated against import-competing agriculture more than against exportable agriculture. In addition, the uniform tariff equivalent of the barriers to trade went from an average of 5.4 percent in 1949–1953 to a peak of 256 percent in 1969–1973. "True" protection for import-competing activities increased from 2 percent to 28 percent, and the "true" tax on exportables from 3 percent to 65 percent.

Franklin and Valdés (Chapter 2, this volume) extended the analysis of Valdés and Leon (1987) to the policy effects on agriculture in Peru—specifically, on the impact of the extreme attempts to close the economy to manufactured imports and isolate domestic prices from world prices. They report that from 1964 to 1968 and 1969 to 1973, a time of intense import substitution, when the equivalent tariff rose from 133 percent to 256 percent, the relative producer prices of nontradable food, importable food, and agricultural exports decreased by 3 percent, 23 percent, and 35 percent, respectively. In turn, the output of nontraded food rose 3 percent, while the output of importable food and exportables decreased 4 percent and 17 percent, respectively. Industrial production increased 18 percent. Because of the decline in the production of agricultural exportables and importables, foreign exchange earnings declined, and Peru needed large amounts of agricultural imports.

In studying the transfers from the beef sector to the rest of the economy in Uruguay, as well as their distribution, Sapelli (1984) found that commercial policy in 1930 generated transfers from exporters equivalent to 9 percent of the gross national product (GNP), of which 0.3 percent went to import-competing firms and 8.7 percent to consumers. In 1961 exporters lost 19 percent of GNP, while consumers-taxpayers gained 11.9 percent of GNP and import-competing firms 7.1 percent. The average transfer from exporters for the period 1956–1978, when there was an equivalent tariff of 100 percent, was 15.6 percent of GNP. Since agriculture's share of GNP was 16 percent and 90 percent of agricultural products were exported, the tax on the sector's output was equivalent to 50 percent.

As Jarvis and Medero (1989) discuss, the government in Uruguay made an effort to control the domestic price of beef by means of a beef export tax and the exchange rate policy. The government related the tax rate for beef exports to the price of beef exports, and the real exchange rate to the international price of beef, the export tax, and other macro-economic variables (rate of increase in the money supply, rate of growth of industrial countries, and the price of wool, Uruguay's other important export). It appears that close to two-thirds of the variation in the tax on beef exports can be explained by the international price of beef and the real exchange rate, which were positively associated with the tax. That is, when international beef prices or the real exchange rate rose, the tax on beef exports increased. Jarvis and Medero also found that a higher beef price tended to reduce the real exchange rate and a higher export tax to increase it. When they tested for the joint effect of export taxes, the real exchange rate, and other variables, they found that these poli-cies stabilized domestic beef prices over time.

The Elasticities Approach

The World Bank used an elasticities approach in a comparative study of the political economy of agricultural policies[3] in Argentina, Brazil, Co-lombia, Chile, and the Dominican Republic.[4] The study focused on a set of agricultural products rather than the entire agricultural sector, as did Oliveira (1981, 1983) in his calculations of the amount of transfers from Brazil's agricultural sector to the rest of the economy. The World Bank study distinguished between the effects of direct and indirect policy interventions: the former affect the price of a product or its inputs di-rectly, while the latter (overall commercial and macroeconomic policies) affect the exchange rate and, in turn, the prices of traded agricultural products and the traded part of the nonagricultural sector. To measure these effects, researchers drew a distinction between prevailing relative prices and relative prices in the absence of direct and total (indirect plus direct) interventions.

Table 11.1 shows that the direct interventions sometimes favored agricultural producers, in some instances by large amounts. Further, and this is a key point, in most cases the indirect interventions substan-tially reduced the incentives for agricultural producers and swamped the positive effects of the direct interventions. Moreover, the negative effects of the indirect interventions magnified the negative effects of the direct interventions.

The strongest cases of taxation occurred in Brazil from 1966 to 1983 and in Argentina from 1960 to 1984, followed by Chile until 1975. The taxation of agriculture in Brazil and Chile was the result mainly of indirect interventions, but in Argentina the mechanism was direct interventions. Also in Brazil and Chile, the direct interventions tended to favor the production of some agricultural products. Because Argentina taxed agricultural exports, the exchange rate rose and offset, in part, the

TABLE 11.1   Divergence between Prevailing Relative Prices and
              Relative Prices in the Absence of Direct and Indirect
              Interventions for Selected Products (percentage)

	Direct intervention			Total intervention		
Argentina						
	Wheat	Meat	Corn	Wheat	Meat	Corn
1960–1965	−20	−35	−5	−42	−53	−31
1966–1970	−12	−27	−14	−38	−48	−39
1971–1975	−42	−29	−39	−56	−46	−54
1976–1980	−29	−11	−22	−48	−40	−48
1981–1984	−17	−14	−19	−47	−53	−48
Chile						
	Wheat	Meat	Milk	Wheat	Meat	Milk
1960–1965	8	−12	215	−43	53	67
1966–1970	9	−25	166	−29	−51	74
1971–1975	−17	−33	86	−50	−59	25
1976–1980	17	−16	113	21	−13	93
Dominican Republic						
	Sugar	Coffee	Rice	Sugar	Coffee	Rice
1966–1972	581	−5	23	144	−33	−10
1973–1977	−51	−14	2	−62	−31	−16
1978–1981	−1	−6	19	−39	−30	−10
1982–1985	183	−40	60	67	−65	19
Brazil						
	Cotton	Corn	Soybeans	Cotton	Corn	Soybeans
1966–1970	−16	42	0[a]	−28	22	−18[a]
1971–1975	−9	42	−17	−26	14	−30
1976–1980	2	26	−28	−19	1	−43
1981–1983	8	17	−16	−7	0	−27
Colombia						
	Wheat	Cotton	Coffee	Wheat	Cotton	Coffee
1960–1965	24	2	−7	−8	−1	−31
1966–1970	24	7	−17	−5	2	−36
1971–1975	−8	−5	−9	−30	−9	−30
1976–1980	5	1	−11	−22	−9	−34
1981–1983	20	9	−8	−24	−6	−41

a. Corresponds to the value for 1970.
SOURCES: For Argentina and Chile, Valdés (1986, Table X-2); for the Dominican Republic, Greene and Roe (1989, Tables 10A, 10B, 11A); for Brazil, Brandão and Carvalho (1987, Tables 3.2 and 3.3); and for Colombia, García García and Montes Llamas (1989, Tables 4.5 and 4.6).

downward effect of the import tariffs. Colombia and the Dominican Republic showed the same pattern as Chile and Brazil: indirect interventions were the main source of discrimination against agriculture.

The main conclusion of these studies was that trade and macro-economic policies were the principal sources of discrimination against agriculture and the main cause of resource transfers out of agriculture.

The large transfers of resources out of agriculture between 1960 and 1983 were mainly due to the indirect interventions. In the Dominican Republic, Argentina, and Colombia, direct interventions in the output and input markets caused net transfers out of agriculture of 14 percent, 8 percent, and 1 percent, respectively. By contrast, direct interventions in Brazil and Chile produced transfers into the agricultural sectors of 22 percent and 2 percent of agricultural GDP. Indirect interventions generated a transfer of resources out of agriculture in all countries but Brazil. Thus, the combined effect of the direct and indirect interventions in the output and input markets was a transfer of resources out of agriculture equivalent to 57 percent, 13 percent, 14 percent, and 32 percent of agricultural GDP in Argentina, Chile, Colombia, and the Dominican Republic. Only in Brazil did the agricultural sector receive transfers, equivalent to 17 percent of agricultural GDP, attributable mainly to the subsidy on agricultural credit.[5]

Oliveira (1983) obtained different results in his study of Brazil. However, he did not include credit subsidies in estimating the income transfers, while including all traditional exports that were systematically taxed. Oliveira estimated the value of transfers between the agricultural sector and the rest of the economy during the period from 1950 to 1974 by constructing an index of the free trade equilibrium exchange rate and then constructing an index of prices and implicit exchange rates for agricultural output and categories of inputs (fertilizers and machinery) and products (traditional exports, nontraditional exports, and raw materials, food, and importables used in the domestic market). Having constructed these indexes and assuming no divergence between foreign and domestic prices in the base year (1950), he calculated the relative rate of the implicit tax incidence (or subsidy) on agricultural output, inputs, and various categories of output.

On the product side, Oliveira found that, in the early 1950s, Brazil subsidized agriculture as a whole but taxed traditional export agriculture (for example, coffee) and agricultural commodities used as industrial raw materials. The subsidy finding was probably the result of his assuming free trade in 1950.[6] Oliveira also found that discrimination against Brazilian agriculture began in the late 1950s, peaked in the mid-1960s, fell somewhat in the late 1960s and early 1970s, and picked up again in the mid-1970s. On the input side, inputs appear to have been subsidized, except for machinery during the years from 1952 to 1958 and from 1964 to 1970. Oliveira then computed the effective tax incidence on agriculture (the net rate of income lost by the sector as a proportion of its value added). Agriculture received a small subsidy (2 percent) in 1950–1952 and was taxed by 11.2 percent in 1953–1957 and by 36 percent in 1958–1974. Average taxation of agriculture during the period was 36 percent, reaching a peak of 48.4 percent in 1964. Because of this taxation, the contribution of agriculture to GDP was undervalued by 20–70 percent of its measured values. Oliveira did not correct the contribution of agriculture to GDP for the undervaluation that resulted from measuring the output of industry and services at domestic rather than international prices.

Macroeconomic Policies, Agricultural Incentives, and Growth

As is now well known, changes in the terms of trade and in macroeconomic policies, in particular fiscal policy, can greatly affect agricultural incentives. Given the substantial macroeconomic disruptions that have taken place in Latin America since the end of World War II, it is surprising that the literature in this area is so limited. Because the research pertains specifically to Argentina, Chile, and Colombia (see Cavallo and Mundlak 1982, 1986; Coeymans and Mundlak 1984; and in this volume, Chapters 8, 9, and 3, respectively), I will focus my remarks on them.

Static Models

The experience of Colombia during the period 1967–1983 provides useful information for analyzing the effects of agricultural incentives and the performance of Latin American countries subject to commodity booms (and busts) and expansionary fiscal policies (see García García 1983; Montes Llamas 1984; Thomas et al. 1985; García García and Montes Llamas 1988). Commodity booms and government expenditures impinge on agriculture through their impact on the real exchange rate. Because a large proportion of agricultural output is tradable, a real depreciation (appreciation) of the currency causes the relative price of agricultural output to increases (decrease) and thereby encourages (discourages) agricultural production and net exports (see Chapter 3).[7]

The results of the estimated equations in García García and Montes Llamas (1988) and in Chapter 3 of this volume support the argument that improvements in the terms of trade and increases in government expenditures reduced the relative price of the noncoffee tradable sector and of the agricultural sector.

In estimating real exchange rate equations for Argentina, Cavallo and Mundlak (1982), Cavallo (1985), and Mundlak, Cavallo, and

Domenech (Chapter 8, this volume) found that the share of government consumption in total income, the deficit of the public sector financed by borrowing in the foreign and domestic markets (as a proportion of total income), and the rate of growth of the money supply in excess of the rate of nominal devaluation tended to produce a real appreciation in the currency. Because agriculture was an exportable sector, agricultural incentives were negatively correlated with the above variables.

Comparative Dynamic Models

Cavallo and Mundlak (1982) were the first to use comparative dynamic models to study the impact of trade and macroeconomic policies on agricultural growth in Argentina for the period 1940–1972. Following up on this work, Mundlak, Cavallo, and Domenech (1989) looked at three sectors (agriculture, nonagriculture excluding government, and government) in the period from 1913 to 1984. Coeymans and Mundlak (1984) incorporated five sectors (agriculture, mining, manufacturing, services, and government) in a similar study for Chile for the period 1960–1982. The models on Argentina and Chile are presented in Chapters 8 and 9 of this volume, respectively.

Summary

In the simulation exercises for Argentina and Chile, the national economy and agriculture in particular were highly responsive to relative price changes. That is to say, policies that produced a real appreciation in the domestic currency had a considerable negative effect on agricultural output, employment, and real wages. Indeed, it appears that the policies of forced industrialization through import substitution did significant damage to the agricultural sector throughout Latin America. At the same time, by reducing real rural wages and employment opportunities in agriculture, they caused a sharp reduction in the real income of the rural population.

Effects on Real Rural Wages

A Model and Some Empirical Evidence

A simple model of supply and demand for labor in agriculture can be used to analyze the impact of trade policy on real rural wages. This model is particularly useful for countries in which data are in poor supply. The absence of data is no doubt one of the reasons for the lack of research on the impact of trade and macroeconomic policies on the incomes of rural labor in Latin America. Another reason is that most efforts to date have concentrated on analyzing agricultural policy by itself.

The advantage of analyzing agricultural policies in a general equilibrium context is that it draws attention to the importance of factor movements between sectors and, hence, to the interaction between the agricultural and nonagricultural markets. In the first attempts to analyze these links, researchers estimated the migration functions. Migration was attributed to an economic decision based on the real income differentials between agriculture and nonagriculture, urban unemployment, and other variables such as health and education in the rural and urban sectors.[8]

The impact of trade and macroeconomic policies on real wages is analyzed here by comparing actual real wages with real wages in the absence of interventions, using a simple model of supply and demand for labor in the agricultural sector (see García García and Montes Llamas 1988 for Colombia; and Hurtado, Muchnik, and Valdés 1990 for Chile).

In Latin America, urban unemployment coexists with a relatively high real wage in the manufacturing sector and a more competitive and informal urban labor market. Despite relatively high and sometimes rising rates of urban unemployment, labor flows from agriculture to the urban sector because people expect to get a higher-paying job there. The probability of doing so depends, among other things, on the rate of urban unemployment. Thus, it can be postulated that the higher the rate of urban unemployment, the lower the probability of finding an urban job, the lower the expected gains from migration, and the higher the supply of labor in the rural sector compared with what it would otherwise be (Todaro 1969). The size of the rural population also affects the supply of rural labor. Therefore, labor supply in the rural sector can be thought of as a function of real wages in the agricultural and urban sectors, the rate of urban unemployment, and the size of the rural population. On the demand side, the demand for labor is negatively related to the real wage and positively related to the stock of capital and the price of agricultural output in relation to its price in the nonagricultural sector (see Chapter 3 for further details of the modeling exercise for Colombia).

Hurtado, Muchnik, and Valdés (1990) followed a similar approach in their study of real agricultural wages in Chile. The explanatory variables that had a positive impact on rural real wages were labor demand for the production of fruits, vineyards, and livestock; area in crops; and nonagricultural wages; while the labor force and the price of fertilizer had a negative effect (Hurtado, Muchnick, and Valdés 1990, Table 4.7).

The study for Brazil (Brandão and Carvalho 1987) estimated a demand for labor function that depended on the price of agricultural output, tractor/land rental prices, and agricultural GDP. In this case, the only significant coefficients were the land/rental price ratio and agricultural GDP (Brandão and Carvalho 1987, Table 7.20).

Impact on Real Wages

As a result of trade and macroeconomic policies, real wages in rural Colombia between 1960 and 1983 were 15 percent below what they would otherwise have been (García García and Montes Llamas 1988). Even this result is probably an underestimation, because the lower agricultural prices discouraged capital accumulation in agriculture and pulled real wages down further.

A detailed model of intersectoral reactions in Chile demonstrates that the trade and macroeconomic policy interventions in that country between 1960 and 1981 depressed agricultural wages by 6 percent below what they would otherwise have been (Hurtado, Muchnik, and Valdés 1990, Table VII-6).

Conclusions

Several conclusions emerge from the literature on Latin America to date. First, to a large extent, the performance of agriculture is more closely tied to trade and macroeconomic policies than to sectoral policies. In general, the negative effects of the former swamped the possible positive effects of the latter.

Second, by implementing policies that reduced agricultural incentives and by forcing countries to follow a path of industrialization based on import substitution, governments have kept the standard of living of the population lower than it would otherwise have been. Because these policies discouraged investment, they also constrained capital accumulation and led to lower labor productivity than would otherwise have occurred. Although the studies reviewed in this chapter did not deal with the accumulation of human capital, it is likely that lower real incomes discouraged such investment because of an expected lower stream of labor incomes compared with what would have been generated by an economic policy more favorable to agriculture.

Third, excessively expansionary fiscal policies have increased expenditures on nontraded goods, especially labor services, and thereby have reduced the real exchange rate and discouraged economic activity in the tradable sectors.

Fourth, the agricultural sector was highly responsive to changes in economic incentives. Because the negative effects of the trade and macroeconomic policies swamped the positive agricultural incentives, it appeared instead that agricultural producers were reluctant to respond to the incentives or to adopt modern technologies and that they had great difficulty adapting to changing economic conditions. Believing this to be the case, many authorities responded with policy interventions that taxed agriculture and thus caused agricultural incentives to deteriorate further.

Fifth, the income transfers out of agriculture have not been small. In Argentina, for example, these transfers reached 50 percent of agricultural output, and in Colombia and Chile they were close to 15 percent. In Brazil, the evidence is contradictory, in part because of the range of products and inputs included in the studies. In the 1950s and 1960s, however, when the subsidy for agricultural credit was not important, the agricultural sector was strongly taxed. Because these transfers were a significant disincentive to agricultural production, they discouraged investment and technological change in agriculture.

Sixth, the trade and macroeconomic policies have led to a reduction in real rural wages: by depressing agricultural prices, in Colombia and Chile those policies left wages 15 percent and 5 percent lower than they would otherwise have been. This situation in turn led to rural-to-urban migration that has sometimes aggravated urban unemployment.

Notes to Chapter 11

1. I wish to acknowledge the financial support received from the Bogota office of the International Development Research Center and from the International Food Policy Research Institute. The views and interpretations are those of the author and not of the World Bank or its affiliated organizations.

2. To simplify, García García did not calculate an import premium from the quantitative restrictions in 1967–1978, although they were still important. Thus, the measured import tariff was underestimated.

3. Although this approach is not fully in line with the modern theory of exchange rate determination, it was adopted because it is straightforward and could be applied to a wide spectrum of countries with wide differences in terms of availability of data.

4. The authors of these studies are Sturzeneger for Argentina; Carvalho and Brandão for Brazil; García García and Montes Llamas for Colombia; Hurtado, de Rubinstein, and Valdés for Chile; and Green and Roe for the Dominican Republic. Valdés (1986) has reviewed some of the results of these studies.

5. In the case of Brazil, the negative effect of price interventions was underestimated because coffee, which had traditionally been taxed, was left out of the study.

6. Because Oliveira compared an index of implicit prices with an index of an equilibrium exchange rate, he found that in 1950 Brazilian agriculture was not discriminated against. If protection was 10 percent and a tariff index was built assuming that protection in the base year was zero, then the level of protection was underestimated.

7. Other authors (Edwards 1984, 1986a; Diaz-Alejandro 1984; Kamas 1986) have also discussed the Dutch disease phenomenon in Colombia. See also García García and Montes Llamas (1988).

8. An early analysis of this issue is found in Sahota (1968). For more recent studies, see Cavallo and Mundlak (1982, 38–39) and Coeymans (1982, 1983).

Effects of Trade and Macroeconomic Policies on African Agriculture

According to most indicators of economic performance, the countries of sub-Saharan Africa are, without doubt, the poorest and most economically distressed in the world. Per capita gross national product (GNP) for the region as a whole averaged US$560 in 1983. For the low-income countries, it was US$220, for middle-income oil importers US$610, and for middle-income oil exporters US$800.

The rate of growth of both gross domestic product (GDP) and per capita GDP declined rather sharply from the 1960s through the early 1980s (Table 12.1). During the 1960s, the overall annual rate of growth of GDP for sub-Saharan Africa averaged 3.8 percent, then fell to 3.6 percent in the 1970s, and recorded negative rates in the first three years of the 1980s. A slight recovery appears to have taken place in the subsequent three years. The average rate of GDP growth from 1980 to 1986 was only 1.1 percent (World Bank 1988). The performance of the three different categories of countries that make up the region paralleled this general pattern. Although the per capita improvement in the standard of living was marginal in the aggregate during the 1970s, in the early years of the 1980s it fell quite sharply. In fact, the low-income countries as a group suffered falling per capita income over the 1980–1983 period and recovered only slightly by 1986.

Agriculture carries a great deal of the economic burden in African

Table 12.1   Indicators of Overall Economic Performance in
Sub-Saharan Africa, 1960–1983 (average annual growth
rate, percentage)

Indicator and category of country	1960–1970	1970–1980	1981	1982	1983
Gross domestic product					
Low-income countries	4.0	1.9	1.1	0.5	2.7
Middle-income oil importers	4.2	4.5	4.0	2.6	−0.1
Middle-income oil exporters	3.5	4.1	−3.7	−1.6	−4.1
Sub-Saharan Africa	3.8	3.6	−1.0	−0.2	−0.7
Per capita GDP					
Low-income countries	1.5	−0.9	−1.9	−2.5	−0.3
Middle-income oil importers	1.5	1.2	0.6	−0.7	−3.4
Middle-income oil exporters	1.1	1.6	−6.7	−4.7	−7.3
Sub-Saharan Africa	1.3	0.7	−4.0	−3.3	−3.8

Source: World Bank (1984c, 16).

economies, and many of their problems can be linked to its performance.[1] Agriculture is the principal sector, accounting for the dominant share of GDP, income, employment, food supply, and export earnings. Indeed, agriculture accounts for about 70 percent of the labor force and provides 30–60 percent of the GDP in most African countries. It also dominates external trade: except in countries such as Nigeria, Zambia, and Zaire, where metals and minerals are significant sources of foreign exchange, agriculture accounts for well over 60 percent of export earnings. Clearly, the performance of agriculture is the most important determinant of overall economic growth in most African countries.[2]

Given the special role of agriculture in Africa's potential for economic growth, it is important to identify the main factors and policies that have hindered its growth in the past. This information should help in determining the extent to which those factors need to be removed and policies changed to help improve performance. It is also useful to analyze whether and to what extent trade and macroeconomic policies have provided overriding incentives or disincentives to agriculture.

This chapter presents a broad survey of Africa's experience, particularly during the 1970s and early 1980s, in terms of the impact of trade, exchange rate, and associated macroeconomic developments and policies on agricultural incentives and growth.[3] This discussion opens with a review of the record of growth of the agriculture sector.

Performance of African Agriculture

The rate of agricultural growth in African economies has declined steadily since the 1960s. For the sub-Saharan African countries as a

TABLE 12.2   Agricultural Growth in Sub-Saharan Africa, 1960–1982
(average annual growth rate, percentage)

Category of country	Total agriculture		Food	
	1960–1970	1970–1980	1960–1970	1970–1982
Volume of production				
Low-income countries	3.1	0.7	3.2	1.0
Middle-income oil importers	3.8	2.5	3.7	3.3
Middle-income oil exporters	1.1	2.3	1.1	2.4
Sub-Saharan Africa	2.5	1.4	2.5	1.7
Per capita production				
Low-income countries	0.9	−1.4	1.0	−1.2
Middle-income oil importers	0.7	−1.2	0.7	−0.6
Middle-income oil exporters	−1.4	−0.7	−1.4	−0.3
Sub-Saharan Africa	0.2	−1.1	0.2	−0.9

Source: World Bank (1984c, 77).

group, the total volume of agricultural production grew at an annual rate of 2.5 percent during the 1960s, but this rate fell by almost 50 percent, to 1.4 percent a year, between 1970 and 1982.

The food component of agriculture shows the same pattern (Table 12.2). In this case, the total volume of food production increased by 3.2 percent a year in 1960–1970 in the low-income countries, 3.7 percent in the middle-income oil-importing countries, and 1.1 percent in the middle-income oil-exporting countries. In the aggregate, the volume of food production rose by 2.5 percent a year during the period. From 1970 to 1982, however, performance worsened: the annual rate of growth for low-income countries fell to 1.0 percent, the aggregate rate to 1.7 percent, as the improved performance of the middle-income oil exporters was swamped by the poorer progress in the other two categories of countries. In per capita terms, marked declines occurred in food production both in the aggregate and with respect to each of the three categories of countries.

Estimates of the index of per capita food production confirm this trend. For low-income countries, the per capita food production index declined from 100 in 1970 to 86 in 1982, and it dropped to 91 for middle-income oil importers, and to 92 for middle-income oil exporters. For all sub-Saharan African countries, the index declined by 12 percent over the 1970–1982 period. Only a handful of countries (including Mauritius, Côte d'Ivoire, Rwanda, and Cameroon) posted small increases in their per capita food production indexes in this period. In sharp contrast, the larger countries such as Kenya, Tanzania, Sudan, Zaire, Ethiopia, and Nigeria recorded substantial declines.

TABLE 12.3   Growth of Africa's Major Agricultural Exports,
              1961–1982

Export	Average annual change in volume (%)		Africa's share of world exports (%)	
	1961–1963 to 1969	1969–1972 to 1980–1982	1961–1963	1980–1982
Cocoa	0.2	−0.3	79.9	68.3
Coffee	3.4	−0.2	25.6	25.9
Tea	9.0	4.1	8.7	9.3
Groundnuts, oil	2.2	−6.0	53.8	27.8
Groundnuts, shelled	−6.1	−13.9	85.5	18.0
Oilseed cake and meal	5.3	−3.8	9.5	2.2
Palm kernel oil	8.9	−1.3	55.2	21.6
Palm kernels	−6.2	−9.6	90.4	75.8
Palm oil	−8.6	−5.1	55.0	3.0
Sesame seed	3.8	−6.2	68.6	40.7
Bananas	1.7	−5.4	10.9	3.0
Cotton	5.6	−3.5	10.8	9.2
Rubber	3.0	−2.9	6.8	4.4
Sisal	−2.1	−8.7	60.7	60.4
Sugar	3.2	1.4	4.7	4.8
Tobacco	−3.1	6.6	12.1	11.8

Source: World Bank (1984c, 80–81).

In view of the heavy reliance on exports of primary commodities, the performance of African agriculture has significant implications for the countries' foreign exchange earnings, as the trend in export volume and market share of Africa's major export crops indicate. There were substantial declines in the volume of virtually all agricultural export crops, particularly during the 1970s and early 1980s (Table 12.3). In the case of some crops—for example, shelled groundnuts, palm kernels, palm oil, bananas, and sisal—the beginning of this sharp downward trend in export volume began in the early 1960s. As a result, Africa suffered significant losses in market shares between the early 1960s and 1980s. Particularly noticeable were the losses for cocoa (from 80 percent to 68 percent), groundnut oil (54 percent to 28 percent), shelled groundnuts (86 percent to 18 percent), oilseed cake and meal (10 percent to 2 percent), palm kernel oil (55 percent to 3 percent), sesame seed (69 percent to 41 percent), and bananas (11 percent to 3 percent). In those few cases where gains were achieved, such as coffee, tea, and sugar, they were marginal.

Africa's agricultural growth record worsened in the early 1980s, and the region's food self-sufficiency declined. The incremental demand for

TABLE 12.4   Food and Agricultural Imports of Sub-Saharan Africa, 1962–1984

Imports	1962–1969	1970–1979	1980–1984
Low-income countries			
Value of imports (millions of US$)	16.5	42.1	83.7
As % of total imports	12.0	13.4	14.7
As % of export earnings	17.0	21.4	29.7
Middle-income oil importers			
Value of imports (millions of US$)	24.4	74.7	158.9
As % of total imports	17.4	15.6	14.1
As % of export earnings	19.5	19.4	19.1
Middle-income oil exporters			
Value of imports (millions of US$)	33.0	215.9	616.3
As % of total imports	7.8	7.1	7.1
As % of export earnings	9.7	8.3	7.8

SOURCE: Oyejide and Tran (1989).

food had to be met increasingly by commercial imports and food aid.[4] As far back as the 1960s, Africa's imports of food and agricultural products had grown rapidly in both volume and value. Several indicators of the size of these imports are given in Table 12.4. In the low-income countries, the average annual value of food and agricultural imports rose from US$16.5 million in 1962–1969 to US$83.7 million in 1980–1984. The figures for the middle-income oil importers ranged between US$24.4 million and US$158.9 million, while for the middle-income oil-exporting countries they rose dramatically, from US$33 million in 1962–1969 to over US$616 million in 1980–1984.

To finance these imports over this period, the low-income countries had to set aside between 17 percent and 30 percent of their export earnings every year. The proportion of those earnings consumed by food and agricultural imports in the middle-income oil-importing countries averaged 19 percent, whereas that for the oil exporters hovered around 8–10 percent. The general pattern of Africa's food and agricultural imports indicates especially sharp increases in 1970–1979 and the dominance of cereals, particularly wheat and rice, in the imports (Oyejide and Tran 1986).[5]

Although imports of cereals by low-income African countries roughly doubled in volume between 1974 and 1986, these countries also received substantial amounts of food aid over the same period (World Bank 1988). Thus, the countries for which an external food supply was particularly important received 38 percent of this in the form of food aid in 1986 compared with 23 percent in 1974.

The Policy Framework

Macroeconomic policies in African countries from 1960s through the early 1980s were driven by both internal and external factors. One of the more enduring internal factors was the deep commitment to industrialization as the key to economic growth, with import substitution under a closely controlled trade regime as the primary means of achieving this development objective. This approach gave rise to trade and exchange rate policy packages that sought to transfer resources out of agriculture and into the industrial sector.

Increases in the world prices of certain primary and mineral products in the early 1970s also led to a number of important developments. As these increases raised export earnings and government revenues, they permitted African countries to launch some expansionary fiscal and monetary policies. When exports weakened by mid-1970 and government revenues fell off following subsequent declines in world commodity prices, expansionary government spending was not (and for sociopolitical reasons could not be) discontinued quickly. Instead, governments financed the resulting fiscal deficits with external borrowing, greater domestic credit to government, and the accumulation of domestic and external trade arrears. A largely inhospitable international economic environment compounded sub-Saharan Africa's economic problems starting in the mid-1970s: the oil price shocks, the economic recession in industrial countries, the steep rise in international interest rates, and the worsening terms of trade made it particularly difficult for the relatively fragile and undiversified African economies to manage their affairs.

Partly as a result of these developments and partly because of the policy reactions to them, annual rates of inflation in Africa almost doubled—from about 15 percent in 1975 to almost 30 percent in 1983. Fiscal deficits rose from 3.2 percent of GDP during 1970–1974 to 6.3 percent in 1980–1985, while debt-service ratios increased sharply from less than 6 percent in 1970 to 25 percent in 1984.

A strikingly similar policy reaction among African countries was their attempt to maintain official domestic exchange rates at constant levels in the face of rising domestic rates of inflation and the widening gap between those and international rates of inflation, as well as other changing international economic conditions. To deal with the scarcity of foreign exchange resulting from both internal and external problems, most African countries resorted to trade and exchange controls and began relying more heavily on external borrowing and foreign aid. In the end, sub-Saharan Africa's real exchange rate appreciated by 31 percent between the late 1960s and early 1980s (Table 12.5).

TABLE 12.5   Index of Real Exchange Rates in Some Sub-Saharan African Countries, 1973–1983 (1969–1971 = 100)

Country	1973–1975	1975–1980	1981–1983
Cameroon	75	58	80
Côte d'Ivoire	81	56	74
Ethiopia	93	64	67
Ghana	89	23	8
Kenya	88	69	86
Malawi	94	85	94
Mali	68	50	66
Niger	80	56	74
Nigeria	76	43	41
Senegal	71	60	85
Sierra Leone	100	90	73
Sudan	76	58	74
Tanzania	85	69	51
Zambia	90	79	86
All sub-Saharan Africa	84	62	69

SOURCE: World Bank (1987b).

The aggregate degree of real exchange rate appreciation in sub-Saharan Africa over this period hides marked differences across individual countries. For instance, the real appreciation was particularly substantial in Ghana and Nigeria, whose real exchange rates fell by 92 percent and 59 percent, respectively. In comparison, the rate in Malawi was only 6 percent over the same period, and by 1983 countries such as Senegal, Kenya, and Cameroon were beginning to achieve a turnaround in the direction of exchange rate policy. These countries notwithstanding, some estimates reveal that the weighted index of the real effective exchange rate for sub-Saharan African countries appreciated by as much as 75 percent between 1974 and 1984 (World Bank 1987b).

How Macroeconomic Policies Affect Agriculture

The difficulties that African agriculture has experienced since the 1960s can be attributed to at least three leading factors. First, at the level of the international economic environment, the prices of Africa's major agricultural exports have exhibited a generally downward trend since the early 1970s, and a substantial loss in the terms of trade. Between 1980 and 1982 alone, this loss was estimated at 1.2 percent of GDP for all sub-Saharan African countries (World Bank 1984c, 12). The average annual changes in the terms of trade for these countries were −1.4 percent in 1980–1984, −5.9 percent in 1985, −23.5 percent in 1986, and 1.1

percent in 1987 (World Bank 1988). Second, Africa's predominantly rain-fed agriculture is frequently exposed to unfavorable weather and other climatic conditions such as the Sahelian drought of the 1970s, and its fragile soils have hindered long-term agricultural growth.

Third, domestic economic policies have played an important part in retarding agricultural development through their impact on the incentives for agricultural production. These incentives derive partly from sector- and commodity-specific government interventions and partly from economywide trade, exchange rate, and general macroeconomic policies. That is, realized (in contrast to intended) agricultural production incentives represent the combined effect of sector-specific interventions with respect to the marketing and pricing of agricultural inputs and output, on the one hand, and trade, exchange rate, and general macroeconomic policies, on the other.

In the 1960s and 1970s, research focused largely on understanding and measuring the impact of sector-specific policies that had a direct bearing on agriculture. More recently, it has been recognized that macroeconomic policies that apparently have no such direct effect may still have a significant positive or negative impact on the sector. Therefore it is essential to examine sector-specific policies that have "direct" effects and macroeconomic policies whose impact is largely "indirect" in order to determine what incentives and disincentives these measures create for agriculture.

Both types of policies impinge on the production incentives for agriculture through their impact on relative prices. Sectoral policies, such as agricultural trade barriers, taxes, subsidies, and marketing margins, as well as agricultural input and product price controls, place a wedge between the domestic farmgate prices of agricultural products and their world prices at the border. When sectoral policies impose net taxes on agriculture, they contribute to the bias against agriculture and may reduce the positive impact of other policies, or exacerbate their negative impact. These other policies consist of general trade, exchange rate, and macroeconomic measures that are designed primarily to implement development strategy and manage the overall economy.

Because of the diverse objectives behind general macroeconomic policies, various kinds of strategies may be proposed. The trade regime may, for instance, reflect a development strategy that seeks to promote industries behind tariff protection. The trade and exchange rate policies that sustain this strategy then shift resources out of agriculture by reducing its profitability in relation to that of industry and thus turn the internal terms of trade against agriculture.[6] In other words, industrialization through protection penalizes agriculture by (1) increasing the prices of import-competing industrial goods relative to the prices of import-competing and export agriculture, and (2) increasing the cost of agricultural inputs.

Macroeconomic policies may include expansionary fiscal and monetary measures designed, perhaps, to generate employment and expand output. At the same time, they may lead to higher domestic inflation, and, unless exchange rates are appropriately adjusted, the local currency could become overvalued. In that event, the bias against agriculture may even cause protection to accrue to the industrial sector. Even if the expansionary fiscal and monetary policies owe their origins to a commodity boom and its associated capital inflows, the effects may still be the same.

Both sector-specific and general macroeconomic policies can, in principle, have positive or negative effects on agricultural incentives. One set of policies may also be adjusted to mitigate the adverse effects of the other. Thus, agricultural policies may be designed and implemented to offset the implicit taxation imposed by general macroeconomic policies. By the same token, however, sector-specific policies may in fact amplify the adverse effects of macroeconomic policies. Whether sectoral trade and pricing policies compensate for any macroeconomic bias against agriculture, their effects cannot be adequately determined in isolation from the impact of macroeconomic policies on incentives.

One way of tackling this problem is to analyze how sector-specific and general macroeconomic policies affect agriculture through their effects on the real exchange rate (Valdés 1985). Defined as the ratio of the price of tradables to nontradables, the real exchange rate plays a key role in the profitability of import-competing and export agriculture. It provides a long-term signal for the allocation and reallocation of resources across and within various sectors of the economy and serves as the primary mechanism through which trade, exchange rate, and macroeconomic policies affect agriculture. Thus, trade policies that sustain protection for the industrial sector may result in, for instance, lower real exchange rates, since protection increases the prices of protected imported goods in comparison with the prices of exportables and home goods. Thus, an appreciation of the real exchange rate penalizes nonprotected import-competing and exportable goods in the agriculture sector.[7]

Similarly, budget deficits that result from chronic balance of payments problems and that are financed by foreign borrowing or assistance reduce the real exchange rate to a lower level than it would otherwise be. This real exchange rate appreciation imposes an implicit tax on agricultural tradables. Moreover, an expansionary fiscal policy that raises total government spending tends to reduce the real exchange rate to the extent that part of the additional expenditures are for home goods, whose prices rise. Further, the large shifts in the terms of trade associated with export booms and the Dutch disease phenomenon, as well as the corresponding capital inflows, lead to an appreciation of the real exchange rate (Corden and Neary 1982). This development occurs because the "spending" effect of the additional income emanating from the boom tends to boost the demand for both tradables and nontradables and to increase the price of the latter.

Both sector-specific and general economywide macroeconomic policies ultimately affect agricultural incentives through their impact on relative prices. Economywide policies affect the relative prices of agricultural products through changes in the real exchange rate. These policies can have particularly strong effects on agriculture in small open economies, effects that may overwhelm more favorable sector-specific agricultural policies.

The Impact of Trade, Exchange Rate, and Macroeconomic Policies

In the 1960s and the 1970s, much of the research on African agriculture concentrated on developments within the sector. Not much was done to link agricultural performance to changing macroeconomic developments and policies. It is clear, however, that even when the analysis is limited to the impact of sector-specific policies, the primary aim of policy in many African countries was not the improvement of agricultural incentives, at least until the mid-1970s.

Two basic factors seem to explain this general pattern. One was the commitment to industrialization and the financing of the industrial sector's development through the transfer of resources from agriculture. The various ambitious development plans launched in Africa through the early part of the 1970s were constructed on the assumption that funds for their financing would be generated from an agricultural surplus, complemented by foreign assistance. Second, many countries depended heavily on taxes from trade as a source of government revenue. Since agricultural exports accounted for such a large proportion of total export earnings, it was inevitable that agriculture would bear a heavy tax burden.

For these and other related reasons, the governments in most African countries have played a leading role in determining the producer prices for all major crops through the use of parastatal crop-marketing authorities, periodic fixing of single pan-territorial prices for scheduled crops, and the imposition of export taxes and, in some cases, input subsidies. As the export taxes increased through the 1970s, parastatal

TABLE 12.6   Nominal Protection Coefficients for Sub-Saharan Africa, 1969–1983

Agricultural crops	1969–1971	1973–1975	1978–1980	1981–1983
Cereals	0.75	0.61	1.04	1.12
Other food crops	0.60	0.40	0.70	0.88
Export crops	0.71	0.68	0.68	0.72
All crops	0.73	0.60	0.87	0.99

SOURCE: Kerr (1985).

marketing margins also widened, so that producer prices tended to fall well below international prices, even when these are converted to local currency at the official exchange rates.

Kerr (1985) has assembled and aggregated estimates of the nominal coefficients of protection (NPC) (that is, ratios of farmgate prices to border prices after adjusting for transportation and related costs) to produce a fairly representative picture for sub-Saharan African countries (Table 12.6).[8] It is clear from the estimates that sectoral pricing, marketing, and trade policies were generally unfavorable to agriculture through the early 1980s. The NPC for all crops remained below 1 throughout the period, although the ratio of producer prices to world prices increased from 1978 onward and approached unity by 1983. Thus, without taking the effects of macroeconomic policies into account, sectoral measures did not provide adequate agricultural incentives.

The crop categories can be distinguished, first, in the treatment of export crops compared to cereals, particularly from the mid-1970s on. Whereas the taxing of export crops at the nominal level continued through the early 1980s, cereals received substantially improved protection, also at the nominal level, between 1978 and 1983.

The effects of macroeconomic policies can be determined in part by reevaluating the rates of protection using estimates of the real exchange rate rather than the official exchange rate, on the assumption that movements in the real exchange rate approximately capture the changes in macroeconomic policy. A comparison of the NPC computed at the official exchange rate with the real coefficient of protection derived using real exchange rates provides some insights into the direction and approximate magnitude of the effects of macroeconomic policies.

With this procedure, it appears that any substantial improvements in agricultural incentives (as measured by the NPC) were sharply eroded by the real exchange rate appreciation between the late 1960s and early 1980s (Table 12.7). In addition, there is a clear difference in incentives, both nominal and real, for the production of cereals and export crops. In the aggregate, although the nominal incentives for cereal production in

TABLE 12.7   Index of Nominal and Real Protection Coefficients for
Cereal and Export Crops in Selected Sub-Saharan
African Countries, 1981–1983 (1969–1971 = 100)

Country	Cereals		Export crops	
	Nominal index	Real index	Nominal index	Real index
Cameroon	140	108	95	95
Côte d'Ivoire	119	87	99	71
Ethiopia	73	49	101	66
Kenya	115	98	98	84
Malawi	106	100	106	97
Mali	177	122	98	70
Niger	225	166	113	84
Nigeria	160	66	149	63
Senegal	104	89	75	64
Sierra Leone	184	143	92	68
Sudan	229	169	105	75
Tanzania	188	95	103	52
Zambia	146	125	93	80
All sub-Saharan countries	151	109	102	72

SOURCE: World Bank (1987b, 68).

sub-Saharan Africa increased by 51 percent between the late 1960s and
early 1980s, in real terms the improvement was only 9 percent. In comparison, the nominal incentives for export crops increased by only 2
percent over the same period, a level that ultimately translated into a net
decline of 27 percent in terms of real incentives. Thus, although net
positive agricultural incentives were provided through various sector-
specific policies, they were not sufficiently high to compensate for the
much stronger disincentives implicit in the macroeconomic policies simultaneously being implemented over the 1970s and early 1980s.

The experience of individual countries gives strong support to this
conclusion. Because of the sharp real exchange rate appreciation in Nigeria, for example, a 60 percent increase in the nominal incentives for
cereal production was transformed into a 34 percent fall in real
incentives.[9] At the same time, while the incentives for export crop production improved by 49 percent in nominal terms, they actually fell by
37 percent in real terms.

Implicit in this analysis is the idea that a given level of real agricultural price protection can be decomposed into at least two parts: one that
reflects the impact of sectoral policies, and one that covers the effects of
macroeconomic policies, operating through changes in the real exchange rate. Following Kerr (1985), this decomposition (Table 12.8)
shows that between 1969 and 1983: (1) the index of agricultural incen-

TABLE 12.8   Components of Real Incentives for Sub-Saharan
African Countries, 1969–1983

	Index of real incentives	Index of incentives from sectoral policies	Index of incentives from macroeconomic policies
Cereals			
1969–1971	100	100	100
1973–1975	68	81	84
1978–1980	90	139	64
1981–1983	115	149	77
Other food crops			
1969–1971	100	100	100
1973–1975	55	67	83
1978–1980	73	117	63
1981–1983	102	147	69
Export crops			
1969–1971	100	100	100
1973–1975	80	96	84
1978–1980	62	96	65
1981–1983	71	101	70
All crops			
1969–1971	100	100	100
1973–1975	68	82	83
1978–1980	75	119	63
1981–1983	96	136	78

SOURCE: Derived from Kerr (1985).

tives attributable to macroeconomic policies fell progressively through 1980 and then in 1981–1983 regained a small part of the loss; (2) the index of agricultural incentives derived from sector-specific policies declined sharply between 1969 and then rose rapidly through 1983 so that, for all crops, an improvement of 36 percent was achieved; and (3) as a result of the combined effects of (1) and (2), the index of real agricultural incentives for all crops fell sharply up to 1975 and then began a gradual upward movement that, by 1983, left it still below its 1969–1971 value. Because substantial improvements in incentives were derived from sector-specific policies for cereals and other food crops, their real incentive levels for 1981–1983 exceeded those of 1969–1971; the reverse applies to export crops. In general, it seems clear that the negative impact of macroeconomic policies was either amplified by the disincentives attributable to sector-specific policies or that the former overwhelmed the latter when positive.

A different and more rigorously derived method of examining the

Table 12.9   Incidence of Macroeconomic Policies on Agriculture in Selected African Countries, 1960–1984

	Côte d'Ivoire (1970–1984)	Nigeria (1960–1982)	Mauritius (1976–1982)	Sudan (1970–1984)	Zaire (1970–1982)
All exports		0.55–0.90			0.52
Agricultural exports	0.82	0.82–0.84	0.85		0.41
Nonagricultural exports	0.43	0.51–0.69	0.59		
Cocoa		0.83–0.86			
Groundnuts		0.61–0.82		0.60	
Palm kernel		0.66–0.71			
Gum arabic				0.80	
Sesame				0.40	
Sorghum				0.25	
Wheat				0.29	

Sources: Côte d'Ivoire and Mauritius (World Bank 1987b); Nigeria (Oyejide 1986a); Sudan (Elbadawi 1988); Zaire (Tshibaka 1986).

impact of macroeconomic policies on agricultural incentives was developed by Sjaastad (1980). He approached the question by estimating the proportion of protection that is provided for import-competing economic activities through trade and macroeconomic measures and that is shifted from a tax on the production of nonprotected tradables. The incidence parameter estimated with this method provides an indication of how macroeconomic policies may override sector-specific measures to penalize a tradable sector such as agriculture.

Estimates of the incidence parameter (Table 12.9) confirm that African agriculture has borne a heavy implicit tax burden as a result of industrial protection, real exchange rate appreciation, and changes in associated macroeconomic policies. For example, in Côte d'Ivoire, Nigeria, and Mauritius, agricultural exports absorbed as a tax more than 80 percent of the protection provided for the industrial sector by the trade and exchange rate regime prevailing in those countries in the 1970s and early 1980s. Similarly, in Nigeria and Sudan more than 60 percent of this protection was shifted as a tax on groundnut exports, while Sudan's exports of gum arabic were subjected to an implicit tax burden equivalent to 80 percent of the incentives provided for protected import-competing tradables.

A further decomposition of the total taxes on export crops into those emanating from explicit sectoral policies and those attributable to implicit macroeconomic policies provides another rough indication of the relative magnitude and direction of these effects. The Nigerian experience demonstrates (Table 12.10) that while the impact of sectoral policies on the major agricultural export crops was gradually transformed from net tax-

TABLE 12.10   Explicit and Implicit Taxes on Major Agricultural
Export Crops in Nigeria, 1979–1981 (percentage)

	1979	1980	1981
Cocoa			
Explicit	38	8	−33
Implicit	42	42	42
Total	80	50	9
Groundnuts			
Explicit	1	11	−18
Implicit	36	36	36
Total	37	47	18
Palm kernels			
Explicit	−3	0	−31
Implicit	36	36	36
Total	33	36	5

SOURCE: Oyejide (1986a, 50).

ation to net subsidy between 1979 and 1981, the direction and magnitude of the implicit impact of general trade and macroeconomic policies were strong enough to ensure that overall agricultural incentives remained negative throughout the period. In the case of cocoa, for example, the overall tax was reduced sharply from 80 percent in 1979 to 9 percent in 1981, but the substantial subsidy of 33 percent provided by sectoral policies was converted into an overall tax of 9 percent by the implicit tax of 42 percent emanating from the macroeconomic policies. A similar pattern is found for exports of both groundnuts and palm kernels.

A recent study that uses a more robust and analytically based methodology derived estimates of the impact of sector-specific and economy-wide policies on agricultural incentives in many less developed countries, including several in sub-Saharan Africa (Krueger, Schiff, and Valdés 1988). This study also decomposed the estimated total impact of policy interventions into "direct" and "indirect" effects (Table 12.11). The study found that both Côte d'Ivoire and Zambia persistently suppressed the producer prices for coffee and cotton, respectively, over the 1975–1979 and 1980–1984 periods through direct policies. In Côte d'Ivoire, the magnitude of this suppression fell from 32 percent to 25 percent, while that for Zambia declined from 13 percent to 5 percent between the late 1970s and early 1980s. In contrast, Ghana provided protection for cocoa through direct policies, the magnitude of which rose from 26 percent in the late 1970s to 34 percent in the early 1980s. What is particularly striking, however, is that in all three countries, the impact of indirect interventions arising from trade, exchange rate, and general macroeconomic policies was negative and large enough to swamp even the positive direct effect

TABLE 12.11   Direct, Indirect, and Total Nominal Protection for Selected Products in Sub-Saharan Africa, 1975–1984 (percentage)

	1975–1979			1980–1984		
	Direct	Indirect	Total	Direct	Indirect	Total
Ghana						
Cocoa	25.6	−66.0	−40.4	34.0	−89.0	−55.0
Rice	79.2	−66.0	13.2	118.0	−89.0	29.4
Côte d'Ivoire						
Coffee	−31.5	−32.6	−64.1	−25.2	−25.6	−50.8
Rice	7.6	−32.6	−24.9	15.5	−25.6	−10.0
Zambia						
Cotton	−13.4	−41.5	−55.0	−4.6	−57.1	−40.1
Corn	−12.8	−41.5	−54.3	−8.8	−57.1	−65.9

SOURCE: Krueger, Schiff, and Valdés (1988, 13, 18).

in the case of Ghana and to increase substantially the negative effects of direct policies in Côte d'Ivoire and Zambia.

Thus, in all three countries the overall effect of policy was negative, ranging from 40 percent to 55 percent in Ghana, 64 percent to 51 percent in Côte d'Ivoire, and 55 percent to 40 percent in Zambia from the late 1970s to the early 1980s. Food products (rice in Ghana and Côte d'Ivoire, and corn in Zambia) were treated more generously by direct policies than were export crops. Hence, the total impact of policy was positive in Ghana, and, although negative in Côte d'Ivoire, the effect was relatively small. Zambia is the exception: although the degree of disprotection for exports and food products was roughly the same from 1975 to 1979, negative protection for corn between 1980 and 1984 was 66 percent compared to 40 percent for cotton.

Policy Reforms

Many of the countries of sub-Saharan Africa have open economies: in most of them, foreign trade as a proportion of GDP is at least 25 percent. This trade is dominated by the export and import of food and agricultural products. It is precisely in this kind of economy that the indirect effects of trade, exchange rate, and general macroeconomic policies can be large enough to overwhelm the impact of more direct sector-specific policies. The evidence presented in the previous section provides strong support for this hypothesis.

Against this background, the lesson from the African experience with the consequences of macroeconomic policies in relation to agricultural incentives and performance seems clear. This lesson partly explains the flurry of reform of economic policy in many countries in sub-Saharan Africa beginning in the early 1980s. Since general economic conditions have worsened in Africa, and no immediately viable alternative prescriptions have appeared to be forthcoming, the movement toward policy reform has gathered momentum.

It should be noted, however, that policy reform has not necessarily been easy to implement or sustain. A fierce debate preceded and continues to accompany the effort in many countries. This debate reflects basic disagreements over the causes of Africa's economic crisis and covers the strategy of policy reform, as well as its content and focus.

Two sharply contrasting views on the crisis emerged in the early 1980s. On the one hand, the Lagos Plan of Action, articulated by the Organization of African Unity, placed most of the blame for the plight of African agriculture on adverse external and climatic environments, specifically the world recession, falling real commodity prices, declining terms of trade, and Africa's drought. On the other hand, the World Bank's Berg Report attributed most of the problem to domestic factors such as poor economic management, inefficient parastatals, and a failure to exploit Africa's comparative advantage in export agriculture, largely because of unnecessarily low producer prices. These contrasting views of the causal factors naturally led to marked differences in policy prescription. Whereas one camp recommended promoting regional cooperation and integration based on an essentially inward-looking strategy, which sought to put some distance between African economies and an "unreliable and hostile" external environment, the other recommended adopting an outward-looking strategy that would become operational through domestic policy reforms.

Actual efforts at policy reform in sub-Saharan Africa through the 1980s give the impression that the countries of this region have either ignored or set aside the prescriptions of the Lagos Plan of Action: their reforms involve a clear shift toward an export-oriented development strategy. The question is, does this radical policy shift reflect a genuine conversion to an outward-looking strategy or does it indicate an involuntary acceptance of an externally imposed "conditionality." Since virtually all of the ongoing domestic policy reform packages have been supported, in one way or another, by arrangements with the World Bank and the International Monetary Fund, it may be assumed that external advice has played an important role in bringing about many of the policy changes.

Whatever their genesis, the reforms are focusing not only on sector-specific policies—such as raising the levels of agricultural producer prices, abolishing agricultural crop procurement by parastatals and marketing authorities or removing their monopsony/monopoly powers, and reducing marketing margins—they are also giving attention to trade and general macroeconomic policies, as indicated by the establishment of market-determined exchange rates, lowering of tariffs, restructuring, general liberalization of external trade, deregulation of domestic product and financial markets, and reduction of current account and fiscal deficits (World Bank 1986a). The five key elements of the policy reform packages adopted by most countries of sub-Saharan Africa are shown in Table 12.12 for a selected sample of countries and periods. In most of these countries, the policy reform has not been completed after three to five years of sustained domestic effort and external assistance.

The policy reforms have concentrated on correcting currency overvaluation and shifting the internal terms of trade in favor of agriculture and export production. Hence, many countries have taken steps to establish more flexible and largely market-determined exchange rate regimes and to deregulate their agricultural marketing systems (Quirk et al. 1987). Between 1983 and 1986, policy reform packages including these two major elements were initiated or implemented to varying degrees in Gambia, Ghana, Guinea, Madagascar, Mauritania, Nigeria, Sierra Leone, Uganda, Zaire, and Zambia. As a result, substantial devaluation of local currencies took place. Between September 1983 and March 1987, local currencies reportedly fell against the U.S. dollar, by 70 percent in Zaire, 77 percent in Tanzania, 79 percent in Nigeria, 81 percent in Gambia, 84 percent in Zambia, 93 percent in Sierra Leone, and 97 percent in Ghana. In addition, several countries raised crop prices substantially (World Bank 1987b). Zambia increased the producer price of maize by more than 35 percent in 1984 and also boosted the price of coffee and cotton. Zaire doubled the producer price of maize and increased that of cassava by about 300 percent between 1983 and 1984. Similarly, Ghana tripled the price of cocoa over the 1983–1985 period, while Guinea increased the wholesale price of imported rice by 400 percent. In Nigeria, the postreform producer prices for the major agricultural export crops increased between 100 percent and 300 percent during from 1985 to 1987.

Preliminary assessments indicate that agricultural production and exporting have responded dramatically to the incentives provided by the new policy environment in many parts of Africa. While a detailed and definitive evaluation of producer responses is not yet possible, the scattered evidence from several countries is sufficiently impressive to provide grounds for optimism. In Tanzania, for instance, the improved policy environment has been given credit for the substantial increases in agricultural production and nontraditional exports between 1983 and 1987 (Ndulu 1988). More specifically, estimated maize production increased by 14 percent between 1983 and 1984 and a further 6.7 percent

TABLE 12.12   Main Policy Reform Measures Undertaken in Sub-Saharan African Countries during the 1980s

Country	Reform period	Exchange rate adjustment	Increased producer price	Liberalized marketing and pricing	Liberalized external trade	Liberalized payments arrangements
Burundi	1986–89	X		X	X	
Congo	1985–88	X	X	X		
Gabon	1986–		X	X	X	X
Gambia	1985, 1986–88	X	X	X	X	X
Ghana	1983–85, 1986–89	X	X	X	X	X
Guinea	1985–86, 1987–90	X	X	X	X	X
Guinea-Bissau	1983–84, 1987–90	X	X	X	X	X
Kenya	1980–85, 1988–90	X	X	X		
Madagascar	1986–87	X	X			
Mauritania	1985–86, 1986–89	X	X			
Mauritius	1982–86	X	X	X	X	X
Mozambique	1987–89	X	X	X	X	
Niger	1983–85, 1987–90		X	X	X	
Nigeria	1986–88	X	X	X	X	X
Senegal	1980–83, 1983–86, 1986–89		X	X	X	
Sierra Leone	1986–89	X	X	X	X	X
Somalia	1985–86, 1987–89	X	X	X	X	X
Tanzania	1982–85, 1986–89	X	X	X	X	
Uganda	1987–	X	X	X	X	X
Zaire	1983–86, 1987–90	X	X	X	X	X

SOURCE: World Bank (1986a).

by 1987. Paddy production went up more sharply, rising by 53.7 percent between 1983–1984 and 1985–1986 and a further 17.7 percent by 1986–1987. Similarly, cotton output more than doubled in the second half of the 1980s and, in the process, established a historical peak in 1987. In terms of exports, the most significant result was the rise in exports of manufactures (37 percent) and other nontraditional exports (46 percent) during 1986–1987; this growth led to a sharp increase in the share of nontraditional exports (in total exports), from 18.6 percent in 1986 to 34.6 percent in 1987. In Guinea-Bissau, agricultural exports increased in value in 1987 by 70 percent and 34 percent in volume. Ghana's cocoa production rose to 230,000 tons in 1986–1987, from 155,000 tons in 1983–1984. The Nigerian experience also shows a generally positive impact of policy reforms on agriculture (Parker 1987). The total value of exports of food in 1987 rose 228 percent over 1986 and 556 percent in comparison with 1985.

The tentative nature of the assessment of the impact of policy reform on agricultural production and export bears repeating, particularly as it leaves some issues unresolved. It is clear, for instance, that some of the increases in agricultural exports reflect diversions from the parallel market rather than new output, and it is unclear how much is diversion and how much is new trade. Another issue is the medium- and longer term sustainability of the increases in production and exports. Excess capacity may soon be used up, climatic conditions are an important factor, and the external environment retains its significance for export expansion. The drought of 1987 in Nigeria had a substantial negative impact on agricultural production, in spite of the policy reforms, and contributed substantially to sharply rising food prices in 1988. In Tanzania, an adverse external environment partly reversed the positive impact of the policy reforms: precipitous declines in the world prices for cotton (20 percent) and coffee (40 percent) during 1987 significantly reduced the potential export revenue from increased agricultural output.

The point is that although reforms of trade, exchange rate, and macroeconomic policies may be a necessary condition to the permanent revival of African agriculture, they are by no means sufficient.

Concluding Remarks

This chapter has concentrated on analyzing the impact of domestic policies that impinge directly or indirectly on agriculture to explain the generally poor performance of African agriculture between the 1960s and early 1980s. Clearly, other factors outside the policy arena have played an important role in the stagnation and decline of this key sector, although this study did not present an analytical framework in which those factors could be taken into account explicitly.

A more complete explanation requires a framework and analytical technique that explicitly introduces the critical structural variables (Delgado and Mellor 1984) while recognizing the essentially complementary nature of the "price incentive paradigm" and the "structural change paradigm" (Oyejide 1984; Schiff 1987). At this stage, it is nevertheless evident that domestic policies, both sector-specific and economywide, have imposed fairly large disincentives on agriculture that penalized the sector sufficiently to be held largely responsible for agriculture's dismal performance through the early 1980s.

Notes to Chapter 12

1. In contrast to the economies of Southeast Asia, where structural changes have made nonagricultural activities the main engine of growth, most African countries have not experienced the kind of transformation that would permit rapid economic growth without correspondingly rapid agricultural growth.

2. No rigorous treatment of the link between agricultural and overall economic growth is attempted in this chapter. Casual empirical evidence appears to point strongly toward a close relationship, however. For example, sub-Saharan Africa's rate of GDP growth averaged 6.6 percent in 1965–1973, 3.3 percent in 1973–1980, and 1.1 percent in 1980–1986. Over the same years, agriculture grew at 3.4 percent, 0.2 percent, and 0.2 percent, respectively; total export volume grew at 15.0 percent, 0.1 percent, and −1.6 percent, largely because the volume of exports of primary goods grew at 15.3 percent in 1965–1973, −0.1 percent in 1973–1980, and −2.0 percent in 1980–1986.

3. I acknowledge with gratitude the useful comments and suggestions provided by several people, particularly Alberto Valdés, Romeo Bautista, and two referees.

4. It is important to note that for the low-income countries in particular, the decline in food self-sufficiency was not associated with a growth-enhancing structural transformation.

5. A recent study shows that the shift in food consumption in favor of wheat and rice is largely explained by urbanization rather than relative price changes, although increases in per capita income are likely to have the same effect. For details, see Delgado and Reardon (1987).

6. Note that the extent to which relative price changes bring about intersectoral resource shifts in a particular economy is an empirical issue.

7. Both the inter- and the intrasectoral impact of real exchange rate appreciation can be significant, although the discussion here largely ignores the intrasectoral effects.

8. It would have been better to use effective protection estimates for this

analysis, but these are not available. The usual caveats hold, given the implied biases.

9. It should be borne in mind that in the particular case of Nigeria, the real exchange appreciation resulted not only from inappropriate macroeconomic policies but also from the effects of the 1973 and 1979 oil price increases.

IV

POLICY ISSUES

Agricultural Price Stabilization and Risk Reduction in Developing Countries

Historically, and especially in the period since World War II, governments have intervened in agricultural markets in ways that cause the domestic incentive structure to deviate systematically from that which would prevail if domestic prices were more or less equal to international prices for all products. The goal of much of the intervention has been to tilt the long-run terms of trade in favor of the industrial sector to encourage its development. To stabilize domestic prices, that is, to ensure that their fluctuations are smaller than those of international prices, governments have used a number of intervention mechanisms that directly or indirectly change the relationship between the domestic and border prices of specific products. Often they have used the same mechanisms both to stabilize prices in the shorter term and to alter the average level in the longer term. These two objectives are conceptually distinct, however, and can be separated in practice. Even when domestic prices follow international trends, they may still be buffered from the shorter-term variability that characterizes agricultural prices in world markets. This chapter focuses on the stabilization issue.[1]

Why Governments Stabilize Prices

In general terms, governmental concerns regarding price instability can be divided into those that relate to the welfare and economic decisions of individual consumers and producers (microeconomic effects) and those that relate to the general economy—inflation, savings, investment, and growth (macroeconomic effects). When the prices of major food products increase, policy makers frequently worry about such microeconomic issues as the effect on the food consumption of the poor. Similarly, when the prices of farmers' crops are highly uncertain and variable, the impact on food production and farmers becomes an issue. On the macroeconomic side, policy makers worry that price increases in major wage goods will generate pressure for wage increases that will fuel inflation and make industries less internationally competitive. The same is true in the case of windfall gains in export earnings, which can affect the stability of exchange rates and the domestic economy. Concerns about food commodities have tended to dominate stabilization policy, although, because of the importance of certain nonfood export crops in export earnings, governments have also initiated stabilization measures for these commodities.

This section looks at some of the theoretical and empirical economic analyses of whether price instability actually has deleterious effects at the micro- and macroeconomic levels.

The Microeconomic Effects of Price Instability

The models traditionally used to analyze the impact of price instability on individual consumers and firms—and the benefits and costs of price stabilization—are based on producers (consumers) who "observe" a price each period, know their own supply (demand) schedule, and make production (consumption) decisions on the basis of this information. Prices change, but there is no uncertainty: economic agents make decisions based on known values of relevant variables. To evaluate the effects of price stabilization, this regime of fluctuating prices and output is compared with a regime of stabilized prices.

Using this general class of model, but with different assumptions about the form of supply, demand, and the stochastic element, some authors have shown that price instability can be preferable to stabilization, even if the financial cost of operating the stabilization program is excluded (see, for example, Waugh 1944; Oi 1961; and Massell 1968). The reason that stabilization may be considered undesirable is that it interferes with the natural welfare-maximizing response of producers and consumers to price fluctuations. Others have concluded that stabilization may or may not be preferable to instability (see Helmberger and Weaver 1977; Turnovsky 1976, 1978; and Just, Hueth, and Schmitz 1977, 1982).[2]

Where the indigent need assured supplies of food, income supplements tied to the cost of foods or targeted programs to give food directly to the poor may be used. This approach is more cost-effective than selective price stabilization.

More recently, attention has shifted away from the effects of instability per se and to the effects of uncertainty or risk, along the lines of some of the literature on "international trade under uncertainty." In the class of model used to analyze these issues, which have been addressed most comprehensively by Newbery and Stiglitz (1981), price and production are each random at the time the once-and-for-all production decision is made.[3] While realized production does change because of a stochastic element, producers cannot change production decisions each period to take advantage of changing price conditions, since prices are not predictable.

With this kind of model, it is likely that stabilizing prices benefits producers, given that risk imposes an additional cost on production.[4] Nonetheless, it is not at all clear that these benefits outweigh the sizable costs of stabilization, in part because the empirical analysis has shown little or no relationship between risk and supply.[5]

Whether the microeconomic effects of price stabilization should be analyzed using the traditional models or the "production under uncertainty" models is open to question. Some price movements are clearly predictable. A Colombian coffee grower knows, for example, that prices will increase following a bad freeze in Brazil and will remain high for several years. At the same time, there is also a purely stochastic element—some risk—in virtually all price movements, a fact which the more traditional framework does not take into account. Empirical work needs to be carried out for specific cases to know which kind of model is most appropriate and whether price stabilization is likely to be beneficial or detrimental. The lesson of economic theory is that—contrary to the assumption of many policy makers—there is no presumption either way.

The Macroeconomic Effects of Price Instability

The economic literature on the adverse effects of instability on the macroeconomy is also rich in a priori theorizing, with the analysis branching in two directions—one concerned with the effects of price instability per se and the other with the related effect of fluctuations in the availability of foreign exchange, created at least in part by export price instability. It is hypothesized that price instability has an impact on inflation because of increases in the prices of the wage goods that comprise a large part of the domestic consumption basket. The argument depends on the presumed asymmetrical effects on wages and prices, with a downward stickiness in their movements that causes price fluctuations to have an upward, ratcheting effect on wages and prices, a condition that creates unemployment. These effects may be magnified by the Keynesian multiplier (see Valdés and Siamwalla 1988). It is argued that export instability deters growth by inhibiting investments, creating uncertainty in foreign exchange earnings and in government revenues and causing instability in domestic income through a multiplier effect. Similarly, booms in commodity prices (and earnings) can cause appreciation of the real exchange rates and suppress other sectors producing tradable commodities (the Dutch disease effect). The empirical studies attempting to measure the effects of this instability have been inconclusive, however (see MacBean 1966; Kenen and Voivodas 1972; Knudsen and Parnes 1975; Bevan, Collier, and Gunning 1987; MacBean and Nguyen 1987; and Pinto 1987).

How Stable Are Domestic Prices?

Surprisingly little attention has been paid to the question of how successful price stabilization efforts have been in reducing the magnitude of domestic price fluctuations in relation to border prices. One study by Krueger, Schiff, and Valdés (1988) included a comparison of an index of producer price instability and an index of border prices for one representative export crop and one import crop in each of seventeen countries. On average, the instability of the domestic prices of both export and import crops was only about 72 percent as great as that of border prices. That pattern changed significantly, however, when the sample of crops was divided into staple food crops (imported grains in all countries plus wheat in Argentina, sugar in the Philippines, and rice in Thailand) and other crops (all other exports). For the nonstaples, the instability of domestic prices was about 82 percent that of border prices, while for the staples the analogous figure was only 66 percent.

Knudsen and Nash (1988) obtained similar results in a study of a larger set of thirty-seven countries and nine commodities. On average, producer prices for grains (which are food staples) were significantly more stable than border prices, whereas for beverages and fibers, on average the domestic prices were less stable than their international counterparts in more than 30 percent of the sample. These results buttress the previous conclusions regarding the relative concerns about the price instability of different kinds of crops.

Price stabilization efforts have concentrated on crops that are important in the consumption basket of urban consumers—so-called wage goods. An examination of individual cases makes it clear that governments have generally not pursued stabilization by a symmetrical smoothing of both the peaks and troughs in price movements, but rather by cutting off the peaks while not raising prices in the troughs. This pattern has characterized much of government intervention in agricultural pricing in developing countries, with powerful urban interests pressuring for subsidization of average food prices, as well as reductions in fluctuations.

Stabilization Schemes: Examples and Experience

Developing countries with a variety of political outlooks have attempted to stabilize producer prices in a number of ways. They range from schemes that address a specific commodity directly by either domestic procurement or importation to principally financial schemes that use buffer stocks or that tax imports or exports. This section reviews some of the mechanisms: taxes (subsidies) on imports and exports; buffer stocks; buffer funds; floor/ceiling prices; and international commodity agreements, a special case.

Taxes (Subsidies) on Imports and Exports

One mechanism sometimes used to reduce the fluctuations in the domestic prices of tradables is a variable tax or subsidy scheme for imports or exports. An export tax, for example, results in a price to producers (and domestic consumers) that is lower than the world price converted into the domestic currency at the prevailing exchange rate. The larger the tax, the greater the difference between the world and domestic prices. If the tax rate is progressive (that is, high when the world price of the commodity is high), it tends to smooth the variations in the world price. Import taxes work in the opposite direction, raising the domestic price over the world price. The higher the tax rate, the greater the difference. Thus, stabilization requires that the rate be low when the world price is high, and vice versa.

A number of developing countries use progressive tax schemes for their exports. They use this kind of scheme less commonly in the case of imports—or at least, make it explicit less commonly—although it is integral to the European Economic Community's Common Agricultural Policy. In some countries, progressivity is not an explicit and systematic characteristic of the export tax regime but rather is established by year-to-year, somewhat ad hoc, adjustments in the tax rates. Papua New Guinea's standard 2.5 percent export tax on many commodities is simply waived when world prices fall to low levels, a provision that makes the system somewhat progressive. Other countries such as Malaysia (for certain crops) have used a predetermined rate schedule that makes the progressivity more uniform over all magnitudes of price fluctuations. Colombia has effectively used a progressive tax schedule for coffee exports to cushion the impact of the price fluctuations in that market.

In designing a progressive export tax schedule, it is important to maintain the marginal tax rates at reasonable levels, so as to permit producers to realize substantial profits when world prices are high. This practice makes up for losses when prices are low and provides an incentive to maintain or expand plantings. In this regard, it is instructive to compare the experiences of Kenya and Sri Lanka in the tea market. Kenya has maintained an export tax regime according to which both average and marginal rates increase moderately as the world price rises, with marginal rates escalating from 10 to 25 percent at world price levels between US$1.80 and US$4.80 per kilogram. In Sri Lanka, this principle was not followed. Tea exports were taxed under a regime with relatively high average rates and a marginal rate that is zero at low prices, but is quite high (50 percent) when prices rise over US$2.40 per kilogram. In this case, the marginal incentives for growers were very low. Not surprisingly, between the early 1960s and early 1980s Sri Lanka's exports fell from 33 percent of world exports to 19 percent, while those of Kenya—whose system offered better incentives—increased from 2.6 to 9 percent.

Another reason to maintain rates at relatively low levels is that the efficiency losses from an export tax increase more than proportionally to its rate (see World Bank 1986b, 82).[6] If, for example, the export supply elasticity is unity and the tax rate is 5 percent, the efficiency cost of collecting the marginal US$1 of revenue is only US$0.056. At a tax rate of 40 percent, however, the marginal US$1 costs US$2 to collect.

For a progressive export tax to be effective in lowering the variability of producer prices, the changes in the tax rate must be passed on to the producer. Some countries question the willingness of exporters or middlemen to pass on these changes. Thailand, for example, uses parastatal rice purchasing agencies to stabilize rice demand (and therefore the producer price), rather than relying on changes in the rate of the export tax, apparently in the belief that changes in the export tax will not be passed on to producers. Generally, however, competition in the wholesale markets ensures that middlemen will have little control over prices. Further, even if they do have some monopsony power over prices, there is little reason to think they would use it to avoid passing on changes in the tax rate, rather than uniformly raising their profit margin whether rates were high or low. At both a theoretical and a practical level, there is reason to believe that a progressive export tax can be effective without direct government procurement in stabilizing producer prices (see, for example, World Bank 1984b).

If, however, the target of stabilization is producer income rather than prices, a progressive export tax may effectively stabilize producer prices but fail to stabilize income. The most obvious example would be a country facing a demand schedule of unitary elasticity for its exports, so that fluctuations in the quantity of the country's exports would be offset by movements in its price, a condition that would hold export revenue constant. In such a case, a nonprogressive export tax would take a constant fraction of the constant export revenue so that the same revenue would be left each year for producers. A progressive tax scheme, on the other hand, would take a different fraction from the constant export revenues each year, depending on the price that year, so that producer income would vary inversely with price. Therefore, although producer prices would be more stable under the progressive tax scheme, producer revenue would be less stable.

Overvalued exchange rates can tax producers, and in some countries this form of taxation is more important than the more direct taxes. Interestingly, however, there is a tendency to use changes in direct trade taxes to offset changes in these indirect methods of taxation, so that the net incentive structure remains at a relatively stable level (see Krueger, Schiff, and Valdés 1988).

Buffer Stocks

Government or parastatal agencies also sometimes use buffer stocks to stabilize prices and perhaps income, as well as to guarantee the availability of some food items for consumption. This measure generally involves the purchase of some quantity of a commodity when it is plentiful (or, equivalently, when its price falls "too low"), storage of these stocks, and their sale or distribution at some time when the commodity is scarce (or its price rises "too high"). If operated effectively, this measure can stabilize the prices for consumers and producers and, to the extent the buffer stock's price targets are known, can make prices more predictable. It may also stabilize producer income, although there is no reason to think it would do so in general. This type of scheme would be the basis of the proposed multicommodity international price stabilization plan known as the Integrated Program for Commodities. India, Pakistan, and Bangladesh, for example, have buffer stocks for wheat, and a number of other Asian countries—among them Bangladesh, the Philippines, Korea, and Malaysia—use this mechanism to stabilize rice prices.

A buffer stock has a number of limitations. It only works with a commodity that is nontradable or when the government controls imports and exports. Otherwise, when international prices rise above the level at which the buffer stock would sell, it would be profitable to buy from the stock and export, a step that would quickly deplete the stock's supplies. Conversely, when world prices fall below the stock's buying price, the incentive is to import the product and sell to the stock, a step that depletes its financial resources.

An effective buffer stock also implies sufficient direct or indirect control over private stockholding to prevent speculative attacks. During a prolonged shortage in the market, for example, the stock would sell enough inventory to maintain the price at its target level. Eventually, however, its stocks would be depleted, and the price would rise. Speculators, anticipating this move, could hasten this process by buying supplies long before they would otherwise be sold.

Theoretical and some empirical work suggests that such "speculative attacks" are inevitable and that the government must take measures to prevent them. The measures can be direct (for example, the government can prohibit private stockholding, although the costs involved are enormous) or indirect (it can maintain a ceiling price, even if doing so means importing the commodity and selling it at a loss), but indirect controls cannot be used for nontradables.

A study of wheat storage policy in Pakistan (see Pinckney and Valdés 1988) demonstrated the limitations and costs of a buffer stock. Although the government preferred price stability, interannual stockholding for stabilization could not be justified except under extremely low international prices. The study found some justification for interseasonal holding of stocks, however, because of the lead time required to import wheat. Nevertheless, any government policy that lowered expected seasonal price rises would reduce the incentive for private stockholding, thereby increasing government procurement and storage and, in turn, fiscal costs. The lesson is that the range of the procurement and release prices for stocks are critical in determining the ultimate amount of private storage displaced and hence the amount and costs of public storage.

Another, more obvious, limitation is that crops must be nonperishable over the time they may have to be stored. Further, efficient operation requires that the commodity have a high value per volume, be fairly homogeneous, and have no close substitutes.

Buffer Funds

A buffer fund is a variation on the general mechanism of trade taxes and subsidies. When the market price of an export is high, a tax is levied to reduce the price received by producers, with the proceeds accumulated in a fund that is used, when the market price is low, to provide producers with a subsidy. Thus, the price producers receive is kept relatively constant, although, once again, their incomes may be made more or less stable. This scheme has one key advantage over a buffer stock—it avoids the need to hold physical stocks of a commodity. At the same time, it is still subject to the opportunity costs of the funds that are tied up.

If the target price chosen is an unbiased estimate of what the world price will be at harvest time, and if the tax or subsidy is designed to tax away or subsidize the difference between the actual and target prices completely, then this scheme is similar to Siamwalla's (1986) proposal for "price insurance." Siamwalla's proposal would not stabilize the price, but rather would remove the uncertainty about what the price would be when the crop is harvested, so that there is no price risk.

Several countries use buffer funds. That in Papua New Guinea is particularly interesting. The original goal was to stabilize incomes. When this goal proved impractical, the government decided to change the goal to price stabilization. One of the most difficult problems for any mechanism that attempts to stabilize prices by setting them—while at the same time recognizing the advantages of not deviating too far from a price consonant with the fundamentals of the market—is how to separate the movements in prices attributable to changes in these fundamental conditions (which should cause a revision in the target prices) from movements attributable to transitory market factors. The buffer funds of Papua New Guinea solved this problem by setting a target price each year equal to the average price for the commodity for the previous ten years in the international market. A tax or subsidy equal to half of the difference between the target price and the actual market price in that year is collected or paid at the point of export. By basing the target price on a moving average of past prices, Papua New Guinea smooths the short-run price fluctuations, while ensuring that the producer price more or less follows any long-term price trends that result from true changes in the fundamental conditions in the world markets. To ensure that private exporters pass on all of the subsidies to producers, the government informs growers by radio and other means what price they should be receiving.

The buffer funds have only been operating a relatively short time, but the initial results look promising. The coffee, cocoa, and copra funds have reduced the instability of domestic prices for these crops by about 34 percent, 46 percent, and 43 percent, respectively, compared with the f.o.b. prices (see Guest 1987). There has, however, been a problem with undercapitalization of the funds.

Because of the random nature of price movements, it is virtually certain that sooner or later any fund will encounter either a large buildup or a depletion of its reserves. These situations can be made less probable by choosing a target price level that does not deviate too far from the actual world price and by keeping the stabilization goals modest. The former criterion argues for choosing an average not only of past prices, but also of the future prices predicted by commodities futures markets and econometric market projections. Such a target is more likely to follow actual prices closely than is an average of past prices alone, especially when there is a long-term trend. The latter criterion argues for keeping bounties and levies in any given year to a relatively small percentage of the difference between the target and actual world prices. Although these valuable lessons come from the experience of Papua New Guinea, in general its buffer fund schemes seem to have achieved their goal of stabilization more efficiently than have alternative schemes in other countries.

The total cost of funds for several commodities could be minimized by combining all the funds, as the resultant fund would be considerably smaller than the sum of the individual funds. The reason is that, in general, the world prices of different commodities are imperfectly correlated. In some years, the tax collected on one commodity can be used in a combined fund to offset the subsidy paid on another. In the case of Papua New Guinea, a simulation experiment estimated that a combined fund would have required net yearly outflows only two-thirds as large as the sum of the payments made by the three separate tree crop funds.[7]

Floor/Ceiling Prices

Many developing countries stabilize prices by establishing minimum or maximum prices (or both) that will be tolerated in the market without government intervention. Various countries intervene through government agencies, marketing boards, or semiautonomous "parastatal agencies." The minimum prices are usually referred to as "price floors" and the maximum prices as "price ceilings." If the government establishes both minimum and maximum prices, the result is called a "price band." These kinds of schemes are used to stabilize producer or consumer prices and to raise the average producer price or lower the average consumer price.

The term "floor/ceiling prices" encompasses a broad spectrum of schemes that differ in a number of ways. In some cases, the floor (ceiling) price may be set so high that the market price will seldom or never be above (below) it, the implication being the government will have to intervene every year.[8] In other cases, the floor/ceiling prices may be effective only in years when market conditions are exceptional. The government-determined prices may be targeted at particular segments of the market (for example, low consumer prices would be available only to the poor), or they may be generally available to all producers or consumers. Most countries do not set the floor equal to the ceiling prices (that is, fix the price), but some do so for major foods or food crops.

Countries differ widely in the bases for the particular prices chosen. One common criterion for setting floor prices for growers is an estimate of production costs (Colombia). The main problem with this method is that the costs of production in a country vary with the location, technology, and skill of individual farmers. Any price will be above the actual cost of some producers and below the cost of others. A closely related issue is that any price chosen will *become* the cost of production for the least efficient farmers. A high (or low) price will encourage the entry (or exit) of farmers until the least efficient ones are more or less breaking even.

For these reasons, the cost of production is not a very satisfactory basis for choosing a floor price. Papua New Guinea originally tried this system, but ran into the above problem and turned to the long-run international market price. In so doing, Papua New Guinea can concentrate on buffering its producers from short-term market fluctuations while avoiding some of the costs associated with maintaining large deviations from international prices. Other countries, such as Pakistan, have recognized the advantage of relying on the long-run international price as a guide to the domestic price and have this criterion as a long-term goal, even though the policies are currently based on production costs.

The choice of price, being basically a political decision, is seldom consistently based on a sole criterion. Tanzania, for example, officially bases its pricing decisions on at least four criteria—producer earnings per man-day, import-export parity, break-even retail prices, and desired official procurement levels.

Countries that set floor or ceiling prices operate under several constraints. First, to make these prices effective for tradable goods, the domestic market must be isolated from the international markets, either by tariffs and subsidies or by quantitative restrictions operated through licenses or state trading monopolies, either of which impose substantial economic costs. The government of the Sudan, for example, maintains a monopsony in the purchase of gum arabic from private traders, who in turn purchase it from producers. The government sets a ceiling price to be paid to the traders. It is constrained in selecting this ceiling price, however, by the fact that traders can, without too much difficulty, smuggle the arabic into Ethiopia and sell it at the world price. In the past, when it has set the price too far below international price levels, large-scale smuggling has resulted.

Second, even among nontraded goods, some crops are poorly suited for floor prices— for example, excess supplies of nontradable perishables must be "dumped" on the domestic market at depressed prices with large losses for the marketing agency. Third, to stabilize prices effectively, the government's policies must be consistent. If the marketing agency periodically suffers from fiscal constraints so that it cannot purchase all the crop offered at the floor price (as is the case for some crops in Brazil), or if the trade policies necessary to enforce the floor price are erratic (as they are for some crops in Nigeria), then prices will be neither stable nor predictable. In extreme cases of underfunding, the government cannot purchase adequate supplies.

Yet another constraint, one that has bearing on the objective of making prices more predictable so as to improve producers' decisions to plant, is that the prices at which the crop will be purchased must be announced *before* the decisions are made. Some countries are concerned about the possibility of speculative stockholding, however, and announce the price close to the planting season. Bureaucratic disagreement over pricing policy sometimes delays the announcement and deprives farmers of guidance in planting decisions.

Various countries have had to deal with two other important issues in setting floor and ceiling prices. The first is the size of the margin between the floor price paid to producers and the ceiling price to consumers. Because of the political imperative of maintaining producer prices as high as possible while keeping food prices to urban consumers low, this margin is frequently set at levels that are quite low and that have a tendency to fall over time. A study of the grain marketing system in Indonesia, for example, indicated that the ratio of the ceiling to floor price for rice eroded from about 1.35 to 1.09–1.20 in the 1970s.

This situation has two adverse consequences. For one, the small margin tends to squeeze private intermediaries out of the market (that is, entrepreneurs who would otherwise handle the collection, storage, processing, and wholesaling of the crop). Marketing agencies are then forced to assume a much greater role in the market.

This expanded role of the public sector is actually quite unnecessary: to establish effective control over the ceiling and floor prices, the government agency has only to operate on the margin, as long as it is understood that the agency will buy or sell all that is necessary to maintain the floor and ceiling prices. In Indonesia and the Philippines, two countries with effective floor/ceiling price programs, the grain marketing agencies generally purchase only 2–4 percent and 7 percent, respectively, of total national production, or 35–40 percent and about 20 percent of the marketable surplus, and even these fractions may be larger than necessary.

The tendency of the marketing agency to assume control over larger than necessary shares of the market leads to the other adverse consequence: these agencies tend to run extremely large deficits after the exit of the private collectors, storers, processors, and traders, because the agency must perform all these functions for the entire crop.

The second crucial issue in setting prices is the extent to which prices are allowed to reflect natural seasonal variations. In most countries and for most crops, harvests are seasonal. Storage is costly, and to reimburse the storage costs, the stored crop must be sold during the interharvest period at a price higher than that paid during the harvest period. In other words, there must be seasonal variations in price, with the price increasing from the end of one harvest period until the beginning of the next. This pattern is generally observed in well-functioning private markets. Many, if not most, marketing agencies attempt to stabilize this seasonal price instability, however, and in the process make it less profitable for the private sector to carry stocks between harvests. Thus, the marketing agency frequently has to store most or all of a crop, a system that leads to large deficits. In the study of Pakistan's wheat policy mentioned previously, it was found that the costs of the wheat stabilization scheme decreased drastically with the expansion of the price band, the fiscal costs dropping by roughly half when prices were allowed to vary by 15 percent and by another half when the price range was increased to 30 percent.

Overzealous seasonal price stabilization has other consequences. It encourages consumption and discourages production in periods when the grain must be stored, so that more storage facilities must be built and more grain stored than is economically or financially efficient. Discouraging off-peak production is especially important in countries such as Peru, which has two quite different agricultural zones, one of which can produce significant quantities of crops—especially rice—in the season when the other is not producing (see Knudsen and Nash 1988).

Alternative Policies for Price Stabilization and Risk Reduction

Apart from programs that directly stabilize prices, a number of policies and more market-oriented mechanisms are available that accomplish the objectives of stabilizing domestic prices or spreading risk. They deserve consideration in designing an optimal policy mix. Those discussed here are lubrication to facilitate smooth agricultural adjustments, diversification of risk, rural credit, compensatory financing, and futures markets.

Lubrication of the Economic Structure

Price stabilization is often used to address the frictional cost of respond-ing to fluctuations. In a period of high prices for crop A, so the argument goes, both farmers and agroindustrial processors will specialize in that crop. When the price of A falls, however, it will be costly and difficult to reduce their specialization. Responses are likely to be extremely slow, and there may be temporary unemployment of labor or other resources.

This problem can be addressed directly by lubricating measures to ensure that change entails the least possible disruption and delay. Pol-icies to improve the rural infrastructure—especially the transportation network—and to aid research and extension services are among them. A primary goal of research and extension should be to help farmers un-derstand their options with respect to crops and cultivation techniques. This knowledge should alleviate their concern when contemplating a shift to an untried crop or technique. A good transport infrastructure helps eliminate an oft-cited constraint on the marketing of certain crops, especially high-value perishables, as well as the large intermediary mar-gins that sometimes characterize distribution. Together, these policies will assist in a relatively easy transition out of a crop when its price falls and into a crop when its price rises. Given appropriate price signals, producers (primary and secondary) can choose the best degree of diver-sification at any time to trade off their own income maximization and risk reduction goals, as well as the best way to change the product mix as relative prices change. Further, in comparison with price stabilization, this kind of policy maximizes the generation of foreign exchange.

Diversification of Risk

Farmers throughout history have practiced an assortment of diversifi-cation techniques. For example, one explanation for the open fields system is that it offers insurance against localized disasters (McCloskey 1976).[9] Similarly, farmers can diversify the price risk by growing several crops with a low covariance of prices. Sometimes, however, they have been reluctant to diversify the risk for a number of reasons. One is the fear of giving up a well-known crop for an unfamiliar one. Many times governments have removed the incentive for diversification. The gov-ernment of Colombia, for example, inadvertently discouraged coffee growers from switching to fruits by stabilizing the price of coffee (re-moving the main reason for diversifying) and by providing subsidized inputs and research and extension support for coffee production. Even-tually, the government recognized the effect of these policies in discour-aging producers from growing crops that were more valuable to society than coffee. Subsequently, it eliminated the input subsidies and inten-sified the research and extension work on alternative crops.

Artificial incentives for diversification should be approached cau-tiously. In the absence of subsidies, farmers may be specializing in a crop because they have a natural advantage in growing it. One study indicated that the governments of Kenya and Senegal promoted diver-sification from the crops in which they had a strong comparative advan-tage (Lele 1988). They paid a heavy price for this strategy.

Rural Credit

Any harm to producers from seasonal or year-to-year fluctuations in income can be ameliorated by smoothing their income streams. Access to rural credit markets allows producers to reduce income fluctuations by saving excess income in better-than-normal years and drawing down their savings in worse-than-normal years. (They can and do save and dissave simply by varying their holdings of cash or chattel, although the transaction costs may be high.) This smoothing was one role of traditional moneylenders, who in many countries have been squeezed out of the market by interest rate ceilings or competition from subsidized credit lines. Unfortunately, the formal institutions that offer subsidized credit are frequently undercapitalized, since they are constantly losing money, and they have been unable fill the void left since the demise of the informal credit markets. One remedy would be to allow local credit institutions to pay and charge realistic (that is, market-determined) in-terest rates to borrowers and lenders. Each producer could then decide how much to smooth his or her income over time.

Compensatory Financing

Two international facilities have been set up to help offset fluctuations in export earnings. Since 1963, the International Monetary Fund (IMF) has operated the Compensatory Finance Facility (CFF) to help offset shortfalls in export earnings caused by factors beyond the recipient coun-try's control. A special provision allows a country to borrow to cover increased needs for foreign exchange to finance imports of cereals, once again when this increase is the result of factors beyond the recipient's control. Authority to use the CFF is conditional on an additional deter-mination by the IMF that the borrower will cooperate in resolving the balance of payments problems. Although the CFF is not commodity-specific, shortfalls in agricultural exports (and increased need for cereal imports) have accounted for a large proportion of its use (see World Bank 1986b).

The second facility, the STABEX scheme, in use since 1985 and financed by the European Communities (EC), finances export shortfalls in forty-eight agricultural products in sixty-six developing countries that are former colonies of EC member states. To qualify for compensation under the present (third) STABEX, a commodity must account for 6.5 percent of export earnings, its export value must be 6.5 percent below the reference level (those limits can be set at 1.5 percent in certain cases), and the shortfalls must not be attributable to policy. The EC has estimated that 69 percent of the transfers under the scheme have been required because of weakening economic conditions and 31 percent because of circumstances such as drought, disease, or flood. All loans are interest-free, and the least developed countries are not required to repay them.

Under the STABEX scheme, recipient governments are to use the funds to compensate export producers and must declare beforehand how they will use the funds and afterward how they did so. There is no similar requirement for CFF borrowings, but if governments are concerned about the effects of export instability on producers, they can establish a domestic facility to pass the funds through to producers, requiring repayment in good years, the proceeds from which would be used to repay the loan. In spite of the appeal of such a mechanism as an alternative to other price stabilization schemes, there appear to be no cases in which such a policy has been used explicitly.

Futures Markets

Policies that encourage primary producers and processors to use futures markets are efficient substitutes for price stabilization schemes where the issue is to reduce or eliminate uncertainty. In contrast to price stabilization plans, futures markets can limit risk by and large without cost to the government and bear no efficiency costs.

Futures markets offer participants the opportunity to choose both the level and type of risk reduction. Hedging with futures contracts locks in a specific price, but if a producer wishes to insure only against price decreases (but not increases), or if an agroindustry wants to insure only against price increases, it can resort to specialized futures contracts called "options."

Participation in futures markets has an important concomitant advantage: the spread between the current spot price and the futures contract price provides valuable information on the way the market expects the price to move, since the futures contract price is a good predictor of the spot price that will prevail at the date the contract matures. This kind of information is valuable in making decisions about storage and inventory control. Some analysts argue that this function of the futures markets is of greater value than the reduction of price uncertainty (Working 1953).

Although many in academic and government circles have recognized the value of futures markets, domestic futures markets are rare in developing countries, which also seldom use the international futures markets, except in the case of large multinational trading companies. One study of this problem in Colombia, which does not appear to be atypical, suggests, first, and perhaps foremost, that government exchange controls make participation difficult. The government has, to some extent, been reluctant to authorize the use of foreign exchange for this purpose for fear that hedgers will begin to speculate and require large quantities of foreign exchange to pay for their losses. Even where governments have allowed hedging, the licensing procedure is time-consuming and does not allow hedgers much flexibility in timing their purchases and the sales of contracts.

Second, controls on imports decrease the usefulness of hedging in world markets, since the domestic price may not be well correlated with the international price of a commodity. In addition, hedging is less effective in reducing risk where the licensing decisions are made a very short time before the import actually occurs, since hedging at that late date reduces the risk very little.

Third, the unpredictability of government trade policy makes hedging riskier. If an importer hedges in the futures market, planning to import a good on the prior-license list, and is subsequently denied a license, he is in effect changed from a hedger into a pure speculator, and his risk is increased greatly.

Fourth, for some agents, hedging is not useful because the government controls the prices.

Finally, information about the value of futures markets is inadequate.

To the list of disincentives found in the Colombian study might be added the existence of "basis risk" for some products in some countries. Basis risk arises because the price of the standard commodity traded on the markets may not move exactly as the commodity being hedged does as a result of differences in quality, changes in transport costs, or other factors.

Most of these obstacles can be removed by policy actions. First, governments can exempt legitimate hedging in certain ways from the rules governing other foreign exchange transactions. As long as the futures market activity is truly hedging—that is, is coupled with a transaction for the physical commodity—the possibility of significant losses in foreign exchange is remote. General rules could be developed that preclude speculation while leaving potential users flexibility to hedge effectively; for example, a country might limit futures market transactions to one set (buying and selling) per transaction in the physical commodity. Second, a commitment might be needed to exempt hedging from changes in trade policy during the period of the transaction. Third, the government could use futures market activity as a substitute for its control of domestic prices as a means of reducing the uncertainty of producers. Guaranteed prices are less efficient and more costly to the government and are perhaps no more effective in reducing the uncertainty of producers. Fourth, import restrictions on agricultural commodities might be gradually eliminated so as to encourage hedging in more commodities.

Concluding Guidelines on Price Stabilization

Theory and experience suggest that price stabilization schemes seldom if ever realize benefits that outweigh their costs. But the political reality is that they are likely to continue to be used. This concluding section presents some broad guidelines for the construction of price stabilization schemes. They can be summarized as follows: (1) whenever possible, rely on normal marketing mechanisms to provide most of the stabilization; (2) avoid having the government directly handle and store a commodity; (3) rely primarily on transparent trade measures, such as variable tariffs and subsidies, whenever possible; and (4) use average international prices as the guide in establishing the ranges for domestic prices.

Market Mechanisms for Price Stabilization

The most reliable market mechanism for buffering the effects of price movements is a flexible production system that permits farmers to produce a variety of crops and then to market or store them as price expectations dictate. Complementing this flexibility should be transparent market mechanisms, such as options and futures markets. Although those conditions are rarely present in developing countries, the first step in determining whether price stabilization is necessary is to determine whether government policies or interventions are obstructing this flexibility and impeding the development of futures markets. In many countries, government subsidies and controls on prices and capital inhibit the market from developing these natural stabilizing mechanisms. Removal of these interventions, along with investments in infrastructure and the adoption of regulations that permit the development of options and futures markets, may be the best price stabilization policy.

One caveat is in order. Exchange rate movements help to buffer domestic prices from international price fluctuations where the commodities account for a large part of export earnings. If the price movements take place over the long term, this adjustment should be permitted as long as the movement would not exacerbate an existing overvaluation of the exchange rate, since it provides a strong signal for the movement of resources between tradable and nontradable activities. When the movements take place over the short term, the consequences may be adverse to certain sectors, and the government may need to take compensatory actions. Although in theory these actions can best be taken through monetary and fiscal policies, in practice governments in developing countries may have imperfect control over the supply of money and budgets. They may need to intervene through trade taxes to buffer the effects of the exchange rate movements on these sectors—that is, to supplement the natural stabilizing mechanism of exchange rate adjustments with other instruments.

Government Handling and Storage of Commodities

One almost universal lesson from price stabilization schemes in developing countries is the high costs associated with interventions that require government purchasing, storage, and sales of commodities, not to mention the severe distortions in the location and timing of production and consumption. It is usually much more desirable and politically less dangerous for governments to rely on indirect mechanisms such as variable tariffs or buffer funds.

Trade Measures to Stabilize Prices

Governments have usually resorted to nontariff barriers (NTBs) to regulate the inflow and outflow of agricultural products. Tariffs, however, provide a more direct and transparent measure of actual protection. Further, the administrative mechanisms surrounding NTBs encourage rent seeking (including outright graft) and impose costs in the form of burdensome paperwork and delays. For these reasons, tariffs are usually preferred to NTBs.

The issue of tariffs versus NTBs is complicated by the movement of the exchange rate. In some developing countries, changes in exchange rates swamp nominal tariffs in terms of protection. (NTBs may also produce varying levels of protection with exchange rate movements.) Nevertheless, several countries, most notably Chile, have administered variable tariffs even under highly fluctuating exchange rates, supplementing them with restrictions on imports during harvests. Thus, in reality tariff mechanisms are not easily administered, and some countries may require temporary NTBs during part of the year.

Pricing for Stabilization

One of the areas in which stabilization schemes universally fail is in establishing the price level for stabilization. Most price stabilization schemes ultimately resort to setting prices based on surveys of the cost of production. Because actual production costs vary across regions and farms and over time, this pricing rule tends to maintain domestic production in crops that have lost their comparative advantage and to discourage the adoption of technology that permits international competitiveness.

The universal rule of price stabilization schemes should be to base prices on average international prices, which represent the long-run economic opportunity cost of imports or exports. If the average price is determined by a weighted average of past prices, then producers are sent pricing signals on a consistent basis, but lagged by several years on average. The longer the period used for calculating the average price, the longer the lag. Since the longer-term trend for agricultural prices is downward, the difference in actual international prices and the averaged price can become significant in schemes using five- or ten-year averaging periods. To counterbalance this lag, forecast prices—for example, from futures markets or the World Bank—could be included in the average price.

The average international price should serve as a reference price about which domestic prices are allowed to vary. Within a prescribed band, the government should not intervene at all but should allow market circumstances to translate into price movements. The width of the price band in which prices can freely vary is difficult to determine. Although simulation models can demonstrate the sustainability of various bands (Miranda and Helmberger 1988), in practice modeling is often difficult to do in developing countries. In general, however, it is clear that the cost of stabilization rises sharply as the degree of stabilization increases. With this point in mind, policy makers should make the band wide enough to allow most moderate price movements to pass on to producers and the economy.

Notes to Chapter 13

1. The authors would like to thank Romeo Bautista, Alberto Valdés, and two anonymous referees for many helpful comments. Any errors are exclusively

attributable to the authors. This essay reflects their views and should be used and cited accordingly.

2. The effects on the poor of a dramatic upward shift in basic food prices is difficult to discuss in the traditional framework because it is more a question of extremes than of averages. Since one year of extremely high prices could mean starvation, long-run average welfare becomes a meaningless concept.

3. Uncertainty is less an issue for consumers, since generally they do not have to make consumption decisions far into the future. These models therefore have concentrated on the production side.

4. Any scheme to stabilize prices and reduce the risks faced by producers increases the risks faced by other economic agents. Although analysts generally argue that governments are—or should be—risk-neutral, this argument is not universally accepted, so that it is unclear whether this compulsory risk transfer actually enhances welfare (see Valdés and Siamwalla 1988).

5. The degree of the effect on output depends on how risk-adverse farmers actually are and how they form expectations (Binswanger 1980; Scandizzo, Hazell, and Anderson 1984). Empirical work on the effect of risk on supply is rather scarce, but in general, the empirical results show no or weak relationships (for example, see Scandizzo, Hazell, and Anderson 1984).

6. The efficiency losses referred to here are the net effect on the welfare of producers and consumers and the government's budget. They do not take into account the administrative costs of the tax.

7. This same principle applies to the operation of multiple buffer stocks. The size of a single fund to finance all the stocks could be smaller than the total for a number of separate stocks.

8. The fact that the government determines the price each year does not necessarily imply the price is more stable or predictable. Shifts in policy and fluctuations in fiscal constraints may make government-determined prices more erratic than they would be if set by the market.

9. In this system, any owner holds his land in small plots scattered over a wide area.

Some Policy Perspectives

One of the stylized facts of the international economy is that developed countries discriminate in favor of their agriculture, and developing countries discriminate against theirs. In developed countries, that discrimination has largely taken the form of price and income support, supply management, and other domestic interventions that affect the output and incomes of agricultural producers. Agricultural economists have been in the forefront in analyzing these policies and demonstrating their negative effects.

In the case of developing countries, agricultural economists have also noted the tendency to suppress producer prices and have demonstrated the negative consequences. They have tended to focus on domestic interventions, however, probably because, traditionally, analysis of these policies in developed countries has emphasized direct domestic interventions. Only in the past ten years has awareness of the impact of trade and exchange rate policies on agriculture in developing countries increased. This shift was the result of pathbreaking work such as that of Cavallo and Mundlak (1982), who recognized the importance of the effect of trade and balance of payments regimes on agriculture. This volume is another step in improving the understanding of the impact of trade and exchange rate policies on agriculture.

In the 1970s international economists also became increasingly aware of the detrimental effects of highly restrictive trade and balance of payments policies. A number (for example, Balassa 1971; Krueger 1983; and Little, Scitovsky, and Scott 1970) demonstrated the importance of these policies, while analysis of the experience of individual countries led to ever-increasing estimates of the costs of trade and balance of payments restrictions in terms of lowered rates of economic growth. However, most of the work of the international economists focused on the impact on the structure of industry. Although these economists recognized that an overvalued exchange rate had a negative effect on agriculture, they concentrated most of their research on analyzing the variability of incentives among manufacturing sectors and its consequences. They seldom disaggregated agriculture.

One of the more unsettling aspects of the economics profession is how compartmentalized it seems to have become. As the chapters of this volume suggest, only recently have agricultural economists, who for so long have understood very well how markets work, begun to recognize that macroeconomic phenomena and policies can have serious effects on the fortunes of farmers and the factors of production employed in agriculture. At the same time, international economists have been busy in their own area of concentration, with its emphasis on the effects of trade and balance of payments regimes on industry; they have ignored some realities with which agricultural economists have long been familiar and thus have ignored the impact of those regimes on agriculture. The strong tendency within international economics to ignore differentiation among agricultural outputs and to regard resources as being fully fungible within agriculture may seem strange to agricultural economists. This tendency is all the more ironic in view of the increasing emphasis placed on models of product differentiation and, more generally, on theoretical models of multiple goods in trade.

As the chapters in this volume attest, agricultural economists now recognize the importance of both direct domestic governmental policies and trade and balance of payments regimes in affecting agricultural incentives and producer behavior. The relative importance of domestic interventions and of trade and balance of payments regimes varies significantly across regions. In most countries of Latin America, exchange rate and protectionist policies appear to have been more important than domestic policies. In Asia, where exchange rates have been more realistic and protection for domestic import-competing activities has generally been much lower, domestic interventions appear to have been quantitatively more significant. Most African countries have faced severe trade and exchange rate problems, whose impact has often been intensified by domestic policies.

As an international economist, I address three issues here from the framework of international economics: (1) How does or should a trade theorist view agriculture within the framework of an open economy? (2) How do trade theorists view the case for government intervention? and (3) If it were judged that policies should be reformulated to reduce discrimination against agriculture, how should that liberalization proceed? Each of these questions is complex, and only an outline of an approach to answering them is possible here.

Do Trade Regimes Discriminate against Agriculture?

A first problem is how to regard agriculture in light of the various models of international trade. To start the discussion, it must be recognized, as shown in this volume, that a wide variety of commodities are produced within the agricultural sector of an economy. To confess the extent of my own prior ignorance, I had assumed that the various agricultural commodities were more clearly identifiable and defined than were manufactured outputs. I now regard that assumption as highly suspect.

If there are import-competing, exportable, and nontradable agricultural commodities, a first question is how a trade theorist views or ought to view the impact of trade and balance of payments regimes on the agricultural sector. Put another way, the question is whether and how a highly restrictive trade regime accompanied by overvaluation of the exchange rate discriminates against agriculture. The natural categories from the vantage point of trade and payments theory are tradable and nontradable goods.[1]

In the context of trade and payments theory, an exchange rate matters only if some price is fixed within a domestic economy. Otherwise, the domestic prices of all goods and services would be flexible domestically, and the exchange rate could be fixed: it could have no effect on real variables. If, however, there is price stickiness somewhere, then fixing an exchange rate can affect relative prices.

The most frequent assumption made about price stickiness is that domestic monetary, fiscal, and exchange rate policies determine the domestic price level for home goods. Given a small country unable to influence its terms of trade, the choice of an exchange rate will affect the price of tradable commodities—under normal arbitrage conditions, the domestic price of each tradable commodity would be the international price (plus transport costs) times the price of foreign exchange.[2]

Thus, for a given exchange rate, the domestic prices of tradables are given. Similarly, given the money supply, the domestic prices of home goods are determined. Increasing the money supply can increase the price of home goods but will not affect the price of tradables, since their world prices are given. If, after a period of rising prices for home goods, the authorities decide to increase the price of foreign exchange, that measure will clearly raise the domestic price of tradables in relation to home goods. In turn, under normal circumstances, that change would reduce the size of the current account deficit or increase the size of the current account surplus.

It is probably safe to say that most international economists have recognized that an overvalued real exchange rate discriminates against agricultural exports, but that conclusion is probably as far as their analysis has gone in most instances. It is necessary, however, to go one step further and consider what happens to relative prices when tariffs on imports are introduced. Consider first the case where, in the presence of home goods and a fixed exchange rate, the authorities impose a uniform and ad valorem tariff of x percent on all imports.

In such a case, the domestic relative price of imports and import-competing commodities will rise by x percent compared with their earlier level.[3] Moreover, the domestic price of importables in terms of exportables will be x percent higher than the world price. That much is clear. What, however, happens to the price of import-competing and exportable goods in comparison with home goods? At a fixed exchange rate and given money supply, the real incomes of consumers will decline, and they will then reduce their consumption of home goods, while they would tend to substitute exportables and home goods for import-competing goods in consumption. It is not a priori certain which effect will dominate.[4]

In many developing countries, however, the situation is typically one in which domestic inflation at a fixed exchange rate (the implication being a higher price for home goods relative to tradables, especially exportables) leads to ex ante balance of payments difficulties. The authorities then attempt to suppress insupportable current account deficits by imposing higher tariffs (and tariff-equivalent quotas) on imports. That is, they support an "overvalued" exchange rate by import licensing and other controls on imports.

In this fairly typical situation, the price of import-competing goods is higher in comparison with home goods and exportables than it would be under a system that permitted the domestic price ratio of importables to exportables to equal the international price ratio. Moreover, the domestic price of exportables is lower in relation to both import-competing and home goods than it would be in the absence of protection. Thus, protection of import-competing goods supports an overvalued exchange rate, and hence a higher price for nontraded goods relative to exports than would otherwise obtain.

On that basis, it is possible to draw inferences about the impact of the trade regime on agriculture. An overvalued exchange rate maintained through quantitative restrictions on imports discriminates doubly against agricultural exportables: it lowers the price of exportables and reduces the purchasing power of the income from sales.[5] This second reduction in income for producers of agricultural exportables may be sizable. If, for example, producers of an exportable crop receive a price 20 percent below what they otherwise would because of overvaluation of the exchange rate, and simultaneously pay 50 percent more than they would under free trade for the 60 percent of their budget devoted to nonagricultural commodities, as a first approximation they would lose about 42 percent of their real income, as contrasted with a situation of free trade and a realistic exchange rate.[6]

Much of the focus in this volume is on the diversity of agricultural commodities and on the fact that some agricultural goods are import-competing, some are exportable, and some are nontradable. How can the categories set forth in international trade be reconciled with the diversity of agricultural products? A necessary first step is to divide a country's agricultural production into terms-of-trade categories. For example, and as a first approximation, it might be estimated that 75 percent of a particular country's agricultural output consisted of exportables, 15 percent home goods, and the remaining 10 percent import-competing goods. In that case, and if it were also estimated that protection for imports resulted in a real exchange rate 20 percent higher than it would otherwise be relative to the free trade situation, exportables might be 20 percent lower in price and import-competing goods 50 percent higher in price, relative to the price of home goods.

Under these circumstances, it is possible to say that the trade regime discriminates against agriculture *on average*: 75 percent of agricultural output would be priced 20 percent lower than it would otherwise be, while 10 percent would be priced 50 percent higher than its free-trade level. Overall, this change would result in discrimination against agriculture (measured in terms of units of home goods) of 10 percent (0.75 times 0.2 minus 0.1 times 0.5).

Applying these rough orders of magnitude to more extreme developing countries yields significantly larger numbers. In Ghana, for example, it was estimated that the real exchange rate was less than 10 percent of its free-trade level, while protection to industry was several hundred percent (see Stryker 1988). If 80 percent of Ghanaian agricultural output was exportable and 10 percent import-competing, the real return to agricultural producers would have averaged about 43 percent (0.8 times 0.9 minus 0.1 times 1.5) of what they would have received under a regime in which international relative prices prevailed.

Although these calculations neither take into account the extent to which cropping patterns may shift in response to relative price changes (and thus understate the drop in income because weights reflecting the shift are used) nor recognize the impact of the trade and payments regimes and policies subsidizing inputs for agricultural producers (so that the extent of discrimination is probably overstated), it is still clear that trade and payments regimes can and do significantly discriminate against agricultural producers. When that discrimination is added to the discrimination that results from the suppression of producer prices, the total impact on agriculture can be large.[7]

In that sense, even once it is recognized that agricultural output falls into all the relevant trade categories, it is probably true that, for many developing countries, the trade and payments regimes discriminate against agriculture *because* such a large fraction of agricultural output in developing countries consists of exportables. While highly restrictive trade and payments regimes with an overvalued real exchange rate supported by tariffs and quantitative restrictions on imports are not inherently discriminatory against agriculture, they are discriminatory against a country's exportables, and when agricultural outputs are heavily weighted by exportables, discrimination against agriculture as a whole results.[8]

Trade Theorists and Government Intervention

Throughout this volume, and more generally in discussions of economic policy, there has been a strong temptation to suggest that a government can offset a negative side effect of its policy by enacting an additional policy. Although the authors in this volume agreed that there had been "too much" discrimination against agriculture, a number of them thought that lower levels of intervention, and more targeted interventions to achieve specific purposes (such as low-cost food for poor people), would be desirable. Moreover, some thought that direct and indirect discrimination against agriculture was, or could be, offset by subsidizing agricultural inputs or increasing investment in agricultural infrastructure. These sorts of policy prescriptions imply an underlying model of a government as a "benevolent guardian." Politicians and officials are assumed to behave in such a way as to maximize social welfare, once they understand it, and to be able to intervene without cost and difficulty.

At least in international economics, and especially with the analysis of protectionist trade regimes, there is growing concern with these assumptions. On the one hand, the political process generates vested interests in support of policies that achieve results different from those intended by the advocates of intervention on "public interest" grounds. On the other hand, administration of direct interventions often entails costs that are significant, again with results different from those intended. In international trade theory, for example, it is well-known that if there is an exogenous distortion in the economy, a variety of government interventions can improve welfare in comparison with a state of laissez-faire. An infant industry where dynamic external economies might be expected to operate over time might be an example. In that case, a first-best policy would be a production subsidy. Trade theorists also recognize that if a subsidy is not feasible, there is some level of tariff, as opposed to laissez-faire, that would improve welfare.

However—and this point is important—the proposition that there is some level of tariff for industry A that might improve welfare does not prove that *any* level of tariff would improve welfare. If a tariff of, say, 10 percent were the welfare-maximizing intervention for a particular infant industry, a tariff of 50 percent might well be inferior to no intervention on welfare grounds. Worse yet, even if there were a valid case for 10 percent protection for industry A, once protection is granted to A, irresistible political pressures for protection may arise from firms in industries B and C. If it is also granted, the situation may be significantly welfare-inferior in comparison with laissez-faire.

In fact, political pressure is the first reason why international economists are leery of arguments for protection: although there may be valid grounds for tariffs, the political process tends to "capture" tariff formation. Not only will pressures arise from the protected industry for a higher level of protection, but once the deserving infant has been protected, other groups will also lobby for, and receive, protection. Although economists have a lot to learn about governmental behavior and the political process, they know enough to be confident that there is such a thing as "governmental failure," in addition to "market failure."

Agricultural economists need to analyze the ways in which these political economy considerations apply to agricultural intervention. In some of the chapters in this volume, the view seemed to be that governments had been seeking legitimate ends and had somehow misjudged the appropriate amount of intervention. This conclusion seemed to raise a question as to whether political institutions and mechanisms will permit only a "little" intervention or whether it is likely to be "excessive"—at least by economists' criteria—once it starts.

The discussion of price stabilization schemes in Chapter 13 is an important illustration. It seems perfectly reasonable for a body politic to decide that the market will lead to greater price instability than is deemed desirable. Governments that have intervened to achieve greater stability have had only limited success, however, and the costs appear to have been considerable. The problem does not lie in the conclusion that some stabilization might be desirable; it lies in assuming that the authorities can, without cost and political repercussions, put into place a price-stabilizing mechanism.

This conclusion immediately leads to the second concern that international economists have with proposals for government intervention: the apparent assumption that the administration of protection is straightforward and low in cost, when it is anything but. Even if a government attempts to undertake an economic function at market-clearing prices, the mechanics of administration are complicated. Purchasing farmers' crops, for example, requires at a minimum quality grading—a task that places significant strains on administrative capabilities and often on the integrity of the purchasing agency's staff. When a government agency is asked to administer the distribution of a commodity (fertilizer, pesticides, water, and the like) at less-than-market value, the situation is even more difficult. Employees of the administrative agency have discretion in the distribution of something of value and are very likely to be influenced by the relative influence of the potential recipients of the good, especially since the employees will probably have to ration the good in one form or another. The strains placed on that administration can be large.[9]

The political economy issues are difficult. Given the many important functions governments undertake, and given the scarcity of administrative capabilities in all countries (and especially developing ones), it seems that these issues merit special attention when economists are arguing that "a little intervention" is all right. The costs of intervention, whether big or small, include a drain on scarce administrative resources. When, in addition, the administering agency is passing out something of value, the costs of intervening a little may not be significantly different from intervening a lot, and the benefits will be commensurately smaller.

There is yet another consideration that is very important in international economics and the analysis of protectionist trade regimes, but whose importance for agriculture is unclear. Many forms of direct intervention open up private opportunities for profit through evasion and disregard of regulations. For example, in the case of trade and balance of payments regimes that involve government intervention to ration scarce foreign exchange and restrict imports, smuggling, over- and under-invoicing, black markets, and a host of other extralegal or illegal activities arise (see Bhagwati 1974 for an analysis).

Not enough is known about the interactions between the political and economic markets to be confident of the political economy of intervention in any particular instance. In any event, governments must perform a wide variety of functions, especially if they wish to stimulate the growth of agricultural productivity. Nonetheless, enough has been learned to provide a warning that it is important to be very careful when advocating interventions of the type that will drive a significant wedge between private and social profitability, directly benefit an identifiable group that will become a lobbyist for enhancement of the program, or place a heavy burden on a government's administrative capacity.

The Process of Liberalization

Many economists recognize the need for substantial reform of the incentives confronting agriculture in developing countries. At the same time, they are fatalistic about the likelihood of appropriate liberalization, not only because of the political economy considerations discussed above, but also because they believe the costs of the transition might be high. The questions surrounding how to liberalize, and the conditions under which liberalization is most likely to succeed, are the subject of a great deal of recent research, especially with respect to foreign trade regimes. It is not possible here to do more than summarize briefly some of the important insights of that research as it pertains to agriculture. Two areas in particular need to be noted: the chief lessons emanating from the study of liberalization, and the role of knowledge in the liberalization process.

Efforts at liberalization are bound to face a number of difficulties. First, regardless of the initial reasons for intervention, interest groups made up of those benefiting from the intervention will have sprung up. Second, protection pulls resources into the highly protected economic activities and out of others. Liberalization, or reducing the protection, will of necessity affect the workers and employers engaged in the highly protected sectors.

Sketching out even briefly the issues surrounding the "best" ways to liberalize or the lessons that appear to have been learned requires far more space than is available.[10] A few quick points can be made, however. First, the degree of dislocation associated with liberalization has usually been overestimated. Second, in countries where the degree of exchange rate overvaluation and discrimination against exports is substantial, the alternative to fairly thoroughgoing policy reforms will probably be stagnation of economic growth. While liberalization may entail some costs, failure to liberalize will also be costly, especially in the longer run. In effect, the real choice may be between current and future liberalization. If that alternative is true, delays incur costs without conferring commensurate benefits.

Third, nothing in theory or historical experience suggests that slower liberalization may reduce the costs, while both theory and historical experience suggest that extremely slow liberalization is likely to fail (see Mussa 1986 for an elaboration of the argument). A slower pace of liberalization gives the political opposition time to form; it raises more doubts as to the likelihood that the liberalization will be carried forward and as such reduces the credibility of the effort. The consequence is that those responsible for allocating resources are uncertain of the payoffs for investing in newly profitable activities; old, highly protected activities may contract, while newly profitable ones do not expand. These circumstances can seriously diminish the ability of a government to carry through the reforms.

Fourth, one of the greatest obstacles to liberalization is a lack of conviction that it will succeed. This attitude takes several forms: noneconomists cannot see the many ways in which highly restrictive trade and payments regimes prevent exportable activities from emerging and expanding; everyone recognizes the immediate costs to himself but fails to recognize the benefits that will accrue from lower prices for importables and more rapid economic growth; and, finally, they misinterpret the relatively weak and inefficient economic performance as a characteristic of the economy, rather than a result of the highly protective trade and payments regimes.

This fourth consideration raises the last issue requiring comment: the role of knowledge. Many economic analysts tend to be both fatalistic and deterministic in their view of the political process. That attitude ignores the role of knowledge in affecting economic policies. Increasing knowledge is likely to help the situation in two ways. First, political decisions are more readily taken when they are seen to have "legitimacy," and are more difficult when they are not so viewed. Second, greater understanding of the benefits of liberalization and of how it is best achieved will influence new governments in their decisions whether to make the effort and will also increase the likelihood of success, as past mistakes can be avoided.

Regarding the first point, when the restrictionist trade and payments regimes were put in place or evolved, economists and others were generally unaware of the extent of the associated costs. As more has been learned, the political pressures against protection have increased. Although the political economy of economic policy is not entirely clear, as discussed above, it does seem clear that there was acceptance of the view that restrictionist trade regimes were in some sense beneficial. To the extent that today's increased understanding of agricultural development shows that restrictionist trade and payments regimes and discrimination against agriculture are harmful, maintaining political acceptance of such regimes will be increasingly difficult.

As to the second point, a number of governments have undertaken policy changes designed to liberalize their trade and payments regimes and lessen the discrimination against agriculture. In some cases, these policy changes have succeeded, but the cost was higher than would have been necessary had a better base of knowledge been available. In other cases, technical mistakes or other problems (including the opposition of those who were not persuaded the liberalization would provide benefits) resulted in the failure of the effort (see Corbo and de Melo 1987 for an analysis of the Southern Cone experience). In these cases, technical mistakes might have been reduced or avoided had sufficient knowledge been available.

Seen in that light, this volume is useful in helping improve the knowledge base for policy makers and analysts. While a great deal remains to be learned about the links between agriculture and the trade regime, about the political economy of intervention, and about the liberalization process, the preceding chapters surely contribute to that understanding.

Notes to Chapter 14

1. The following discussion draws on Sjaastad (1980).

2. It is usually assumed that a competitive wholesale-retail set of activities exists and that distribution adds only a normal, competitive charge to the landed cost of imports.

3. It is assumed that the country is so small that the tariff does not affect international prices, an assumption reasonable for most developing countries facing world markets.

4. With a flexible exchange rate, some appreciation of the currency can be expected, which would lower the real return to exporters in relation to the return to producers of home goods. Since few developing countries have flexible exchange rates, this case is ignored here. In the long run, however, officials have a choice between changing the restrictiveness of their import regime and altering the exchange rate (or domestic monetary and fiscal policies). To the extent that they adjust the exchange rate eventually, for most purposes the analysis can proceed as if the exchange rate were flexible.

5. This reduction is analytically distinct from the negative effective protection for agricultural exportables that could result if the trade regime protects inputs for agriculture.

6. To be paying 50 percent more for nonagricultural consumer goods would require a tariff of 70 percent, since, by hypothesis, a realistic exchange rate would increase the imported price of these goods.

7. See Krueger, Schiff, and Valdés (1988) for documentation as to the relative importance of the direct interventions as contrasted with that of the trade and payments regimes.

8. Even in countries with a significant amount of import-competing agri-

cultural production, the authorities often attempt to suppress the prices of those commodities because of political pressures from urban consumers. In these instances, even the part of agriculture that is import-competing may not benefit from the trade and payments regimes. In the extreme case where imports are permitted at the official (overvalued) exchange rate, commodities competing with those imports are discriminated against in the same way as are exportables. In Morocco, for example, wheat is an import-competing staple whose price has historically been suppressed to satisfy urban consumer interests. See Salinger and Tuluy (1988).

9. Evidence is emerging in the World Bank Comparative Study on the Political Economy of Agricultural Pricing that large landowners almost invariably benefit disproportionately from programs to subsidize inputs and that most specific domestic interventions generate significantly greater benefits for large producers than for small ones, who may not benefit at all. See Krueger (1988) for a discussion.

10. The interested reader could consult Choksi and Papageorgiou (1986) and Krueger (1978).

V

CONCLUSION

Toward More Rational Trade and Macroeconomic Policies for Agriculture

The empirical findings presented in the country studies and regional surveys in this volume indicate that the trade, macroeconomic, and sector-specific pricing policies adopted in developing countries since the early 1950s have given rise to strong incentive biases: (1) against the production of tradable goods and in favor of nontradables; (2) within the tradable goods sector, against exports compared with import-competing goods; (3) within the export sector, against agricultural products compared with manufactured goods; and (4) within agriculture, against export crops compared with food crops. In failing to provide a more neutral incentive structure that could have encouraged a more efficient allocation of scarce resources in both static and dynamic terms, these policies have had an adverse effect not only on agricultural performance, but also on the economy as a whole and thus have inhibited overall economic growth.

It appears that improved policies could be a significant boon to future growth, particularly in the area of agricultural income and foreign exchange earnings. Institutional changes, new agricultural technologies, the development of rural infrastructure, and other productivity-enhancing public investments, as well as access to foreign markets, may be necessary to boost the growth of agriculture to any degree. Such changes are likely to prove inadequate, however, if the relative incentives continue to be heavily biased against agricultural production.

The complementary nature of improved incentives for farm producers and increased public investment in agriculture is often neglected in discussions of their relative effectiveness in raising agricultural output. In most developing countries, each of these two policy instruments is likely to increase the effectiveness of the other. Moreover, where agricultural products are heavily taxed and rural infrastructure is severely underdeveloped, it would not be wise to address only one of these two problems.

Because this book has concentrated on trade and macroeconomic policies, it has said little about the need to develop the "trade infrastructure." Most low-income developing countries will find it virtually impossible to realize their potential comparative advantage unless they improve the existing organizational framework of the economy. In Myint's (1985, 26) model of organizational dualism, this would require "investment in social overhead capital, including the 'invisible' infrastructure of the marketing, credit, and information network" aimed at reducing the differential transaction costs between the "traditional" and "modern" sectors. An important implication of that model is that organizational adaptations to achieve comparative advantage represent a movement toward the "neoclassical production possibility curve." Thus, instead of facing a trade-off between food and export crops, countries that expand export crop production can also expect to increase their food crop output.

What cannot be generalized is the capacity of developing country governments to reform the incentive structure and expand agricultural investment. In view of individual budgetary constraints, the repercussions of adopting alternative policy packages involving different levels and types of public investment and reform of price policy need to be considered at the country level. There, a number of pertinent questions merit close attention. For example, can certain forms of public expenditures (such as subsidies for credit, fertilizer, and irrigation) be reduced without a significant decline in output? What are the revenue effects of replacing a "cascading" tariff structure with a uniform tariff set at alternative levels?

Although this is not a book about economic development, some mention should be made of the implications of trade and macroeconomic policy reform (to improve agricultural incentives) for the national economy and its long-run growth. The increased rural incomes that would arise from higher agricultural prices can be expected to to stimulate the demand for nonagricultural production, setting in motion a sequence of employment and income multiplier effects on the rural, regional, and national economies. This form of interconnected growth is at the heart of an agriculture-based development strategy (for an early statement, see Mellor 1976). The basic assumption is that both large and small agricultural producers are capable of responding to improvements in the economic environment by adjusting output supply and factor inputs to reflect prices and technology. In addition to increasing public investment in the rural sector, an agriculture-based development strategy would do well to eliminate policy-induced price biases against agriculture. The removal of taxes on agricultural exports and of any direct price disprotection for food crops would be a significant step in the right direction for many developing countries. Attention should focus not only on explicit export taxes levied on farm products, but also on the implicit taxation resulting from the pricing policy of state marketing boards. Developing countries need to check the tendency to tax excessively and to develop costly bureaucracies.

For the sake of efficiency, it is preferable to rely as much as possible on land, value added, or consumption taxes, rather than on trade taxes that distort production incentives. If revenue considerations dictate that export taxes and import tariffs cannot be avoided, governments should at least try to make the tax rates more uniform across commodities. They should also recognize that quantitative restrictions on trade are inferior to a system of equivalent taxes and subsidies; aside from the higher administrative cost and loss of government revenue, direct trade controls create rent-seeking opportunities, induce noncompetitive behavior, and magnify the dynamic efficiency losses. Beyond the standard neoclassical propositions, recent research on trade externalities, scale economies in production, and growth of total factor productivity indicate that expanded export and import activities allow many other benefits to accrue to the national economy.

The greatest price penalty usually imposed on agriculture is the implicit (or indirect) tax on tradable agricultural products arising from the overvaluation of the real exchange rate. Therefore, apart from paying attention to sector-specific pricing policies, governments should monitor and carefully examine the effects of trade and macroeconomic policies on the real exchange rate. Officials at the Ministry of Agriculture could play a larger role in promoting agriculture's interests by placing themselves on the side of policy reform to reduce industrial protection, strengthen the financial system, foster fiscal discipline, and manage the nominal exchange rate rationally. A great challenge for developing country governments is to develop the institutional arrangements necessary to ensure that agricultural policy makers are not left out in the formulation of trade and macroeconomic policies.

Related Policy Issues

Policy makers in developing countries frequently express concern about two expected repercussions of liberalizing the trade regime in order to move to a more neutral structure of incentives. One is that under less restrictive trade policies the instability of world commodity prices would be transmitted more fully to domestic prices. Consumer expenditures on staple foods would then become more unstable, as would agricultural income, the tax revenues from export crops, and possibly the real exchange rate. Unrestricted trade is politically unattractive in part because world commodity markets are perceived to be incapable of providing a satisfactory degree of price stability.

Second, some transitional difficulties would arise in adjusting to a less restrictive trade regime. Lower tax rates on imports and exports would have a particularly harsh effect on low-income countries in which trade taxes are the most important source of public finance. Exports may not expand quickly enough to offset the likely increase in imports and thus may create a balance of payments problem in the immediate term. Unless the government is in a strong budgetary position, it would need external financing, at least until the fiscal and foreign exchange benefits from the trade liberalization are realized.

Both of these concerns are surrounded by complex issues, as explained in the following sections.

Domestic Price Stabilization

In many developing countries, the domestic prices of agricultural products have indeed been more stable than their border prices, as can be seen from the calculated standard deviation and coefficient of variation of the annual price levels (Krueger, Schiff, and Valdés 1988). Moreover, domestic price instability is somewhat lower in the staple group—which is made up of the food products in the consumption basket of urban consumers. In other words, the urban bias in developing country agricultural pricing policy pertains not only to the subsidization of average food prices but also to the reduction in price variability.

Because the stability of food prices is a politically sensitive issue in most developing countries, it is not uncommon to observe governments increasing or decreasing the levels of protection or taxation for staple food grains from year to year to compensate for sharp changes in foreign prices (Intal and Power 1990; and Chapter 7, this volume). Typically, governments use three mechanisms to stabilize domestic prices: a buffer stock system, a government monopoly over the country's foreign trade in staple food grains, and enforced price targets for consumers and producers.

If international supplies are reliable, which seems to be the case for most major food staples (rice and white maize are the possible exceptions), it is more cost-effective to rely on foreign trade than on public stockholding as a way to cope with the fluctuations in both domestic output and world prices from year to year (Reutlinger and Bigman 1981; Pinckney 1989). The rationale for interseasonal holding of stocks is stronger, since trade and seasonal storage are not close substitutes—although proper timing of trade flows can also generate some savings (Siamwalla 1988).

The fiscal cost of operating a price stabilization program is also related to the size of the targeted price band. A narrower band provides a greater degree of stabilization but allows fewer private traders to earn normal profits from holding stocks. Therefore the government has to expand its storage capacity and marketing operations to achieve the desired degree of price stability. The trade-off between the government's objective— which is to reduce the fiscal cost and stabilize the food price from one year to the next—has been examined empirically in two recent studies on Bangladesh and Pakistan. A simulated stabilization program for rice in Bangladesh indicates that lowering the price band from 20 percent to 15 percent would entail an additional cost of US$17.3 million (Ahmed and Bernard 1989). In Pakistan, holding the price of wheat between Rs 73.0 and Rs 87.0 per 40 kilograms would cost about Rs 200 million (US$11 million) less per year in comparison with a price band between Rs 78.9 and Rs 81.1 (Pinckney 1989).

In many developing countries, government intervention has also helped reduce domestic price instability for export crops. The price fluctuations have not been reduced symmetrically, however: especially in the 1970s, governments tended to reduce the peaks without raising prices in the troughs. In the Philippines, for example, various "stabilization tax" measures partly siphoned off the gains to agricultural export producers from the currency devaluation and increased world commodity prices during the first half of the 1970s. When export prices fell precipitously later in the decade, the government provided no corresponding price subsidies (Bautista 1987a).

Many developing countries have employed variable tax rates for primary exports (that is, high rates when export prices are high) to reduce the domestic price instability for export producers (Chapter 13, this volume). This approach to agricultural price stabilization avoids the high fiscal costs associated with interventions that involve government handling and storage of commodities. The progressivity of such export tax schemes is not always explicit or even systematically applied. Although a few countries have made use of a predetermined structure of rates (as Colombia did on coffee exports), others have simply waived the fixed export tax rate when world prices declined significantly. In all cases, the government budget is rendered more unstable.

Governments can avoid the adverse budgetary effect by operating a variable export tax or subsidy scheme in conjunction with a buffer fund—

which would collect the tax proceeds when export prices are high and give subsidies to producers when export prices are low. Some developing countries already use buffer funds, including Papua New Guinea (for cocoa, coffee, copra, and palm oil). In that country, each fund has an annual target price for the commodity, which is based on the average of world prices in the previous ten years; a tax or subsidy is applied equal to one-half the difference between the target price and actual price for the year. It has been suggested that, where a government maintains separate buffer funds for several commodities, it can reduce the total cost considerably by combining them into a common fund. Because the world prices of different commodities are imperfectly correlated, the cost of operating such a common fund would be smaller than the sum of the individual funds.

If the target price is determined by a moving average of past world prices, a variable export tax or subsidy cum buffer fund not only dampens the short-run variability of world prices but also ensures that domestic prices more or less follow the long-run trend in world prices. In the latter sense, this price stabilization scheme is superior to ones that ignore the longer-term relationship between domestic and foreign prices.

There are other means of stabilizing agricultural prices and reducing the risk from fluctuations in world prices for both food and export crops (see Chapter 13). The lack of private, risk-diffusing mechanisms in most developing countries suggests that government assistance would have a high social payoff from the development of commodity futures markets and rural capital markets. It may well be that policy-induced and institutionalized distortions prevent the natural development of these markets, in which case they may need to be corrected before government interventions can be rationalized. Further, it is vital to monitor the dynamics of government mediation and to closely examine the effectiveness with which the price stabilization objective is being met to ensure that the system being used does not merely add another layer of rent-creating market distortion or induce other interest groups to promote costly government interventions elsewhere.

In any case, it seems clear that there is no inherent conflict between the idea of adopting a more open trade regime to improve agricultural production incentives and efforts to reduce agricultural price instability. As argued persuasively by Knudsen and Nash in Chapter 13, the two objectives are distinct in concept and can be kept separate in practice.

Trade Liberalization, Structural Adjustment, and Agriculture

In the main, trade and exchange rate liberalization improve producer incentives for exportable and import-competing farm products. Over time, liberalization will shift resources toward the production of agricultural tradables and increase both traditional and nontraditional agricultural output and exports. The greater allocative efficiency of a more liberal trade regime can also be expected, in the long term, to boost overall economic growth, improve the country's balance of payments, and place the government in a stronger budgetary position.

Even where product and factor prices can adjust quickly to the changed policy environment, there will be some costs and delays in reallocating resources to the newly profitable sectors and in expanding exports to world markets. Significant output losses in the industries that used to be highly protected offset the short-run gains from the improved incentive structure, and thereby slow down economic growth. If imports increase faster than exports in the short run, the current account will deteriorate before it improves. To overcome any supply constraints and hasten the expansion of domestic output and exports, it may be necessary to increase government expenditures on rural and export infrastructure. Public resources may also be required to compensate for any adverse effects of trade liberalization on the poor (for example, to offset higher food prices with temporary food subsidies). On the revenue side, the lowering of trade taxes will have a negative fiscal effect in the short run that can add to an existing budget deficit.

Macroeconomic policies can make these short-run difficulties both better and worse (Mussa 1987). If trade liberalization is deflationary in the short run (because of a domestic price reduction in the import-competing sector), or if the economy is already in a recession, expansionary monetary and fiscal policies would be warranted. Many developing country governments, however, have great difficulty finding ways to offset the decline in revenue resulting from lower trade taxes.

The success of trade liberalization efforts may also depend on the external economic environment. A rapidly expanding international economy not only has a positive influence, through the additional demand stimulus on domestic production, but it also facilitates the conduct of macroeconomic policies complementary to trade liberalization. Liberalization efforts are therefore less likely to fail in times of buoyant export markets than during a slowdown of the world economy.

The initial conditions in developing countries contemplating trade policy reform have considerable influence on the severity of the transitional problems. Low-income countries in which trade taxes account for a large proportion of government revenue would be particularly vulnerable to the negative fiscal effect of lower tax rates on exports and imports. To the extent that they can replace quantitative import restrictions with tariffs (even at relatively low rates), however, they can alleviate the short-run losses in revenue. These countries may also have low supply elasticities in the short run, which means they would have to improve infrastructure a great deal before they could expect to expand domestic output and exports substantially. In many cases, these countries will need immediate external financial assistance.

Unfavorable initial conditions may also be present in countries that availed themselves of considerable external financing in the 1970s and later failed to fulfill their debt-service obligations when interest rates increased in the 1980s. Once these countries lost their creditworthiness, they found their access to commercial loans closed. To restore their creditworthiness, they need to reform their trade and exchange rate policies and reduce their deficits and thereby improve their external asset position over time. Many economists believe that countries with high inflation rates and large budgetary deficits should undertake macroeconomic stabilization as a necessary precondition to implementing trade liberalization and other policies for long-run growth (see, for example, Sachs 1987). Again, external finance (with some debt relief, it is hoped) would facilitate the transition. Among other things, it would permit countries to bring in higher levels of imports than would otherwise be possible and thus avoid the additional inflationary and recessionary pressures of trade liberalization.

Many countries have obtained financial assistance from multilateral sources, primarily the International Monetary Fund and the World Bank, in the form of macroeconomic or structural adjustment loans. These loans are meant to help countries implement the policy reforms necessary to achieve financial stability, balance of payments equilibrium, and sustainable economic growth. Reform of the foreign trade regime is invariably a key element in structural adjustment programs aimed at making incentives more equal across all production sectors. In view of the incentive biases against agricultural production, these adjustment policies should be favorable to agriculture. Producers of tradable agricultural goods—not only export products but also import-competing ones—should benefit directly and indirectly from the lowering of industrial protection required by a more uniform incentive system through trade liberalization. As the agricultural sector responds over time to the trade policy reform, a country's overall economic performance should also improve, given the large share of agriculture in GDP and strong links between agricultural growth and the rest of the economy. The agricultural output in some low-income countries is not too responsive to price incentives, owing to various supply constraints (related to technological backwardness, limited access to required inputs, inadequate transport and marketing facilities, and so on), but this situation could change as other (nonprice) aspects of the structural adjustment program take effect and enhance the effectiveness of the price and trade policy reforms (Koester, Schafer, and Valdés 1989). At the same time, the fiscal retrenchment associated with structural adjustment can have a particularly adverse impact on agricultural production where the level of government expenditures for agriculture is excessively high. In Brazil, for example, agricultural producers were so accustomed to negative rates of interest on abundant rural credit that the credit squeeze during the first half of the 1980s contributed heavily to the decline in output grains and oilseeds (Días 1988).

The actual performance of developing countries during episodes of trade liberalization in the course of structural adjustment will be affected by more than the liberalization measures themselves, since other policy elements are bound to be included in the reform package or structural adjustment. As pointed out throughout this volume, even nonpolicy influences can have a vast influence on the outcome. India is a case in point. After implementing a devaluation-cum-import liberalization package in June 1966, the government was disappointed to find that export performance did not improve, output of the principal crops fell short of their trend values, and in the next two years the general inflation merely grew worse. As Bhagwati and Srinivasan (1975) have argued, however, better export performance did not follow because the country did not achieve real devaluation: the newly imposed export duties on several traditional exports and the removal of the export subsidies on "new" exports neutralized the nominal devaluation. Moreover, the shortfalls in the production of agricultural crops and the increased rate of inflation were largely due to exogenous events—the droughts of 1965–1966 and 1966–1967.

The crisis atmosphere in which governments frequently undertake trade liberalization is exemplified by the Philippine experience in the early 1970s. During the second half of the 1960s, imports grew rapidly, exports stagnated, and the country's balance of payments difficulties intensified, sustained by expansionary monetary and fiscal policies. Things came to a head in late 1969 in the form of a foreign exchange crisis. The government decided to float the exchange rate of the Philippine peso in February 1970, permitting a nominal devaluation of 61 percent in that year. Since it did not liberalize its import policy, however (owing to the the strength of the import-competing industry's lobby), the domestic inflation rate jumped sharply (Bautista, Power, and associates 1979). The government had also introduced some stabilization measures that lowered the effective nominal exchange rate for agricultural exports and thus further undercut the improved competitiveness of agricultural export production. The exchange rate policy reform did not, therefore, lead to a sustained improvement in the incentives for agricultural exports. To make matters worse, the agricultural food sector was also being buffeted by typhoons and floods and the *tungro* disease, which proved particularly damaging to the high-yielding rice varieties that had just been introduced.

When Argentina launched its stabilization and adjustment program, the Plan Austral, in June 1985, it was on the verge of hyperinflation. The government froze prices and salaries, created a new currency unit (the Austral) and made its goal a substantial reduction in the government deficit—steps that enabled it to reschedule its foreign debt payments. Initially the stabilization effort was successful, but it was not sustained. The inflation rate and the nonfinancial public sector deficits, although they had fallen considerably in the first fifteen months of the program, while output and the trade balance recovered, showed significant increases during the last quarter of 1986 and all of 1987. These developments were related, as Reca and Garramon (1989) have argued, to the deteriorating performance of agricultural output and exports, which in turn was caused by (1) the sharp decline in the world prices of grain products, (2) the significant rise in the effective agricultural export tax, (3) the increased financing costs and scarce credit resulting from the Plan Austral, and (4) unfavorable weather conditions. It was only in mid-1987, when the government lowered the export taxes on agricultural products and initiated other policy measures to improve the expectations of profitability in agriculture, that structural adjustment began to take place in earnest.

By way of contrast, the gradual reform of the exchange rate and import policies in Taiwan from the late 1950s to the mid-1960s, a period of expanding world trade, resulted in a successful transition to a liberalized trade regime (Tsiang 1984). Earlier, from 1950 to 1958, the government had laid the groundwork for stabilization by introducing monetary reform to change the inflationary expectations, reforming the interest rate to expand domestic savings, and maintaining a balanced government budget (Kuo 1983). Exports not only expanded rapidly (they averaged 25 percent a year during the 1960s) but also changed in composition significantly in response to the changing resource endowment and foreign demand. In the mid-1950s, for example, rice and sugar together accounted for nearly 80 percent of Taiwan's exports. In the mid-1960s they gave way to new agricultural exports such as mushrooms, asparagus, eels (for Japan), and edible snails (for France), which are all labor-intensive and land-saving. New manufactured exports also appeared on the scene, such as textile products, clothing, shoes, umbrellas, toys, and other labor-intensive consumer goods.

Without doubt, the external economic environment greatly influences the extent to which trade liberalization and structural adjustment in developing countries can be sustained. The economic and political difficulties of the transition can be mitigated by an expanding world economy and better access to export markets. For developing countries in a debt-service crisis, an adequate inflow of foreign resources, favorable interest rate movements, and liberal debt rescheduling terms would also be helpful. It is equally clear that domestic policy should support trade liberalization and structural adjustment. Developing countries with a long history of industrial protectionism and policy bias against agriculture in particular need to provide a credible commitment to a liberalized trade regime. Moreover, they need to make the public better aware of the consequences of alternative trade and macroeconomic policies and to generate the coalition of interests that can make policy reform politically feasible.

REFERENCES

Adelman, Irma, and Sherman Robinson. 1978. *Income distribution policy in developing countries: A case study of Korea.* Oxford: Oxford University Press.

Ahmed, Raisuddin, and Andrew Bernard. 1989. *Fluctuations of rice prices and an approach to rice price stabilization in Bangladesh.* Research Report 72. Washington, D.C.: International Food Policy Research Institute.

Ahmed, Raisuddin, and John W. Mellor. 1988. Agricultural price policy: The context and the approach. In *Agricultural price policy for developing countries,* edited by John W. Mellor and Raisuddin Ahmed. Baltimore: Johns Hopkins University Press.

Akrasanee, Narongchai. 1981. Trade strategy for employment growth in Thailand. In *Trade and employment in developing countries,* edited by Anne O. Krueger, Terry Monson, and Narongchai Akrasanee, Vol. 1, *Individual studies.* Chicago: University of Chicago Press.

Amat y Leon, C., and D. Curonisy. 1981. *La alimentación en el Perú* [Food in Peru]. Lima: Universidad del Pacifico.

Amranand, P., and Wafik Grais. 1984. *Macroeconomic and distributional implications of sectoral policy interventions: An application to Thailand.* World Bank Staff Working Paper 627. Washington, D.C.: World Bank.

Anderson, Kym. 1986. Economic growth, structural change and the political economy of protection. In *The political economy of agricultural protection,* edited by Kym Anderson and Yujiro Hayami. Sydney: Allen and Unwin.

Athukorala, P. 1986. The impact of the 1977 policy reforms in domestic industry. *Upanathi* (Journal of the Sri Lanka Association of Economists) 1 (1).

Bacharach, M. 1970. *Biproportional matrices and input change.* New York: Cambridge University Press.

Balassa, Bela. 1971. *The structure of protection in developing countries.* Baltimore: Johns Hopkins University Press.

Baldwin, Robert E. 1975. *Foreign trade regimes and economic development: The Philippines.* New York: National Bureau of Economic Research.

Banque du Crédit Agricole. 1985. La politique du crédit agricole [Agricultural credit policy]. A paper presented by Deputy Director Ilela, October 22, Kinshasa.

Banque Nationale du Congo. 1964. *Rapport de 1963* [Report for 1963]. Kinshasa: Banque Nationale du Congo.

_____. 1968. *Rapport de 1967* [Report for 1967]. Kinshasa.

Banque Nationale du Zaire (Congo). Various years. *Rapport Annuel* [Annual Report]. Kinshasa: Banque Nationale du Zaire.

Barandiarán, E. 1974. Inflación durante el gobierno de la UP [Inflation during the UP regime]. *Documento*. Santiago: Instituto de Economía, Universidad Católica de Chile.

Barker, Randolph. 1984. *The Philippine rice program: Lessons for agricultural development*. Cornell International Agriculture Monograph 104 (September). Ithaca, N.Y.: Department of Agricultural Economics, Cornell University.

Bautista, Romeo M. 1977. The effects of major currency realignment on Philippine merchandise trade. *Review of Economics and Statistics* 59 (May): 152–60.

_____. 1981. The 1981–85 tariff changes and effective protection of manufacturing industries. *Journal of Philippine Development* 8 (1 and 2): 1–20.

_____. 1983. *Industrial policy and development in the ASEAN countries*. Monograph 2 (October). Manila: Philippine Institute for Development Studies.

_____. 1985. Effects of trade and exchange rate policies on export production incentives in Philippine agriculture. *Philippine Economic Journal* 24(3).

_____. 1986a. Domestic price distortions and agricultural income in developing countries. *Journal of Development Economics* 23 (1).

_____. 1986b. Multisectoral analysis of trade liberalization: The Philippines, 1978. *Philippine Economic Journal* 25 (3 and 4).

_____. 1987a. Instability in food and export crop incomes: The Philippine case. In *Agriculture and economic instability*, edited by M. Bellamy and B. Greenshields. Aldershot, England: Gower.

_____. 1987b. *Production incentives in Philippine agriculture: Effects of trade and exchange rate policies*. Research Report 59. Washington, D.C.: International Food Policy Research Institute.

Bautista, Romeo M., John H. Power, and associates. 1979. *Industrial promotion policies in the Philippines*. Manila: Philippine Institute for Development Studies.

Behrman, J. 1977. *Macroeconomic policy in a developing country: The Chilean experience*. Amsterdam: North-Holland.

Bevan, David L., Paul Collier, and Jan W. Gunning. 1987. Consequences of a commodity boom in a controlled economy: Accumulation and redistribution in Kenya 1975–83. *World Bank Economic Review* 1 (May).

Bhagwati, Jagdish N. 1974. *Illegal transactions in international trade*. Amsterdam: North-Holland.

_____. 1987. Outward orientation: Trade issues. In *Growth-oriented adjustment programs*, edited by Vittorio Corbo, Morris Goldstein, and Mohsin Khan. Washington, D.C.: International Monetary Fund and World Bank.

Bhagwati, Jagdish N., and T. N. Srinivasan. 1975. *Foreign trade regimes and economic development: India*. New York: Columbia University Press.

Bhalla, Surjit S. 1988. The politics and economics of agricultural price policies in Sri Lanka. Paper prepared for the World Bank, Washington, D.C., February.

Binswanger, Hans P. 1980. Attitudes toward risk: Experimental measurement in rural India. *American Journal of Agricultural Economics* 62 (3): 395–407.

Binswanger, Hans P., and Pasquale L. Scandizzo. 1983. Patterns of agricultural protection. Agricultural Research Unit Report 15. Washington, D.C.: World Bank.

Binswanger, Hans P., Yair Mundlak, Mow-Cheng Yang, and A. Bowers. 1985. Estimation of aggregate agricultural response. Agricultural Research Unit Report 48. Washington, D.C.: World Bank.

Bond, Marian E. 1983. Agricultural responses to prices in sub-Saharan African countries. *IMF Staff Papers* 30: 703–26.

Brandão, Antonio Salazar, and Jose L. Carvalho. 1987. *A comparative study of the political economy of agricultural pricing policies: The case of Brazil.* Paper prepared for the World Bank, Washington, D.C.

Canlas, Dante B., et al. 1984. An analysis of the Philippine economic crisis: A workshop report. School of Economics, University of the Philippines, Quezon City.

Cavallo, Domingo. 1985. Exchange rate overvaluation and agriculture: The case of Argentina. Background paper for the *World Development Report 1986*. Washington, D.C.: World Bank.

———. 1986. Argentina. In *The open economy: Tools for policymakers in developing countries*, edited by Rudiger Dornbusch and F. L. Helmes. EDI Series in Economic Development, Chapter 12. Washington, D.C.: World Bank.

Cavallo, Domingo, and Yair Mundlak. 1982. *Agriculture and economic growth in an open economy: The case of Argentina.* Research Report 36. Washington, D.C.: International Food Policy Research Institute.

———. 1986. On the nature and implications of factor adjustment: Argentina 1913–1984. Paper presented at the World Congress of the International Economic Association, December 1–5, New Delhi.

Choksi, Armeane M., and Demitrios Papageorgiou. 1986. *Economic liberalization in developing countries.* Oxford: Basil Blackwell.

Clements, K. W., and Larry A. Sjaastad. 1984. *How protection taxes exporters.* Thames Essay. London: Trade Policy Research Centre.

Coeymans, Juan Eduardo. 1982. Determinantes de la migración ocupacional agrícola–no agrícola en Chile [Determinants of the migration of agricultural/nonagricultural labor in Chile]. *Cuadernos de Economía* 57 (August): 177–93.

———. 1983. Determinantes de la migración rural-urbana en Chile, según origen y destino [Determinants of rural-urban migration in Chile by origin and destination]. *Cuadernos de Economía* 59 (April): 43–65.

———. 1986. Determinants of sectoral annual real wages in a developing economy. *Documento de Trabajo* 106. Santiago: Instituto de Economía, Universidad Católica de Chile.

Coeymans, Juan Eduardo, and Yair Mundlak. 1984. Un modelo econométrico para el análisis del crecimiento del sector agrícola chileno [An econometric model for analyzing growth in Chile's agriculture sector]. *Documento de Trabajo* 90. Santiago: Instituto de Economía, Universidad Católica de Chile.

_____. 1987. Agricultural and economic growth: The case of Chile, 1960–1982. Washington, D.C.: International Food Policy Research Institute. Mimeo.

_____. 1992. *Sectoral growth in Chile: 1962–1982*. Research report manuscript. Washington, D.C.: International Food Policy Research Institute.

Colombia, Departamento Administrativo Nacional de Estadística (DANE). 1977. La migración interna y el proceso de concentración de la población en los departamentos [Internal migration and the process of population concentration in states]. *Boletín Mensual de Estadística* 314.

_____. 1984. *Cuenta nacionales de Colombia: 1970–83* [National accounts of Colombia: 1970–83]. Bogotá: DANE.

Colombia, Ministerio del Trabajo, Servicio Nacional de Empleo. 1979. *La dinámica interna de los movimientos migratorios en Colombia* [The dynamics of internal migration in Colombia]. Bogotá: Ministerio del Trabajo.

Corbo, Vittorio. 1974. *Inflation in developing countries: An econometric study of Chilean inflation*. Amsterdam: North-Holland.

_____. 1983. Desarrollos macroeconómicos recientes en la economía chilena [Recent macroeconomic developments in the Chilean economy]. *Cuadernos de Economía* 20 (59): 5–20.

Corbo, Vittorio, and Jaime de Melo. 1987. Lessons from the Southern Cone policy reforms. *World Bank Research Observer* 2 (2).

Corden, W. Max. 1971. *The theory of protection*. Oxford: Clarendon Press.

Corden, W. Max, and J. Peter Neary. 1982. Booming sector and deindustrialization in a small open economy. *Economic Journal* 92 (December): 825–48.

David, Cristina C. 1983. *Economic policies and Philippine agriculture*. Working Paper 83-02. Manila: Philippine Institute for Development Studies.

de Janvry, Alain, and K. Subbarao. 1986. *Agricultural price policy and income distribution in India*. Oxford: Oxford University Press.

de la Cuadra, Sergio, and Dominique Hachette. 1988. The timing and sequencing of a trade liberalization policy: The case of Chile. *Documento de Trabajo* 113. Santiago: Instituto de Economía, Universidad Católica de Chile.

Delgado, Christopher L., and John W. Mellor. 1984. A structural view of policy issues in African agricultural development. *American Journal of Agricultural Economics* 66 (5): 665–70.

Delgado, Christopher L., and Thomas Reardon. 1987. Policy issues raised by changing food patterns in the Sahel. In *Cereal policies in Sahel countries*, Comité Inter-Etat de Lute contre la Sécheresse au Sahel/Club du Sahel. Paris: Organization for Economic Cooperation and Development.

Departamento de Economía Agraria, Universidad Católica de Chile. 1979. 15 años de reforma agraria en Chile [15 years of agrarian reform in Chile]. In *Panorama Económico de la Agricultura* 2.

Días, Gilherme. 1989. The role of agriculture in the structural adjustment process of Brazil. In *Agriculture and governments in an interdependent world*, edited by Allen Maunder and Alberto Valdés. Proceedings of the 20th International Conference of Agricultural Economists. Aldershot, England: Dartmouth.

Diaz-Alejandro, Carlos. 1982. Exchange rates and terms of trade in the Argentine

Republic, 1913–1976. In *Trade stability, technology and equity in Latin America*, edited by Moshe Syrquin. Orlando, Fla.: Academic Press.

———. 1984. Latin American debt: I don't think we are in Kansas anymore. *Brookings Papers on Economic Activity* 2. Washington, D.C.: Brookings Institution.

Dornbusch, Rudiger. 1974. Tariffs and nontraded goods. *Journal of International Economics* 4 (May): 177–85.

———. 1980. *Open economy macroeconomics.* New York: Basic Books Inc.

Dorosh, P. A. 1986. Linkage between the macroeconomy and agriculture: A study of Indonesia's food sector from 1949 to 1984. Ph.D. diss., Department of Food Research, Stanford University, Stanford, Calif.

Dorosh, P. A., and A. Valdés. 1990. *Effects of exchange rate and trade policies on agriculture in Pakistan.* Research Report 84. Washington, D.C.: International Food Policy Research Institute.

Edwards, Sebastian. 1984. Coffee, money, and inflation in Colombia. *World Development* (November/December): 1107–17.

———. 1986a. A commodity export boom and the real exchange rate: The money-inflation link. In *Natural resources and the macroeconomy*, edited by J. Peter Neary and Sweder van Wijnbergen. Cambridge, Mass.: MIT Press.

———. 1986b. Commodity export prices and the real exchange rate in developing countries: Coffee in Colombia. In *Economic adjustment and exchange rate in developing countries*, edited by Sebastian Edwards and Liaquat Ahamed. Chicago: University of Chicago Press.

———. 1988. *Exchange rate misalignment in developing countries: Analytical issues and empirical evidence.* Baltimore: Johns Hopkins University Press.

Edwards, Sebastian, and M. Aoki. 1983. Oil boom and Dutch disease: A dynamic analysis. *Resource and Energy* 5: 1–24.

Edwards, Sebastian, and A. Cox-Edwards. 1987. *Monetarism and liberalization: The Chilean experiment.* New York: Ballinger.

Elbadawi, I. A. 1988. *Foreign trade, exchange rate, and macroeconomic policies and the growth prospects for Sudanese agriculture.* New Haven, Conn.: Economic Growth Center, Yale University.

Elías, Victor J. 1985. *Government expenditures on agriculture and agricultural growth in Latin America.* Research Report 50. Washington, D.C.: International Food Policy Research Institute.

Fields, Gary S. 1979. Lifetime migration in Colombia. Tests of the expected income hypothesis. *Population and Development Review* (June): 247–66.

Findlay, Ronald. 1984. Trade and development: Theory and Asian experience. *Asian Development Review* 2 (2).

Food and Agriculture Organization of the United Nations. 1978. FAO food balance sheets, 1961–65 average to 1977. Rome: FAO.

———. Various years. *FAO production yearbook.* Rome: FAO.

———. Various years. Trade yearbook tapes. Rome.

Franklin, D. L., et al. 1983. *An assistance strategy towards the improvement of nutrition in Peru.* Raleigh, N.C.: Sigma One Corporation.

French-Davis, R. 1973. *Políticas económicas en Chile 1952-1970* [Economic policies in Chile 1952–1970]. Santiago: Editorial Nueva Universidad.

Frenkel, Jacob, and Michael Mussa. 1985. Asset markets, the exchange rate and the balance of payments: The reformulation of doctrine. In *Handbook of international economics*, edited by R. Caves and R. Jones. Amsterdam: North-Holland.

Galang, Jose. 1985. Economic husbandry. *Far Eastern Economic Review* 31 (January): 46-49.

Gallant, R. A., and J. J. Goebel. 1976. Nonlinear regression with autocorrelated errors. *Journal of the American Statistical Association* 71 (December): 961–67.

García García, Jorge. 1981. *The effects of exchange rates and commercial policy on agricultural incentives in Colombia: 1953–1978*. Research Report 24. Washington, D.C.: International Food Policy Research Institute.

_____. 1983. Aspects of agricultural development in Colombia: 1970–1982. Paper prepared for the World Bank, Colombia Division, Bogotá.

García García, Jorge, and Gabriel Montes Llamas. 1988. *Coffee boom, government expenditure and agricultural prices: The Colombian experience*. Research Report 68. Washington, D.C.: International Food Policy Research Institute.

_____. 1989. *Trade, exchange rate, and agricultural pricing policies in Colombia*. Washington, D.C.: World Bank.

Gomez, Hernando J. 1988. La economía ilegal en Colombia: Tamaña, evolución e impacto económico. *Coyuntura Económica* 18 (3): 93–113. Also The Colombian illegal economy: Size, evolution, characteristics and economic impact. Washington, D.C.: Brookings Institution. Mimeo.

Greene, Duty D., and Terry L. Roe. 1989. *Trade, exchange rate, and agricultural pricing policies in the Dominican Republic*. Vol. 1, *The Country Study*. Washington, D.C.: World Bank.

Gregory, R. G. 1976. Some implications of the growth of the mineral sector. *Journal of Agricultural Economics* (Australia) 20 (2): 71–91.

Guest, J. 1987. *The cocoa, coffee, and copra price stabilization funds in Papua New Guinea's post-independence macroeconomic policy framework*. Port Moresby: Bank of Papua New Guinea.

Guisinger, S., and G. Scully. 1988. The timing and sequencing of a trade liberalization policy: The case of Pakistan. Paper prepared for the World Bank, Washington, D.C.

Gulati, A. 1987. Effective protection and subsidies in Indian agriculture: Case of wheat and rice. *Indian Journal of Agricultural Economics* 42 (4).

Hachette, D., and P. Rozas. 1992. *The liberalization of Chilean agriculture: 1974–1990*. Documento. Santiago: Instituto de Economía, Universidad Católica de Chile.

Hamid, Naved, Ijaz Nabi, and Anjum Nasim. 1990. *Trade, exchange rate, and agricultural pricing policies in Pakistan*. Washington, D.C.: World Bank.

Harberger, Arnold C. 1971. On measuring the social opportunity cost of labor. *International Labour Review* 103 (June): 559–79.

_____. 1983. Dutch disease: How much sickness, how much boom? *Resources and Energy* 5.

_____. 1985. Observations on the Chilean economy, 1973–1983. *Economic Development and Cultural Change* 3 (3).

Harris, J., and M. Todaro. 1970. Migration, unemployment and development: A two-sector analysis. *American Economic Review*: 60 (3): 126–42.

Harvey, A. C. 1981. *The econometric analysis of time series*. New York: Halsted Press.

Helleiner, G. K. 1964. The fiscal role of marketing boards in Nigerian economic development, 1947–61. *Economic Journal* 74 (September): 582–610.

Helmberger, P., and R. Weaver. 1977. Welfare implications of commodity storage under uncertainty. *American Journal of Agricultural Economics* 59 (November): 639–51.

Herdt, Robert W. 1970. Disaggregate approach to aggregate supply. *American Journal of Agricultural Economics* 52 (4).

Honma, Masayoshi, and Yujiro Hayami. 1987. Agricultural protection of East Asia international perspective. *Asian Economic Journal* 1 (March): 48-69.

Hurtado, Hernan, Eugenia Muchnik, and Alberto Valdés. 1986. Effects of price intervention in Chilean agriculture: A progress report. World Bank, Washington, D.C., and Departamento de Economía Agraria, Universidad Católica de Chile, Santiago.

_____. 1990. *Trade, exchange rate, and agricultural pricing policies in Chile*. Washington, D.C.: World Bank.

Ilahi, K. Mushtaq. 1978. *Sugar industry of Pakistan*. Research Report Series 108. Islamabad: Pakistan Institute of Development Economics.

Instituto de Estudios Económicos sobre la Realidad Argentina y Latinoamericana. 1986. Estadísticas de la evolución económica Argentina, 1913–1984. *Estudios* (39).

Intal, Ponciano S., Jr., and John H. Power. 1986. The political economy of agricultural pricing policies. The Philippines. Paper prepared for the World Bank, Washington, D.C. Mimeo.

_____. 1990. *Trade, exchange rate, and agricultural pricing policies in the Philippines*. Washington, D.C.: World Bank.

International Food Policy Research Institute. 1981. Food aid tape. Washington, D.C.

International Monetary Fund (IMF). 1984. *International Financial Statistics Yearbook 1984*. Washington, D.C.: IMF.

_____. 1985a. *International Financial Statistics*. Supplement no. 9, Exchange rates. Washington, D.C.: IMF.

_____. 1985b. *International Financial Statistics Yearbook 1985*. Washington, D.C.: IMF.

Ishikawa, Shigeru. 1967. *Economic development in Asian perspective*. Tokyo: Kinokuniya Bookstore.

Jarvis, Lovell S., and Maria del Rosario Medero. 1989. Domestic beef price stabilization in a beef exporting country: Uruguay, 1961–1986. In *Agriculture and governments in an interdependent world*, edited by Allen Maunder and Alberto Valdés. Proceedings of the 20th International Conference of Agricultural Economists. Aldershot, England: Dartmouth.

Jenkins, Glenn P., and Andrew K. Lai. 1989. *Trade, exchange rate, and agricultural pricing policies in Malaysia.* Washington, D.C.: World Bank.

Junguito, Roberto, and Carlos Caballero. 1978. La otra economía [The illegal economy]. *Coyuntura Económica* (December): 103–39.

Just, R. E., D. L. Hueth, and A. Schmitz. 1977. The distribution of welfare gains from international price stabilization under distortion. *American Journal of Agricultural Economics* 59 (November): 653–61.

———. 1982. *Applied welfare economics and public policy.* Englewood Cliffs, N.J.: Prentice-Hall.

Kamas, Linda. 1986. Dutch disease economics and the Colombian export boom. *World Development* (September): 1177–98.

Kenen, P. B., and C. S. Voivodas. 1972. Export instability and economic growth. *Kyklos* 25 (December): 791–804.

Kerr, T. C. 1985. Trends in agricultural price protection, 1967–1983. Washington, D.C.: World Bank.

Knudsen, O., and J. Nash. 1990. Domestic price stabilization schemes in developing countries. *Economic Development and Cultural Change* 38 (April): 539–58.

Knudsen, O., and A. Parnes. 1975. *Trade instability and economic development.* Lexington, Mass.: D. C. Heath.

Koester, Ulrich, Hartwig Schafer, and Alberto Valdés. 1989. External demand constraints for agricultural exports: An impediment to structural adjustment policies in sub-Saharan African countries? *Food Policy.* 14 (3): 274–83.

Krueger, Anne O. 1978. *Foreign trade regimes and economic development: Liberalization attempts and consequences.* Lexington, Mass.: Ballinger Press.

———. 1983. *Exchange rate determination.* New York: Cambridge University Press.

———. 1989. Some preliminary findings from the World Bank's project on the political economy of agricultural pricing. In *Agriculture and governments in an interdependent world,* edited by Allen Maunder and Alberto Valdés. Proceedings of the 20th International Conference of Agricultural Economists. Aldershot, England: Dartmouth.

Krueger, Anne O., Maurice Schiff, and Alberto Valdés. 1988. Agricultural incentives in developing countries: Measuring the effect of sectoral and economy-wide policies. *World Bank Economic Review* 2 (3): 255–71.

Kuo, Shirley. 1983. *The Taiwan economy in transition.* Boulder, Colo.: Westview Press.

Lele, Uma. 1988. Agricultural growth, domestic policy, and external assistance to Africa: Lessons of a quarter century. Paper presented at the Eighth Agricultural Symposium of the World Bank, January 6–8, Washington, D.C.

Lerner, Abba. 1936. The symmetry between import and export taxes. *Economica* 3 (August): 306–13.

Lim, David. 1981. Malaysia. In *Capital utilization in manufacturing,* by Romeo M. Bautista, Helen Hughes, David Lim, David Morawetz, and Francisco E. Thoumi. Oxford: Oxford University Press.

Lipton, Michael. 1982. *Why poor people stay poor: Urban bias in world development.* Cambridge, Mass.: Harvard University Press.

Little, Ian M. D., Tibor Scitovsky, and Maurice Scott. 1970. *Industry and trade in some developing countries.* Oxford: Oxford University Press.

Lucas, R. 1988. On the mechanics of development planning. *Journal of Monetary Economics* 22: 3–42.

MacBean, A. I. 1966. *Export instability and economic development.* Cambridge, Mass.: Harvard University Press.

MacBean, A. I., and O. T. Nguyen. 1987. *Commodity policies: Problems and prospects.* London: Croom Helm.

Massell, B. F. 1968. Price stabilization and welfare. *Quarterly Journal of Economics* 83 (May): 285–98.

McCloskey, D. N. 1976. English open fields as behavior towards risk. *Research in Economic History* 1: 124–70.

McGreevy, William. 1968. Causas de la migración interna en Colombia [Sources of internal migration in Colombia]. In *Empleo y desempleo en Colombia* [Employment and unemployment in Colombia]. Bogotá: Centro de Estudios sobre Desarrollo Económico (CEDE).

Mellor, John W. 1976. *The new economics of growth: A strategy for India and the developing world.* Ithaca, N.Y.: Cornell University Press.

Michaely, Michael, Armeane M. Choksi, and Demetris Papageorgiou. 1989. The design of trade liberalization. *Finance and Development* 26 (March): 2–5.

Miranda, M. J., and P. G. Helmberger. 1988. The effects of commodity price stabilization programs. *American Economic Review* 78 (March): 46–57.

Montes Llamas, Gabriel. 1984. Políticas macroeconómicas y desarrollo agropecuario [Macroeconomic policies and agricultural development]. *Revista Nacional de Agricultura* (Colombia) (December): 125–49.

Moon, Pal Y., and Bong S. Kang. 1989. *Trade, exchange rate, and agricultural pricing policies in the Republic of Korea.* Washington, D.C.: World Bank.

Mundlak, Yair. 1979. *Intersectoral factor mobility and agricultural growth.* Research Report 6. Washington, D.C.: International Food Policy Research Institute.

————. 1985a. The aggregate agricultural supply. Center for Agricultural Economic Research, Rehovot, Israel. Mimeo.

————. 1985b. *Agricultural growth and the price of food.* Working Paper 8505. Rehovot, Israel: Center for Agricultural Economic Research.

————. 1987. Endogenous technology and the measurement of productivity. In *Agricultural productivity: measurement and explanation*, edited by Susan M. Capalbo and John M. Antle. Washington, D.C.: Resources for the Future.

————. 1988. Capital accumulation, the choice of techniques, and agricultural output. In *Agricultural price policy for developing countries*, edited by John W. Mellor and Raisuddin Ahmed. Baltimore: Johns Hopkins University Press.

Mundlak, Yair, and R. Hellinghausen. 1982. The intercountry agricultural production function: Another view. *American Journal of Agricultural Economics* 64 (November): 664–72.

Mundlak, Yair, Domingo Cavallo, and Roberto Domenech. 1989. *Agriculture and economic growth: Argentina, 1913-1984.* Research Report 76. Washington, D.C.: International Food Policy Research Institute.

Mussa, Michael. 1986. The adjustment process and the timing of trade liberalization. In *Economic liberalization in developing countries*, edited by Armeane Choksi and Demetris Papageorgiou. Oxford: Basil Blackwell.

_____. 1987. Macroeconomic policy and trade liberalization: Some guidelines. *World Bank Research Observer* 2 (January): 61–77.

Myint, Hla. 1985. Organizational dualism and economic development. *Asian Development Review* 3 (1): 24–42.

_____. 1988. Comments on *Patterns in processes of intersectoral resource flows: Comparison of cases in Asia*, by Shigeru Ishikawa. In *The state of development economics*, edited by Gustav Ranis and T. Paul Schultz. New York: Basil Blackwell.

Naqvi, Sywed N. H., and A. R. Kemal. 1983a. *The structure of protection in Pakistan: 1980–81*, Vol. 1. Islamabad: Pakistan Institute of Development Economics.

_____. 1983b. *The structure of protection in Pakistan: 1980–81*, Vol. 2. Islamabad: Pakistan Institute of Development Economics.

Ndulu, B. J. 1988. Notes on medium-term development issues for Tanzania. Helsinski: World Institute for Development Economics Research (WIDER).

Neary, J. Peter, and Sweder van Wijnbergen, eds. 1986. *Natural resources and the macroeconomy*. Cambridge, Mass.: MIT Press, Center for Economic Policy Research.

Nelson, Gerald C., and Mercedes Agcaoili. 1983. *Impact of government policies on Philippine sugar*. Working Paper 83-04. Manila: Philippine Institute of Development Studies.

Nerlove, Marc. 1958. *Distributed lags and demand analysis for agricultural and other commodities*. Washington, D.C.: U.S. Department of Agriculture.

Newbery, D. M. G., and Joseph E. Stiglitz. 1981. *The theory of commodity price stabilization: A study in the economics of risk*. Oxford: Clarendon Press.

Nigeria. Various years. *Annual Report*. Central Bank of Nigeria.

Nogues, Julio. 1991. A study of Peru. In *Liberalizing foreign trade*, edited by Demetris Papageorgiou, Michael Michaely, and Armeane Choksi. Vol. 4, *The experience of Brazil, Colombia, and Peru*. Oxford: Basil Blackwell.

Oi, W. Y. 1961. The desirability of price instability under perfect competition. *Econometrica* 29 (January): 58–64.

Oliveira, João do Carmo. 1981. An analysis of transfers from the agricultural sector and Brazilian development: 1950–1974. Ph.D. diss., Cambridge University, Cambridge, England.

_____. 1983. Resource transfers from agriculture in Brazil. Paper presented at the Fourth Meeting of the Latin American Econometric Society, July, Santiago.

Ordóñez, Myriam. 1977. Migración y desempleo en las cuidades colombianas [Migration and unemployment in Colombian cities]. In *Empleo y desempleo* [Employment and unemployment]. Bogotá: Asociación Nacional de Instituciones Financieras.

Oyejide, T. Ademola. 1984. Accelerating agricultural growth in sub-Saharan Africa, Discussion. *American Journal of Agricultural Economics* 66: 684–85.

_____. 1985. *Agricultural marketing and pricing policies in Nigeria*. Managing Agricultural Development in Africa (MADIA) Research Project Report. Washington, D.C.: World Bank.

_____. 1986a. *The effect of trade and exchange rate policies on agriculture in Nigeria*.

Research Report 55. Washington, D.C.: International Food Policy Research Institute.

————. 1986b. *World Bank assistance to Nigerian agriculture: A review of policy analysis, policy advice, and lending operations.* MADIA Research Project Report. Washington, D.C.: World Bank.

Oyejide, T. Ademola, and Lien H. Tran. 1989. Food and agricultural imports of sub-Saharan Africa. In *The balance between industry and agriculture in economic development,* edited by Nurul Islam. Proceedings of the Eighth World Congress of the International Economic Association, New Delhi, India.

Paauw, D. S. 1981. Frustrated labour-intensive development: The case of Indonesia. In *Export-led industrialisation and development,* edited by E. Lee. Geneva: International Labour Organisation.

Pakistan, Agricultural Prices Commission (APCOM). 1986. *Cost of production of field crops: Methodology and empirical results (rice, cotton, and wheat).* APCOM Series 52. Islamabad: APCOM.

————. Ministry of Finance. Various years. *Economic Survey.* Islamabad: Ministry of Finance.

Parker, K. E. 1987. The impact of structural adjustment on Nigerian agriculture. Food Research Institute, Stanford University, Stanford, Calif. Mimeo.

Peru, Instituto Nacional de Estadística (INE). 1983. *Cuentas Nacionales del Perú 1950–1982* [National accounts of Peru 1950–1982]. Lima: INE.

Pinckney, Thomas C. 1989. *The demand for public storage of wheat in Pakistan.* Research Report No. 77. Washington, D.C.: International Food Policy Research Institute.

Pinckney, T. C., and Alberto Valdés. 1988. Short-run supply management and food security: Results from Pakistan and Kenya. *World Development* 16 (9): 1025–34.

Pinto, Brian 1987. Nigeria during and after the oil boom: A policy comparison with Indonesia. *World Bank Economic Review* 1 (3): 419–45.

Quirk, Peter J., Benedicte Vibe Christensen, Kyung-Mo Huh, and Toshihiko Sasaki. 1987. *Floating exchange rate in developing countries.* Occasional Paper 53. Washington, D.C.: International Monetary Fund.

Ramos, J. 1984. Estabilización económica en el Cono Sur [Economic stabilization in the Southern Cone]. *Estudios e informes de la Cepal* (ECLA) (38).

Ranis, Gustav, and Frances Stewart. 1987. Rural linkages in the Philippines and Taiwan. In *Macro-policies for appropriate technology in developing countries,* edited by Frances Stewart. Boulder, Colo.: Westview Press.

Reardon, Thomas. 1984. *Agricultural price policy in Peru.* Ph.D. diss., University of California, Berkeley, Calif.

Reca, Lucio. 1980. *Argentina: Country case study of agricultural prices and subsidies.* World Bank Staff Working Paper 386. Washington, D.C.: World Bank.

Reca, Lucio, and Carlos Garramon. 1989. Argentine interactions and the adjustment program and the agricultural sector. In *Agriculture and governments in an interdependent world,* edited by Allen Maunder and Alberto Valdés. Proceedings of the 20th International Conference of Agricultural Economists, Aldershot, England: Dartmouth.

Reutlinger, Shlomo, and David Bigman. 1981. Feasibility, effectiveness, and costs of food security alternatives in developing countries. In *Food security for developing countries*, edited by Alberto Valdés. Boulder, Colo.: Westview Press.

Reyes, A. 1975. *Efectos de la migración rural urbana sobre el desarrollo económico y demográfico* [Effects of rural-urban migration on economic and demographic development]. Bogotá: Corporación Centro Regional de Población.

Ribe, Helena. 1981. La posición económica de los migrantes y no migrantes en Colombia [The economic situation of migrants and non-migrants in Colombia]. *Desarrollo y Sociedad* 5 (January).

Rodríguez, Carlos A. 1982. Gasto público, déficit y tipo real de cambio: Un análisis de sus interrelaciones de largo plazo [Public expenditure, the deficit and the real exchange rate: An analysis of their interrelationships in the long term]. *Cuadernos de Economía* 19 (57): 203–16.

Rosegrant, Mark W., Faisal Kasryno, Leonardo A. Gonzales, Chairil Rasahan, and Yusuf Saefudin. 1987. *Price and investment policies in the Indonesian food crop sector*. Washington, D.C.: International Food Policy Research Institute, and Bogor, Indonesia: Center for Agro Economic Research.

Sachs, Jeffrey D. 1987. Trade and exchange rate policies in growth-oriented adjustment programs. In *Growth-oriented adjustment programs*, edited by Vittorio Corbo, Morris Goldstein, and Mohsin Khan. Washington, D.C.: International Monetary Fund and World Bank.

Sahota, Gian S. 1968. An economic analysis of internal migration in Brazil. *Journal of Political Economy* 2 (March-April): 218–45.

Salinger, Lynn, and Hasan Tuluy. 1988. A comparative study of the political economy of agricultural pricing policies: The case of Morocco. Paper prepared for the World Bank, Washington, D.C.

Sandilands, Roger. 1971. La modernización del sector agropecuario y la migración rural urbana en Colombia [Modernization of the agricultural sector and rural-urban migration in Colombia]. *Revista de Planeación y Desarrollo* 3 (3): 25–517.

Sapelli, Claudio. 1984. *Government policy and the Uruguayan beef sector*. Ph.D. diss., University of Chicago, Chicago, Ill.

Scandizzo, Pasquale, P. Hazell, and J. Anderson. 1984. *Risky agricultural markets: Price forecasting and the need for intervention policies*. London: Westview Press.

Schiff, Maurice. 1987. A structural view of policy issues in African agricultural development: Comment. *American Journal of Agricultural Economics* 69 (2): 384–88.

Schultz, T. Paul. 1969. *Population growth and internal migration in Colombia*. Santa Monica, Calif.: Rand Corporation.

Schultz, Theodore W. 1978. On economics and politics of agriculture. In *Distortions of agricultural incentives*, edited by Theodore W. Schultz. Bloomington: Indiana University Press.

Scobie, Grant M. 1981. *Government policy and food imports: The case of wheat in Egypt*. Research Report 29. Washington, D.C.: International Food Policy Research Institute.

Senga, Kunio. 1983. A note on industrial policies and incentive structures in the Philippines: 1949–80. *Philippine Review of Economics and Business* 20 (September-December): 299–305.

Siamwalla, Ammar. 1986. Approaches to price insurance for farmers. In *Crop insurance for agricultural development: Issues and experience*, edited by Peter Hazell, Carlos Pomareda, and Alberto Valdés. Baltimore: Johns Hopkins University Press.

_____. 1988. Public stock management. In *Agricultural price policy for developing countries*, edited by John W. Mellor and Raisuddin Ahmed. Baltimore: Johns Hopkins University Press.

Siamwalla, Ammar, and Suthad Setboonsarng. 1989. *Trade, exchange rate, and agricultural pricing policies in Thailand*. Washington, D.C.: World Bank.

Siebert, H., ed. 1984. *The resource sector in an open economy*. Berlin: Springer-Verlag.

Sjaastad, Larry A. 1980. Commercial policy, "true tariffs" and relative prices. In *Current issues in commercial policy and diplomacy*, edited by John Black and Brian Hindley. London: Macmillan for the Trade Policy Research Centre.

Sjaastad, Larry A., and K. W. Clements. 1981. The incidence of protection: Theory and measurement. Paper presented at the Conference on the Free Trade Movement in Latin America, June 21–24, Hamburg.

Société Financière de Développement (SOFIDE). 1984. Evolution de la politique d'intervention de la SOFIDE [Evolution of the intervention policy of SOFIDE]. Document 315/84/TMV/SAS. Kinshasa, Zaire.

Solow, Robert M. 1967. Some recent developments in the theory of production. In *The theory and empirical analysis of production*, edited by Murray Brown. Studies in Wealth and Income, Vol. 31. New York: National Bureau of Economic Research.

Stern, J. J., R. D. Mallon, and T. L. Hutcheson. 1988. Foreign exchange regimes and industrial growth in Bangladesh. *World Development* 16 (12): 1419–40.

Stryker, Dirck. 1988. A comparative study of the political economy of agricultural pricing policy: The case of Ghana. Paper prepared for the World Bank, Washington, D.C. Mimeo.

Swamy, G., and H. P. Binswanger. 1983. Flexible consumer demand systems and linear estimation: Food in India. *American Journal of Agricultural Economics*, 64 (4): 675–84.

Tan, Norma A. 1979. The structure of protection and resource flows in the Philippines. In *Industrial promotion in the Philippines*, edited by Romeo M. Bautista, John H. Power, and associates. Manila: Philippine Institute for Development Studies.

Thomas, Vinod, Sebastian Edwards, John Nash, Jorge García García, José B. Sokol, Ai Cheen Wee, and Mateen Thobani. 1985. *Linking macroeconomic and agricultural policies for adjustment with growth: The Colombian experience*. Baltimore: Johns Hopkins University Press.

Todaro, M. 1969. A model of labor migration and urban unemployment in less developed countries. *American Economic Review* (March): 138–48.

Tshibaka, Tshikala B. 1986. *The effects of trade and exchange rate policies on agricul-*

ture in Zaire. Research Report 56. Washington, D.C.: International Food Policy Research Institute.

Tshuinza, Muamba. 1982. Allocation et utilisation des ressources dans l'agriculture traditionelle: Cas de la collectivité rurale Turumbu [Allocation and use of resources in traditional agriculture: The case of the Turumbu rural collective]. Institut Facultaire des Sciences Agronomiques, Yangambi, Zaire.

Tsiang, S. C. 1984. Taiwan's economic miracle: Lessons in economic development. In *World economic growth*, edited by Arnold C. Harberger. International Center for Economic Growth. San Francisco: ICS Press.

Turnovsky, S. J. 1976. The distribution of welfare gains from price stabilization: The case of multiplicative disturbance. *International Economic Review* 17: 133–48.

_____. 1978. The distribution of welfare gains from price stabilization: A survey of some theoretical issues. In *Stabilizing world commodity markets*, edited by F. G. Adams and S. Klein. Lexington, Mass.: Heath.

Valdés, Alberto. 1985. Exchange rates and trade policy: Help or hindrance to agricultural growth? In *Agriculture in a turbulent world economy*, edited by Allen Maunder and Ulf Renborg. Proceedings of the 19th International Conference of Agricultural Economists. Aldershot, England: Gower.

_____. 1986. Efecto de las políticas comerciales y macroeconómicas en el crecimiento agropecuario: La experiencia sudamericana [Impact of trade and macroeconomic policies on agricultural growth: The South American experience]. In *Progreso económico y social en América Latina: Informe 1986* [Economic and social progress in Latin America: 1986 Report]. Washington, D.C.: Inter-American Development Bank.

Valdés, Alberto, and Javier Leon. 1987. Política comercial, industrialización y su sesgo antiexportador: Perú 1940–1983 [Commercial policy, industrialization, and the antiexport bias; Peru 1940–1983]. *Cuadernos de Economía* 24 (71): 3–28.

Valdés, Alberto, and Ammar Siamwalla. 1988. Foreign trade regime, exchange rate policy, and the structure of incentives. In *Agricultural price policy for developing countries*, edited by John W. Mellor and Raissudin Ahmed. Baltimore: Johns Hopkins University Press.

Warr, P. G. 1984. Exchange rate protection in Indonesia. *Bulletin of Indonesian Economic Studies* 20 (2): 53–89.

Waugh, F. 1944. Does the consumer benefit from price instability? *Quarterly Journal of Economics* 58 (4): 602–14.

Westphal, Larry E., and Kwang Suk Kim. 1981. Korea. In *Development strategies in semi-industrial economies*, edited by B. Balassa and associates. Baltimore: Johns Hopkins University Press.

Wie, T. K. 1987. Industrial and foreign investment policy in Indonesia since 1967. *Tonan Ajia Kenkyu* (Southeast Asian Studies) 25 (3): 83–96.

Working, H. 1953. Futures trading and hedging. *American Economic Review* 3: 314–43.

World Bank. 1980. *Country study: Zaire*. Washington, D.C.: World Bank.

_____. 1982. *World Development Report 1982*. New York: Oxford University Press.

_____. 1984a. *Commodity trade and price trends*. Baltimore: Johns Hopkins University Press.

_____. 1984b. *Thailand: Pricing and marketing policy for intensification of rice agriculture*. Washington, D.C.: World Bank.

_____. 1984c. *Toward sustained development in sub-Saharan Africa: A joint program of action*. Washington, D.C.: World Bank.

_____. 1986a. *Financing adjustment with growth in sub-Saharan Africa, 1986–90*. Washington, D.C.: World Bank.

_____. 1986b. *World Development Report 1986*. New York: Oxford University Press.

_____. 1987a. *Pakistan sixth plan progress and future prospects*. Report 6533-PAK. Washington, D.C.: World Bank.

_____. 1987b. *World Development Report 1987*. New York: Oxford University Press.

_____. 1988. Design, implementation, and adequacy of fund programs in Africa. In *Africa and the International Monetary Fund*, edited by G. K. Helleiner. Washington, D.C.: International Monetary Fund.

Zaire, Département de l'Agriculture. 1982. Unpublished data. Direction des Etudes. Kinshasa.

_____. n.d. Unpublished data, Division des Statistiques Agricoles. Kinshasa.

Zaire, Département de l'Economie Nationale. Various years. *Conjoncture Economique*. Kinshasa: Département de l'Economie Nationale.

Zaire, Institut National des Statistiques. Various years. *Annuaires Statistiques*. Kinshasa: Institut National des Statistiques.

About the Contributors

ROMEO M. BAUTISTA has been a research fellow at the International Food Policy Research Institute (IFPRI) in Washington, D.C., since 1983. He was a professor and chairman of the Department of Economics at the University of the Philippines and served as deputy director-general for policy of the National Economic and Development Authority in the Philippines.

DOMINGO CAVALLO is minister of economy and public works of Argentina. He was president of the Central Bank of Argentina, director of the Institute of Economic Studies of the Fundación Mediterránea in Córdoba, Argentina, and minister of foreign relations.

JUAN EDUARDO COEYMANS is professor of economics at Pontificia Universidad Católica de Chile.

ROBERTO DOMENECH is adviser to the minister of the economy and editor of the Newsletter of the Fundación Mediterránea. He was senior researcher at the Institute of Economic Studies of the Fundación Mediterránea and professor of macroeconomics at the University of Córdoba.

PAUL DOROSH is a senior research associate in the Food and Nutrition Policy Program of Cornell University in Washington, D.C. He was a postdoctoral fellow at IFPRI in 1988.

DAVID E. FRANKLIN is president of Sigma One Corporation in Raleigh, N.C. He was a staff economist at the Research Triangle Institute, also in Raleigh.

JORGE GARCIA GARCIA is a senior agricultural economist at the World Bank. He was a visiting research fellow at IFPRI and a professor at the Universidad de los Andes in Bogotá. He also served as deputy director of the National Planning Commission in Colombia and as an adviser to Colombia's Monetary Board.

ODIN KNUDSEN is a division chief in the Agriculture Operations Division for North Africa, at the World Bank.

ANNE O. KRUEGER is Arts and Sciences Professor of Economics at Duke University. She was vice president of economics and research at the World Bank and a research associate at the National Bureau of Economic Research.

YAIR MUNDLAK is a research fellow at IFPRI, F. H. Prince Visiting Professor of Economics at the University of Chicago, and professor emeritus of agricultural economics at the Hebrew University of Jerusalem, Israel.

JOHN NASH is a senior economist in the Trade Policy Division, Country Economics Department, at the World Bank. He is also codirector of the United Nations Development Program/World Bank Trade Expansion Program.

T. ADEMOLA OYEJIDE is a professor and head of the Department of Economics at the University of Ibadan, Nigeria. He was a visiting research fellow at IFPRI in 1985.

TSHIKALA B. TSHIBAKA has been a research fellow at IFPRI since 1984. He was a professor and vice dean of research at the Institut Facultaire des Sciences Agronomique (IFA) in Yangambi, Zaire.

ALBERTO VALDES is a principal economist in the Technical Department, Latin America and the Caribbean, at the World Bank. He served as director of the International Trade and Food Security Program at IFPRI in 1976–1990. Previously, he was an economist at the International Center for Tropical Agriculture (CIAT) and a professor at the Pontificia Universidad Católica de Chile.

INDEX

ICEG Academic Advisory Board